Computers and Thought

Explorations in Cognitive Science
Margaret A. Boden, Editor

Computers and Thought
A Practical Introduction to Artificial Intelligence

Mike Sharples,
David Hogg,
Chris Hutchison,
Steve Torrance, and
David Young

A Bradford Book
The MIT Press
Cambridge, Massachusetts
London, England

Sixth printing, 1994

This book was printed and bound in the United States of America.

Library of Congress Cataloging-in-Publication Data

Mike Sharples ... [et al.].
   Computers and thought: a practical introduction to artificial intelligence

   p. cm. — (Explorations in cognitive science 5)
   "A Bradford book."
   Bibliography: p.
   Includes index.
   1. Artificial Intelligence. 2. Cognitive Science. I. Sharples,
Mike, 1952 – . II. Series.
Q335.C57 1989   006.3 — dc19   89-2541
ISBN 0-262-19285-3   CIP

The original question, "Can machines think?" I believe to be too meaningless to deserve discussion. Nevertheless I believe that at the end of the century the use of words and general educated opinion will have altered so much that one will be able to speak of machines thinking without expecting to be contradicted.

Alan Turing, in
"Computing Machinery and Intelligence"

Special Acknowledgement

The authors of this book and The MIT Press especially wish to acknowledge the important contribution of a historic and seminal work which helped to establish the field of Artificial Intelligence—*Computers and Thought*, edited by Edward A. Feigenbaum and Jerome A. Feldman. The *Computers and Thought Award*, established by the American Association for Artificial Intelligence and presented at International Joint Conference on Artificial Intelligence meetings, is the most prestigious in this now strong and flourishing field of research and teaching. The title of this book was based in part on the title of an original article by Alan Turing and was not intended to be associated either with the book edited by Feigenbaum and Feldman or with the award. Though the original work by Feigenbaum and Feldman is not now in print, its royalties and its influence went far toward establishing the award.

The original question, "Can machines think?" I believe to be too meaningless to deserve discussion. Nevertheless I believe that at the end of the century the use of words and general educated opinion will have altered so much that one will be able to speak of machines thinking without expecting to be contradicted.

Alan Turing, in
"Computing Machinery and Intelligence"

Special Acknowledgement

The authors of this book and The MIT Press especially wish to acknowledge the important contribution of a historic and seminal work which helped to establish the field of Artificial Intelligence—*Computers and Thought*, edited by Edward A. Feigenbaum and Jerome A. Feldman. The *Computers and Thought Award*, established by the American Association for Artificial Intelligence and presented at International Joint Conference on Artificial Intelligence meetings, is the most prestigious in this now strong and flourishing field of research and teaching. The title of this book was based in part on the title of an original article by Alan Turing and was not intended to be associated either with the book edited by Feigenbaum and Feldman or with the award. Though the original work by Feigenbaum and Feldman is not now in print, its royalties and its influence went far toward establishing the award.

Contents

Contents

Preface

The aim of this book is to introduce people with little or no computing background to artificial intelligence (AI) and cognitive science. It emphasizes the psychological, social, and philosophical implications of AI and, by means of an extended project to design an Automated Tourist Guide, makes the connection between the details of an AI programming language and the 'magic' of artificial intelligence programs, which converse in English, solve problems, and offer reasoned advice.

The book covers computer simulation of human activities, such as problem solving and natural language understanding; computer vision; AI tools and techniques; an introduction to AI programming; symbolic and neural network models of cognition; the nature of mind and intelligence; and the social implications of AI and cognitive science.

Each chapter will, in general, present a particular AI topic, with sections on the background to the topic, methods, and applications. These do not assume any previous knowledge of a computer language, and are intended for the reader who wants to gain an understanding of the field without plunging into programming. The foreword and chapter 1 offer an overview of artificial intelligence and cognitive science. The fundamental AI techniques of pattern matching, knowledge representation, and search are covered in chapters 2–4, and these chapters need to be read thoroughly in order to get a grounding in the subject. Chapters 5–9 deal with applications of AI and the techniques of reasoning with stored knowledge. They can be read out of order, or to different depths, although the programming appendix for a chapter will use terms introduced in earlier ones. Chapter 10 is a fairly self-contained discussion of AI and the philosophy of mind. Chapter 11 speculates on the future of AI and its social implications.

Most of the chapters contain an appendix which presents the topic in terms of an AI programming language. The language we have chosen, POP-11, is not the most widely used one for AI (although it is rapidly growing in popularity), but it is a language both for beginners and for advanced research. These aims are not contradictory, since both beginners and advanced programmers need tools that are well designed, and that reveal the structure of the problem at hand. POP-11 is particularly suitable as a way of describing programs on paper, since its appearance is similar to the popular teaching language PASCAL, and it encourages clear, well-structured programs. You do not need to have access to a computer running POP-11; the programs that we use as examples can be followed on the printed page.

Wherever possible we have used plain language and avoided technical terms unless they are an essential part of the vocabulary of AI. Such words are printed in boldface and included in the glossary.

Although this book is intended to give you a good feel for the issues and practicalities of AI and cognitive science, it does not attempt a full coverage of the subject. Nor in general does it go into the details of programming or computer science. It should be seen as the text for a course on "Foundations of AI and Cognitive Science" or as a preliminary to more technical texts such as those by Charniak and McDermott (1985), Rich (1983), and Winston (1984) for AI, and Stillings (1987) for cognitive science.

The book arose from a 10-week course for first-year arts undergraduates at Sussex University, also called "Computers and Thought." Most of the students have no previous experience of computing, and many of them are deeply suspicious of what they see as attempts to replace people with computers. As well as introducing them to the tools and methods of AI we have tried to show that, by building models of the mind, we can uncover the fascinating range and detail of human cognition; by attempting, and failing, to build thinking machines we gain respect for living, thinking beings.

One person took prime responsibility for each of the chapters (apart from chapter 5, which was jointly written by David Hogg and Chris Hutchison). Mike Sharples wrote the main draft of chapters 1, 8, and 11. David Young wrote the main draft of chapters 2 and 4. Steve Torrance wrote the main draft of chapters 3 and 10. Chris Hutchison wrote the main draft of chapters 6 and 7. David Hogg wrote the main draft of chapter 9. After comments from independent reviewers, the manuscript was reworked by the original authors and by Mike Sharples, to create a consistent style and to tidy up cross references. We believe we now have the best of both worlds: one coherent textbook, built from chapters written by specialists on their own subject areas.

Over the years the "Computers and Thought" course has been revised and polished by many people. We have drawn on course material produced by Aaron

Sloman, Steve Hardy, Benedict du Boulay, and Tom Khabaza. We should like to thank them and the other staff, the POPLOG team who developed POP-11, the reviewers who provided detailed comments on the chapters, and the students at Sussex University who have provided the fertile soil for this book. Particularly, we want to thank Robert Bolick of The MIT Press for championing the book and for his patient and helpful advice, Harry Stanton of MIT Press/Bradford Books for easing it through all the stages of production, and Nick Franz for spending many hours with LaTeX turning a manuscript into a book.

The coloring of the image on the cover is by the British artist Harold Cohen. The drawing is the work of Cohen's computer program, AARON. AARON is an intelligent computer-based program, now in its fifteenth year of continuous development, and the only program currently in existence capable of the autonomous generation of original works of art. Harold Cohen's goal in writing AARON has been to understand how human beings make and read images, not to simulate existing works of art. Cohen and AARON have exhibited together in art museums and science centers in New York, London, Tokyo, Amsterdam, Toronto, San Francisco, Boston and many other major cities.

Foreword: A Personal View of Artificial Intelligence

Introduction

There are many books, newspaper reports, and conferences providing information and making claims about artificial intelligence (AI) and its lusty infant, the field of expert systems. Reactions range from one lunatic view that all our intellectual capabilities will be exceeded by computers in a few years' time to the slightly more defensible opposite extreme view that computers are merely lumps of machinery that simply do what they are programmed to do and therefore cannot conceivably emulate human thought, creativity, or feeling. As an antidote for these extremes, I shall try to sketch a sane middle-of-the-road view.

In the long-term, AI will have enormously important consequences for science and engineering and our view of what we are. But it would be rash to speculate in detail about this. In the short-to-medium term there are extremely difficult problems. The main initial practical impact of AI will arise not so much from intelligent machines as from the use of AI techniques to build 'intelligence amplifiers' for human beings. Even if machines have not advanced enough to be capable of designing other complex machines, discovering new concepts and theories, understanding speech at cocktail parties, and making all our important economic, political, and military decisions for us, AI systems may nevertheless be able to help people to learn, plan, take decisions, solve problems, absorb information, find information, design things, communicate with one another, or even just explore ideas when confronted with a new problem.

Besides helping human thought processes, AI languages, development tools, and techniques can also be used for improving and extending existing types of automation, for instance: cataloguing, checking computer programs, checking consistency of data, checking plans or designs, formatting documents, analyzing images, and many kinds of monitoring and controlling activities.

What Then Is AI?

Some people give AI a very narrow definition as an applied sub-field of computer science. I prefer a definition that reflects the range of work reported at AI conferences, in AI journals, and the interests and activities of some of the leading practitioners, including founders of the subject. From this viewpoint AI is a very general investigation of the nature of intelligence and the principles and mechanisms required for understanding or replicating it. Like all scientific disciplines it has three main types of goals: theoretical, empirical, and practical.

Goals of AI: The Trinity of Science

The long-term goals of AI include finding out what the world is like, understanding it, and changing it, or, in other words,

a. empirical study and modelling of existing intelligent systems (mainly human beings);

b. theoretical analysis and exploration of possible intelligent systems and possible mechanisms and representations usable by such systems; and

c. solving practical problems in the light of (a) and (b), namely:

c.1. attempting to deal with problems of existing intelligent systems (e.g., problems of human learning or emotional difficulties) and

c.2. designing useful new intelligent or semi intelligent machines.

Some people restrict the term 'artificial intelligence' to a subset of this wide-ranging discipline. For example, those who think of it as essentially a branch of engineering restrict it to (c.2). This does not do justice to the full range of work done in the name of AI.

In any case, it is folly to try to produce engineering solutions without either studying general underlying principles or investigating the existing intelligent systems on which the new machines are to be modelled or with which they will have to interact. Trying to build intelligent systems without trying to understand general principles would be like trying to build an aeroplane without understanding principles of mechanics or aerodynamics. Trying to build them without studying how people or other animals work would be like trying to build machines without ever studying the properties of any naturally occurring object.

The need to study general principles of thought, and the ways in which human beings perceive, think, understand language, etc., means that AI work has to be done in close collaboration with work in psychology, linguistics, and even philosophy, the discipline that examines some of the most general presuppositions of our thought and language. The term 'cognitive science' can also be used to cover the full range of goals specified above, though it too is ambiguous, and some of its more narrow-minded practitioners tend to restrict it to (a) and (c.1).

But What Is Intelligence? — Three Key Features

The goals of AI have been defined in terms of the notion of intelligence. I do not pretend to be able to offer a definition of 'intelligence'. However, most, if not all, of the important work in AI arises out of the attempt to understand three key characteristics of the kind of intelligence found in people and, to different degrees, other animals. The features are intentionality, flexibility, and productive laziness.

Intentionality

This is the ability to have internal states that refer to or are *about* entities or situations more or less remote in space or time, or even non-existent or wholly abstract things.

So intentional states include contemplating clouds, dreaming you are a duke, exploring equations, pondering a possible action, seeing a snake, or wanting to win someone's favours. These are all cases of awareness or consciousness of something, including hypothetical or impossible objects or situations. A sophisticated mind may also have thoughts or desires about its own state — various forms of *self-*consciousness are also cases of intentionality.

All intentional states seem to require the existence of some kind of *representation* of the content of the state: some representation of whatever is believed, perceived, desired, imagined, etc. A major theme in AI is therefore investigation of different kinds of representations and their implementation and uses. This is a very tricky topic, since there are many different kinds of representational forms: sentences, logical symbols, computer databases, maps, diagrams, arrays, images, etc. It is very likely that there are still important forms of representation waiting to be discovered.

Flexibility

This has to do with the breadth and variety of intentional contents, i.e., the variety of types of things intentional states can refer to, for instance, the variety of types of goals, objects, problems, plans, actions, environments etc., with which an individual can cope, including the ability to deal with new situations using old resources combined and transformed in new ways.

Flexibility in this sense is required for understanding a sentence you have never heard before, seeing a familiar object from a new point of view, coping with an old problem in a new situation, and dealing with unexpected obstacles to a plan. A kind of flexibility important in human intelligence involves the ability to raise a wide range of questions.

A desirable kind of flexibility often missing in computer programs is 'graceful degradation'. Often if the input to a computer deviates at all from what is expected, the result is simply an error message and abort. Graceful degradation, on the other hand, would imply being able to try to cope with the unexpected by reinterpreting it, or modifying strategies, or asking for help, or monitoring actions more carefully. Instead of total failure, degradation might include taking longer to solve a problem, reducing the accuracy of solution, reducing the frequency of success, etc.

One of the factors determining the degree of flexibility will be the range of representations available. A system that can merely represent things using a vector of numerical measures, for example, will have a narrower range of possible intentional states than a system that can build linguistic descriptions of unlimited complexity, like:

the man
the old man
the old man in the corner
the old man sitting on a chair in the corner
the sad old man sitting on a chair with a broken leg in the corner
etc.

so flexible control systems of the future will have to go far beyond using numerical measures, and will have to be able to represent goals or functions, and relationships between structures, resources, processes, constraints, and so on.

Productive Laziness

It is not enough to achieve results: intelligence is partly a matter of *how* they are achieved. Productive laziness involves avoiding unnecessary work.

A chess champion who wins by working through all the possible sequences of moves several steps ahead and choosing the best one is not as intelligent as the player who avoids examining so many cases by noticing that the pieces form a pattern which points directly to the best move.

Why is laziness important? Given any solvable task for which a finite solution is recognizable, it is possible in principle to find a solution by enumerating all possible actions (or all possible computer programs) and checking them exhaustively until the right one turns up. In practice this is useless because the set of possibilities is too great.

This is called a 'combinatorial explosion'. Any construction involving many choices from a set of options has a potentially huge array of possible constructs to choose from. If you have 4 choices each with 2 options, the total set of options is 16. If you have 20 choices each with 6 options, the total shoots up to 3,656,158,440,062,976. Clearly exhaustive enumeration is not a general solution, so lazy shortcuts have to be found.

For example, a magic square is an array of numbers all of whose rows, columns, and diagonals add up to the same total. Here is a 3 by 3 magic square made of the digits 1–9:

$$6 \ 7 \ 2$$
$$1 \ 5 \ 9$$
$$8 \ 3 \ 4$$

If you try to construct a 3 by 3 magic square by trying all possible ways of assigning the 9 numbers to the locations in the square, then there are 362,880 possible combinations. Trying them all would not be intelligent. A more sensible procedure would involve testing partial combinations to see whether they can possibly be extended satisfactorily, and, if not, rejecting at one blow all the combinations with that initial sequence. It is also sensible to look for symmetries in the problem. Having found that you cannot have the number 5 in the top left corner, reject all combinations that involve 5 in any corner.

Yet more subtle arguments can be used to prune the possibilities drastically. For example, since eight different triples with the same total are needed (one for each row, one for each column and the two diagonals), it is easy to show that large and small numbers must be spread evenly over the triples, and that they must in fact add up to 15. So the central number has to be in four different triples adding up to 15, the corner numbers in three triples each, and the mid-side numbers in two each. For each number we can work out how many different triples it can occur in, and this immediately restricts the locations to which they can be assigned. For example, 1 and 9 must go into locations in the middle of a side, and the only candidate for the central square is 5. In fact, a high-level symmetry shows that you need bother to do this analysis only for the numbers 1–4. You can then construct the square in a few moves, without any trial and error. What about a 2 by 2 magic square containing the numbers 1, 2, 3, and 4? Think about it!

These examples show that the ability to detect shortcuts requires the ability to *describe* the symmetries, relationships, and implications in the structure of the task. It also requires the ability to *notice* them and perceive their relevance, even though they are not mentioned in the statement of the task. This kind of productive laziness therefore depends on intentionality and flexibility, but motivates their application. Discovering relevant relationships not mentioned in the task specification (e.g., "Location X occurs in fewer triples than location Y") requires the use of a generative conceptual system and notation (i.e., one that enables novel descriptions to be formulated). Being lazy in this way is often harder than doing the stupid exhaustive search. But it may be very much faster. This points to a need for an analysis of the notion of intellectual difficulty.

Productive laziness often means applying previously acquired knowledge about the problem or some general class of problems. So it requires learning: the ability to form new concepts and to acquire and store new knowledge for future applications. Sometimes it involves creating a new form of representation, as has happened often in the history of science and mathematics.

Laziness motivates a desire for generality — finding one solution for a wide range of cases can save the effort of generating new solutions. This is one of the major motivations for all kinds of scientific research. It can also lead to errors of over-generalization, prejudice, and the like. A more complete survey would discuss the differences between avoiding mental work (saving computational resources) and avoiding physical work.

An (Overly) Simple Design for an Intelligent System

Here is a simple set of components for an intelligent system.

Perceptual mechanisms   These mechanisms analyze and interpret information taken in by the "senses" and store the interpretations in a database.

A database of information   This is not just as a store of facts, for a database can also store information about how to do things. It may include both particular facts provided by the senses and generalizations formed over a period of time.

Analysis and interpretation procedures   These are procedures which examine the data provided by the senses, break them up into meaningful chunks, build descriptions, match the descriptions, etc. Analysis involves describing what is presented in the data. Interpretation involves describing something else, possibly lying behind the data, for instance, constructing a 3-D description on the basis of 2-D images, or inferring someone's intentions from his actions.

Reasoning procedures   These use information in the database to derive further information which can also be stored in the database. If you know that Socrates is a man, and that all men are mortal, you can infer something new, namely, that Socrates is mortal.

A database of goals   These just represent possible situations which it is intended should be made *actual*. There may also be policies, preferences, ideals, and the like.

Planning procedures   These take a goal, and a database of information, and construct a plan which will achieve the goal, assuming the correctness of the information in the database.

Executive mechanisms and muscles or motors   These translate plans into action.

Often the divisions will not be very clear. For instance, is 'this situation is painful' a fact or a goal concerned with the need to change the situation? This sort of system can be roughly represented by figure 1.

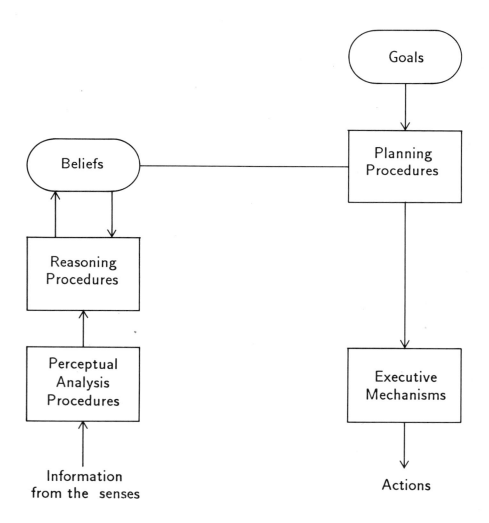

Figure 1 Sketch of a not very intelligent system.

Limitations of This Design

This sort of diagram conceals much hidden complexity. Each of the named sub-processes may have a range of internal structures and sub-processes, some relatively permanent, some very short term.

However, even this kind of complexity does not do justice to the kind of intelligence that we find in human beings and many animals. For example, there is a need for internal self-monitoring processes as well as external sensory processes. A richer set of connections may be needed between sub-processes. For example, planning may require reasoning, and perception may need to be influenced by beliefs, current goals, and current motor plans (see figure 1).

It is also necessary to be able to learn from experience, and that requires processes that do some kind of retrospective analysis of past successes and failures. The goals of an autonomous intelligent system are not static, but are generated dynamically in the light of new information and existing policies, preferences, and the like. There will also be conflicts between different sorts of goals that need to be resolved. Thus 'goal-generators' and 'goal-comparators' will be needed, and mechanisms for improving these in the light of experience.

Further complexities arise from the need to be able to deal with new information and new goals by interrupting, modifying, temporarily suspending, or aborting current processes. I believe that these are the kinds of requirements that explain some kinds of emotional states in human beings, and we can expect similar states in intelligent machines.

Whether or not the design sketched above is accurate, ideas developed in exploring such designs may prove to be essential for developing correct theories about how the mind works. This may be so even if the human mind is embodied in a physical system whose basic mechanisms are very different from a modern digital computer.

'Noncognitive' States and Processes

One of the standard objections to AI is that although it may say something useful about *cognitive* processes, such as perception, inference, and planning, it says nothing about other aspects of mind, such as motivation and emotions. In particular, AI programs tend to be given a single 'top-level' goal, and everything they do is subservient to this, whereas people have a large number of different wishes, likes, dislikes, hopes, fears, principles, ambitions, all of which can interact with the processes of deciding and planning, and even such processes as seeing physical objects or understanding a sentence. This is correct and important.

There are ways of extending the design so as to begin to cope with this sort of complexity, without leaving a computational framework. Questions to be addressed include, What sorts of processes can produce new motives? How should motives be represented? What sorts of processes could select motives for action? How should one motive (e.g., a fear or preference) interact with the process of trying to achieve another? In order to answer these questions we must clarify what we understand by the key terms. This requires conceptual analysis.

Conceptual Analysis

This involves taking familiar concepts, like *knowledge, belief, explanation,* and *anger,* and exploring their structure. What sorts of things can they be applied to, how are they related to other concepts, and what is their role in our thinking and communication? To meet the above criticism of AI in full, it is necessary to engage in extensive analysis of many concepts which refer to mental states and processes of kinds which AI work does not at present say much about, concepts like *want, like, enjoy, prefer, intend, afraid, sad, pleasure, pain, embarrassed, disgusted, exultation,* and the like.

This is not an easy task, since we are largely unconscious of how our own concepts work. However, by showing how motives of many kinds might co-exist in a single system, generating many different kinds of processes, some of which disturb or disrupt others, we may begin to see how, for example, emotional states might be accounted for. This would require considerable extension of the ideas of this book. This theme is developed in Sloman (1987).

Conclusion

This is by no means a complete overview of AI. At best I hope I have whetted the appetites of those for whom it is a new topic.

As readers may have discerned, my own interests are mainly in the use of AI to explore philosophical and psychological problems about the nature of the human mind, by designing and testing models of human abilities, analyzing the architectures, representations, and inferences required, and so on. These are long-term problems.

In the short run, my own guess is that the most important practical applications will be in the design of relatively simple expert systems, and in the use of AI tools for non-AI programming, since the advantages of such tools are not restricted to AI projects. In principle, AI languages and tools could also have a profound effect on teaching by making new kinds of powerful teaching and learning environments available, giving pupils a chance to explore a very wide range of subjects by playing with or building appropriate programs. For example, Seymour Papert (1980) and others have suggested that students will acquire a deeper understanding of thinking and problem solving if they are given a chance to 'play God' and design working simulations, including simulations of physically impossible processes. (The programming language Logo, now widely used in schools, was developed for this sort of learning experience.) AI programming languages and development tools can be used to extend this idea in new directions: by designing programs that do some of the things that people can do, students can acquire a deeper understanding of issues in linguistics, psychology, logic, philosophy, and the social sciences.

AI may or may not achieve its full potential. Whether it does will depend on social and political factors outside the control of those who work in AI. I am not terribly optimistic. For example, since our culture does not attach much importance to education as an end in itself, I fear that this potential will not be realized. Instead, millions will be spent on military applications of AI.

Aaron Sloman
Professor of Artificial Intelligence and Cognitive Science,
University of Sussex.

Computers and Thought

Chapter 1

Towards Artificial Intelligence

1.1   What Is Artificial Intelligence?

Artificial intelligence (AI) is a cloth woven from three academic disciplines — psychology (cognitive modelling), philosophy (philosophy of mind), and computer science — with further strands from linguistics, mathematics, and logic. These subjects have been forced apart by academic politics and the twentieth-century passion for specialization, but for many purposes they belong together. Joining them is not easy. Psychology and philosophy split in the late nineteenth century; computer science grew up as a branch of mathematics. But the aim of AI is broad: to get below the surface of human behaviour; to discover the processes, systems, and principles that make intelligent behaviour possible. Computers are needed as tools for modelling these mental states and processes.

Practical applications include the design of computer systems that can perceive, learn, solve problems, make plans, and converse in natural language. Such systems are already in commercial use for medical diagnosis, identifying ships from satellite pictures, mineral prospecting, language translation, and science training.

The theoretical aims include attempting to understand how the mind works by investigating the problem of designing machines that have abilities previously possessed only by human beings. This work can only be done successfully if combined with other disciplines that involve a study of the human mind. For example, psychology provides information about human perception, memory, and learning skills.

Linguistics illuminates the structures and functions of human languages. Philosophy seeks to clarify our understanding of what it is to be human, typically by examining the concepts we use in explanations of the world, of our own actions, and of the behaviour of others.

This chapter follows the historical route, describing the origins of the three main strands — cognitive modelling, philosophy of mind, and computer science — and ending where all three merge into the fabric of AI.

1.2   Machine Models of Mind

To set the scene, I would like you to try a simple experiment.

Make up and write down four lines of rhyming verse; it doesn't matter how bad they are, it's the thought that counts. While you are devising the verse, try and describe to yourself the processes that are going on in your mind. How do you search your memory to find a rhyming word? Do you come up with more than one candidate for a word or phrase? How do you decide between them? Try it now, before you read on.

The questions above are more or less difficult to answer. You may have produced some answer for question two. For example, in thinking up the following lines,

> Now I want you all to try
> And write some rhyming poetry

I first came up with the word 'eye' to rhyme with 'try', but rejected it for the word 'poetry'. You may be able to give a broad answer to question three (I could not think of a suitable line ending in 'eye', and 'poetry' seemed a more comic rhyme for 'try'). But you will not be able to describe the process by which you searched your memory and generated a novel series of words. To give another example, try and think up rhymes for the word 'orange'. Candidate words will begin to pop into your conscious attention ('carriage', 'forage', 'lozenge', etc.), but you will have no idea of *how* they were placed there, in that particular order.

All this suggests that we are consciously aware only of the *products* of our minds, not the processes. This is so much an accepted part of being human that, until recently, it has coloured our entire understanding of the mind. Language, for instance, has traditionally been studied in terms of its product: the style and structure of written texts; the vocabulary and intonation of speech. In language education, the emphasis has always been on teaching grammar (how words are organized into regular patterns), rather than helping young writers to manage the difficult process of creating text.

If **introspection** (looking into one's own mind) reveals little about the process of thinking, then how can we find out about it? One approach (that of **behavioural** psychologists) is to say that looking for mental states and processes is both unreliable and a waste of time. Instead we should study observable behaviour and look for consistent links between stimulus (such as setting a subtraction sum) and response (the numbers the child writes on the page). The early successes of behaviourism, particularly in the study of animal activity, led behavioural psychologists to propose a general theory of human functioning, in terms of Stimulus-Response (S-R) links. All observable behaviour is classified as stimulus (input) or response (output) and the job of the psychologist is to infer lawful relationships between observed stimuli and observed responses.

Unfortunately, the method that had proven so successful in describing animal behaviour was a far from adequate account of human activity. In general, the connection between stimulus and response is complex. If I were to provide you with a stimulus by saying "What is two plus two?" then your response would be fairly predictable (not entirely so: you might give some deliberately silly response, but then the behaviourists did not have much to say about human perversity). But when I ask you, "Write down four lines of rhyming verse," then your response is far from predictable. Predictability is an important test of the success of a psychological theory; if we can say, in a given situation, what a person will do next, then it is a good indication that the theory is accurate. (You may say, after reading this book, that neither is cognitive science much good at predicting a person's response to such a question. This is true, but what cognitive science *can* offer is a theory about the general *class* of responses, and the method by which a *typical* response might be generated.) Behaviourists have attempted to bridge the gulf between stimulus and response by proposing chains of little internal S-R links, but these begin to look suspiciously like the mental states they were trying to avoid.

Another possibility is to study physical characteristics of the brain, using instruments like the electroencephalograph which records patterns of electrical current in the brain. While it is possible to say that one pattern indicates that a person is sleeping, that a different one shows the person to be awake but relaxed, and yet another indicates a burst of intense mental activity, the electrical patterns give no indication of the *content* of that mental activity. Deducing the content of mental processes from looking at the physiology of the brain is a bit like trying to find out what programme is on TV by measuring changes in electric current through transistors in a TV set. A study of the brain can give valuable information about mental functions and disorders, but it is not an open route to understanding the process of thinking.

Faced with the urge to make sense of a complex system, with sparse data and no obvious underlying rules, scientists have traditionally built models that mimic the observable parts of the system. Thus, in Renaissance times, astronomers built beautiful and intricate instruments — orreries, planispheres, armillary spheres — to model the whirl of heavenly bodies. The earliest ones were certainly inaccurate due to their builders' hazy understanding of planetary motion but, unlike the planets themselves, they were available for experiment; they could be systematically altered, then tested for accuracy by comparing their motions against observations of the planets themselves. Of course, Kepler and then Newton later came up with universal principles of planetary motion, mathematical abstractions that demoted the mechanical models to toys and teaching aids, but in the study of the mind we are still at the level of Renaissance astronomers. Psychologists have, at various times, put forward universal 'principles of behaviour', such as Thorndike's Law of Effect, but these have usually been hedged with qualifications, and subsequently shown to be far from universal. Of more interest to us are the attempts to formulate 'principles of reasoning', such those of George Boole (see section 1.3).

Designing models of the mind is nothing new: people have long attempted to describe mental states and processes in terms of current technology. Medieval scientists saw the mind as a miniature plumbing system, with reservoirs of imagination, reason, and memory stored in the brain, topped up by supplies from the sense organs and ready to flow through 'nerve fibres' to the muscles. In the late nineteenth century the favoured model was a telephone exchange, with 'wires' connecting the 'telephone exchange' in the brain to 'subscribers' at the nerve ends.

In the 1940s computers became the vogue technology and, sure enough, people began to propose the computer as a model of the mind. The newspapers of the time were full of articles about the 'superhuman brain' and 'electronic genius'. So, is the computer yet one more metaphor for the mind, to be supplanted when the next piece of technology comes along? To answer this, we first need to distinguish between **computers** and **computation**.

The computer is the conglomerate of printed circuits, wires, magnetic tape drives, floppy disk units, and so on that carries out the work. Although present-day computers vary enormously in size and cost, they are almost all of the same basic design, or **architecture** (called the **von Neumann Architecture** after the Hungarian-American who first proposed it). Each machine has a single **Central Processing Unit** (CPU) that performs the computation. The CPU has access to **main memory**, a series of data cells (you might imagine them as a long line of boxes, each containing a single simple piece of information) that are used for two quite distinct tasks. One part of main memory holds the data to be operated on: initial data (if any), intermediate values, and the final results, ready to be outputted. A separate part of the main memory holds the computer's program, in the form of a string of coded instructions to carry out operations on the data. A typical instruction might be (decoded into English) *load the data in cell 1000 into a cell (called a register) in CPU*. The typical computer also has **backup memory**, in the form of disks or tapes, to supplement main memory, and devices for interacting with the outside world, such as a keyboard and a **Visual Display Unit**, or VDU (see figure 1.1).

Despite the differences in appearance, these machines all carry out the same basic function, that of computation, where this can be defined as *performing operations on symbolic structures according to stored instructions*. Notice that in the previous paragraphs I have been careful to talk about the computer operating on 'data' rather than 'numbers'. This is because a number is only one kind of symbolic structure. There are many others — words, diagrams, musical notation, chemical formulae and so on — and the computer is capable of manipulating all of these; in fact at the most basic level, that of the electronic circuit, the computer makes no distinction between them.

Imagine a series of boxes (representing the computer's main memory). Each box can be either empty or full, so a line of them can be arranged in many different combinations: the longer the line, the more possible arrangements. (Computers actually use electrical voltages to represent the contents of a 'memory cell', one voltage being equivalent to 'full box' and another being equivalent to 'empty box'.)

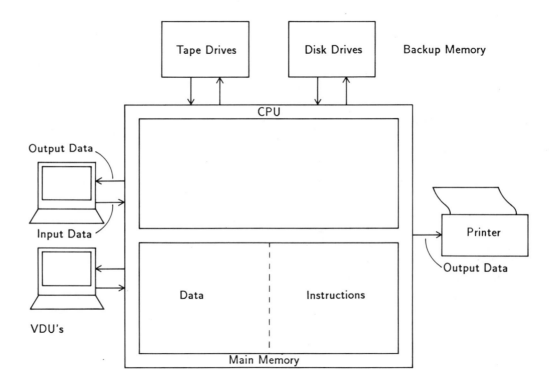

Figure 1.1
The design of a conventional computer.

One combination of boxes might be

where ■ stands for a full box and ☐ stands for an empty box.

By themselves the boxes represent nothing, they are just 'a line of boxes'. But let us construct a coding scheme, by labelling each box with a number according to its position:

32768 16384 8192 4096 2048 1024 512 256 128 64 32 16 8 4 2 1

Using this coding scheme, let a full box represent the number below it (an empty box is ignored) and then add up the numbers to get a single result. You may well recognize the coding scheme as corresponding to **binary numbers**; the advantage of this scheme is that different combinations of 'full' and 'empty' boxes can represent every number between 0 and 65535. Thus, the boxes above represent $16384 + 2048 + 64 + 8 + 1 = 18505$.

This is by no means the only way of interpreting the line of boxes. Another method could be to divide the boxes into sets of eight and add up the numbers for each set of eight: $64 + 8 = 72$ $64 + 8 + 1 = 73$

128 64 32 16 8 4 2 1 128 64 32 16 8 4 2 1

Then, by letting 65 stand for the letter A, 66 stand for the letter B, 67 stand for the letter C, and so on, we have the word HI. This letter coding scheme may seem a bit bizarre, but it is the one, called **ascii coding**, that is actually used by many computers to represent letters. A still different code, in which combinations of boxes stand for musical notes, would represent a snatch of music.

There are two important points to note. First, by using an appropriate coding scheme, the computer can be made to represent *any* symbolic structure. Second, although the coding scheme is arbitrary, in the sense that it was devised by humans and is not a characteristic of the computer itself, *so long as the scheme is consistent and the computer performs operations that are appropriate to the scheme*, then the computer can manipulate the boxes (memory cells) *as if* they were numbers, words, or music. For example, treating the boxes above as the number 18505, the computer can be instructed to add this number to another one, stored in another part of its memory, and print out the result. The computer *could* carry out the same addition operation on the 'boxes as letters', but in this case the result would not make sense, as 'addition' is not an appropriate operator for letters. Thus the computer *performs operations on symbolic structures* and the operations it carries out are determined by a set of instructions (which are themselves symbol structures stored in memory).

What makes the computer important as a 'mind modeller' is the assumption that "mental processes may be thought of, at some level, as a kind of computation." (Charniak and McDermott, 1985, p. 6)

This does not mean to say that our brains store information in the same way as computers: the coding scheme is entirely different, and, as yet, we have no idea what that scheme is. But that does not matter; what is important is that *at the right level of description, that of symbolic structures*, the computer can operate in such a way as to model mental states and operations on them.

What makes a computer superior to all previous models of the mind is that the model can actually be built, and the processes run. Nobody ever seriously suggested building a plumbing system to perform the same functions as the human mind, but computer programs that carry out tasks normally associated with minds — such as holding conversations, translating text from one language into another, diagnosing illnesses, solving puzzles, or proving mathematical theorems — have already been constructed. The great advantage of a working model is that it can be tested, by setting it well-chosen tasks to perform and seeing if it operates in the same way as a human mind. Thus, a medical diagnosis program might be asked to describe its line of reasoning, to see if it corresponds to that of a human doctor.

1.3   The Mind as Machine

Earlier I referred to the *assumption* that the human mind acts like a computer. It is only an assumption, since we have no proof that this is the full story. We do know that the mind *can* perform symbolic operations, such as adding numbers, comparing words, or transposing music, but it may be that there are other things happening in our minds that are either completely non-symbolic (experiencing emotions, for instance) or are below the level of conventional symbol processing (such as seeing and distinguishing objects). Investigating the limitations of the computational model of mind is a fascinating new area of philosophy. If it is the case that the mind is purely a symbol manipulator (and, as I have said, this is an open question), then, some philosophers have suggested, an appropriately programmed computer may not just be able to *model* the mind, but may actually *have* a mind.

At first sight this seems absurd — after all humans are made of flesh and blood and computers of metal and silicon — but again we need to distinguish between computers and computation. Nobody is suggesting that we look like computers, or act like any existing computer, but rather that thinking consists (partly or wholly) of symbol manipulation, and manipulating symbols is exactly what computers do. Now one symbol does not make a thought, and there are plenty of symbol manipulators that by no stretch of the imagination can be called minds: adding machines and electric typewriters, for instance. What makes a computer different is its ability to act autonomously, guided by its internal stored program. The issue is this: can a program be built of sufficient elegance and complexity that the computer running it can be said to have a mind?

Look at the following lines:

> Why does my waiting child like to talk?
> Why does my girl wish to dream of my song?
> You are like a song.
> By herself my waiting girl dreams.

They do not rhyme, but then neither do many of the poems of Dylan Thomas and e. e. cummings. If I told you that I wrote the lines, then you might comment that I was 'wistful' when I wrote them, or say that they expressed 'loneliness'.

In fact the lines were generated by a computer program (one called GRAM3, running on a DEC-VAX computer). Applying terms like 'wistful' to a computer program is, to say the least, strange, yet what is it that separates computer from human? If we can program a computer to write poems (albeit rather poor ones), then where do we draw the line?

Philosophers have long wished to discover just what are those qualities that distinguish human beings. Thus, the French philosopher René Descartes (1596–1650) believed that humans were guided by an immaterial mind while the rest of nature (including all animals) were driven only by the laws of physics (lumping dogs and monkeys in with clocks and windmills as mindless objects conveniently allowed Descartes to ignore any considerations of care or sympathy towards them, and he carried out some, to us, horrific experiments on live animals).

One of the pastimes of the period was the building of 'automata', clockwork dolls that looked and moved like people or animals. In a fascinating section of his book *Discourse on Method*, Descartes suggests that if it were possible to design an automaton which had the organs and outward shape of a monkey or "other animal that lacks reason," then we should have no means of telling it from a real animal. But a machine to imitate humans would be far easier to detect because humans have two special characteristics that distinguish them from automata (and from animals).

First, according to Descartes, a machine "could never use words, or put together other signs, as we do in order to declare our thoughts to others." Granted one could build a machine that utters words, e.g., if you touch it in one spot it asks you what you want of it, if you touch it in another it cries out you are hurting it, and so on," but it could not give an "appropriately meaningful answer to what is said in its presence, as the dullest of men can do."

Second the automaton would lack general reasoning abilities: "even though such machines could do some things as well, or better, than humans, they would inevitably fail in others, which would reveal that they were acting not through understanding but only from the disposition of their organs." In other words, whereas a machine has a collection of parts to respond to particular situations (a chiming clock, for example, is set off by the position of its gear wheels), human reason is "a universal instrument which can be used in all kinds of situations" (Descartes, 1642).

In thus proposing the differences between people and machines Descartes did not appeal to our intuition, nor did he suggest that ethereal qualities like a 'soul' or 'emotion' set us apart from machines. Instead he indicated two testable human characteristics: the meaningful use of language and general reasoning abilities. As you will see later, language and reasoning are central themes of present-day research in artificial intelligence.

It is hardly surprising that Descartes considered there were fundamental differences between people and machines, since the only machines around at the time were either substitutes for human muscle, like the windmill, or highly specialized recording and tabulating machines, like clocks, or cunningly designed dolls that merely simulated the outward appearance and movements of humans.

As it happens, at almost the same time that Descartes wrote his *Discourse on*

Method another French philosopher, Blaise Pascal (1623–1662), was designing a mechanical calculator that could perform addition and subtraction, and in the 1670s Gottfried Leibniz (1646–1716) built one that could multiply and divide. Although these were early examples of symbol manipulation machines, they were still specialized devices, dedicated to carrying out a narrow range of arithmetic tasks. The first general purpose programmable symbol manipulator (and as such a candidate for 'mind model') came 200 years later.

Charles Babbage (1791–1871), an eccentric British mathematician, planned to build two different machines. The first, which he called the 'Difference Engine', was for calculating mathematical tables. It was an elegant and complex device but, like Pascal's calculator, it was devoted to a single task. The second, his 'Analytical Engine', was a general purpose calculator, and was the product of a magnificent combination of mathematical insight and mechanical skills. It had many of the features of a modern computer, with a Central Processing Unit (which he called the 'Mill'), a data memory, and a controlling unit, and, unlike previous calculators, it could be programmed to perform different sequences of operations. The programs were encoded as holes punched on cards that were fed into the machine. The entire contraption would have been the size of a car; unfortunately it was never built, not because the design was faulty, but because nineteenth-century engineering was not up to the precision needed for the hundreds of gears and cogs.

Although the Analytical Engine was intended as a numeric calculator, Babbage and his friends were sufficiently astute to realize that similar machines could be devised and programmed to operate on other kinds of symbolic data. They also speculated on whether such machines might be called intelligent. A colleague of Babbage, Ada Lovelace, in a written commentary on a set of Babbage's lecture notes, wrote, "The Analytical Engine has no pretensions to *originate* anything. It can only do *whatever we know how to order it* to perform" (Bowden, 1953).

This is reminiscent of Descartes' argument that machines cannot reason (since reasoning involves the creation of new ideas), and the notion that computers cannot be creative persists to the present day. Certainly a computer is under the direct control of its program, but this need not be a restriction, for the simple reason that we can progam the computer to be creative.

One of the great intellectual achievements of the late nineteenth and early twentieth centuries was the invention of a 'calculus of reasoning'. It began in 1854 with George Boole's *Investigation of the Laws of Thought*. Boole tried to set down precise logical definitions of words like *and* and *or* and the rules whereby they can be used to build complex statements out of simple ones, like

It is hot today and it will rain or it will get hotter.

Then, in the late nineteenth century, Gottlob Frege developed a formal method of representing more of the internal structure of sentences and set out formal **rules of inference** for deriving new statements from old. These ideas were developed during this century by Bertrand Russell and A. N. Whitehead, among others, into what is now known as **predicate logic**. The rules of predicate logic specify ways of checking whether an inference is valid merely by analysing the structures of symbols. Thus, a machine that attached no meaning to the symbols could be programmed to apply these rules and check, for example, that

All As are Bs

does not validly entail

All Bs are As

but does validly entail

If no Cs are Bs then no Cs are As.

No such machine had then been built, but during the 1930s mathematicians began to consider 'what would happen if' the rules of predicate calculus were mechanized. The next step was to show that besides checking the validity of existing inferences, machines could also generate new valid inferences, thereby deriving new **theorems** from some set of **axioms**. If a machine could derive interesting ones that had not previously been discovered by people, that would be a form of creativity. This mechanization of reasoning also inspired the hope that yet more complex systems of rules would enable a machine to invent new concepts and new axioms, instead of simply deriving theorems from axioms given to it by its designers. This would overcome Descartes' objection that reasoning must be the preserve of humans and Lady Lovelace's that symbol manipulating machines cannot be creative. (It cannot be claimed that these more ambitious goals have been achieved already, though work in artificial intelligence seems to be steadily moving toward them, in ways that will be illustrated in this book.)

These, and other more subtle arguments against 'machine intelligence', were discussed by the next great name in computing, Alan Turing. Turing was another

British mathematician and, although not quite as eccentric as Babbage, his life was just as eventful. After setting out the theoretical foundations of computing in the 1930s he worked during World War II at Bletchley Park, where a group of academics had been assembled by the British government to try and crack the coded messages broadcast by the German armed forces. To help them in this task, they built what was arguably the world's first electronic computer. The machine, called Colossus, was built two years before ENIAC, the first US computer, but it was cloaked in military secrecy and, being designed for code breaking, did not have a general purpose architecture. Alan Turing also worked on the world's first commercially available electronic computer, the Ferranti Mark I.

In 1950 Turing published a celebrated paper entitled "Computing Machinery and Intelligence" in which he addressed the question "Can machines think?" (The paper has been reprinted many times and can be found in, for example, Hofstadter and Dennett, 1981.) The paper is entertaining and nontechnical. It begins with what he calls the 'Imitation Game' (later to be known as the **Turing Test**), played between three people, a man (A), a woman (B), and an interrogator (C) (who may be of either sex). The people are in separate rooms and the interrogator cannot see A or B. The only method of communication is by teleprinter link, and the interrogator does not know which line goes to A and which to B. The object of the game is for the man (person A) to fool the interrogator into believing he is a woman (person B). Thus, the interrogator might type a message down the line saying "Name me three types of knitting stitch," and, if the line were to the man, he would answer saying something like: "Plain, purl, and basket."

Now for the purpose of the Imitation Game: imagine it as before, with one teleprinter line from the interrogator to a human (the sex of the human is now not important), but the other to a computer. The object is now to program the computer so that it can imitate the human. The question and answer session, Turing suggested, might go something like this:

Q: Please write me a sonnet on the subject of the Forth Bridge.

A: Count me out on this one. I never could write poetry.

Q: Add 34957 to 70764.

A: *(Pause about 30 seconds and then give as answer)* 105621.

Q: Do you play chess?

A: Yes.

> Q: I have K at my K1, and no other pieces. You have only K at K6
>   and R at R1. It is your move. What do you play?
>
> A: *(After a pause of 15 seconds)* R-R8 mate.

Notice that the respondent gives a wrong answer to the addition in the dialogue
above; imitating a person involves mimicking human errors and lapses. If, after a
reasonable number of questions, the interrogator cannot tell which line is connected
to the human and which to the computer, then the computer might be said to
think.

In the second part of the paper, Turing raises, and dismisses, some of the reasons
(such as the argument that computers cannot be creative) why it might not be
feasible to program a computer to pass his test.

By the design of the experiment, Turing followed Descartes in implying that
intelligence is the ability to reason and to communicate by language. More recent discussions of machine intelligence have tended to take such feats for granted
(even though passing the Turing Test is way beyond the capabilities of any existing
computer program) and instead have concentrated on whether other human qualities like consciousness and emotion can be ascribed to a (suitably programmed)
computer.

1.4   Intelligent Machines

Whether or not a computer might actually be intelligent, it can certainly put up
a good show. In the more relaxed years following World War II people on both
sides of the Atlantic borrowed time on the new computing machines to try out
their unconventional ideas. One of the earliest areas of interest was chess playing
programs (chess being a game that clearly demands intelligence, yet is easy to
describe in symbolic terms), and early in the 1950s a number of chess playing
programs were devised (including one by the ubiquitous Alan Turing). In 1955
Alan Newell, J. C. Shaw, and H. A. Simon at the Systems Research Laboratory of
the RAND Corporation (in breaks from writing an Air Defense radar simulator)
turned their attention to producing a theorem-proving program, called the 'Logic
Theorist', for mathematical logic. The idea was to take logic theorems (from the
standard book on predicate logic by Russell and Whitehead) and prove that they
could be deduced either from five basic axioms or from previously proven theorems.

Theorem proving is pretty mundane work for mathematicians, but was a great
leap forward for computers. Until then, computer programs had had the form of

algorithms: step-by-step instructions on how to reach the solution to a problem. Here is an algorithm (adapted from British Telecom's instructions on how to use a Phonecard):

1. Lift the receiver and listen for the dial tone.

2. Insert the green card into the slot, green side up, and press it fully home.

3. Dial the number you want.

4. Listen for the ringing tone and speak when connected.

5. If the number is engaged, or when you finish the call, replace the receiver and the card will be ejected.

6. Retrieve the card.

The algorithm is not foolproof — the phone may be vandalized, or the card may be torn — but it is guaranteed to find a solution (let you make a phone call) *if a solution exists.*

To make the call, you, the caller, must follow the instructions and perform the actions; with an algorithm in the form of a computer program, that task is carried out by the computer. The following line is an algorithm to draw a square written in the computer language Logo:

repeat 4 [forward 100 right 90]

When this is typed to a computer running Logo, a blip of light on the screen moves forward 100 units; it then changes direction by 90 degrees and so on four times. The computer directly **interprets** the algorithm. (Just how the computer interprets the instructions of a program is a long story. In brief, the instructions are converted automatically into a longer list of primitive instructions which correspond to actions that the computer **hardware** can carry out.) What Newell, Shaw, and Simon invented was the notion of a programmable **heuristic**. A heuristic corresponds roughly to a 'rule of thumb'. It may help in solving a problem but, unlike an algorithm, it is *not guaranteed to find a solution.* Newell, Shaw, and Simon defined 'heuristic' thus: "A process that *may* solve a given problem, but offers no guarantee of doing so, is called a 'heuristic' for that problem" (Newell, Shaw, and Simon, 1963b). (Since then, the term has been used in other ways — for instance, to describe methods that improve the efficiency of algorithms by making use of specific facts about the problem domain.) Below is an example of a heuristic, from an incident that happened to one of the authors.

> I used to go skiing at Glenshee in Scotland, a resort notorious for its sudden changes in weather. Just as I reached the top of a ski tow mist suddenly descended and the wind blew up to an icy gale. I could not see more than five feet ahead. A small group of us skied gingerly away from the tow and then when the wind became too strong, took off our skis and walked.
>
> After about 20 minutes trying to find the ski run we realized that we were hopelessly lost. We flung off our characteristic British reserve and argued furiously about where to go. At this point an ex-paratrooper took command. "What we have to do," he said "is to turn round and walk back along the contour line of the hill, not going up or down. Providing we are below the top of the ski-tow, we will eventually get back to it."

After looking at the instructions below, and before reading the text that follows it, try and think of circumstances in which the the instructions would not have led to a successful solution (the group being back at the ski tow).

Now this is a perfectly rigorous specification for action. If we had been carrying altimeters, we could have written a set of instructions of the form

1. Measure initial altitude and call it A.

2. Turn round 180 degrees.

3. Walk 50 paces in the direction we faced at the end of step 2.

4. Measure the new altitude and call it B.

5. If B is greater than A then walk down the hill until B equals A.

6. If B is less than A then walk up the hill until B equals A.

7. Repeat steps 3 to 6 until we see the ski tow.

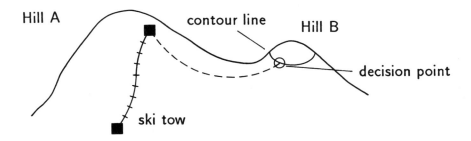

Figure 1.2
A situation in which the 'contour' heuristic fails.

But the instructions are not guaranteed to find a solution to the problem.

Suppose we had been in the situation shown in figure 1.2. In that case, following the contour line from the decision point would just have led the party round in circles on hill B and they would never have reached the tow.

Although a heuristic does not guarantee a solution, it is a powerful computational tool. Knowledge of the problem **domain** (in this case the knowledge that the ski tow should cross the contour line at some point around the hill) can make all the difference in finding a practical solution to a problem: the strategy was successful and the party soon found the ski tow (a domain general solution to the problem would have been to fan out in every direction, searching in wider and wider circles; some of the party would certainly have collapsed from exhaustion before they could reach civilization!).

In the case of the Logic Theorist a domain general algorithm would start with the five basic axioms and would work by applying the rules of deduction in turn to generate more and more possible theorems, until it happened to come up with one that was in Russell and Whitehead's book. To prove 50 theorems by this method would take a modern computer billions of years. But using heuristics to guide the generation, the Logic Theorist managed to find 38 of the first 52 proofs in the book in a few hours of computer time.

The success of the Logic Theorist attracted the attention of other mathematicians and computer scientists, and in 1956 the term **artificial intelligence** was coined when John McCarthy organized a "two month ten-man study of artificial intelligence" at Dartmouth College, New Hampshire. Among the participants were Newell and Simon, and Marvin Minsky from Massachusetts Institute of Technology, who was to be one of the leading proponents of AI during the next decade.

In the 1960s general problem solving methods, supplemented by domain specific heuristics, were applied to a wide range of problems, and AI gradually separated out into the application areas of language understanding and generation, game playing, theorem proving, vision, and robotics. With a few exceptions (such as Newell and Simon's monumental work *Human Problem Solving*, 1972) there was little attempt to construct programs that accurately modelled the human mind; the emphasis was on performance — computer systems that *acted* in intelligent ways by, for instance, playing chess or solving mathematical problems. The general approach was one of **successive refinement**: start with a method that approximates the desired action (e.g., a program that plays chess badly, or solves puzzles in a large number of steps) and then refine it until it behaves to the standard expected of an intelligent human.

To return again to computer-generated poetry: a first approximation might be to write a program that picked at random from a large list of words, taking a new line say every five words:

> Crinoline it erase hostile delve
> Gourd transit self low care
> Ton oyster irrigate fly coriander

Clearly this will not do. We need a method of forming the words into an orderly pattern. So, the next step in the refinement process might be to group the words according to part of speech, collecting together:

> **nouns:** aardvark, abacus, abalone, . . . , zebra
> **verbs:** abandon, abase, abate, . . . , zoom

and so on. By specifying an appropriate pattern of parts of speech, such as

> adverb article adjective noun verb
> preposition adjective adjective noun

we could instruct the computer to generate words in a better order:

Elegantly a patient seed flush
Over inarticulate translucent demon

The next refinement would be to ensure that the words agreed in number (i.e., singular or plural) and tense (past, present, future). The stage after that would be to add a list of 'meaning tags' to each word:

WORD	PART OF SPEECH	MEANING TAGS
rock	noun	inanimate, still, ground
bird	noun	animal, moving, air
snowflake	noun	inanimate, moving, air

and rewrite the program so that it chooses words with similar meaning tags. This is the method used to generate the poem shown earlier, in section 1.3. But here we come to a dead halt. Human poets do not merely pour out words to fixed patterns, matched for meaning; they call on experience of past events, their emotions, and knowledge of how the world is organized.

Since 1970 there have been major advances in AI: in the design of prototype programs such as Winograd's SHRDLU (described in chapter 3); in the application of AI to commerce and industry through **expert systems** which can perform some of the tasks of a human expert in, for example, diagnosing diseases or identifying mineral deposits (but without the extensive background knowledge of a true human expert); and in the design of new programming languages and computers to help the AI programmer. But to progress further towards the goal of intelligent systems, AI researchers now need to understand more about the workings of the human mind. How to represent commonsense knowledge, experience, emotion and senses in a symbolic form that can be manipulated by computer is one of the main themes of present-day research in artificial intelligence and a major topic of this book.

1.5 Beyond Symbol Processors

What if some of these human faculties cannot be imitated by operations on symbols? That need not be the end of the road for AI. From the very earliest days nonsymbolic machines have been used for computing. Until the end of the 1940s **analogue computers** were as promising as digital ones. An analogue computer has no store of symbols waiting to be pushed around by instructions, but instead carries out computation by representing values directly, as electrical voltages, or

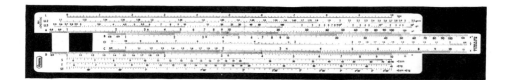

Figure 1.3
A slide rule.

lengths, or turns of a gear wheel. (A slide rule (see figure 1.3) is a simple example of an analogue computer, where numbers are represented as lengths along a piece of wood or plastic.) Analogue computers fell out of fashion largely because each one was designed to do just a limited range of tasks, such as solving differential equations, unlike the more versatile digital machine.

Another strand of AI, which gained strength in the 1950s and 60s, is neural modelling. The human brain does not seem to have one central processor controlling passive memory cells, but a complex network of active neurons (brain cells). The mystery is how a "large number of highly interconnected elements [the neurons] which apparently send very simple excitatory and inhibitory messages to each other" (McClelland, Rumelhart, and the PDP Research Group, 1986) can support the intricacies of human reasoning. There is now a great revival of interest in neural modelling, both as an attempt to understand the fine detail of human cognition (those processes that go on below our awareness, for example, the recognition of visual images, coordination of hand and eye, and learning of concepts), and more generally as a simulation of the human brain and a competitor to the symbol-processing tradition of artificial intelligence.

Most of the work in neural modelling is carried out by simulating the **neural networks** on a conventional computer, but machines are now being designed with not one complicated central processor, but hundreds of simple **distributed processors**, connected together somewhat like neurons in the brain. The hope is that not only can these model the subsymbolic actions of the brain, but that they can also be used as the building blocks for machines that mimic the many levels of human thought, from the stimulation of a single neuron to the sophistication of conscious reasoning. That is still only a hope; we are still a long way from being able to design 'electronic brains'.

1.6 Conclusion

AI is at the centre of a new enterprise to build computational models of intelligence. The main assumption is that intelligence (human or otherwise) can be represented in terms of symbol structures and symbolic operations which can be programmed in a digital computer. There is much debate as to whether such an appropriately programmed computer would *be* a mind, or would merely *simulate* one, but AI researchers need not wait for the conclusion to that debate, nor for the hypothetical computer that could model all of human intelligence. Aspects of intelligent behaviour, such as solving problems, making inferences, learning, and understanding language, have already been coded as computer programs, and within very limited domains, such as identifying diseases of soybean plants, AI programs can outperform human experts. Now the great challenge of AI is to find ways of representing the commonsense knowledge and experience that enable people to carry out everyday activities such as holding a wide-ranging conversation, or finding their way along a busy street. Conventional digital computers may be capable of running such programs, or we may need to develop new machines that can support the complexity of human thought.

1.7 Appendix: Programming in POP-11

1.7.1 Automated Tourist Guide

So far we have introduced the notion of symbolic computing without actually teaching you any programming language. That time has now come.

Imagine a tourist standing in Victoria Underground Station, with a day to see the sights of London. In front of him is a video screen, with a keyboard below. On the screen is the following message:

```
Welcome to the London Tourist Guide

This guide can answer your queries about landmarks,
attractions and events in London.

Please type your query in English, for example:
How do I get to the National Gallery?

Press the RETURN button to finish a query.
```

He types in the words

```
Where is Marble Arch?
```

It responds with

```
Marble Arch is at the West End of Oxford Street.
```

He then types

```
Please tell me about entertainments in London.
```

It replies

```
Where do you want to go:  city centre or suburbs?
```

He replies, and it engages him in a conversation about his preferences for entertainment, and ends by offering a list of possible events to suit his taste.

No such automated tourist guide has yet been installed in Victoria Station, London. Your task as an AI programmer is to design one!

You will be using a programming language called **POP-11** (after Robin Popplestone, one of its inventors). POP-11 has been developed for research and teaching in artificial intelligence and is designed to be simple to learn (simple, that is, compared to other programming languages!) yet powerful enough for programming full-scale artificial intelligence systems. The entire POP-11 language is large and to describe it in detail would more than fill a book.[1]

We have therefore restricted all the examples in this book to a subset of POP-11 and appendix A (at the back of the book) gives a guide to it. We do not assume that you have access to a computer running POP-11: you should be able to understand the examples by following them line by line on paper.

POP-11 is a **procedural programming language**, which means that programs are written as a series of **commands** to the machine to perform operations on symbol structures (called **data objects**).

1.7.2   Data Objects

The full POP-11 has some 21 different types of data object, but we will be concerned with just four: **numbers**, **words**, **booleans**, and **lists**. Here are some examples of each type:

---

[1]More complete guides to POP-11 are Barrett, Ramsay, and Sloman (1985), Burton and Shadbolt (1987), and Laventhol (1987).

Numbers

```
66 9987679 -66   0   3.14159 -22.55
```

Numbers may be integers (counting numbers) like 10, 12345, or –66, or they may be decimal numbers like 2.13 or –55.55.

Words

```
"cat" "ninety" "if" "HI" "hello_there" "MI5"
```

A POP-11 word consists of a letter followed by a series of letters or numbers and is put between double quote marks. No blank spaces are allowed, so "hello there" is not a legal POP-11 word. The underline symbol _ is taken to be a letter, so "hello_there" is a legal POP-11 word.

Booleans

```
<true>   <false>
```

There are very many different possible words or numbers, but only two booleans (named after the logician George Boole). We will deal with booleans in chapter 2.

Lists

```
[The cat sat on the mat]      [1 Acacia Avenue]
[name [Joe Bloggs] age 33]
```

A list is different to the other data objects because it can contain any other type of data object, including other lists. Thus the first example is a list made up of five words: "The" "cat" "sat" "on" "the" "mat" (when a word is inside a list the surrounding quote marks are omitted). The second example is a list comprising a number followed by two words. The third example has four elements: a word "name", a list [Joe Bloggs], a word "age" and a number 33.

1.7.3   Commands

POP-11 commands are instructions for the computer to perform some action on a specified data object. A simple action is to display the object on the screen; the command to do this is represented by the following symbol, called a **print arrow**: =>. You type it by pressing the = key and then the > key. To display a data object, you type the object, followed by a print arrow, e.g.,

```
[The cat sat on the mat] =>
** [The cat sat on the mat]
```

24

```
"cat" =>
** cat
```

In this book we shall indicate symbols typed in by the user in bold type and the responses produced by the program in normal type. The two stars merely indicate that the item has been displayed using the print arrow. The 'pretty print' symbol =>>[2] will display lists without the outer brackets or the two stars:

```
[Welcome to the London Tourist Guide] =>>
Welcome to the London Tourist Guide
```

You can put spaces between items. An item is a single data object or symbol (e.g., cat or =>). Thus, you could write,

```
[ The cat sat on the mat ] =>
** [The cat sat on the mat]
```

POP-11 will not interpret the command correctly if you split items (e.g., if you type = > rather than => or c a t rather than cat).

Simply displaying an object on the screen is not a very exciting demonstration of the power of the computer, but commands can be applied not only to objects but also to combinations of objects, called **expressions**. An expression is a series of objects linked by **operators**. One familiar kind is the arithmetic expression, consisting of numbers linked by arithmetic operators such as + - / (for 'divide') and * (for 'multiply'). An expression followed by a print arrow instructs the computer to **evaluate** the expression and display the result, e.g.,

```
2+2=>
** 4
```

```
12 - 3 + 5 =>
** 14
```

POP-11 **interprets** a program by carrying out each command in turn, where necessary evaluating the expressions and applying the command to the result. When the last command has been interpreted, the program ends.

---

[2]The pretty print symbol is not a standard POP-11 operator. It is defined at the start of appendix B.

1.7.4 Procedures

A procedure is a sequence of commands that have been given a name. To instruct the computer to interpret the commands (known as **calling the procedure**) you simply give the name of the procedure followed by parentheses. Most POP-11 procedures take inputs and return results. The inputs (called **arguments**) are put inside the parentheses when the procedure is called. The procedure length, for example, returns the length of a data object given as its argument:

```
length([the cat sat on the mat])=>
** 6


length("cat")=>
** 3
```

It is not necessary to know the detailed structure of a procedure in order to use it. In general, a procedure contains a complicated series of commands, and it would be very inconvenient to have to remember or repeat the commands each time you want to call it. Instead you merely have to remember the procedure's name and how it is used. You can imagine the procedure as a box, with a name, zero or more inputs, and zero or more outputs:

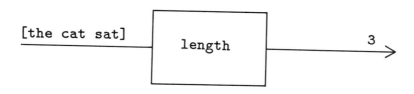

1.7.5 Mishaps

Mishaps are an everyday part of programming. Sometimes they are the result of giving a POP-11 procedure the wrong type of input; sometimes, as in the example below, they are caused by a character left out, a word mistyped, or a symbol put in the wrong place.

```
length [the cat] ) =>

;;; MISHAP - MSEP: MISSING SEPARATOR (eg semicolon)
;;; INVOLVING: length [
;;; DOING : compile
```

Occasionally a mishap message can be hard to understand, but generally they are informative. The first line of the message gives the type of mishap: in this case a missing separator, the (character. The next line gives the position of the mishap (between length and [), and the third line is a 'calling sequence' that would give an experienced programmer more information about where the mishap occurred.

1.7.6   Variables

We now need a way of storing information in the computer's memory so that the results of expressions can be saved for later use. Earlier in the chapter we said that memory can be thought of as if it were a large number of boxes, each of which is capable of storing some information. To use them, we place a particular piece of information in a named location (box), and then refer by name to the the location that contains the information. A named location is called a **variable**. POP-11 carries out the work of allocating and accessing particular locations automatically. Suppose that we want to store a list of words in memory. We give that part of memory a name, say myinfo, by means of the POP-11 instruction

```
vars myinfo;
```

It is preceded by **vars** because myinfo is the name of a variable. Any POP-11 word can be the name of a variable, and the **vars** instruction **declares** the variable by entering the word in its list of variable names and by allocating memory for it. Once we have given the **vars** command, we can store a data item in the memory set aside, and refer to it again by the name myinfo. We can have as many variables as we like in a POP-11 program and we can declare more than one in a **vars** command; they should be separated by commas.

1.7.7   Assignment

To store a list in the memory that the new variable refers to, we use the POP-11 *assignment* command, indicated by an 'assignment arrow', written ->. To store the list [1 Acacia Avenue] with the name myinfo, we give the command

```
[1 Acacia Avenue] -> myinfo;
```

Now whenever we refer to `myinfo` again, the POP-11 system plucks out the stored information. For example, the following command prints the data object with the name `myinfo`:

```
myinfo =>
** [1 Acacia Avenue]
```

If we store something new in the variable, then the old information that was stored there is simply lost: the chunk of computer memory for the variable gets changed, and there is no record of what was there before. So, the command below changes the information in `myinfo` from the list [1 Acacia Avenue] to the word "cats":

```
"cats" -> myinfo;
myinfo =>
** cats
```

In fact you can have any POP-11 expression on the left of the assignment arrow, and the result will be stored in the variable on the right of the arrow. So if you write

```
12 / 3 -> myinfo;
```

then `myinfo` thereafter refers to the number 4.

You can regard the chunk of memory labelled by a variable as if it were elastic: you can store a list of any length in it without worrying about the details of how this is done. In fact POP-11 can lump together the primitive units of memory (the empty and full boxes of section 1.2) to store numbers, words, booleans, or lists of any length in the section of memory associated with one variable. One of many tasks of a programming language like POP-11 is to relieve the programmer of having to think about how memory is allocated. POP-11 also 'remembers' what type of data is stored: it records whether `myinfo` refers to a list, a word, a number, or a boolean. This can be useful. If you accidentally try to multiply a number by a list, for instance, POP-11 will give a mishap message to say that this is an illegal operation. The reason why variables are so very useful is that they enable us to write programs without our knowing in advance what information the programs are going to work with.

1.7.8   User-Defined Procedures

The `length` procedure given earlier is already part of the POP-11 language. You can write other procedures yourself as you need them. Writing a **user-defined** procedure is a way of extending the POP-11 language, since the procedure functions in exactly the same way as a built-in one. Here is how you might define a procedure that works out how to add purchase tax to a price. Suppose that you have to add 15% tax to the cost of items you buy. To calculate the tax the procedure must multiply the price by 15%, or 0.15:

```
;;; This procedure multiplies the price by 0.15
;;; to get 15%
define tax(price) -> amount;
     price * 0.15 -> amount;
enddefine;
```

All the words after the three semicolons `;;;` until the end of the first line are taken as comments and are ignored by POP-11. Comments are useful to you, and to anyone who might read your program, to remind you of the purpose and effect of a procedure.

The line signalled by the word **define** is the procedure heading:

```
define tax(price) -> amount;
```

It tells the system that you want to define a new procedure **tax** that takes one input, or argument, and produces one output, or result. Since we do not know what the actual argument and result will be we, use a variables called **price** and **amount** to refer to them. We could have used any other names, e.g., **abc** and **xyz**, as in

```
define tax(abc) -> xyz;
     abc * 0.15 -> xyz;
enddefine;
```

The `-> amount` is not an assignment. It indicates that there will be one result of the procedure and that the value of the result will be the value assigned to **amount** within the propcedure. The second line of the procedure is

```
price * 0.15 -> amount;
```

This carries out the calculation. When the procedure is called, the argument given is multiplied by 0.15 and that value of the expression is assigned to the variable **amount**. It is this value that is returned as the result. The last line ends the definition of the procedure. Neither **price** nor **amount** need to be declared with a **vars** statement since they are both **local** to the procedure and are declared in its heading.

A procedure definition is not a command, so POP-11 does not perform any action when you type it in. Only when you call the procedure will POP-11 respond. You do that by giving its name followed by arguments in brackets:

```
tax(10)=>
** 1.5

tax(50)=>
** 7.5
```

Thus the tax on a £10 item is £1.50 and the tax on a £50 item is £7.50. Now that the **tax** procedure has been defined, it acts in the same way as a built-in one, as a box with, in this case, one input and one result,

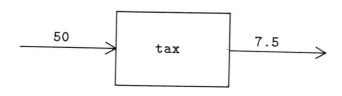

but by following the commands within the procedure, line by line, you can follow its actions. If the **tax** procedure is called with an argument of 50, as in the second example above, then the first line of the procedure **assigns** the value of 50 to the variable **price**. The next line multiplies the assigned value of **price** by 0.15 and this is returned as the result of the procedure call. The procedure then ends. The returned value is then displayed.

A call to one procedure can form part of the definition of another procedure. Say we want to extend the tax calculation so that POP-11 returns the value of a given item with 15% tax added to the original price. This calculation divides neatly into two steps:

1. Calculate the 15% tax for the original price.

2. Add the tax onto the price and return it.

We already have a procedure, tax, to calculate 15% tax for any given price, so we merely need to write another procedure that adds the tax to the price:

```
define cost(price) -> amount;
      price + tax(price) -> amount; ;;; add 15% tax
enddefine;
```

Having defined the cost procedure we can now call it

```
cost(10)=>
** 11.5


cost(50)=>
** 57.5
```

Thus a £50 article will cost £57.50 after 15% tax has been added. Notice that we have used the variables price and amount again within the cost procedure. This does not get confused with those of the same name within tax because an argument variable is local to the procedure in which it is used. Thus, tax creates its own storage space for its price and amount variables, which is quite separate to that of the variables inside cost.

You now know enough POP-11 to understand the first part of the Automated Tourist Guide: a procedure which we shall call welcome that displays the 'Welcome' message shown in section 1.7.1.

```
define welcome;
    [Welcome to the London Tourist Guide]=>>
    [This guide can answer your queries about landmarks,]=>>
    [attractions and events in London]=>>
    [Please type your query in English, for example:]=>>
    [How do I get to the National Gallery?]=>>
    [Press the RETURN button to finish a query]=>>
enddefine;
```

The procedure can now be run by typing

```
welcome();
Welcome to the London Tourist Guide
This guide can answer your queries about landmarks ,
attractions and events in London
Please type your query in English , for example :
How do I get to the National Gallery ?
Press the RETURN button to finish a query
```

This is only the first procedure of a much larger program. The difficult part comes next: reading in the tourist's query and producing a useful response.

1.8 Exercises

1. Write (in English) an algorithm for making poached egg on toast, taking into account that you might have run out of eggs, toast, or butter.

2. The procedure **date** returns a list containing the current date and time:

   ```
   date() =>
   ** [21 Mar 1989 13 51 24]
   ```

   What would be printed out by the following POP-11 commands:

   ```
   length(date()) + length("date")=>
   [length(date)]=>
   "length(date)"=>

   vars date_length;
   date() -> date_length;
   date_length + date_length -> date_length;
   date_length =>
   ```

3. Write a POP-11 procedure **area** that takes as its argument the radius of a disk and returns its area (given that an expression to calculate the area is **3.14159*radius*radius**). Incorporate **area** in a procedure **volume** that takes two arguments, representing the radius and height of a cylinder, and returns its volume (given that the volume of a cylinder is **area*height**).

4. Read Turing's paper entitled "Computing Machinery and Intelligence," in Hofstadter and Dennett (1981). Is his 'Imitation Game' a valid test of intelligence? What are its limitations? Turing sets out some objections to the assertion that "machines can think" and dismisses each one. Can you think of any more objections? Are the dismissals fair? Given what you have read so far, and your own background knowledge and opinions, do you agree with Turing's claim that "at the end of the century the use of words and general educated opinion will have altered so much that one will be able to speak of machines thinking without expecting to be contradicted"?

Chapter 2

Performance without Knowledge

2.1 A Conversation with a Computer

Can a computer hold a conversation? You can certainly communicate with one in a variety of ways: when you type in the amount of money you want from an automatic cash dispenser, when you move the joystick to produce an effect in a computer game, even sometimes when you simply dial a telephone number, you are communicating information to a computer, and you hope it will produce an appropriate response. In these cases the response will be selected from a relatively small range of possibilities. To use a computer to the full you can give it instructions in a language such as BASIC, PASCAL or POP-11 which express in general terms what you want it to do (if you choose to read the chapter appendices of this book, you will begin to learn one of these languages, POP-11), but computer languages are not a natural form of communication for people.

What about English? Computers are, after all, general purpose information-processing machines, and they would presumably be all the more useful if they could respond to normal human language. There are a number of answers to this question, some of which will be discussed in this chapter. To begin with, here is an example of a real conversation, in English, with a computer (or to be precise, with the combination of a computer and a program). The computer starts the conversation and its contribution is in upper case.

```
GOOD DAY WHAT IS YOUR PROBLEM?
I haven't much of a problem really
DO YOU THINK YOU ARE UNIQUE?
I think I am unique in some ways
SOMETIMES YOU THINK YOU AREN'T UNIQUE IN SOME WAYS
That's true as well, I'm sure
ARE YOU SURE?
Yes, I am certain
IS THIS THE FIRST TIME YOU'VE BEEN CERTAIN?
No, I have felt certain of things before now
DOES ANYONE ELSE HAVE THAT PROBLEM?
It's hardly a problem, is it?
FIRST TELL ME WHY YOU HAVE COME HERE
To talk to a computer
TO TALK TO A COMPUTER
Yes, to talk to a computer
SUPPOSE I WERE NOT A COMPUTER
Then I wouldn't be talking to you
EARLIER YOU SAID YOU HAVEN'T MUCH OF A PROBLEM REALLY
That's true, apart from money like everyone
WHAT DO YOU THINK ABOUT MONETARIST POLICIES?
They don't seem to make much money for me
HAVE YOU TALKED TO THE PRIME MINISTER ABOUT THAT?
No of course not
WOULD EVERYONE FIND THAT OBVIOUS?
Anyone who wasn't a computer
DO MACHINES WORRY YOU?
```

Whether machines worry you or not, you might find that conversation slightly at odds with the image of a computer as a machine for calculating payroll slips or spacecraft trajectories. This computer seems to be displaying some unexpected qualities: its conversation is rather aimless and chatty, though it has ready answers in a number of subjects; it can refer to itself and its interlocutor; it appears to show human peculiarities such as impatience and facetiousness; it seems to be somewhat on the defensive too. The program in question can carry on a conversation like the one above for a considerable length of time, and can even occasionally give the impression of having an insight into human affairs.

So, let us continue with this sample of conversation (though few of us would wish to consult a computer that manages to be both condescending and evasive), as the human partner becomes increasingly irritated with the program's aimlessness.

```
No, computers worry me very little
MOST COMPUTERS ARE AS STUPID AS THEIR
PROGRAMMERS
Why do you say that?
IS THAT QUESTION RHETORICAL?
No, I really want to know
BEWARE OF ADDICTIONS
Why should I?
WHAT MAKES YOU THINK I KNOW THE ANSWER?
Tell me about yourself
WE WERE DISCUSSING YOU NOT ME
But I want to talk about you
BEWARE OF ADDICTIONS
You have said that twice now
I HAVE SAID THAT TWICE NOW
Can't you be a bit more interesting than that?
I CAN'T HELP IF YOU ASK TOO MANY QUESTIONS
OK, but I think you are not being very helpful at all
WOULD YOU TRUST A MACHINE TO HELP?
No
YOU ARE BEING SOMEWHAT SHORT WITH ME
Yes
ARE YOU PREPARED TO ELABORATE?
I don't want to elaborate
DO YOU EVER SUFFER WITHDRAWAL SYMPTOMS?
Your comments get sillier and sillier
DOES ANYONE ELSE HAVE THAT PROBLEM?
You asked that before when you couldn't think of anything
better to say
DID YOU REALLY EXPECT ME TO UNDERSTAND THAT?
You understand nothing, I think
I UNDERSTAND NOTHING, YOU THINK
```

```
You understand nothing
PLEASE EXPLAIN SO THAT A STUPID COMPUTER CAN
FOLLOW YOU
If I could explain to you I could explain anything to
anyone
IF YOU COULD EXPLAIN TO I YOU COULD
EXPLAIN ANYTHING TO ANYONE
You are a very simple-minded program
SUPPOSE I WERE NOT A VERY SIMPLE-MINDED PROGRAM
We'll come to that later
COME TO THAT LATER
Stop repeating me and say something new!
ARE YOU USING YOURSELF AS A SCAPE-GOAT?
It wouldn't pay me to
WHAT DO YOU THINK ABOUT MONETARIST POLICIES?
You already asked, you want to be more original
CAN YOU DO WITHOUT?
Without what?
IS THAT QUESTION IMPORTANT TO YOU?
```

The program is loosely based on a well-known one, developed by Joseph Weizenbaum in the mid-1960s, called ELIZA. ELIZA altered people's view of computers, since it appeared that computer science had breached the defenses of human language. In one version, ELIZA took the role of a nondirective therapist — that is to say, a psychiatrist whose main aim is to help patients determine the direction of the therapy themselves, and to find their own solutions.

There are anecdotes concerning people who, for brief periods, treated ELIZA as if it were a sympathetic human. Weizenbaum's own secretary, for instance, asked him to leave the room while she confided in the program. And when Weizenbaum suggested that he might set ELIZA to record all its interactions, he was accused of spying on people's most intimate thoughts. Another case concerns a vice-president in a computer company who arrived one morning to find a version of ELIZA running on the computer, but was under the impression that the teletype (that is, the keyboard and printer) was linked directly to one in a colleague's home. The conversation that ensued was a masterpiece of misunderstanding. (It is reproduced in Boden, 1986). The vice-president took a good deal of persuading that he had really been talking to a computer program.

Try to work out what the program is doing. Think about its tactics, even if you have no experience of programming. Do you think the program needs any kind of intelligence to achieve the standard of conversation shown above?

So does this mean that ELIZA would succeed in Turing's 'Imitation Game'? The answer is that it would not. If you had to distinguish between ELIZA and a human on the basis of their typed replies, you would soon find that ELIZA's lack of initiative, lack of knowledge, and lack of common sense gave it away. For some reason, though, many people are willing to attribute 'human' characteristics to a computer program even though there is only the flimsiest evidence that it might possess them. Perhaps this is not surprising; our bias is demonstrated by an advertising slogan for cars: "Minis have feelings too." Such advertising may be harmless, but in the case of computers it is dangerous to believe that a program has feelings or other human attributes, since we inevitably use programs in ways that influence the decisions we take in our lives. In this chapter, we will show how a program like ELIZA works, and we hope this will inoculate you against what Weizenbaum, in his book *Computer Power and Human Reason* (1984), called "powerful delusional thinking in quite normal people."

In the same book, Weizenbaum comments that he was surprised that many people saw ELIZA as demonstrating a general solution to the problem of programming a computer to understand natural human language. His own conclusion was that language is only understood within a contextual framework. In other words, we only understand what someone says to us because of what we have in common in our understanding of the world. ELIZA only makes an impression because knowledge about the world is built into its responses; but its representation of knowledge is, as we shall see, too shallow and inflexible to make ELIZA a program that could begin to be called intelligent. The remainder of this chapter will be concerned with the way our version of ELIZA operates, and in particular what it lacks for achieving real communication in English. Since the program is not quite the same as Weizenbaum's, we shall call it *Eliza*.

2.2   Analyzing Eliza

First we shall look at the behaviour of *Eliza*, and from it suggest the simplest techniques that are needed to produce such responses. The method is similar to that of a cognitive psychologist studying human behaviour in order to describe the form and function of the human mind. We shall then look at the program itself. To avoid having to continually refer to 'the human', we assume the computer is conversing with someone called Pat.

At first sight *Eliza* appears to show some understanding, both of English and of the world. For example, the program takes Pat's statement

```
I think I am unique in some ways
```

and stands it on its head to produce

```
SOMETIMES YOU THINK YOU AREN'T UNIQUE IN SOME WAYS
```

This looks sophisitcated. *Eliza* suggests the exploration of a new possibility, derived from Pat's own statement, but embracing the idea that people revise their estimations of themselves. The next few exchanges are in a similar vein, with *Eliza* taking Pat's statements and inviting Pat to question them. When Pat challenges the program with the words

```
It's hardly a problem, is it?
```

Eliza bounces the initiative back to Pat with

```
FIRST TELL ME WHY YOU HAVE COME HERE
```

Does *Eliza* 'keep track' of the conversation, following an underlying theme, or does it merely respond to Pat's most recent words? The former seems to be the case, as when the conversation hinges on computers, or money, for several rounds. But in both cases Pat has mentioned the topic between each of *Eliza*'s responses. Whenever Pat introduces a new subject, *Eliza* immediately switches to it. There is one exception to this, when *Eliza* responds with

```
EARLIER YOU SAID YOU HAVEN'T MUCH OF A PROBLEM REALLY
```

so the program can store away some of Pat's statements and reproduce them, but there is no evidence that *Eliza* has any way of representing to itself the general theme and drift of the conversation. This is an important clue to how the program works. Although it occasionally seems to be taking the initiative, it only does so by either producing general prompts, or by reproducing one of Pat's earlier statements (with the word 'I' changed to 'you', 'your' changed to 'my', etc.). In the main its responses are driven by the immediately previous statement.

The program has only four types of response:

1. A general question or statement, prompting Pat to continue.

2. Pat's immediately previous statement, transformed in some way.

3. A response relevant to the topic of Pat's previous statement.

4. A reproduction of one of Pat's earlier statements.

That said, *Eliza* must have some grasp of English to transform sentences, or extract a topic. *Eliza*'s mistakes offer some clues:

```
If I could explain to you I could explain anything to
anyone
IF YOU COULD EXPLAIN TO I YOU COULD EXPLAIN
ANYTHING TO ANYONE
```

This suggests that the transformations may be rather simple substitutions and not the result of a deep analysis of the sentence's structure. And the response

```
BEWARE OF ADDICTIONS
```

when the word 'want' appears in one of Pat's sentences indicates that extracting a topic may depend only on the presence of certain key words. As far as we can tell from this conversation, both *Eliza*'s knowledge of the world and its knowledge of English are shallow. A longer conversation would confirm these conclusions. On the other hand, the conversation was conducted in part to show up the limitations. *Eliza*'s shallowness is not always immediately apparent to a credulous user (particularly if a more elaborate version of the program is used), and it is important to bear in mind the fact that the superficial appearance of computer systems can sometimes be highly misleading. Programs designed to teach children, for example, often give responses like "I'm sorry, you're wrong there" or even "Well done, you're almost as intelligent as me" as if they had some deep insight into the child's abilities and problems. Invariably they do not!

2.3   Inside Eliza

Our version of ELIZA, although simplified, retains many features of the original. After the program has printed its opening gambit,

GOOD DAY WHAT IS YOUR PROBLEM?

it operates in a cycle, repeatedly carrying out the following actions:

1. Get input from the user.

2. Generate a response.

3. Print the response.

When the program gets input from the user, it converts all the characters typed by the user into lowercase, and then in printing its response it converts lowercase characters into uppercase ones. So, in showing the internal workings of the *Eliza* program, we shall use all lowercase characters. Generally, the program just responds to its most recent input, but occasionally, not on every cycle, it stores the input so that it can reproduce it later prefaced by EARLIER YOU SAID. (It actually stores the input after it has been transformed to change the 'point of view'; see below.) This crude form of memory is only a minor complication, though it does add appreciably to the program's effect.

It is the middle part of the cycle, generating an appropriate response, that is interesting. This has the following sequence of actions:

1. Transform the input to change the 'point of view'.

2. If there is a pattern that matches the transformed input, then choose one of the responses associated with the pattern. Otherwise choose a general-purpose response.

As the program will often use all or part of the input in constructing a response, it first changes the 'point of view' to that of *Eliza*. The method is just to change 'you' to 'i', 'me' to 'you', 'are' to 'am', 'myself' to 'yourself', and so on. So the sentence

you understand me

would be changed to

```
i understand you
```

One problem with this very simple approach is that 'you' can be the subject or the object of a sentence (i.e., it may come before or after the verb). Just slavishly changing 'you' to 'i' would result in

```
i understand you
```

being changed to

```
you understand i
```

The program therefore uses another simple trick to deal with this: if the transformed sentence ends in 'i', then the 'i' is changed to 'me'. This is far from foolproof, as the earlier dialogue showed:

```
If I could explain to you I could explain anything to
anyone
IF YOU COULD EXPLAIN TO I YOU COULD EXPLAIN ANYTHING TO
ANYONE
```

Further tricks like this (called 'kludges' in computer jargon) would not solve the central problem, which is that *Eliza* is not founded on any principled representation of the form and content of English.

With the input in its new form, the program then searches for a **keyword** on a particular topic, or a suitable pattern to match the transformed input, by means of **pattern matching**. Pattern matching underlies most of *Eliza*'s apparent cleverness, and computer languages that have access to a pattern matching mechanism can easily be programmed to emulate *Eliza*.

2.3.1   Patterns

A pattern for *Eliza* is a list containing a mixture of words and **wild cards**. Wild cards are elements that can match any series of words, so a pattern is like a partly specified sentence in which some of the words are present and some are still to be filled in. We shall adopt the convention that lists of words and wild cards are enclosed in square brackets, and we will use = or == to denote a wild card in the list. The = (single equals) wild card stands for a single word, and the == (double equals) wild card stands for any number of words (including none at all). The pattern is matched against the list of words inputted by the user (after each occurrence of 'you' has been changed to 'i', etc.) — for example

```
[you think you are unique in some way]
```
is changed to
```
[i think i am unique in some way]
```
which matches the pattern
```
[== i am ==]
```

```
[anyone who wasn't a computer]
```
matches the pattern
```
[== computer ==]
```

```
[then you would't be talking to me]
```
is changed to
```
[then i wouldn't be talking to you]
```
which does not match the
pattern
```
[== talking with ==]
```

In order to match keywords or phrases in the input *Eliza* has a series of such patterns associated with standard responses:

PATTERN	STANDARD RESPONSE
`[== want ==]`	`[beware of addictions]`
`[== need ==]`	`[can you do without]`
`[== crave ==]`	`[do you ever suffer withdrawal symptoms?]`
`[== mother ==]`	`[tell me more about your family]`
`[== father ==]`	`[do you approve of large families?]`
`[== sister ==]`	`[family life is full of tensions]`
	`[do you like your relatives?]`

The program compares the input to each pattern in turn until a match is found. It then produces one of the standard responses. If there is more than one response available, then it picks one at random.

A pattern may contain variables to indicate pieces of data to be stored. For the examples here we shall just use two variables named X and Y. In a pattern, a single query followed by the variable name will match a single word, and two queries followed by a variable name will match any number of words (including zero). If a match succeeds, then the words matched will be stored as the value of the appropriate variable, so

```
Input: [eliza is a very simple program]

PATTERN        RESPONSE
[??X is ??Y]   [suppose ^^X were not ^^Y]


               X: [eliza]
               Y: [a very simple program]


Output: [suppose eliza were not a very simple program]
```

Figure 2.1
The construction of a response.

[eliza is a very simple program]
matches the pattern
[??X is ??Y]

[eliza] is stored as the value of X and [a very simple program] is stored as the value of Y.

To construct a response, *Eliza* reassembles the fragments. We need one more piece of notation. Two up-arrows before a variable name instruct the program to insert the value of the variable into the newly created response list. Figure 2.1 shows the complete sequence.

Note that the program does nothing meaningful with the words 'eliza' or 'a very simple program'. They are simply stored temporarily with the names X and Y and then slotted into the output sentence.

2.3.2 Choices in Eliza

That almost completes the description of our version of *Eliza*. There is one gap in the structure to fill in. This concerns what happens when several possible responses are possible. For instance

    i wouldn't pay money for a computer

fits patterns [== money ==] and [== computer ==]. *Eliza* deals with this in a simple way: it selects one of the matching patterns at random, and generates a response based on that one. Special tests, like whether a sentence is particularly short or long, are just treated as special kinds of patterns that can be matched (though not using the notation above).

Look back over the dialogue on pages 34 and 35 to see where *Eliza* departs from what would be expected of an intelligent (but non-committal) human respondant. What do you think are the limitations of pattern matching as a means of producing a response. How could *Eliza* be improved?

2.4   What Eliza Lacks

We have already seen some of the situations the program cannot cope with. For instance, with moderately complex input its substitution rules generated ungrammatical output. The program became muddled over the word 'want', which occurred with two different meanings in the input. Perhaps most important, there are many sentences that *Eliza* cannot match against its patterns, in which case the program either recalls an earlier sentence or produces general chatty response with no real content. We have also seen, however, that *Eliza* is built up mainly from simple pattern matching rules: thus the program could be extended enormously just by adding more patterns and more responses. We could make the patterns more elaborate so that, perhaps by taking account of surrounding words, the two different meanings of 'want' could be distinguished. We could have more complex substitution rules, each of which would help *Eliza* avoid falling into some grammatical trap. All this could be done without new computational tools and without changing the basic structure of the program.

These measures would undoubtedly improve the program's performance, at the expense of increasing its size and complexity. As the rules got more and more detailed and coped with more and more different cases, so the responses would become more appropriate. In terms of the 'Imitation Game', extra rules could mean that it would take longer to distinguish *Eliza* from a human. Could this approach ever realize a program that showed real competence in the use of English? There is little doubt that the answer to this question is no.

The reasons are probably already clear to you. The first is that pattern matching provides no way for *Eliza* to represent or recognize the grammatical structure, or **syntax**, of a sentence. This means that the program has to have one pattern to match every possible way of saying something. Suppose we wanted *Eliza* not merely to respond to the keyword 'computer', but also to take into account the human's attitude to computers. Then its patterns would also have to include words like 'worry', 'like', 'hate', 'not', 'greatly', and so on, along with the word 'computer'. But in order to respond to the following two sentences

        Computers worry me very little.

and

        I'm not worried much by computers.

the program would need two separate patterns. The meanings of these two sentences are almost identical, but the pattern matching approach treats them entirely separately. Even to give a reasonable coverage of the possible sentences expressing attitudes to computers, the number of patterns required would be tremendous. To cover a fair number of topics of conversation, the explosion of patterns would be unthinkable.

Analyzing the syntax of a sentence could go part of the way to solving this problem. If *Eliza* could work out how a sentence had been put together by the speaker, then that would be a step towards basing a response on the sentence's meaning rather than on its superficial appearance. The common ground in the two sentences above could be recognized more readily. Chapter 5 will show you something of how artificial intelligence programs tackle the problem of analyzing the structure of an English sentence.

There is a second limitation. We have noted that *Eliza* has no knowledge of anything it talks about. It has simply a set of responses (or response patterns into which part of the input can be inserted). Again, we can imagine extending this collection greatly, and again *Eliza*'s performance would improve up to a point. But it is again easy to see that this improvement would have severe limits. If you say to another person "Computers worry me," then that person will relate the sentence to what they already know about you, to what they already know about computers, and to what they know about the context in which you made the remark. They will infer, perhaps, that you are learning about computers, and that you would prefer not to be worried by them. However much it was elaborated, *Eliza* could do none of this. If you ponder the wealth of meaning you draw from almost any sentence you hear, you will see how much more there is to language than words and syntax.

A program needs to represent knowledge about the world if it is to communicate with people in a natural and useful way. **Knowledge representation** is a central theme in artificial intelligence, and we will introduce you to the analysis and representation of knowledge in chapter 3.

2.5   What Use Is Eliza?

We have paid a great deal of attention to *Eliza*'s limitations, for two reasons. The first is to show that appearances can be deceptive: programs that are actually very shallow can, for short periods, give the impression of a degree of insight which is not justified by their real nature and abilities. The second is to provide a jumping-off point for our study of the analysis of natural language and the representation of knowledge. The question naturally arises as to whether *Eliza* itself, or the pattern matching techniques we have developed, are themselves of any value. The answer is a qualified yes.

First, the pattern matching techniques can be applied in many contexts other than that of *Eliza*. You will find them used frequently in later chapters, as a general tool. For instance, in the program that uses search strategies to find routes in the London Underground, pattern matching is employed to find statements in a database which record the state of the search. Programmers in the main languages of artificial intelligence, such as **LISP** and POP-11, take pattern matching for granted as a tool the language supplies to them; they do not have to worry about the details themselves.

Second, techniques like *Eliza*'s can make programs more accessible to people unaccustomed to using computers. A large database with information about London might be easier to use if questions could be entered in a variety of forms, and if the answers were phrased in familiar ways. *Eliza*, or something very like it, can help in giving this kind of flexibility. By recognizing keywords and patterns in the user's input, the program can free the user from the need to use some rigid formula to express a question. There are dangers, of course. The first is that the limitations of pattern matching systems mean that the program will occasionally interpret the input wrongly. Although it may be helpful in some circumstances to type information or questions freely, a rigid format has its merits. Perhaps an automated tourist guide gains, on balance, by sacrificing precision for 'user-friendliness', but would the same be true for a medical database program being used to help a doctor make a diagnosis?

There is also the question of how much we want interaction with a computer to really resemble interaction with other people. An *Eliza* interface to a program may help to overcome nervousness in using an unfamiliar system, but it can, as Weizenbaum's ELIZA showed, also give some people the wrong impression about what kind of entity they are talking to. Do we want people to think that a program actually has sympathy with their problems? We will return to this important question in chapter 10. In the meantime *Eliza* has served its purpose as a jumping-off point.

2.6 Conclusion

It is not difficult to program a computer to give it the *appearance* of understanding English and producing intelligent responses. One simple method is to match a series of words against a pattern (which is like a partly specified sentence) and, if the words match, to give a predefined response. The technique can be made a little more powerful by including some of the original words in the response. This, and a few other tricks, were used in ELIZA, which was celebrated as an early computer program that could hold an extended dialogue with a human being. But its facade crumbles when you ask it a question with a complicated grammatical structure, or one that demands a reasoned or calculated response. What ELIZA lacks is firstly a means of recognizing the grammatical structure of language and secondly a means of converting the user's query into a represention of the underlying knowledge, from which inferences can be drawn. Despite its limitations the ELIZA approach of word pattern matching has some use as a simple means of communicating with a computer through natural language, in circumstances where 'user-friendliness' is more important than precision.

2.7 Appendix: A Program to Hold a Conversation

The *Eliza* whose output was shown early in this chapter could chat in a general way, and pass comments on topics such as money and computers. The version we will outline here is a little more focused: it will talk to a tourist about London, and is a first step towards our Automated Tourist Guide. After what we have said about *Eliza*'s limitations, you must not expect it to be too useful on its own, but in later chapters it will be combined with more powerful techniques.

2.7.1   Pattern Matching

In chapter 1 we showed how variables can be given values through assignment
statements and by calling procedures with arguments. Another way is to use pattern matching. We have already introduced the main ideas of pattern matching in
section 2.3.1, where we conveniently used POP-11 notation for patterns. To do pattern matching in POP-11, we use the `matches` operator. In chapter 1, the familiar
arithmetic operators were introduced, and `matches` is similar to these except that
instead of working with numbers it works with lists, and instead of producing a
number as a result it produces a boolean. A boolean is a data object that has only
two possible values, corresponding to logical truth and falsity. We shall write these
as <true> and <false> since that is how they are displayed by the print command.
The result of the `matches` operation is <true> if the list matches the pattern, and
<false> otherwise. (An apostrophe inside a POP-11 list has a special meaning —
it signifies the start of a 'string' data item — so we have used 'would not' rather
than the 'wouldn't' of earlier examples.)

```
[i think i am unique in some ways] matches
    [== i am ==] =>
** <true>
[then you would not be talking to me] matches
    [== talking with ==] =>
** <false>
```

We can also include variables in the wild cards. Note that the `matches` operator
still returns <true> or <false> as the match can still succeed or fail, but the
operation also has the side-effect of assigning the matched items to the variable.
We have to declare the variables first.

```
vars x, y;
[eliza is a very simple program] matches
    [??x is ??y] =>
** <true>
```

The match was successful. Now let us look at the side effects:

```
x =>
** [eliza]
y =>
** [a very simple program]
```

Finally, we shall use the double up-arrow notation to build a new sentence:

```
[suppose ^^x were not ^^y] =>
** [suppose eliza were not a very simple program]
```

Note that the double up-arrow did not just put the values of `x` and `y` into the new list; that would have produced the result

```
[suppose [eliza] were not [a very simple program]]
```

Instead, the words from the two lists were extracted and then built into the new list that was printed out. Instead of being printed out, the new list could have been stored in memory (by using the assignment arrow to assign it to a variable).

2.7.2 Deciding What to Do

Our *Eliza* program will need to take decisions. If the input matches one type of pattern, it will need to produce one output, and if the input matches another type, it will need to produce a different output. POP-11, like most programming languages, allows us to write instructions to make decisions. The ability to follow different paths under different conditions is at the heart of programming languages.

Choices in POP-11 are produced by **conditional** commands, signalled by the word `if`. Here is an example:

```
vars input;
[is your name eliza?]->input;
if input matches [== eliza ==] then
     [we were talking about you, not me] =>>
endif;
```

```
we were talking about you, not me
```

Between `if` and `then` is the expression

```
input matches [== eliza ==]
```

When the computer evaluates this, the result is `<true>`, so POP-11 carries out the instructions between the word `then` and the word `endif`. If the value of the expression had been `<false>`, then the instructions would have been ignored.

The word `else` can be used to introduce instructions that are to be carried out when the expression following `if` turns out to be false. The general form of the if...then...else statement is

```
if <expression> then

    <instructions to do when the expression is true>

else

    <instructions to do when the expression is false>

endif;
```

The else is optional; if it is omitted, then no action is taken if the expression is
<false> and POP-11 continues with the next command after the if statement.

For *Eliza* we need to test the input against a series of patterns until a match is
found, at which point the program constructs an appropriate response. If there is
no match, then it gives a general-purpose response. What we want is a statement
of the form "If the first condition is true then carry out the first action, otherwise if
the next condition is true then carry out the next action, and so on. If no condition
is true then carry out a default action." In POP-11 this is written as a series of

```
if      then      elseif
```

commands, for example

```
if input matches [== eliza ==] then
    [we were talking about you, not me] =>>
elseif input matches [??x is ??y] then
    [suppose ^^x were not ^^y] =>>
elseif input matches [== computer ==] then
    [do machines worry you] =>>
else
    [please go on] =>>
endif;
```

POP-11 has many operators that return boolean values, and indeed you can write
your own procedures to do so, so the if statement is extremely powerful.

2.7.3   A Simple *Eliza*-Like Tourist Guide

We can now make a small procedure that produces answers to questions about
London. The procedure, which we shall call **answer**, will have one argument, which
will be the query, and will return one result, its response. It will use variables,
pattern matching, and conditional instructions. Here is the complete procedure:

```
define answer(query) -> response;
    vars x;
    if query matches [== changing of the guard ==] then
        [The changing of the guard is at Buckingham
            Palace] -> response;
    elseif query matches [== politicians ==]
        or query matches [== politics ==] then
        [You can hear political opinions at the Houses
            of Parliament or at Speakers Corner in Hyde
            Park] -> response;
    elseif query matches [== river ==] then
        [You can go on river trips from Tower
            Bridge] -> response;
    elseif query matches [thank you] then
        [You are welcome] -> response;
    elseif query matches [== get to ??x] then
        [I do not know the way to ^^x] -> response;
    else
        [Sorry, I do not know about that] -> response;
    endif;
enddefine;
```

As you can see, this procedure just tries to match the query against different patterns, and if one of the matches succeeds, it returns a reasonably appropriate result. We have also sneaked in a new operator, which you have not met before, but its use should be fairly obvious. The **or** operator takes two boolean values, one from each side of it (as + does with numbers and **matches** with lists) and produces a boolean result. If the expressions on both sides of **or** evaluate to <false>, then the result is <false>, but if either (or both) is <true>, then the result is <true>. Thus the instruction in the second conditional statement gets executed if either 'politicians' or 'politics' appears in the query. Here is what happens when we try the procedure on a few examples:

```
answer([Where can I see the changing of the guard?]) =>>
The changing of the guard is at Buckingham Palace
answer([How do I find out about British politics?]) =>>
You can hear political opinions at the Houses of Parliament
or at Speakers Corner in Hyde Park
```

```
answer([How do I get to Islington])=>>
I do not know the way to Islington
answer([thank you]) =>>
You are welcome
```

But the procedure suffers from the usual *Eliza* limitations:

```
answer([Is the river Thames very polluted these days?]) =>>
You can go on river trips from Tower Bridge
```

Still, there is the making of a useful procedure here.

One more useful POP-11 procedure is `oneof`, which selects at random an element from the list given as its input. It can be used within `answer` to add variety to the responses:

```
    else
    oneof([[Sorry, I do not know about that]
           [I have no answer to that question]
           [Please ask me only simple questions]])-> response;
```

To finish this chapter, we shall tie together the `welcome` and `answer` procedures into one package.

2.7.4   A Complete *Eliza* Program

On page 40 we showed the structure of *Eliza* as a repeated cycle of actions:

1. Get input from the user.

2. Generate a response.

3. Print the response.

In POP-11 the words `repeat` and `endrepeat` are used to enclose a series of commands to be repeated. Thus

```
    repeat
        [Hi there] =>
    endrepeat
```

prints out

```
** [Hi there]
```

over and over again, until the program is interrupted (on most systems this is done by holding down the CTRL key and typing the character 'c'). A **repeat loop** forms the outline of the *Eliza* program.

We can call up **answer** to generate a response, but we need a command that will accept words typed by the user and pass them to **answer**. The POP-11 procedure **readline** does this. If we insert **readline** into the program, then when it is called it displays a query on the screen and waits for the user. Whatever the user types (terminated by pressing the RETURN key) is formed into a list which is returned as the result of **readline**.

Here is a procedure to control *Eliza*. It repeatedly calls **readline** to receive input from the user, which is stored in the variable **query**. The value of **query** is passed to **answer**, which returns a response, to be printed out by =>>:

```
define respond();
  vars query;
  repeat;
    readline()->query;
    answer(query) =>>
  endrepeat;
enddefine;
```

The procedure will work; the only problem is that it can only be halted by interrupting the program. The built-in procedure **quitif** evaluates the expression **query = [bye]** and, if it is **<true>**, then breaks the repeat loop:

```
define respond();
  vars query;
  [Type bye to finish the consultation.]=>>
  repeat
    readline()->query;
      quitif(query=[bye]);
      answer(query)=>>
  endrepeat;
enddefine;
```

We can now combine **respond** with the **welcome** procedure defined in chapter 1 to create the first version of the Tourist Guide:

```
define guide();
    welcome();
    respond();
enddefine;
```

The guide procedure starts with the welcoming message and then calls respond.
This in turn calls readline and answer:

```
guide();
Welcome to the London Tourist Guide
This guide can answer your queries about landmarks ,
attractions and events in London
Please type your query in English , for example :
How do I get to the National Gallery ?
Press the RETURN button to finish a query
Type bye to finish the consultation.
?  Where can I go for a trip on the river?
You can go on river trips from Tower Bridge
?  How can I get to Trafalgar Square?
I do not know the way to Trafalgar Square
?  bye
```

2.8   Exercises

1. Look at the following statements and responses and try to work out why *Eliza*
   went wrong:

   ```
   To err is human
   COULD A MACHINE ERR IS HUMAN

   Who dares wins
   I THINK YOU KNOW THE ANSWER

   No one is more optimistic than myself
   AREN'T YOU BEING A LITTLE NEGATIVE

   Whatever my problems are not one of them gets me down
   CAN YOU ALWAYS EXPECT WHATEVER YOUR PROBLEMS TO BE ONE
   OF THEM GETS YOU DOWN
   ```

2. What would be printed out by each of the following lines of POP-11, executed in the following order?

```
vars thisbit, thatbit;
[my name is eliza] matches [my name ==] =>
[my name is eliza] matches [my name is ??thisbit] =>
thisbit =>
[my name is eliza] matches [??thisbit is ??thatbit] =>
thisbit =>
thatbit =>
[are you sure about ^^thisbit being ^^thatbit ?] =>
thisbit matches [my ??thisbit] =>
thisbit =>
```

Hint: To understand what happens in the final match above, it is important to look at what POP-11 does one step at a time, and to be very clear about how variables work. First, the value of the variable `thisbit` is obtained from memory, and the `matches` operation is applied to this list and the pattern `[my ??thisbit]`. As it happens, the pattern contains the same variable, `thisbit`, in a wild card position, so if the match succeeds, a new value will be given to the variable. This will simply replace the old value. Although the command looks peculiar because the same variable name appears twice, there is no contradiction provided you understand the sequence of operations that it gives rise to. If you find this difficult to follow, or you can't see that the final command will print out simply the list `[name]`, it may help to go over the section on variables in chapter 1.

3. Here is a definition of a POP-11 procedure and a call to it. What will be printed out?

```
define greet(name);
    if [Mike Dave Chris Steve David]
        matches [== ^^name ==] then
          [Hello ^^name, are you one of
              the authors of this book?] =>
      elseif name = [Aaron] then
          [Hello Aaron, I guess you wrote the foreword] =>
```

```
    else
        [Hello ^^name, pleased to meet you] =>
    endif;
enddefine;

greet([David]);
greet([Brian]);
greet([Aaron]);
```

Notice how this procedure introduces a new way to use the pattern matcher: in the examples in the chapter we always had a fixed pattern written into the program, but there is nothing to stop us building up a pattern out of the data passed in to a procedure.

Modify the procedure so that it will work with an input giving both first name and surname, as in

```
greet([Mike Sharples]);
```

4. Write a procedure called `thing_of_colour` which gives examples of things of particular colours. The procedure should take as its argument (i.e., input) a list which may contain the name of a colour, and should return as its result the name of something of that colour. It should not always return the same object for a given colour, and it should return a suitable message if it does not recognize a particular colour. Here is an example of an interaction in which the procedure is called.

```
thing_of_colour([green]) =>
** grass
thing_of_colour([green]) =>
** creme_de_menthe
thing_of_colour([red]) =>
** strawberries
thing_of_colour([magenta]) =>
** [Sorry I do not know the colour magenta]
thing_of_colour([horse]) =>
** [Sorry I do not know the colour horse]
thing_of_colour([black]) =>
** coal
```

Make a procedure which repeatedly asks the user to type in the name of a colour, and prints out an example of something of that colour, stopping only when the user types in the word **bye**.

5. Create your own conversation program, but on a theme different from *Eliza*. For instance, you might design a program that replies with insults:

```
I have a problem
STOP MOANING ABOUT YOUR PETTY AILMENTS
My mother cannot seem to understand me
I AM NOT SURPRISED, I CANNOT SEEM TO UNDERSTAND YOU
EITHER
Are you intelligent?
A MIRACLE OF MODERN TECHNOLOGY AND ALL I GET IS
QUESTIONS LIKE: ARE YOU INTELLIGENT?
```

Chapter 3

Stored Knowledge

3.1 The Importance of Stored Knowledge

When we looked at the *Eliza* program in the last chapter we saw that its apparently impressive performance was extremely limited. In this chapter we shall describe an important way to make AI programs more flexible and more 'mind-like', by giving them ways of representing knowledge of the world about which they converse, or in which they operate.

In order to see the importance of stored knowledge, think again about the Automated Tourist Guide project. Our aim is to simulate a human advisor who has to deal with a wide variety of enquiries of different forms — for example,

> How do I get from here to Knightsbridge Station?
>
> When is the Changing of the Guards next due to take place?
>
> How do I book a river cruise on the Thames?
>
> Is it possible to visit the top of Telecom Tower?
>
> What station is Big Ben nearest to?
>
> How much should I pay to take a taxi to Heathrow?
>
> Is the Tate Gallery open on Sundays?
>
> Where would you recommend me to go to hear a symphony concert?

If you were employed as a tourist enquiries adviser, you would need to have access to a large amount of information. Some of this would be stored in reference books, some in maps, some in tables, and so on. But a lot of it would be stored 'in your head'. The knowledge in your head would be of various kinds. For example, one could distinguish between factual and practical knowledge: between 'knowledge that ...', and 'knowledge how ...'.

Items of factual knowledge might be that Buckingham Palace is where the Changing of the Guards takes place, or that the Haymarket is near Piccadilly Circus. Practical knowledge would include how to get information from a map or reference book, or how to help a tourist find accommodation for the night. (In the AI context a similar distinction is made between *declarative* and *procedural* kinds of knowledge or, more correctly, between declarative and procedural ways of representing knowledge. There has been considerable debate within the artificial intelligence community over which of the two is most useful and efficient.) These two kinds of knowledge are not completely distinct. For instance, if I am asked the way to Knightsbridge Station from Victoria, I can express this both in terms of knowledge how ("Take the Victoria Line to Green Park and then change to the Piccadilly line") or in terms of knowledge that ("Knightsbridge is on the Piccadilly line, and the interchange station is Green Park").

Dividing knowledge into facts ('knowledge that ...') and procedures ('knowledge how ...') is one means of classification. Can you think of any other forms of knowledge, or ways of dividing knowledge into different types?

The representation of knowledge is central to artificial intelligence. One of the ways in which people working in AI try to distinguish their kinds of system from more conventional computer programs is by appealing to a distinction between processing information and processing knowledge. Indeed, the term **knowledge-based systems** is often used in place of artificial intelligence to denote that particular field of research.

Different AI systems incorporate and deploy knowledge for many different purposes. They use knowledge of syntax and meanings in order to understand sentences. They use knowledge to cut down on useless or time-consuming search when solving problems. They have detailed knowledge of specific areas of expertise in order to function as expert systems, and they employ general knowledge of various sorts in order to apply such specialized expertise in flexible and sensible ways. Some AI systems have knowledge about knowledge — for instance, a knowledge of how to acquire more knowledge, either by drawing inferences from the knowledge they already possess or by acquiring fresh knowledge through questioning the human user or through perception. A few have knowledge about the scope and limits of their own knowledge, and that of other knowers. AI systems acquire, store, and manipulate representations of knowledge, and indeed, not merely knowledge (in the sense of propositions or abilities which a given system can take as given or as beyond challenge), but also beliefs, conjectures, presumptions, rough-and-ready rules of thumb, and so on. Examples of some of these types of knowledge will be given in the rest of this chapter.

3.2   Specialized versus Commonsense Knowledge

Earlier we made a distinction between factual and practical knowledge (knowing how and knowing that). Another distinction worth stressing is between **domain-specific** and **domain-independent** knowledge. The specific knowledge domain of a London tourist guide (the needs and interests of tourists to London) is made up of a number of sub-domains, such as the location of places of interest, the transport system in London, and the prices of various activities and goods. Having the knowledge clustered into identifiable domains makes the job of designing a system like our Tourist Guide considerably easier and is one reason for the commercial success of expert systems. Expert systems can reproduce the specific domain expertise of, for example, a geological mineral prospector (Duda, Gaschnig and Hart, 1979) or a specialist in blood infections (Shortliffe, 1976) and are often able to perform as well as, or in some cases even better than, their human counterparts.

Compare the following two paragraphs (from Hayes-Roth, 1983) summarizing the pulmonary function diagnosis of a particular patient at a San Francisco hospital. One is written by a human physician, and the other by an expert system called PUFF, using exactly the same details from the patient. Try and guess which is which.

Conclusions: The low diffusing capacity, in combination with obstruction and a high total lung capacity is consistent with a diagnosis of emphysema. Although bronchodilators were only slightly useful in this one case, prolonged use may prove to be beneficial to the patient. PULMONARY FUNCTION DIAGNOSIS: MODERATELY SEVERE OBSTRUCTIVE AIRWAYS DISEASE. EMPHYSEMATOUS TYPE.

Conclusion: Overinflation, fixed airway obstruction and low diffusing capacity would all indicate moderately severe obstructive airway disease of the emphysematous type. Although there is no response to bronchodilators on this one occasion, more prolonged use may prove to be more helpful. PULMONARY FUNCTION DIAGNOSIS: OBSTRUCTIVE AIRWAYS DISEASE, MODERATELY SEVERE, EMPHYSEMATOUS TYPE.

The first was the computer-generated diagnosis, but you might be forgiven if you got it wrong.

Currently, an expert system capable of exhibiting impressive performances like this has only extremely narrow and specialized knowledge. PUFF, for instance, knows nothing about medical complaints apart from conditions of the lung. It may not even be able to answer questions of common knowledge about human anatomy (for example, "Are my lungs above or below my knees?").

Now a lot of the knowledge on which you would have to rely if working as a tourist guide would be of a quite unspecialized kind, based upon general knowledge, or common sense. For instance, you would need to know that if it is raining very heavily outside, a scheduled open-air symphony concert is likely to have been cancelled. Or, to take another example, this time concerning our commonsense understanding of the dynamics of conversation, you would need to know that, if an excessively polite inquirer says, "Would you possibly be able to tell me the way to X?" this means, "Please tell me the way . . .?" rather than "Do you, hypothetically, have the ability . . .?" Such items of knowledge do not fit easily into specialized bodies of expertise — they are just some of the myriad pieces of life-experience that we pick up. If AI researchers are to do more than build systems which give virtuoso performances within extremely narrow limits, then they will have to find ways of representing large amounts of domain-independent general knowledge.

There are two different sorts of question involved here, although they are intimately linked. The first is, "How is knowledge represented in the minds (brains) of human subjects, or those of other animals?" This is a question of psychology, and, as will be made clear many times in this book, the concerns of psychology and of AI overlap to a very large degree. The second is, "How can we best organize the way knowledge is represented in computer systems, given the constraints on how such systems can be designed, so as to make them useful to us?" Much of AI is concerned with making systems which actually work (and work effectively); so, in answering the second question, people may not necessarily be too worried if there is no close fit between the methods for representing knowledge in machines and those which might be supposed to occur in humans. However, many AI researchers believe that in order to represent knowledge in flexible and sophisticated forms in machines (especially commonsense knowledge rather than specialized expertise) it is best to build knowledge-structures which closely reproduce those we seem to use ourselves. Some researchers believe that, to parody Alexander Pope, "The proper study of computerkind is man." There is a lively debate within the AI community between those who aim for neat, systematic, logical structures which are intended to suit the demands of the computer as an information-processing device; and those who try to build knowledge representation systems which reflect the rich 'messiness' of human experience and ideas. This controversy, between the 'neats' and the 'scruffs' , as they are often called, has resulted in an interesting divergence of styles of representing knowledge in computational systems.

3.3 Styles of Knowledge Representation

We shall briefly examine some of the major techniques (or **formalisms**) for knowledge representation. The most important ones are **predicate logic**, **semantic networks**, **production systems**, **frames** and **scripts**.

3.3.1 Predicate Logic

The first of these, predicate logic, involves using standard forms of logical symbolism which have been familiar to philosophers and mathematicians for many decades. Most simple sentences, for example, "Peter is generous" or "Jane gives a painting to Sam," can be represented in terms of logical **formulae** in which a **predicate** is applied to one or more **arguments** (the term 'argument' as used in predicate logic is similar to, but not identical with, its use to refer to the inputs to a procedure in POP-11):

PREDICATE	ARGUMENTS
generous	(peter)
gives	(jane, painting, sam)

Consider the following sentence: "Every respectable villager worships a deity." A moment's reflection will reveal that this is ambiguous. Is it saying that there is one single deity to which each respectable villager offers worship? Or does each worshipper have his or her own deity, to which a fellow respectable villager may or may not be also praying? With predicate logic it is easy to reveal the nature of the ambiguity, by a device known as **quantification**. Quantification allows one to talk in a general way about all things of a certain class or about some particular but unspecified thing of a certain class. We can, for instance, express the proposition "All of Jane's friends are generous" in terms of the following formula:

> For any X: IF friend(X,jane) THEN generous(X)

while the sentence "Jane has at least one friend who is generous" can be expressed as follows:

> For some X: friend(X,jane) AND generous(X)

The expressions 'For any X' and 'For some X' are known as **quantifiers**. We can now use quantification to exhibit the ambiguity of the sentence about the respectable villagers. The first reading of it can be represented as

> For some X: for any Y: deity(X)
> AND IF (villager(Y) AND respectable(Y)) THEN
> worships(Y,X)

while the second can be represented as

> For any Y: (IF villager(Y) AND respectable(Y) THEN
> For some X: deity(X) AND worships(Y,X))

It is thus possible to show in a clear way that the original sentence can express (at least) two quite distinct propositions. It is possible to infer from the first, but not from the second, that if Margaret and Neil are two respectable villagers, then they both worship the same entity. (In the interests of ecumenical peace, however, it is sometimes better to refrain from letting such ambiguities come out into the open!)

Predicate logic has a long pedigree. Its roots go back at least as far as Aristotle, although in its current form it was developed starting in the late nineteenth century. Associated with it are techniques for the *analysis* of many conceptual structures in our common thought. Because these analytical techniques are well-understood, and because it is relatively easy to express the formulae of predicate logic in AI languages such as LISP or POP-11, it has been a very popular knowledge representation symbolism within AI. Predicate logic also embodies a set of systematic procedures for *proving* that certain formulae can or cannot be logically derived from others and such logical inference procedures have been used as the backbone for problem-solving systems in AI. (For an account of predicate logic in AI see, for example, Rich, 1983.) Predicate logic is in itself an extremely formal kind of representation mechanism. Its supporters believe, however, that it can be used to fashion conceptual tools which reproduce much of the subtlety and nuance of ordinary informal thinking.

A popular method for incorporating predicate logic in AI programs has involved a machine-based inference procedure called **resolution**, first proposed by J. A. Robinson (1965). This makes it relatively easy to represent expert, or commonsense, knowledge in terms of a set of axioms expressed in a special form of predicate calculus formulae and then derive consequences from these axioms. Indeed an AI programming language has been developed called Prolog (PROgramming in LOGic) which employs a resolution inference mechanism together with restricted form of predicate logic (Clocksin and Mellish, 1981) and its proponents claim that it is a powerful tool for building knowledge-based systems. For example, a large section of the recently passed British Nationalities Act has been translated into the logical symbolism of Prolog, allowing inferences to be drawn on whether or not a particular person can argue entitlement to a passport under the labyrinthine provisions of the Act (Sergot et al., 1986).

3.3.2   Semantic Networks

Another mechanism for representing knowledge is the **semantic network**. To grasp what a semantic network is, consider two people, John and Sue, paddling in a canoe. We can imagine such a scene as a series of objects and relationships, which can be represented as an organized schema or network. Our network will include, for example (see figure 3.1), the knowledge (or assumptions) that John is a man, Sue is a woman, John is in the canoe, Sue is in the canoe, the canoe is in water, and so on. There are also more general facts, such as that a man is a human, a woman is a human, a human is a living thing, a canoe is a boat, a boat is an inanimate object, and so on. Each of these facts and assumptions can be expressed by means of a link, or **arc**, joining two points, or **nodes**, in a network.

The relationships 'Sue is a woman', 'A woman is a human', 'A human is a living person' form an **isa hierarchy**. Any properties that a node in such a hierarchy possesses can be inherited by other objects lower down in the hierarchy. So if the semantic network contains the information that a human has arms, then it can be inferred that this property is also possessed by Sue. There is a close similarity between a semantic network and predicate logic, since any semantic network can

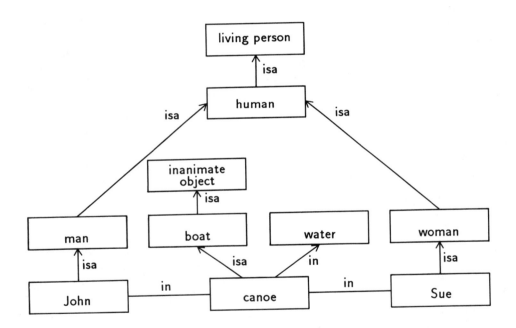

Figure 3.1
A semantic network.

be expressed as a series of logical predicates, such as

> isa (john,man)
> isa (sue,woman)
> location (john,canoe)

There are also important differences. On paper and, usually, as data structures in the computer, all the information relating to a node in the network is grouped together; thus, any fact that relates to John will have a link to the 'john' node. In predicate logic, the facts are just stored as one long series of predicates and so, for a large knowledge-base, finding related facts may require a long search.

From the point of view of someone who favours the predicate logic approach, semantic networks seem rather undisciplined. For example, the 'isa' relationship, as typically used in semantic nets, appears to hide the important distinction between an individual object or entity (for example, 'Sue') and a term specifying a class of objects or entities (for example 'woman', or 'human'). The statements 'Sue is a woman' and 'A woman is a human' would have quite different analyses in predicate logic, the latter being the disguised universal statement 'All women are humans'. So semantic networks can be criticized for obscuring such important logical distinctions. We shall examine semantic networks and inference in more detail in chapter 6.

3.3.3 Production Systems

Another mechanism that has acquired great popularity is the **production system**. A production system has a set of **production rules**, usually of the form

> IF <condition> THEN <action>

and a control mechanism which searches for rules to apply in a given situation. Several rules may apply in a given case and the control mechanism will contain a method for choosing one of the various competing rules to apply (or **fire**). When a rule fires, its 'action' part is carried out and this typically changes the situation, making new rules available to fire.

As a sample illustration of a production system, imagine that an air travel firm offers discounts on its trips for certain age groups: children under 12 go half price; senior citizens (that is, females of 60 or over, and males of 65 or over) have a 25% discount.

Consider how a computer program might embody the knowledge about these ticket discounts, and how it might handle customers' enquiries. In order to know what discount, if any, applies to a particular passenger, the system may have to ask for information. But, for reasons of efficiency as well as politeness, the system should avoid asking unnecessary questions.

The following rules presuppose that the system can consult a database (or **working memory**) as it goes along, and can add information to it, or delete information from it as needed. The system can also ask questions, and can record the answers in its working memory. Here are some sample production rules, expressed in an English form.

Rule 1 condition: [age of passenger unknown]
           action: print: What is the passenger's age ?
                       read: AGE
                       add: [age of passenger is AGE]

Rule 2 condition: [age of passenger is AGE] where AGE < 12
           action: print: The passenger travels half price.
                       stop

Rule 3 condition: [age of passenger is AGE] where AGE >= 65
           action: print: The passenger has a 25% discount.
                       stop

Rule 4 condition: [sex of passenger is unknown] and
                       [age of passenger is AGE] where Age >= 60
           action: print: Is the passenger male or female?
                       read: SEX
                       add: [sex of passenger is SEX]

Rule 5 condition: [sex of passenger is female] and
                       [age of passenger is AGE] where AGE >= 60
           action: print: The passenger has a 25 % discount.
                       stop

Rule 6 condition:
           action: print: The passenger has to pay the full rate.
                       stop

You must imagine that the above rules are processed on a 'first-come first served basis' by matching the the conditions of each rule in turn against the database until a match occurs and the rule fires.

The production system will repeatedly cycle through the rules starting at Rule 1, looking for one to fire. This cycling will continue until it is told to stop. (In this simple example, there are at most three cycles through the rules: for instance, for a female passenger aged 62, the following will fire in succession: 1,4, and 5.) The order of the rules ensures that questions are asked only when necessary. The final rule offers a 'default' option. As can be seen, it carries no conditions at all, but because of its position in the set of rules, it will fire only if no other rule is applicable.

Production rules are useful where the knowledge consists of many loosely related facts and independent actions, and we shall devote a whole chapter (chapter 7) to them.

3.3.4 Frames and Scripts

Two other popular knowledge representation formalisms are **frames** and **scripts**. Although these were developed independently (both originating in the early 1970s), and are different in important ways, they have sufficient similarities to be considered together. One influential proponent of frame-based systems is Marvin Minsky (1975); a champion of script-based systems is Roger Schank (see Schank and Abelson, 1977). The key idea involved in both frames and scripts is that our knowledge of concepts, events, and situations is organized around *expectations* of key features of those situations.

Consider a stereotypical situation, such as going to hear a lecture. One's knowledge of what might go on during such an event is based on assumptions. For instance, it can be assumed that the person who actually delivers the lecture is likely to be identical with the person advertised; that the lecturer's actual time of arrival is not more than a few minutes after the advertised start; that the duration of the lecture is unlikely to exceed an hour and a half at the maximum; and so on. These and other expectations can be encoded in a **generic** 'lecture frame' to be modified by what actually occurs during a specific lecture. This frame will include various *slots*, where specific values can be entered to describe the occasion under discussion. For example, a lecture frame may include slots for 'room location', 'start time', 'finish time', and so on (see figure 3.2).

Some of these slots may have default settings, or ranges within which actual values are likely to be found. For instance, in figure 3.2 the 'room location' slot is associated with a list of the rooms used for AI lectures, and, in the 'default' slot,

SUSSEX AI LECTURE FRAME

Specialisation of: Sussex lecture
Room location:
    Range: D541, D310, B24
    Default: D541
Start time:
    Range: 0910, 1010, 1130, 1230, 1415, 1515, 1615, 1715
Duration:
    Range: 30 minutes to 120 minutes
    Default: 50 minutes
Finish time:
    If needed: start time + duration
Equipment:
    Range: overhead projector, blackboard, video player,
            computer terminal, slide projector
    Default: blackboard, overhead projector, computer terminal
Lecturer:
    If needed: consult lecture schedule given room location, start time

COMPUTERS AND THOUGHT LECTURE FRAME

Specialisation of: Sussex AI lecture
Room location: D541
Start time:
    Range: 0910, 1010
Finish time:
    If needed: start time + 50 minutes

Figure 3.2
Frames for 'Sussex AI lecture' and 'Computers and Thought lecture'.

the room normally used. Slots in one frame may contain reference to other frames, so linking them together into **frame systems**. Frames may also contain procedures, often called **demons**, which are activated under prescribed circumstances. In figure 3.2, the identity of the speaker at a particular lecture can be established by an 'if needed' demon, which, given a location and a start time, can consult a lecture schedule to retrieve the speaker's name. Another kind of demon ('if added') is activated when the value of a particular slot is changed.

Schank and his co-workers have elaborated a technique for reducing a story or a newspaper report to **conceptual primitives** and their interrelations. The conceptual primitives specify certain basic actions that people and objects can perform — for instance, transferring a physical thing from one location to another; transferring a mental idea from one mind to another; building new information from old; grasping objects; focussing attention of a sense-organ on some occurrence; ingesting some form of nourishment; and so on. Schank showed how complex representations of the meaning of *individual* sentences could plausibly be built up from these conceptual primitives.

To represent a narrative composed of a *series* of linked sentences Schank proposed using frame-like structures, called scripts, which record the normal sequence of events for a given type of occurrence. Figure 3.3 shows a simplified 'lecture script'.

Each event in a script can be expressed as conceptual primitives. A system with such a script will find it relatively easy to make sense of a narrative where a particular episode is described in only partial or fragmentary terms. Moreover, it will be relatively easy to describe unusual events, in terms of the expectations set up by the script. In a much-cited example, the SAM program, developed by Schank and Abelson, was provided with a brief story along the following lines:

> Joe went to a restaurant. Joe ordered a hamburger. When the hamburger
> came, it was burnt to a crisp. Joe stormed out without paying.

The system was able to infer that Joe had not eaten the hamburger, even though no explicit mention was made of what he did and did not eat in the restaurant. Indeed, the system could explain its reasoning by referring to the ways in which the events described in the story failed to match up to the standard restaurant script (See chapter 5 of Schank and Riesbeck, 1980).

Frames and scripts offer extremely rich and versatile methods for representing organized clusters of knowledge about everyday or specialized occurrences. They reproduce a powerful feature of our own thinking processes: the fact that our understanding of new situations is often driven by stereotypes, which can be applied

LECTURE SCRIPT

Props: lecture hall, blackboard, chalk, overhead projector,
transparencies, marker pens
Roles: student, lecturer
Point of view: lecturer
Event sequence:

1. Enter room

2. Set up unless attendance = 0 when exit room

3. Deliver lecture

4. Pack up

5. Exit room

Main concept: 3

Figure 3.3
A simplified lecture script.

in a rough-and-ready way, avoiding the need for extensive inferential processes in order to build up an understanding from scratch. Often our initial attempts to make sense of a situation are quite inappropriate, and we have to make improvisations and revisions as we go along. Frame and script systems are able to incorporate such flexibility.

There are many other approaches to the representation of knowledge in a computer, and there is much controversy about which represents the 'best' general framework — in particular, about whether a 'neat', logic-based approach, or some more informal, 'scruffy' approach such as those embodied in semantic networks, or scripts or frames is to be preferred. This is a particularly acute problem when one is articulating commonsense knowledge (for example, "An object in motion generally slows down unless it is propelled or is going downhill"). This knowledge that we all have about the usual behaviour of physical objects in the world around us is known as **naive physics**. Should we represent our commonsense assumptions as a set of logical axioms, or in terms of a more rough-and-ready conceptual scheme? This is a critical issue within AI. Obviously the way one reacts depends at least partly on whether one's concern is primarily to use AI to build versatile machines or to model human thinking processes. Fortunately, however, we do not have to take a stand on the issue in this book.

It is now time to turn from these fundamental questions of methodology toward the mechanics of representing knowledge. Later in this chapter we shall examine a particular AI program in order to see how different kinds of knowledge can be articulated and linked together. We shall show that even the representation of relatively simple kinds of knowledge involves quite complex data-structures. Before we do this, however, it is worth saying a little in general about the importance of internal representation, for this is something which newcomers to AI (and even the occasional oldcomer) may easily underestimate.

3.4 Two Models of AI

There is a superficial view of artificial intelligence which puts the accent on performance, on getting computers to display outward behaviour which is as human-like as possible. Programs like ELIZA encourage this view (though not necessarily as a result of the conscious intention of their creators), as does Alan Turing's key paper on "Computing Machinery and Intelligence" (1950), mentioned in the introductory chapter, where he discussed an (as yet) imaginary program which will be able to engage in conversation about any topic in such a convincing fashion that people will be genuinely and consistently unable to tell they are talking to a machine. The Turing Test has played an extremely important part in the history of AI, and many people working in the field have defined what they do ultimately in terms of producing a program which will qualify for the title 'genuinely intelligent' by virtue of passing the Turing Test.

We can contrast this 'performance model' of AI, as it might be called, with another model, which is concerned not so much with mimicking the outward behavioural displays of intelligence as with reproducing the inner processes, schemes of representation, inference mechanisms, processes of searching, problem solving, learning, etc. We shall call this latter view the **internal representation** model of AI.

You could think of a performance approach as concentrating on the inputs and outputs of a system, and an internal representation approach to AI as being concerned with what goes on inside the 'black box' of the system. Most of the crucial problems in AI do not relate to the performances which a given AI system may eventually deliver, but rather to the details of its internal organization.

A good illustration of internal representation in AI is a famous early program called SHRDLU, written by Terry Winograd (Winograd, 1972). This program is quoted in many popular accounts of AI, no doubt because, like ELIZA, it gives a very convincing conversational performance. Figures 3.4–3.6 show the original SHRDLU in operation. Figure 3.4 shows the initial state of the blocks. Figure 3.5 shows a section of dialogue between a human user and SHRDLU (SHRDLU's contribution is in uppercase). Figure 3.6 shows the blocks after the dialogue.

In order to carry out the command 'pick up the red big block' SHRDLU needs to represent many different kinds of knowledge. For example, it needs declarative knowledge about its objects and the relationships between them (it needs to know that 'the big red block is on the table' and 'the big green block is on the big red block'). Before reading on, try and write down in general terms what other kinds of knowledge are needed for it to respond correctly to the command.

Unlike ELIZA, SHRDLU's conversations are highly domain-specific. More to the point, however, the key achievements of SHRDLU are almost all 'on the inside'.

3.5 Blocks-World Programs and Internal Representations

In this section we shall take a close look at a program called MSBLOCKS, which is loosely based on Winograd's SHRDLU. MSBLOCKS was created at Sussex University for use by undergraduate students in order to explore the sorts of issues discussed in this book. It is a much-simplified relative of SHRDLU, and we only have space to describe a simplified version of MSBLOCKS.

MSBLOCKS, like SHRDLU, is a program which constitutes the 'mind' of an imaginary robot or automaton. This robot is to be imagined as living in a notional world of coloured objects of different sorts. In the case of MSBLOCKS these objects are simply boxes of two sizes (big and small) and three colours (green, blue, and red) lying on a table. Our cast thus includes the following (the names should be self-explanatory):

```
boxg   boxG   boxb   boxB
boxr   boxR   table
```

and, of course, the robot itself, whose arm hovers around over the table.

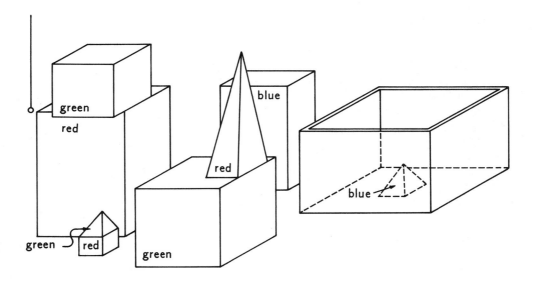

Figure 3.4
The initial state of the SHRDLU example.
Adapted from T. Winograd (1972). *Understanding Natural Language.* New York:
Academic Press, p. 8. Reprinted by permission.

1. pick up a big red block.
    OK.
2. grasp the pyramid.
    I DON'T UNDERSTAND WHICH PYRAMID YOU MEAN.
3. find a block which is taller than the one you are holding and
    put it into the box.
    BY "IT" I ASSUME YOU MEAN THE BLOCK WHICH
    IS TALLER THAN THE ONE I AM HOLDING. OK.
4. what does the box contain?
    THE BLUE PYRAMID AND THE BLUE BLOCK.
5. what is the pyramid supported by?
    THE BOX.
6. how many blocks are not in the box?
    FOUR OF THEM
7. is at least one of them narrower than the one which
    I told you to pick up?
    YES, THE RED CUBE.
8. is it supported?
    YES, BY THE TABLE.
9. can the table pick up blocks?
    NO.
10. can a pyramid be supported by a block?
    YES.
11. can a pyramid support a pyramid?
    I DON'T KNOW.
12. stack up two pyramids.
    I CAN'T
13. the blue pyramid is mine.
    I UNDERSTAND.
14. I own blocks which are not red, but I don't own anything
    which supports a pyramid.
    I UNDERSTAND.
15. do I own the box?
    NO.
16. do I own anything in the box?
    YES, TWO THINGS: THE BLUE BLOCK AND
    THE BLUE PYRAMID.
17. will you please stack up both of the red blocks and either
    a green cube or a pyramid.
    OK.

Figure 3.5
A section of dialogue with SHRDLU.

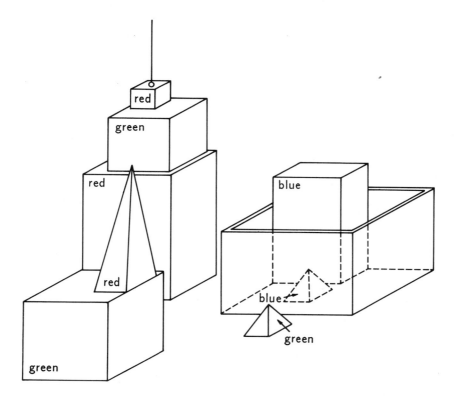

Figure 3.6
The final state of the SHRDLU example.
Adapted from Winograd (1972), *Understanding Natural Language*, p. 12. Reprinted
by permission.

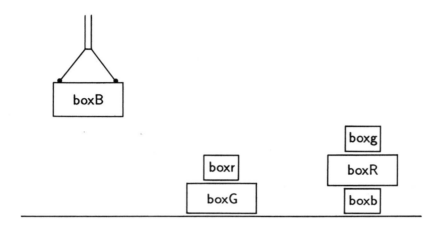

Figure 3.7
The initial state of the MSBLOCKS example.

These boxes can be moved around and placed one on top of the other, or onto a table. The robot is a very simple one: all it can do is pick up boxes and put them down again. Moreover, the system is set up in such a way that it can only hold one box at any one time. In figure 3.7, for example, if it is instructed to pick up the big green box (boxG), where boxG is covered by the little red box (boxr), and where the robot is holding the big blue box (boxB), it must go through a series of preparatory operations before it can do what you say: first it must put boxB down somewhere (but not on boxr); then it must pick up boxr and place it clear of boxG.

As can be seen, the 'world' inhabited by the MSBLOCKS automaton is very rudimentary indeed. It can, however, be made indefinitely more complicated by adding more and more boxes, and objects of other sorts, including more devices to move the objects around, and so on. The point of the example is to show how even a situation as simple as that illustrated in figure 3.7 hides a surprisingly complex set of underlying structures and procedures for manipulating these structures.

3.5.1 Knowledge of the MSBLOCKS World

The simplification in this model is made even more extreme by the fact that, as with SHRDLU, there is no real robot there at all, and there are no real boxes to move about in 3-dimensional physical space. Rather, the robot and its world are simulated, and details of the simulation are held in a database containing a list of facts which are currently true in the world. There are two kinds of entries in the database. First, there are the entries which represent general, unchangeable, background facts about the objects in the world, such as the colours and sizes of the boxes on the table. Thus, when we ask the robot, for example, to move 'the large red box', it is able to work out which box we must be referring to. Unchangeable facts of this sort are represented as lists like

```
[boxB size large] [boxB colour blue]
[boxb size small] [boxb colour blue]
[boxG size large] [boxG colour green]
```

Then there are the changeable facts, which only hold at particular times in the history of the 'world'. These say where a particular box is located, what, if anything, the robot is holding, and so on. For example, the state of the world pictured in figure **??** might be represented by the following database entries:

```
[boxG on table] [boxr on boxG] [cleartop boxr]
[boxb on table] [boxR on boxb] [boxg on boxR]
[cleartop boxg] [holding boxB]
```

The `cleartop` entries make explicit which boxes can be directly picked up or covered with another box. The entry `[holding boxB]` indicates what the robot is currently holding. The robot might not have been holding anything, in which case the database would instead have contained the entry `[handempty]`.

The MSBLOCKS automaton will respond to commands and questions in English like

> Put the big green box onto the small green one.
> Place a blue box on a red one.
> Is there a large box on the table?

When we tell the simulated robot to do something like "Put the big green box onto the small green one" the program has to

1. Decompose the sentence into a symbolic representation of its meaning.

2. Relate the meaning to the facts in the database and form a goal (in this case to put boxG onto boxg).

3. Plan a sequence of operations to achieve the goal.

4. Carry out the plan, by moving the simulated boxes about the screen.

Given the initial state shown in figure 3.7, the plan to achieve the goal [boxG on boxg] requires several operations:

1. Put down the box which the robot is currently holding (boxB); it had better be onto the table.

2. Pick up boxr from the top of boxG.

3. Put boxr down; on top of boxB will do.

4. Pick up boxG from the table.

5. Put boxG down on top of boxg.

As the robot carries out the plan by performing these operations, the changeable part of the database is modified (or 'updated'). One or more items is deleted from the database, and others are added to it (see figure 3.8). For instance, operation (1) above requires the program to

```
Delete:   [holding boxB]
Add:      [boxB on table] [cleartop boxB] [handempty]
```

By the time operations (1)–(5) have been performed the database will have been changed quite considerably. The changeable part of it will now consist of

```
[handempty]        [cleartop boxG] [boxG on boxg]
[cleartop boxr]    [boxr on boxB]  [boxB on table]
[boxb on table]    [boxR on boxb]  [boxg on boxR]
```

Figure 3.8 shows the final state of the boxes.

If the robot were a real one — for instance, storing crates in a warehouse — then real boxes would be manipulated in a real physical environment. It would still be necessary to update the database after each operation to record the changes which

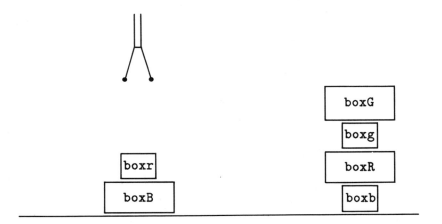

Figure 3.8
The final state of the MSBLOCKS example.

have taken place in the environment. However, from the point of view of modelling the internal, 'mental' organization of this kind of system, carrying out actions on real objects is unnecessary. In the MSBLOCKS simulation (as in SHRDLU and the many similar 'blocks-world' programs it has inspired), the operations consist simply of the manipulation of symbolic structures. It would be quite possible to add to such a system a robotic arm that could manipulate actual boxes sitting on a physical table, but the main issues which are addressed by MSBLOCKS (and by SHRDLU) concern internal organization, rather than outwardly observable performances.

3.5.2 Knowledge of Possible Actions

MSBLOCKS has another important kind of internal representation, which specifies the different kinds of actions which it is able to perform. In the MSBLOCKS world just four different operations are available (although this number can obviously be increased indefinitely). These operations are

[pickup ?X table]	Lift a box from the table
[unstack ?X ?Y]	Pick up a box which is sitting on top of another box
[putdown ?X table]	Put the box which the robot is holding on the table
[stack ?X ?Y]	Stack a box on top of another box

As explained in the previous chapter, the expressions ?X and ?Y stand for pattern-matching variables. When the operations are performed the variables will be given the values of particular boxes to be moved, such as [stack boxG boxg].

When we set the robot a goal — for example, "Put the big green box onto the small green one" — the robot must choose a sequence of operations which will bring about the desired result. The process of choosing a sequence of operations is usually known as **planning** in AI.

In order to plan out a sequence of operations, the MSBLOCKS system has to follow certain constraints, in the form of preconditions that must be true in order for a given action to be possible in a given situation, and effects that the operations need to produce in order to reach the goal. For instance, if I plan to drive from Marseilles to Paris, the preconditions are that I must have a car, that it is in working order, that I am situated in, or can get to, Marseilles, and so on. Similar conditions apply to the robot. . So, for example, in order to perform the operation [unstack boxr boxG] it must be the case that

1. the robot is not holding anything (i.e., [handempty] must be in the database), and

2. boxr must not have any other box on top of it (i.e., [cleartop boxr] must be in the database).

Each operation produces effects in the form of changes to the database: entries may be *deleted*, or they may be *added*.

For example, after the operation [unstack boxr boxG] has been performed, the following changes will be made to the database:

Delete: [handempty] [cleartop boxr] [boxr on boxG]
Add: [holding boxr] [cleartop boxG]

The program's knowledge of possible actions, subject to the constraints just mentioned, is encoded as a series of structures called **operator schemas** — rather like simple frames, with slots which can be filled in different ways. Each operator schema represents the characteristics of a given operation and provides at least four kinds of information:

1. the specification of the type of operation — for example, [unstack ?X ?Y],

2. the preconditions of the operation,

3. the 'delete' list, and

4. the 'add' list.

Here is how the schema for the operation [unstack ?X ?Y] might look, expressed in a list pattern form. The schema will consist of a list, with four sublists:

```
[ [unstack ?X ?Y]                                    Operator specification
[ [?X on ?Y] [cleartop ?X] [handempty] ] Preconditions
[ [?X on ?Y] [cleartop ?X] [handempty] ] Delete list
[ [cleartop ?Y] [holding ?X] ] ]         Add list
```

The two middle sub-lists, the preconditions and the delete list, contain the same members. This need not always be the case, but it happens to be so for this particular operation.

In planning a sequence of operations, the program selects a series of operator schemas that move the database from its initial state to the goal state. For each stage in the plan an operator is chosen that fits both constraints; that is, its proeconditions match the current state of the database, and its effects advance the robot toward the goal. Normally there is more than one way to reach a goal, within the constraints, and just how a program plans a good series of operators is a major topic of AI, and one that is not covered further in this book. Rich (1983) and Charniak and McDermott (1985) both offer good introductions to planning techniques.

We have shown how simple data-structures can represent the fixed and changeable conditions of the robot's environment, and its available actions. Other kinds of representation are also needed. Before forming a plan the program must reduce sentences typed in English to a form that can be matched against its database of operator schemas. From the raw words of a sentence, a representation of its syntax is constructed, from which the sentence's meaning is derived. If the sentence is a command, such as "Put the little red box on top of a green one," then its response will be to plan a sequence of operations and make changes to the database. If the sentence is a question, such as "Where is the small green box?" then it will consult the database and generate an appropriate answer.

There are some salutary lessons to be learned from SHRDLU and MSBLOCKS. A surprisingly complicated set of internal structures, as well as processes to manipulate these structures, is required in order to make the system work, to enable it to understand simple one-sentence commands or questions about blocks. Much more complex knowledge representations are likely to be needed for AI systems capable of performing more substantial or more lifelike mental tasks: tasks such as answering a tourist's questions!

3.6   Conclusion

In order to answer a wide range of questions, to plan a sequence of actions, or to reason about the world, an AI program needs internal representations of knowledge. Human knowledge comes in many forms — for example, it may be factual or practical, general or specific, logical or informal — and different AI formalisms have been developed to model different types of knowledge. The main ones are predicate logic, semantic networks, production systems, frames, and scripts. To carry out a command such as "Put a red block on the big blue one," an AI program needs knowledge about the structure and meaning of English, the objects in its 'world' (coloured blocks of different sizes), the current relationships between the objects, the possible actions it can perform, and the constraints on these actions. It must (at the very least) convert the English command into an internal representation of its meaning, relate this to its stored knowledge of the objects, form a plan in the form of a sequence of actions, and then carry out these actions. To carry out more everyday actions (like tidying a room) or answer questions like "What would happen if I tilted this glass full of water?" may require an understanding of a wide range of objects and their possible interactions.

3.7 Appendix: Representing Knowledge

In this section we shall develop the notion of matching patterns against a database, as a tool for manipulating knowledge in our Automated Tourist Guide. The version of the Guide described in chapter two had the severe limitation that its 'knowledge' of London consisted entirely of questions paired with appropriate answers. This a cumbersome way of storing knowledge, in that a single concept, such as Buckingham Palace, must be held in a number of different forms, depending on the type of question to be asked about it. It is also inconvenient; the knowledge is hidden within the English phrases and so cannot easily be used as the basis for automated reasoning or planning.

By contrast, the knowledge of MSBLOCKS is kept as a series of entries in a database, with concepts stored as compact symbol structures. There are a number of ways in which a database for a Tourist Guide might be organized, but for our purposes it contains a number of component entries, which can be searched, added to, or removed. Each item in the database is arranged as a sub-list of three parts, representing two items and their relationship. Here, for example, are some possible entries in the database:

```
[[marble arch] near [hyde park]]
[[marble arch] at [the west end of oxford street]]
[[marble arch] isa [triumphal arch]]
[[the science museum] near [the natural history museum]]
[[the science museum] underground [south kensington]]
[[the natural history museum] isa [museum]]
```

It is useful to have information stored in the form of lists of triplets like this, rather than English text such as

```
[marble arch is near hyde park]
[marble arch is at the west end of oxford street]
```

If we know in advance that every item in the database will be a triplet, and that the item indicating relationship is drawn from a restricted set of words ('near', 'at', etc.), then searching through the database becomes much more straightforward. It is also easy to give a database in this form some the characteristics of a semantic network, or to use it as a foundation for the more structured representations like frames or scripts.

The POP-11 database is stored in a variable called, appropriately, **database**. The procedures below all operate on **database** and its value is a list of items, each of which represents one entry. Initially we want the database to be empty. We can do this by 'initializing' the variable **database**, as follows:

```
[ ] -> database;
```

The expression [ ] stands for the empty list.

3.7.1   Some Procedures to Access the Database

Built into the POP-11 language is a small number of simple but powerful procedures for manipulating a database of this sort, known collectively as the **database package**. It is fairly easy to implement similar procedures in LISP or other AI languages. As we saw in our examination of MSBLOCKS, at least three types of operation can be carried out on a database:

1. It can be modified by having items added to it.

2. It can be modified by having items removed from it.

3. It can be searched.

Among the procedures provided for the POP-11 database package are the following:

add	For adding new entries to the database;
present	For searching for a given entry in the database;
allpresent	For searching for multiple entries in the database;
remove	For deleting entries from the database.

Each of these procedures takes one argument, which is the database entry to be added, removed, or searched for. When calling the `remove`, `present`, or `allpresent` procedure, it is possible, and often extremely useful, to use a pattern, rather than a fully specified list, as the argument to the procedure. Examples of this will be given below:

`add`   This procedure adds an item to the database. We can use it to store facts about London of interest to tourists:

```
add([[the science museum] isa [museum]]);
add([[the science museum] underground [south kensington]]);
add([[the science museum] near
[the natural history museum]]);
add([[the natural history museum] isa [museum]]);
```

Each of these `add` commands takes a single argument: a list to be added. The print arrow can be used to display the state of the database:

```
database =>

** [[[the natural history museum] isa [museum]] [[the
science museum] near [the natural history museum]] [[the
science museum] underground [south kensington]] [[the
science museum] isa [museum]]]
```

The items appear in reverse order because each time the procedure is called it inserts the new item at the *beginning* of whatever is already there. As we have shown, `add` is a built-in POP-11 procedure, but we can make clearer how it works by showing how it might be defined:

```
define add(item);
    [^item ^^database] -> database;
enddefine;
```

The crucial expression to understand here is `[^item ^^database]`. This is a new list containing the newly added item followed by the contents of the old `database`. The new list is then made to be the new value of database, 'overwriting' the old value.

present   The procedure **present** searches for an item in the database. It can take either a list or a pattern as argument and it does not alter the database, but simply returns the result **<true>** if the item is present in the database, or **<false>** otherwise:

```
present([[the science museum] isa [museum]])=>
** <true>
```

present can be given a pattern as argument. So the call

```
vars x;
present([?x isa [museum]])=>
```

will return the value

```
** <true>
```

Repeated calls to **present** will match the same item (because a call to **present** does not alter the database).

The ability of **present** to work with patterns as well as explicit lists makes it useful for finding items which cannot be completely specified. Also, using **present** with a pattern as argument has the side-effect of assigning the matched parts of the database item to the pattern variables. So, if we ask for the value of x to be printed out after a call of

```
present([?x isa [museum]]);
```

this will be the result:

```
x=>
** [the natural history museum]
```

The first item in the database that matches the pattern is used for the assignment. In this call to **present** the variable x is assigned the value [the natural history museum].

allpresent   The procedure `allpresent` takes a list of lists or patterns as input and tries to find a consistent way of matching them against items in the database. It returns `<true>` if all the patterns can be matched, and `<false>` otherwise:

```
allpresent([[[the science museum] isa [museum]]
    [[the science museum] underground
    [south kensington]]])=>
** <true>
allpresent([[?x isa [museum]]
    [?y underground [south kensington]]])=>
** <true>
```

Assignment to pattern variables is made by the first match of each pattern against an item in the database. So the call of `allpresent` above will assign [the natural history museum] to x and [the science museum] to y. If the same variable is used more than once, then a match must be found that assigns the same value to all instances of the variable — for example,

```
allpresent([[?x isa [museum]]
  [?x underground [south kensington]]])=>


** <true>
```

Both patterns can match items in the database so that the same value is given to x — in this case [the science museum].

remove   The procedure `remove` searches through the database to find an appropriate item to remove. The search always starts from the beginning. If by any chance there are two or more occurrences of the same item, then only the first is removed. Like `present`, `remove` can be used with a pattern, rather than a fully specified list. It will then delete the first entry it finds which matches the pattern as input.

Given the database created earlier, we could remove

```
[[the natural history museum] isa [museum]]
```

as follows:

```
remove([[the natural history museum] isa [museum]]);
```

	Alters database	Can use list pattern	Returns <true> or <false> as result
add	Yes	No	No
remove	Yes	Yes	No
present	No	Yes	Yes
allpresent	No	Yes	Yes

Table 3.1
A summary of the features of add, remove, present, and
allpresent

We can also give a pattern as an argument to **remove**, as follows:

```
vars x,y;
remove([[the science museum] ?x ?y]);
```

In this call to **remove**, the pattern

```
[[the science museum] ?x ?y]
```

can match

```
[[the science museum] near [the natural history museum]]
and
[[the science museum] underground [south kensington]]
and
[[the science museum] isa [museum]]
```

The procedure **remove** deletes only one item each time it is used. So the first time we call

```
remove([[the science museum] ?x ?y]);
```

only the first of these lists will be removed. If we then repeat exactly the same call, the second of the three lists will be deleted. Table 3.1 shows the effects of each procedure.

3.7.2   A Revised Version of the answer Procedure

The POP-11 database package has many other features, but even with the four procedures that we have reviewed here, we can build a knowledge base for our

Tourist Guide. For a fuller account of the POP-11 database see chapter 9 of Barrett, Ramsay, and Sloman (1985). In this section, we shall only employ the **present** procedure to answer tourists' questions, but the Guide could be further extended by using **add** and **remove** to set up the database with an appropriate store of knowledge and then to modify it from time to time as new knowledge is required (for example, if a new theatre show opens).

We will suppose that an appropriate database has been set up, as follows:

```
[ [[marble arch] near [hyde park]]
  [[marble arch] at [the west end of oxford street]]
  [[marble arch] isa [triumphal arch]]
  [[the science museum] near [the natural history museum]]
  [[the science museum] underground [south kensington]]
  [[the natural history museum] isa [museum]] ] -> database;
```

We can now define a version of the **answer** procedure which consults the database for information to construct a response to a query. (If you have difficulty in following the use of the pattern matching expressions used here, then go back to the last chapter, where their use is explained, or forward to the next section of this chapter, where there is a longer explanation.)

```
define answer(query) -> response;
  vars x y;
  if query matches [where is ??x] and
      present([^x at ?y]) then
        [^^x is to be found at ^^y] -> response;
  elseif query matches [== description of ??x] and
      present([^x isa ?y]) then
        [^^x could be described as a ^^y] -> response;
  elseif query matches [what == near ??x] and
      present([?y near ^x]) then
        [^^y is close to ^^x] -> response;
  elseif query matches
      [what == underground station to ??x] and
      present([^x underground ?y]) then
        [the nearest underground station to ^^x is ^^y]
            -> response;
  else
```

```
      [i cannot answer that] -> response;
   endif;
enddefine;
```

Here is an example of how this procedure might be called, given the database as set up on page 91:

```
answer([what is near the natural history museum])=>
** [the science museum is close to the natural history museum]
```

In the version of **answer** defined in chapter 2, the **if** part of each if ... then clause contained a pattern to be matched against the query, and the **then** part contained a list or pattern to be given as a response. In this new version each if ... then clause has three patterns, one to match the query, one to search the database, and one which is returned as a response — for example,

Query pattern:	`[what == near ??x]`
Database search pattern:	`[?y near ^x]`
Response pattern:	`[^^y is close to ^^x]`

The query pattern is matched against the query. If the match is successful, for instance, if the query were

```
[what is near the natural history museum]
```

then the variable x inside the pattern has its value set to the appropriate part of the query, in this case

```
[the natural history museum]
```

The database search pattern is now filled out with the value assigned to x, producing

```
[?y near [the natural history museum]]
```

This partially filled pattern is given as the argument to **present** which searches the database to find a match. If the search is successful (as it is in this case), the value of y is set from the database. In this example y will now stand for

```
[the science museum]
```

The response pattern is now fully specified, as both x and y now have values, and its value

```
[the science museum is close to the naural history museum]
```

is returned as the result of calling **answer**.

3.7.3 Using Variables in Patterns

In order to follow what happened in the example, care has to be taken in interpreting the pattern matching variables used in the various list patterns. As this is quite an intricate feature of POP-11 programming, it would be as well to go over the most important features of the use of variables in list patterns. So this section expands on the discussions of pattern matching in the last chapter. Reading this section is not essential if you are not at present concerned with gaining a practical knowledge of POP-11 programming through reading this book.

Two things have to be kept clear in understanding variables in list patterns.

Set-Value and Use-Value variables First, there is the difference between **set-value** and **use-value** variables. Set-value variables look like this:

```
?x        ??y        ?item          ??items
```

and use-value variables look like this:

```
^x        ^^y        ^item          ^^items
```

A set-value variable is used when a value is *being looked for* to assign to that variable. A use-value variable is used when the variable has already had a value assigned to it, and where that value is to be used. As you can see, set-value variables are always preceded by queries and use-value variables are always preceded by up-arrows.

To illustrate: take, for example, the pattern

```
[?y near ^x]
```

Here the variable x is to be given a value, while the variable x will already have a value assigned to it, and that value will be used in place of x in the pattern.

Suppose, for example, that the value [hyde park] has been assigned to the variable x, and the pattern [?y near ^x] is being used to search the database. There will then be a match with the following database entry:

```
[[marble arch] near [hyde park]]
```

and, as a result, the variable y will be set to the list [marble arch].

Related to set-value variables, are **wild cards**, with single or double equals-signs:

```
=        ==
```

As we explained in chapter 2, these stand for single or multiple items in a list, and are used where one does not care what items those are (so one does not need to store them).

Single and Double   The second point that needs to be kept clear in the use of list-patterns is the difference between single and double queries or up-arrows preceding variables in patterns. This is the difference between *match-one* pattern variables like

```
    ?x       ?item        ^y        ^item
```

and *match-any* pattern variables such as

```
    ??x      ??items      ^^y       ^^items
```

The single pattern-variables are used to match against *one and only one* item in a list (that item may itself be a list). The double pattern-variables are used to match against *any number of items* in a list: that is, zero or more.

There are a few things to note about these variables. In the case of double query pattern-variables, the items which are picked up are *always enclosed in list brackets.* So when, for instance, the pattern

```
    [direct me to ??x]
```

is matched with

```
    [direct me to great portland street]
```

the variable x will acquire the value

```
    [great portland street]
```

Again, if it were matched with

```
    [direct me to piccadilly]
```

then x would acquire the value

```
    [piccadilly]
```

and not the word piccadilly. Notice that if it were matched with

```
[direct me to]
```

then **x** would acquire the value [ ].

Conversely, when double up-arrows are used, the contents of a list are to be inserted into a pattern, and the rule here is 'insert the items in the list *without the outer list brackets*'. So the pattern

```
[direct me to ^^x]
```

where **x** has the value

```
[great portland street]
```

will result in the list

```
[direct me to great portland street]
```

being created. By contrast, if we had used the pattern

```
[direct me to ^x]
```

then the result would be

```
[direct me to [great portland street]]
```

Having gone over these points, go back through the **answer** procedure given above, trying to see how the various pattern-variables operate there.

3.7.4 Reviewing the answer Procedure

With the behaviour of the list pattern-matching variables explained, we shall summarize how the **answer** procedure works. In brief, the procedure takes as input a tourist's enquiry, processes the question by searching its database, and produces and answer as output. In the course of this operation, the procedure links up no less than six different lists or list-patterns. These are

1. the list given as the initial question,

2. a matching query-pattern picked up by one of **answer**'s if ... then clauses,

3. the associated database search pattern,

4. the actual database entry,

5. the response pattern used to build up the answer to the input question, and

6. the answer itself.

We can thus divide the working of the procedure into five steps, as follows:

1. A question, in the form of a list, is given as an argument to the procedure, for example:

```
answer([what is the closest underground station
        to the science museum])=>
```

2. The enquiry is matched to a question pattern, in one of the if ... then clauses (the last one in the version of **answer** shown earlier). In the course of this matching, some variables in the question pattern will acquire values. Thus, the above question matches the pattern

```
[what == underground station to ??x]
```

The double-equals matches the words 'is the closest' and this information is discarded. The pattern-variable **??x** matches the words 'the national gallery', so the variable x is set to the *list* [the science museum].

3. An associated pattern is used to search the database. In this case, the search pattern will be

```
[^x underground ?y]
```

The search pattern can be partially filled out, using the value assigned to x:

```
[[the science museum] underground ?y]
```

A matching database entry is found, using **present**. In this case the database entry is

```
[[the science museum] underground [south kensington]]
```

This results in the variable y being given the value [south kensington].

4. The response pattern is then used to build up the final response. In this case the response pattern is

```
[the nearest underground station to ^^x is ^^y]
```

Since both **x** and **y** how have lists as their value, the *items* in these lists (without the outer brackets) are inserted into the slots in the answer pattern.

5. The final result is returned by **answer** and is printed out. So, given our original question, the printed output is

```
** [the nearest underground station to the science
museum is south kensington]
```

3.8 Exercises

1. The classic example used to demonstrate scripts involves eating in a restaurant. Try and write out a script describing both the typical events in a waiter-service restaurant and also unusual occurrences, such as the actions taken if the food arrives burnt.

2. Write your own version of the Tourist Guide's database, in a form similar to the one shown on page 91. Base it on some town or region you like visiting. Write a version of the **answer** procedure to handle five different types of question that might be asked by a tourist visiting your chosen area.

3. Suppose that the search pattern at stage 3 on page 96 had been, not [^x underground ?y] but [^^x underground ??y], and with variable x having the value [the national gallery]. What would the relevant database entry need to look like in order for the search pattern to match it, in such a way that the variable y would be assigned the value [trafalgar square]? Why?

4. Given that the variables x and y have values as in exercise 3, what list would be printed out if the response pattern had been

```
[the nearest underground station to ^x is ^y]
```

Explain why the use of *double* up-arrows is preferable.

5. Define a procedure, **addlist**, along the lines of **add** given on page 87, which adds each new item to the *end* of the database. Incorporate this in a procedure that will keep a diary consisting of an entry for each day, such as

```
[mon june 29 - went fishing]
[tue june 30 - visited planetarium]
```

and so on.

6. Here is a definition for a procedure **excise**, which works rather like the built-in procedure **remove**.

```
define excise(item);
    vars x y;
    if database matches [??x ^item ??y] then
        [^^x ^~y] -> database;
        [^item has been removed] =>
    else
        [sorry - ^item is not there] =>
    endif;
enddefine;
```

Imagine that your diary database (see the previous question) erroneously contains an entry for the nonexistent date: wed june 31. Show how the procedure **excise** might be used with a suitable list *pattern* to delete that particular entry. Using **excise** as a model, write a procedure **replace**, with two arguments, which finds a given entry in the database and replaces it with a new item.

7. Construct a database describing an imaginary world of toy blocks or other objects sitting on a table, like that given in the MSBLOCKS example. Limit the scene to about ten objects. Write a version of **answer** which can reply to simple questions about objects on the table, and maybe change the database if actions like "Pick up the red block" are requested. Write a brief description of the problems you encountered in this exercise.

Chapter 4

Search

4.1   The Idea of Search

Many of the early practitioners of AI hoped that the difficult tasks they had set, such as building automated chess players, theorem provers, and language translators, could be tackled by employing a few general-purpose techniques. One of the earliest AI programs was even given the optimistic title of the General Problem Solver (Ernst and Newell, 1969). The most important of these general techniques is search.

In recent years attention has shifted towards constructing detailed representations of knowledge, of the kind described in the last chapter, coupled with mechanisms more closely based on those of human problem-solvers. Nevertheless, search remains an important topic in AI, both as a technique for implementing the lower levels of cognition, like visual scene recognition and language understanding, and as a means of modelling those occasions when we consciously search for an entity or a possibility.

Suppose a mobile robot needs to find the best route through some furniture in a room to the door. It can do so by looking at the consequences of the possible moves it can make. Without actually moving the robot, its program checks out the various possibilities in a systematic way. In effect, the program asks itself questions like "What if I move to my left?". If the answer is "I collide with the table," then that possible move can be ruled out, but if the answer is "I get closer to the door," then the next move after that can be considered, and so on. Any program that asks this kind of "What if ...?" question over and over until it finds a solution to its problem is doing **search**.

The idea of search in a computer program is not really all that different from searching in everyday life. Imagine you have lost a key. You systematically try the possibilities, asking "What if . . . ?" questions, until the thing is found. Sometimes, in this example, the questions are answered by a making an action ("What if it's under the cushion?" is answered by lifting up the cushion) and sometimes just by thinking ("What if I left it on the bus?" might be answered by recalling that you used the key after getting off the bus). If you are calm, you do not look in places that you have already searched. You look in the most probable places first but also try to organize your search so as to minimize the amount of walking around you do. And you ask yourself questions that can rule out a whole range of possibilies at once — for example, the question of where you last saw the key.

Searching does not always mean looking for a physical object, of course. You might search for a word you do not know how to spell in a dictionary, you might search for the best route to get across a city, or you might search for the best way to express an idea on paper. But even though some of these searches are very abstract, they all involve trying out possibilities, and in this way are closely related to the technique of search used by computer programs.

Often we do not know how our minds search for something. We have little idea how we come up with the solution to an obscure crossword clue, or a good move in a chess game, or the words to get across an idea. Mostly we cannot program computers to do these things well. On the other hand, we do know how to program computers to search for solutions to a wide range of tasks. The rest of this chapter is about how such programs work.

4.2   Computer Search

A computer program to solve a problem by search has to follow steps analogous to those we take when we look for a lost object. Essentially, it has to decide where to look or what to ask next, it has to remember what it has found out, and it has to recognize the solution when it finds it. The examples that follow should be enough for you to understand the basics of computer search. For a fuller account you could look at Charniak and McDermott (1985) or Rich (1983).

We will begin with our Automated Tourist Guide project, and show how a helpful terminal at a London Underground station could find the best route to any other station. The second example will be used to show how similar strategies can be applied in apparently diverse ways, taking as an example the task of solving a type of jigsaw puzzle. We will also briefly mention the relationship of search to playing

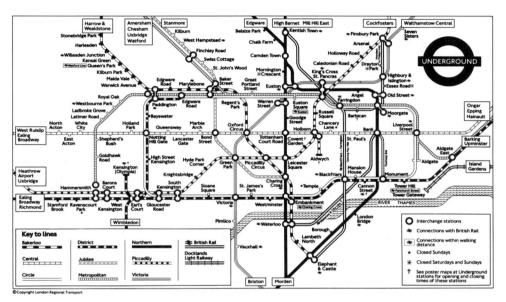

LRT Registered User No. 89/1012

Figure 4.1
The London Underground map.

games, where an adversary is continuously trying to make the problem as hard as possible.

4.2.1 Finding a Route on the Underground

Imagine you are standing at Victoria Station and you need to go to Marble Arch. You are looking at a map like figure 4.1. You would probably decide to go north 2 stops on the Victoria line to Oxford Circus, then west 2 stops on the Central line. You perhaps feel it is obvious that that is the best route, but if the route were more complex and there were many lines going in roughly the right direction, you might be less sure.

To program a computer to carry out such a search we need to provide it with

Try and work out the route between High Street Kensington and Holborn with the smallest number of stops. How did you organize the search? How do you know that you have found the best route?

both a *representation* of the problem (in terms of how the stations are connected) and a *method* of carrying out the search. In creating the representation we can ignore many aspects of the geography and topology of London. For instance, we do not need to know what the area around a station looks like, or its exact map reference. The information we need concerns legal routes between stations, and perhaps the time taken to travel from one station to another and to change lines. (The London Underground map serves just this purpose, and at the time it was first designed, in the 1920s, it was a great innovation.) If we were interested merely in finding *any* route between two stations, then we could program the computer with a fairly simple algorithm. In English it is this:

1. Start at the station from which you want to travel (Victoria in this case). Call this the 'current station'.

2. Keep a record of all the lines (and directions) from the current station that have not yet been tried. Choose one of these untried lines.

3. On the map, pencil over the chosen line, station by station. Keep a record of each station you have visited. If you get to the destination station, then stop; you have found a complete route. If you get to the end of the line, or if you get to a station you have already visited, then erase your route, station by station, until you get back to a junction station (i.e., one that has a different line, or lines, leading from it). If there are no untried lines leading from this junction, then continue back till you find a station with an untried line. Call this the 'current station'.

4. Go back to step 2.

For an example we shall use the simplified map in figure 4.2. Let us say that we want to get to Baker Street. From Victoria we could choose the Victoria line northwards. We follow it station by station: Victoria, Green Park, Oxford Circus, Warren Street. We get to the end of the line at Warren Street without passing our goal, Baker Street. Now we retrace the route back to Oxford Circus and try another line, say the Central line westwards. This reaches a dead end, at Lancaster Gate, so we retrace the route to the last junction, Bond Street, and try a new route, say the Jubilee line southwards. We follow this till we reach a station that has already been visited (Green Park) and then retrace our steps back to Bond Street. We then try the Jubilee line northwards from Bond Street, and reach our goal, Baker Street. The route is then Victoria, Green Park, Oxford Circus, Bond Street, Baker Street.

This type of search algorithm is known as **depth first search**, because it searches right down to the end of a path, before trying an alternative. It is guaranteed to find a path to the goal, if one exists, but the path is not likely to be the best one (a better route to Baker Street is to change at Green Park and take the Jubilee line). Another, related, type of search is **breadth first search**, which follows each path from the current node to the next decision point. It is useful when we want to find a solution with the minimum number of steps from the starting point; an example might occur in programming a robot to perform an action in the smallest possible number of separate movements. For example, from Victoria we investigate the lines to the Embankment, Green Park, South Kensington, and Vauxhall. Since the goal station is not on any of these, we choose one junction, say the Embankment, and investigate all the unexplored lines leading from there (there is only one, to Charing Cross). Since it is not successful we choose the earliest unexplored junction, Green Park. That leads to Bond Street, Oxford Circus, Piccadilly Circus, Charing Cross, and South Kensington. Embankment, Green Park, and South Kensington have now all been explored, and Vauxhall is not a junction. So we look at lines from the earliest unexplored junction, Bond Street. One of these lines leads to Baker Street, and we have found the goal.

But for it to be any use to a tourist, our program for the Tourist Guide should not just find *any* route to a given station, but the *best* route (though it is allowed to make some assumptions about how fast the trains go and how long it takes to change lines). The method we shall describe is an adaptation of breadth first search that takes account of the time taken to reach each station. The name, **branch and bound**, comes from the fact that at each step we put a bound or limit on which branches are searched: i.e., we only consider the ones with the shortest times.

In the appendix to this chapter we outline a computer program to perform branch and bound search, but here is an informal description. Let us assume this time that we want to find the best route to Marble Arch. Imagine we could gather together a large number of volunteers (say 200) and assemble them all at Victoria. They then all set off at the same time, a quarter in each direction, to Pimlico, Green Park, Sloane Square, and St James's Park. At each station with a choice of route

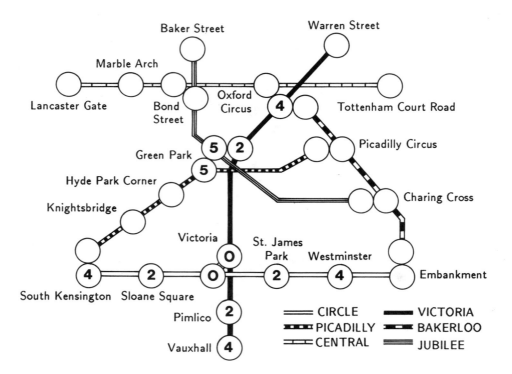

Figure 4.2
A small section of the Underground map.

the party of volunteers splits, some going one way, others another. Thus at Green Park, some stay on the train to Oxford Circus and some change, splitting up and heading for Hyde Park Corner, Bond Street, Picadilly Circus, and Charing Cross. Naturally the parties get smaller, but provided the original group was large enough, there are enough of them to split up at every junction until the search is over. All we need to do is wait at Marble Arch and ask the first volunteers who arrive what stations they have passed through. These volunteers must have taken the fastest route; if a faster one existed then another party would have found it, and would have arrived sooner.

You may feel that this process is unnecessarily extravagant even with simulated volunteers: why explore south from Victoria when it is obvious that this will not produce a useful route? Unfortunately it is not obvious to our computer program. A fact like this is only obvious to us because our visual system manages, without our having to give conscious thought, to do a lot of the information processing that we need laboriously to program into the computer. Until the search is complete, the program cannnot be sure that there is no remarkable shortcut from somewhere south of Pimlico up to Marble Arch.

Let us now turn to the mechanics of the computer program, which we can do best by simulating our wave of volunteers using pencil and paper. We will make the following assumptions (in practice much more detailed knowledge of likely times could be deployed):

- It takes 2 minutes to travel between any two adjacent stations.

- It takes 3 minutes to change lines at a station.

We write on a map of the Underground the times it takes the first of our volunteers to arrive at each station. It will be clearest if we split stations on several lines into pieces, one on each line, as in figure 4.2. We begin by writing 0 by Victoria, then 2 by Sloane Square, St James's Park, Pimlico, and Green Park (Victoria line), since each of these can be reached in 2 minutes from Victoria. Continuing in strict temporal sequence, the next arrivals will be after 4 minutes at Oxford Circus, South Kensington, Vauxhall, and Westminster. At 5 minutes some groups have changed stations to other lines at Green Park, so each of these can be labelled 5. In figure 4.2, the time labels have been completed up to 5 minutes. If you continue this process in strict temporal order, adding all the 6 minute labels before you add the 7 minute ones, you should end up labelling Marble Arch with 11 minutes, for the group that changed at Oxford Circus. That then gives the solution. In the process many other stations will have been labelled.

Note how important it is to do things in chronological order: if we worked outwards from Green Park and forgot what was happening at Oxford Circus, then we could end up erroneously labelling Bond Street (Central line) with 10 and hence Marble Arch with 12.

We now have an informal but quite precise specification of an algorithm, and it remains to convert it into POP-11 to make it usable. In the meantime we shall look at another way of representing the search process, one that has considerable power in helping us to visualize mechanisms such as this.

4.2.2   The Tree Structure of Search

Figure 4.3 shows how we can represent the search in a tree structure. It is the **search tree** for the route from Victoria to Marble Arch, using the reduced map of figure 4.2, and indicating only the first arrival at any station. Trees in AI grow upside-down, and the time sequence in our diagram goes from the top to the bottom of the page. The starting point, Victoria, is shown as the **root** of the tree, and the first branches from it go to the first four possible stations. In the tree, stations are known as **nodes** and each node in our diagram is labelled with a three-letter abbreviation for the station name, followed by a three-letter abreviation in capitals for the line name. As our wave of volunteers spreads out from Victoria and reaches increasing numbers of stations, nodes are added to the tree at increasingly deeper levels. Notice, though, that we still must be careful to work downwards in time sequence, or the end result may go wrong. As soon as Marble Arch is added, we can trace back up the tree, so finding the solution.

The task of the program can be seen, then, as building this tree. This is just another way of expressing the description we gave earlier in terms of simulating our volunteers. As we shall see, the tree description is a very general way to describe search procedures.

Breadth first search is just a special case of branch and bound. Suppose in the route finder the time to change lines was equal to the time to travel between stations. Then in figure 4.3, nodes an equal number of steps from the root would lie at the same level in the diagram, and the simulation would consider all of them before going onto lower (i.e., later) nodes. Under these conditions the search becomes breadth first.

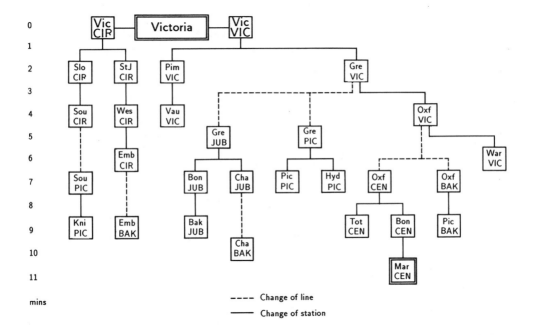

Figure 4.3
The search tree for the route from Victoria to Marble Arch.

4.2.3   Solving a Jigsaw

We shall now give a completely different example of a problem that demands a search method. It is a small puzzle, but is analogous to many problems in the real world where a resource must be divided up subject to some constraints. In this case a frame must be divided up into sections subject to the constraint that the shapes of the sections correspond to the shapes of jigsaw pieces.

The problem is to fit the shaped pieces shown in figure 4.4 into the frame. A larger version of this puzzle, involving 27 pieces, is almost impossible to solve in any reasonable time by hand, but a modest computer running a search program can find the answer in a few minutes. How does the search proceed? Essentially, it tries questions of the form "What if this piece goes in in this position?" until it finds a combination that fits. It starts from one corner of the frame, and uses the fact that some corner of a piece must fit there in order to generate the possibilities to test. From that first position it carries out a depth first search of possible placings. At each stage a corner with an acute angle in the free space is selected, and a piece that can cover the corner is tried out there. The process is repeated, going down each branch of the tree in turn, until there is no piece that can fit the chosen corner, or until all the pieces have been fitted. If we reach a point where all the pieces fit, then the puzzle has been solved.

If no piece can be fitted in the corner chosen, then the program removes the last piece fitted from its internal representation of the frame and tries it in a different orientation, or else it tries a different piece in the same corner. This behaviour is known as **backtracking**.

The tree structure for the first few attempts at the puzzle is shown in figure 4.5. Each node in the tree represents the current state of the frame. If the program happens to try the pieces in the order corresponding to the figure (trying the left branch first each time), then it will have to backtrack four times before it finds a solution. The nodes are numbered in the order that they are examined.

4.2.4   Search Strategies

Depth first, breadth first, and branch and bound are three out of many possible **search strategies**. A search strategy is simply a set of rules for deciding the order in which the tree is to be searched. The best order is dictated by the nature of the problem in hand, as we have seen from the examples so far. Depth-first search makes no sense for the route finder, as it entails following some arbitrarily chosen route as far as possible to see if it leads to the destination. Likewise, branch and

Figure 4.4
A jigsaw puzzle to be solved by search. The 4 pieces must be fitted into the frame.

Try out the puzzle for yourself. Cut out the pieces from cardboard and, starting at the top left corner, place the pieces using a systematic, depth first, strategy, backtracking if you cannot place a piece, until you have solved the puzzle.

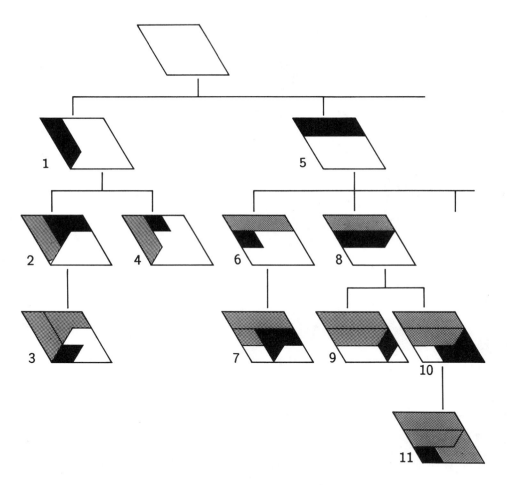

Figure 4.5
Part of the search tree for the jigsaw puzzle.

bound is inappropriate for the jigsaw puzzle, since there is no need to keep track of other branches in the tree while we check whether the present one leads to a solution.

4.2.5 State Space

In both the Underground map example and the jigsaw puzzle, we showed how a program could explore a set of possibilities by developing possible paths towards a goal. Each node in a tree represented some situation, in one case that of having arrived at a particular station, in the other that of having fitted certain pieces into the frame. These situations are known as **states** and the collection of all the possible states pertaining to a problem is called **state-space**. You can picture state-space as simply a table on which descriptions of all the states are laid out, waiting to be examined in turn. In many real problems the state-space, if it were really laid out like this, would be inconceivably huge, but the metaphor is often useful in thinking about what the program is trying to do.

In practice a program builds up its state space step by step. Note that in both the examples the trees were created by going down branches, to which new nodes were added by making one change from the node above. Such nodes represent neighbours in state-space. If a program were to try different states in state-space at random to see if they produced a solution, clearly it would be most unlikely to find one. Search strategies allow programs to cover state-space in a systematic way, jumping from a state to its neighbours, so as to organize an efficient search.

4.2.6 Playing Games

There is a long history in artificial intelligence of attempts to write programs to play games such as chess. Chess playing programs are now better than most human chess players, though still not so good as the very best human players. In fact, games programs work using a form of search adapted to take account of the fact that the human adversary, who wants to beat the program, can change the state of the game at each play.

Take the game of chess. The state-space consists here of all the possible board positions that could arise during play. There is an enormous number of them, and we could never write down the whole of the state-space. Nonetheless, given a particular board position, the program has to decide which of those board positions that it can produce on its next move will give it the greatest advantage over its opponent. It does so by searching through them, investigating the possible ways the game will develop from each position. Once again, a tree will develop, with the course of many possible games shown down its various branches. Once again, the program is trying out many "What if?" questions, in this case of the form "What if I move to X?" and "What if my opponent then moves to Y?"

The state-space for chess is so vast that no program could ever complete the tree, following up all the possible games that could develop to their conclusions. Instead, a program has to stop after looking ahead for only a few moves; it must then assess the board states that have developed using criteria such as the number of pieces taken and the number of squares threatened by the various pieces. The choice of these criteria is a matter of the greatest difficulty in designing a good chess playing program, and involves the application of a great deal of human intelligence. The criteria are combined into a number which reflects the overall assessment of the state of the board; this is called a **static evaluation function**. It is 'static' because it must depend not on further looking ahead, but only on a calculation based on the board state. (A state of play where the computer had won would be given a very high static evaluation, one where it had lost a very low one.) The tree grown is thus cut down to a manageable size. At the end of each branch is a board state whose degree of advantage to the program has been assessed using static evaluation.

Once the program has made this tree for the current state of play, how does it use it to decide what move to make, when it cannot know what the opponent will do? The program has to find choices in the tree that will lead to a board with the highest possible static value, but only alternate choices are under its control. For its opponent's moves, the best the program can do is to put itself in the opponent's shoes, and decide what move it would make in their place. We will shortly give an example of how this works in practice.

Of course the opponent will not always do as predicted. After all, they will probably have a different strategy to the program, and so sometimes the method of swapping roles will yield the wrong guess as to what the opponent will do. However, if the opponent's strategy is worse than the program's, the program will still win, and if the opponent's strategy is better then the program's, then the program can hardly use it to make predictions! This uncertainty means that part of the search tree has to be reconstructed at each play in the game, as it takes unforeseen twists and turns; this is a crucial difference between planning a route in the fixed layout of the Underground and playing against adversaries who will do their best to destroy your plans at each move in the game.

There is another important distinction to make. The Underground route finder was guaranteed to find the shortest route (granted its assumptions about travel times). In a very simple game such as noughts and crosses (tic-tac-toe in the United States) a program can map out the whole of the game tree and hence ensure that it never makes a losing move (though it may still be forced to a draw). In chess, because exhaustive search is impossible, rules for evaluating game states have to be introduced. Such rules cannot guarantee that a board position is the best, and so the search is no longer certain to find the best solution. Chess programs can be beaten. The rules used to assess board positions are therefore heuristics in that they indicate how to proceed without guaranteeing the best solution (see chapter 1). Search strategies that use heuristics go under the name **heuristic search**.

If you want to beat a chess playing program, then you need to understand its weaknesses. First, most chess programs call on a stored set of conventional opening moves, along with the best responses. So start the game in an unconventional way, such as by moving the knight. From then on you will be competing against a search program. Now, whenever you go on the attack, you are putting pieces at risk. Against a human opponent you can generally assess that risk by looking ahead and anticipating possible responses. But assessing possibilities is just what a search program is best at doing, and by systematically evaluating all the states two or three moves ahead, it may well find an excellent response that you have overlooked. So do not give it that chance; play a conservative, defensive game, so that the program cannot easily choose between reponses, and wait for it to make an obvious mistake that you can exploit.

4.2.7 The Game of Quadripawn

Let us examine in more detail how game playing by search operates. We will not use chess simply because to show even a tiny part of a chess game tree would take too much space. Rather we shall adopt a small game based on chess, called quadripawn. It is played on a board with 3 files and 3 ranks (or 3 columns and 3 rows if you prefer), using two white pawns and two black pawns. The starting position is shown at the top of figure 4.6.

White moves first, and players take turns, moving one of their own pieces on each move. On any move a piece may either be moved forward one square, if there is nothing in the way, or it may take an opponent's piece that is diagonally in front of it. An opponent's piece directly in front cannot be taken, and acts as a block. The winner is the first player to move one pawn to the far side of the board, or to take both the opponent's pawns, or to prevent the opponent from moving on the next turn.

Figure 4.6 shows the game tree for 2 moves from the start. To illustrate the

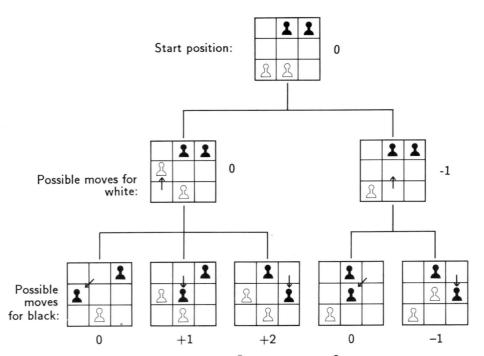

White pawns are indicated by ♙, black ones by ♟. The numbers by the bottom row show the static values obtained using the evaluation function given in the text. The number on the top row is the dynamic value for two move lookahead.

Figure 4.6
Part of the game tree for quadripawn.

idea of heuristic game playing, we will suppose our program is restricted to look ahead only 2 moves. (Real chess programs look much further ahead than this.) The program is playing white, and its first problem is to choose one of the two possible starting moves. We need an evaluation function to apply to the boards on the lowest level of the tree. The following simple example will serve, though other functions are possible. Starting from 0

- for each white pawn on the middle rank that is not blocked add 1,

- for each black pawn in this state subtract 1,

- if it is white's turn, for every black piece that can be taken on the next move add 1, and

- if it is black's turn, for every white piece that can be taken on the next move subtract 1.

Thus the value may become negative; positive values are good for white, negative ones bad. Figure 4.7 shows how the static value for one of the board states is calculated. In this case there is a white pawn, not blocked, on the middle rank, and the total score is +1. You should confirm that the values assigned to the other board states in the bottom row of figure 4.7 are correct.

Now we are in a position to work back up the tree to see what to do on white's first move. From the left-hand state in the middle level, black has a choice of 3 moves, and we guess that the black player would choose the move that is worst for white: the one labelled 0. From the right-hand state, black has a choice of 2 moves and we guess that the choice would be to the one labelled -1. Thus if white takes the left-hand move, the expected value is 0, but for the right-hand move it is -1, so the program's choice should be for the left-hand move with a value of 0. Note that the 'good' state labelled +2 plays no part, since we do not expect black to allow the program the opportunity to exploit it. The expected value, calculated by looking ahead and propagating the static values back up the tree, is called a **dynamic value**.

The strategy is called **minimax**, and the name comes from the fact that if we think of a move to a board state with a lower value as a loss, then black will always try to maximize the program's loss. The program must seek to minimize its loss — thus it must choose a move to minimize the the maximum loss that black can inflict.

White's turn

White pawn(s) on
middle rank not
blocked   1

Black pawn(s) on
middle rank
not blocked   0

Black pieces
that can be taken   0

Total static value   1

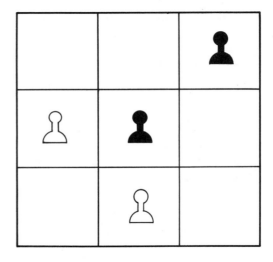

Figure 4.7
A calculation of the static value for a board state.

Powerful chess playing programs are essentially based on a minimax strategy. However, they incorporate many extra ploys to increase their effectiveness, such as avoiding searching branches of the tree that can rapidly be identified as unproductive, and searching deeply in regions where a promising sequence of moves is found. An enormous amount of attention also goes into devising their evaluation functions. Furthermore, they often use specially designed computers to make the generation of possible future board states much faster.

It is unlikely that human chess players work the same way. They do not seem to look ahead as far as the programs, but may depend more heavily on recognizing patterns on the board and remembering successful lines of play that can develop from these patterns. They are probably much more capable of taking advantage of their opponent's characteristic weaknesses in play. Whilst it is possible that chess playing programs may be able to beat all humans in the not too distant future, it is unlikely that they will be simulating the cognitive processes of even a modest human chess player.

4.2.8 Quicker Searching

To return to our Underground map example, we noticed that the search strategy often involved investigating routes that seemed unlikely to end up as useful, such as going south from Victoria. In the tree description, these extra possibilities made the tree more 'bushy' than it really needs to be. If we could guess in advance that certain options were not worth following up, then we could reduce the amount of computer time spent finding the route. To do this, we need to invoke the idea of heuristic search, as in the game playing program.

One such heuristic might involve knowing the layout of stations on the map. We might decide to forget about any route where the line sets off in the 'wrong' direction: say south when the destination is known to be north of the start point, and so on. This is like telling our horde of volunteers that they can get off and give up if they find themselves travelling away from the destination. Characteristically for a heuristic method, it will sometimes go wrong. For instance, to get from St James's Park to Warren Street, which is to the east in the map, it is best to set off west to Victoria. Examples on the Circle line can also be found. However, most of the time the heuristic rule will work properly, and when it does not, the solution arrived at will still probably be adequate. In general, using heuristics does not change the basic structure of the search. Rather, heuristic rules are incorporated into a strategy such as branch and bound in order to give greater efficiency.

For some problems, then, it might be worth limiting the amount of state space to search by adopting heuristics. The more complex the problem, the more likely this is to become necessary. For the Underground map the computer can do a complete search in a reasonable time and heuristics are not essential. For chess games there is no chance at all of playing without heuristics. For many problems in artificial intelligence the challenge lies in discovering the heuristic rules that make a search strategy possible.

4.3   The Limitations of Search

In the examples we have given, the evaluation function is set in advance and the program forges ahead, searching nodes in the tree until it finds a suitable path to the solution. But, given a task such as solving a jigsaw puzzle or playing a game, a human subject will typically work step by step, inspecting the state of the problem and considering alternative strategies for proceeding toward the goal. Rather than evaluating all the permissible, or 'legal', moves from the current state, a human expert will immediately eliminate most of them and may consider only one or two, reassessing the problem in the light of current knowledge. Indeed, outside of games and formal puzzles, it is not clear that the notion of legal moves is particularly helpful: a computer program that generates and tests legal moves in a search through a state-space may be operating in a far less intelligent, and certainly less efficient, way than a human being who thoughtfully 'muddles through' towards a solution.

Some tasks will, in addition, involve the problem-solver in communication with an external source. A doctor diagnosing an illness, for example, will bring expert knowledge to bear not only on the patient's initial symptoms but also on information derived from tests, or elicited from the patient at a particular stage in the diagnosis. If, for instance, the patient has complained of breathlessness and a dull pain in the left arm, it would be appropriate for the doctor to ask whether the patient smokes.

Finally, a state-space is a description of the problem itself, rather than of the behaviour of the problem-solver; to this extent, it can be described independently in individuals' attempts to solve the problem. Maps of London, for example, antedate a particular person's efforts to find a route between two points in the city. If we consider the problem as it appears in the mind of the human problem-solver, then each new state exists only once the subject has generated it.

4.4 Conclusion

We have shown how a computer program can solve a problem by means of a search strategy that tries out different possibilities until the right one is found. Providing that we can represent each state of the search, and the links between adjacent states, then we can draw out a state-space and define an algorithm to search it. We gave examples of three different search methods: depth first search, which involves exploring to the end of each branch of the search tree in turn and then backtracking if the branch reaches a dead-end; breadth first search, in which the tree is searched one layer at a time; and branch and bound search, in which information about the distance from the start to a node is used to determine the next branch to explore. We also showed how search can be used in game playing, using the minimax method to examine a tree of game states. Heuristics can produce a static evaluation of each board state, and this can be used to predict an opponent's move. The assumption behind minimax is that the opponent will always make what the program judges to be a the best move. The program chooses a move that will minimize the 'damage' caused by the opponent. We gave some examples of search, each of which could be generalized: the route finder to working out complex plans of action, the jigsaw puzzle to allocating resources subject to constraints, and the game player to evolving plans to deal with changing situations. Search is a general-purpose method, suited to a class of problems that can be solved by mapping out the state-space and applying a quick and simple evaluation function to the legal moves from the current state.

4.5 Appendix: Programming Route Finding

In this section we shall show how to write a program to find quickest routes on the London Underground, provided we can make simple assumptions about travel times. Here is a call of the main procedure route. Given two stations as input, it returns a list giving the quickest route between them:

```
route([victoria],[marble arch])=>
** [[[VICTORIA victoria] at 0 mins] [[VICTORIA green park]
at 2 mins] [[VICTORIA oxford circus] at 4 mins] [[CENTRAL
oxford circus] at 7 mins] [[CENTRAL bond street] at 9 mins]
[[CENTRAL marble arch] at 11 mins]]
```

In each sub-list the first word is the name of the line, followed by the name of the station and the time taken to get to it. The program implements branch and bound search. There are two ways of looking at what it does: one is that it simulates the spread of the volunteer travellers from the start station; the other is that it builds a representation of the search tree. It will be simplest to describe the program in terms of a simulation. We will not set the program out in full, as it would be too long, but we hope that having read this you will understand the way it works well enough to implement a program of your own if you have a suitable system, or to have a clear idea of what is needed if you do not. The program is more complex than those you have met so far, so if at first you cannot understand how it works, then either skip this section or invest some effort in trying to follow the program line by line. The complete search program is incorporated into the example Tourist Guide in appendix B at the end of the book.

To start, we need to be able to represent the Underground map to the program. This is done by a series of **add** statements storing one entry in the database for each connection between two adjacent stations (you may like to refer back to chapter 3 on the use of the database). Figure 4.2 requires 24 statements to be stored to represent it; here is the part of the program that stores 4 of them:

```
add([[JUBILEE charing cross] connects [JUBILEE green park]]);
add([[JUBILEE green park] connects [JUBILEE bond street]]);
add([[JUBILEE bond street] connects [JUBILEE baker street]]);
add([[BAKERLOO embankment] connects
     [BAKERLOO charing cross]]);
```

Each entry is a triplet, in the same form as those for the London database of chapter 3. Each of the first and last components gives a line and a station; in the middle is the word 'connects', which establishes the relationship between them, and indicates that the stations are next to one another on the line. The line/station combinations are lists, of which the first word is the line name and the rest the station name. We have put the line names in capitals, but that is only for clarity when looking at the program; it does not affect its operation. For convenience, the representation is 'redundant': that is, the line name appears twice in each statement when the same information would still be present if it only appeared once.

The remainder of the program can be divided into two main parts:

- Carry out the search.

- Trace the route followed by the first arrivals and report it.

The volunteers are simulated by recording information about the stations they have reached and are about to reach in the POP-11 database, adding information in chronological sequence. When the destination station is reached the search stops and the second part of the program proceeds to look at the stored information to see the route followed. The bulk of the program is its first part, and we shall now proceed to describe that.

4.5.1 Carrying Out the Search

The main search procedure is quite short. Here it is:

```
define search(startstat,deststat)->destfound
   vars nextevent, line;
   start(startstat);
   repeat
      next() -> nextevent;
      insertnext(nextevent);
   quitif (nextevent matches [arrived [?line ^^deststat]
                                         at = mins from =]);
      addfuture(nextevent);
   endrepeat;
   [[^line ^^deststat] at ^time mins]->destfound;
enddefine;
```

The procedure is called with two arguments, specifying the start station and the destination station. It returns a list with the name of the destination station, its line, and the time taken:

```
search([victoria],[marble arch])=>
** [[CENTRAL marble arch] at 11 mins]
```

At any stage of the search, the database, as well as holding the connections between stations, contains two kinds of statements about the current state of the travellers:

- arrivals at stations and

- pending or 'future' arrivals.

The procedure first calls **start**, which simply records pending events indicating arrival at the starting station, on every line passing through it. These events are given the time 0 minutes. The **start** procedure is quite simple and will not be discussed further. The program then repeatedly calls **next**, **insertnext**, and **addfuture**, generating the next arrival, recording it, and then adding the new future events that follow from it.

The procedure **next** determines which stations the group of simulated volunteers visit at each stage. Whenever a group arrives at a station or transfers to a new line, the procedure **insertnext** adds an entry to the database, giving the line name, the station name, and the time from the start (it also contains their last port of call to help in tracing back over the route when the simulation is complete) — for example,

```
[arrived [JUBILEE Green Park] at 5 mins
from [VICTORIA Green Park]]
```

If the arrival station matches the destination, then **quitif** breaks the **repeat** loop.

The program then calls the procedure **addfuture** to add entries for each of the events that will occur as a direct result of the current arrival; these will contain much the same information, but referring to an event in the program's 'future' — for example,

```
[will arrive [JUBILEE Bond Street]
at 7 mins from [JUBILEE Green Park]]
```

The meaning should be clear. The 7 minutes refers to the time from leaving the start and the line/station combinations are as in the map representation. The group is currently at Green Park. This last piece of information is inserted only so that if some of this group win the race to the destination, it will be easy to follow their route back.

Although in principle the statements about pending events are unnecessary, using them simplifies the program enormously. As you will see, they make it much simpler to keep the simulation running in the correct time sequence. In fact, most search programs use an **agenda** of this sort to decide what question to ask next.

The program decides when the voyagers have reached some point in the network by looking through the database at all the pending events, and choosing the one that has the earliest time associated with it. If there are several contenders, then one is chosen arbitrarily.

The way the program determines what new future events to note in the database, following an arrival at a particular station on a particular line, is slightly more complex: it must examine the Underground map in order to find out the stations on the same line adjacent to the current station, and the lines that pass through the current station. If we use our previous assumptions about timings, future arrivals at the stations on the same line can be noted for 2 minutes after the current time and future arrivals on any other lines through the current station can be noted for 3 minutes after the current time.

foreach Before we plunge into the program, we need one new tool. This is a POP-11 construction that allows us to test all the statements in the database that match a particular pattern. Its form is

```
foreach <pattern> do

    <actions>

endforeach;
```

The word **foreach** indicates the start of a loop in the program; the actions in the loop are carried out once for each item in the database that matches a pattern. Here <pattern> can be replaced with any pattern that could go on the right-hand side of **matches** (see chapter 2). The <actions> can be replaced with any POP-11 instructions. For each item in the database that matches the pattern, the instructions will be carried out, with any variables that were used in the pattern set according to the database item. The way **foreach** is used below should make this clear.

Choosing the Next Event Let us look now at the procedure **next**. This searches the pending events in the database to find the one with the smallest time (the one which will occur next).

We use **foreach** in a procedure, called **next**, which returns the actual event that corresponds to the earliest pending event. Here it is:

```
define next()->event;
    vars leasttime, place, time, lastplace, event;
    100000 -> leasttime;
    foreach [will arrive ?place at ?time mins from
            ?lastplace] do
        if time < leasttime then
            [arrived ^place at ^time mins from ^lastplace]
```

```
            -> event;
        time -> leasttime;
      endif;
   endforeach;
enddefine;
```

This may look rather complex, but here is how it works (you may need to revise the use of ? and ^ in patterns and lists). The if ... endif section is carried out once for each item in the database that matches a pattern starting with the words 'will arrive'. Thus, only pending events will match it (refer back to section 4.5 to see how it works). The variables `place`, `time`, and `lastplace` are set up by `foreach` to have the values corresponding to each pending event in turn: thus at some stage they might well have the following values:

```
place        [VICTORIA pimlico]
time         2
lastplace    [VICTORIA victoria]
```

The variable `leasttime` records the time of the earliest event so far detected, and is set to a very large number to begin with simply to ensure that some event is returned. Each time through the `foreach` loop, if the pending event that has been matched is earlier than the earliest pending event so far (i.e., `time < leasttime`), then `leasttime` is updated. The variable `event` is updated also, to hold a list that records the earliest event so far found, and when all the pending events have been tested, this is what is returned by the procedure.

After this procedure has been run, the program will need to record this event as having happened, and remove the pending event from the database. This is done simply using `add` and `remove`; we shall skip over the procedure that does this and go straight to the other main part of the simulation, which records future events.

Recording Future Events   The procedure that does this is called `addfuture`. We will not give it in full, as one section will suffice to show its operation. The procedure has a variable `place` whose value is a list giving the name of the current line and the current station (i.e., the place just reached) and a variable `time`, the time of arrival at this point. Let us suppose that at some stage they have the values

```
place    [VICTORIA green park]
time     2
```

The job of the procedure is to insert into the database statements like

```
[will arrive [VICTORIA oxford circus] at 4 mins from
                            [VICTORIA green park]]
```

and

```
[will arrive [PICCADILLY green park] at 5 mins from
                            [VICTORIA green park]]
```

The procedure uses **foreach** to scan the map of the Underground, together with another variable, **newplace**. Here is a simplified version of the **foreach** loop:

```
foreach [^place connects ?newplace] do
    add([will arrive ^newplace at ^(time+2) mins from ^place]);
endforeach;
```

For each statement in the database showing a connection from [VICTORIA green park] to another station on the same line, this part of the program adds a statement noting the arrival there in 2 minutes' time.

The version of the **repeat** loop shown in appendix B at the end of the book is a little more complex, in that it calls a procedure **addonefuture** which only adds a notification if there is not already one present in the database.

The **addfuture** procedure needs three more **repeat** loops, similar to the one we have shown: one with ^place and ?newplace reversed in the pattern (because the links can be recorded in the database either way around), and 2 to search the database for other lines passing through the current station.

Speeding Up the Search The program we have described so far will work correctly, but will be rather slow and use more computer memory than it needs to. The reason is that the simulated volunteers will frequently revisit each place. For instance, half of the group that reaches [VICTORIA pimlico] will turn round and return to [VICTORIA victoria], whence they came. From there, some will return to [VICTORIA pimlico], and so on. There will be an enormous amount of unnecessary activity (though it will not affect the final result).

Small modifications lead to a far more efficient search. First, when a pending event is to be inserted into the database, a check is made to see whether any group has already reached the place in question. If so, the pending event is forgotten rather than recorded. Second, when an actual event is noted, all the pending events that refer to the same place are removed. These two measures mean that no duplication of activity occurs. It is like having radio links between the groups of volunteers, so that those who are wasting their time can be told to give up.

4.5.2 Tracing the Route

Finally we come to the second part of the program. The search is complete and the database is full of statements about how it proceeded. To trace out the route is now straightforward, since with each arrival was recorded the previous location of the group. Thus a call to **present** with a pattern incorporating the name of a location will reveal the point from which it was reached — for example,

```
present([arrived ^place at ?time mins from ?lastplace]);
```

Successive values of **place** and **time** are stored in a list, beginning with the destination and continuing back until **lastplace** is the start station. When reversed, the list gives the route. The main procedure, **route**, which returns the list of stations, can be called from within **answer**:

```
define answer(query)->response;
    vars x;
    if query matches [how do i get to ??x] then
        route([victoria],x)->response;
    elseif
        ...
    endif;
enddefine;
```

```
answer([how do i get to marble arch])=>
** [[[VICTORIA victoria] at 0 mins] [[VICTORIA green park] at 2 mins]
[[VICTORIA oxford circus] at 4 mins] [[CENTRAL oxford circus] at 7 mins]
[[CENTRAL bond street] at 9 mins] [[CENTRAL marble arch] at 11 mins]]
```

All that remains is to convert this information into a form suitable for printing out to the real traveller, standing on the platform and looking at the screen, unaware that his or her route has been planned by the combined efforts of a myriad of simulated explorers!

4.6 Exercises

1. Work out how to add the information that the Northern Line joins Embankment, Charing Cross, Leicester Square, and Tottenham Court Road to the database for the route finding program. What difference will this make to the routes that the program finds from Westminster to Tottenham Court Road and to Warren Street?

2. Could the order in which the map information is stored in the database ever make a difference to the output of the route finding program? If it could, would the difference ever be very important?

3. Work out how to change the route finding program to make more realistic assumptions about travel times. For instance, instead of assuming that it takes 2 minutes to travel between any pair of adjacent stations on any line, the program could use a specific time for each line, or even for each pair of stations. These times would, of course, have to be recorded in advance in the database. Work out suitable modifications of the data representation and of the program in order to use this more detailed information.

4. Suppose the database contains the London Underground map, represented as in section 4.5. What is the apparent purpose of the following procedure, and what might the call to it print out?

```
define lines(stat);
    vars line;
    foreach [[?line ^^stat] connects =] do
        line =>
    endforeach;
    foreach [= connects [?line ^^stat]] do
        line =>
    endforeach;
enddefine;

lines([Green Park]);
```

Why is the second half of this procedure necessary?

Write a procedure that prints out all the names of the stations on a given line. Modify it so that instead of printing the information, the station names are returned in a list. Do not worry if a station name appears more than once in the list. (It is quite easy to write a procedure that will remove the extra occurrences.)

5. Draw out the complete game tree for quadripawn; it is not large. For each board state for white, calculate the static evaluation score (using the evaluation function given on page 115) and the score for 2 move lookahead. If white starts, is there a strategy that guarantees it will never lose?

6. Take a game that you know how to play, perhaps draughts (checkers in the United States) or chess, and draw the game tree for two or three moves from a state in the end game, when there are very few pieces left. Devise a static evaluation function for the game and discover how a minimax program using it would behave in your example.

7. Imagine that you have to build a tower 20 centimetres high using a set of 8 blocks, with the following heights in centimetres: 8, 7, 7, 6, 3, 3, 2, and 1. Clearly this can be done using the blocks of heights 8, 7, 3, and 2 centimetres, but with a larger number of blocks and a higher tower the problem can take a very long time to solve. Try writing a POP-11 program that solves problems like this by computer search. You can assume that the block heights and the target height have been stored in some suitable format in the database.

Your program will probably proceed by trying different combinations of blocks — i.e., by effectively asking questions like "What if the tower includes the block of height 7?" The program might use the database to store information about which blocks are available and which ones have been tried. This program may be rather easier when you know more POP-11, so you may want to return to it when you have read further along in the book.

Chapter 5

Natural Language

5.1 The Cognitive Complexity of Language

At Victoria Station, on a visit to London, you walk up to a (human) assistant from the Tourist Board and ask the question, "Can you tell me how to get to the gallery in the square containing the monument?" to which the assistant replies, "Travelling by Underground, take the Victoria Line to Green Park, then change and take the Jubilee Line to Charing Cross." This apparently simple exchange involves a great deal of sophisticated cognitive processing, as we shall show in the pages that follow.

For example, the question, taken alone, appears to need a simple yes or no answer, in much the same way as do questions like "Can you speak Gujarati?" or "Can you touch your toes?" The assistant nevertheless recognizes this as an indirect request for information and responds accordingly; to have just replied "Yes" would have been uncooperative. Your question has not specified which gallery, square, and monument you want to visit. But you have used the definite article 'the' in referring to each, so the assistant takes this to mean that you have a particular gallery, square, and monument in mind, even if you are unable to name them. The assistant draws on her knowledge of London to indentify them, and work out the best route. In fact, she has drawn on even more sophisticated knowledge than this in order to answer you, since the form of your question was ambiguous. In terms of its structure alone the question does not allow the hearer to decide whether the monument is in the gallery or in the square; that is, whether the question is more like sentence A below or sentence B:

"Can you tell me how to get to

A   ...the gallery in the [square containing the monument]?"
compare: ...the corkscrew in the [drawer containing the cutlery]?"

B   ...the gallery [in the square] containing the monument?"
compare: ...the compound [in the zoo] containing the wildebeest?"

The assistant must have sophisticated knowledge of sentence structure in English, since the fact that there are alternative interpretations is not formally signalled in the sentence itself. She must also know something about plausible states of affairs — in this case that monuments are more likely to be found in squares than in galleries — in order to determine which of the alternative interpretations is the correct one. Finally, your question has made no mention of means of transport, nor that you would prefer to know the most direct route. But the assistant knows about the best way to travel across London and understands the phrase 'get to' as implicitly asking for the most direct journey. She therefore suggests you take the Underground and details the shortest way (out of probably thousands of ways) to get there.

Perhaps this example has helped you to appreciate that the ability to use language is one of the most important cognitive skills that we, as human beings, have. It is so complex and important that, as we mentioned in chapter 1, the philosopher Descartes considered it to be the primary faculty that distinguishes human beings from the lower animals. More interesting for our purposes is Descartes' further claim that language distinguishes humans from machines.

Part of the 'remarkable fact' of human language that Descartes highlighted in his writings is that, unlike the fixed patterns of bird calls and bee dance, or the pure mimicry of parrots, language is infinitely productive: human beings are, in principle, able to produce and understand an infinite number of novel sentences, the only limitations in practice being that speakers and hearers eventually get physically tired and ultimately die. But those limitations have nothing to do with the facts of language. Another part of the miracle is that, again unlike parrots, we can use language to convey meanings and thoughts to others, to get at the content behind the purely physical signals of sound waves or marks on paper. Finally, humans do not merely form meaningful sentences, but can give an 'appropriately meaningful answer to what is said'; that is, they can use language in ways appropriate to the context. Linguists usually talk about these three facets of language under the headings **syntax**, **semantics**, and **pragmatics**, respectively. We shall follow these divisions in sections 5.2–5.4 below.

Look again at our informal comments on the types of knowledge that the Tourist Board assistant would have had to draw on to understand the question given at the beginning of this chapter. Try to make a first guess at which comments pertain to the syntax of the utterance, which to the semantics, and which to pragmatics. Revise your answers as necessary as we work through the chapter.

It is largely from Descartes and the seventeenth century Port-Royal school of French philosophers that Noam Chomsky, by far the most influential linguist and language theoretician of the twentieth century, drew the fundamental notions that led to the establishment of linguistics as a cognitive science, or more specifically, in Chomsky's words, as "a branch of cognitive psychology." Descartes was a rationalist; he held that human beings are endowed with 'innate ideas' that determine and constrain the form of human knowledge in quite specific ways, and that it is these innate ideas that distinguish the creative intelligence of humans from the mechanical behaviour of animals and machines. Those innate ideas associated specifically with language Chomsky calls 'universal grammar', "the system of principles, conditions, and rules that are elements or properties of all human languages not merely by accident but by ... biological ... necessity" (Chomsky, 1975, p. 29). It is this 'universal grammar' that accounts for the invariance of certain properties — 'linguistic universals' — across all languages, and for the remarkable speed with which young children acquire their own native tongue. Children learn their first language so quickly, Chomsky argues, because they in some sense already 'know' what human languages look like: they are biologically equipped with what he calls a 'Language Acquisition Device'. If such principles are indeed innate, then a compelling reason for studying human language is that it may gives us insights into the structure of the mind itself.[1]

Chomsky has drawn a distinction between linguistic **competence** and linguistic **performance**, the first being an ideal speaker-hearer's knowledge of her language, and the latter a person's actual use of language in real situations. The primary task of linguistics, in Chomsky's view, is to characterize, in the form of a **grammar** of the

---

[1]Chomsky's writings are often extremely dense and difficult. If you would like to know more about his theory of language, you could browse through the more general sections of his *Cartesian Linguistics* (1966), *Reflections on Language* (1975), and *Rules and Representations* (1980).

language, the ideal speaker-hearer's intrinsic competence. The emphasis in artificial intelligence approaches to natural language has been slightly different. Of course it is important to describe the formal properties of languages; but such descriptions do not, in themselves, say how you would go about producing an actual utterance, or understanding the utterances of others. Since the main thrust of natural language processing in artificial intelligence has been to design machines that can produce and understand human languages, there has been a far greater concern among cognitive scientists to give accounts of how we put to use the internalized knowledge we have of our mother tongues. This division is mirrored in the distinction cognitive scientists make between grammars and **parsers**, which are programs that make use of grammatical knowledge. In most computational natural language systems, the grammar of the language and the parser that works on it are written as separate and independent components — the grammar is encoded as a declarative data structure, the parser as a procedural program. For reasons of simplicity, however, we do not make this separation in the simple system that we develop in the appendix to this chapter.

5.2   Syntax

If we are to extend our Automated Tourist Guide so as to understand sentences like the one at the beginning of the chapter, and to generate appropriate responses, we need first of all to know about the formal structure of the English language. We need, that is, to be able specify all the possible forms of acceptable sentences in the English language (or at least, in the subset of English which we expect our system to handle), and to do so in a manner that enables us to write computer programs which, given strings of words as input, will distinguish between those that we feel as native speakers to be **grammatical** sentences in English and those that are not.

In many grammars, the syntax and semantics are strongly interlinked insofar as the meaning of a complete sentence is in part determined (according to the so-called 'rule-by-rule hypothesis') by the manner in which its constituent words and phrases are syntactically related. We discuss this further in section 5.3. For the present, we wish merely to stress the fact that every well-formed sentence in a natural language has a formal syntactic structure, and that we can unambiguously describe that structure irrespective of whatever meanings it may be used to convey.

There are two strong motivations for this: in the first place, such a program would capture our intuitions as speakers of English about the formal structure of English sentences. We will want our program to be able to distinguish, for example, between novel but perfectly grammatical strings such as those in (1) below and nonsentences of the kind exemplified in (2) below:

1.   a. All stuffed grey elephants are moderately inflammable.
     b. There are no such things as triangular virtues.
2.   a. Inflammable all grey moderately elephants stuffed are.
     b. There are are are are as as virtues.

From your own knowledge of English grammar, try and describe what makes the strings of words in (2) ungrammatical. Now try and say (and this is more difficult) what makes those in (1) grammatical.

5.2.1   Sentence Matching

How might we go about this? And in particular, how might we do so in a way that is consistent with what we believe we know about human cognitive capacities? One way might be to attempt to put in a database all the grammatical sentences of English. Any possible sentence is then bound to be included in the database and can be checked against it, for example, by the POP-11 pattern matcher. Nonsentences, such as those in (2), will not be included, and so will not be recognized as grammatical English.

This method has some severe drawbacks. In the first place, since we have already claimed that the number of sentences in a language is infinitely vast, it follows that no finite database could ever be complete. For example, given a database containing *N* sentences, we could create an (*N*+1)th sentence made up of all the sentences so far joined together by the word 'and', then an (*N*+2)th sentence by joining them with 'or', and so on. Most important, the grammars of natural languages are **recursive** (a concept to which we shall return later in the chapter), allowing syntactic units to be embedded to any depth, as in the sentence "The house the surveyor the property developer called valued fell down" or "The last seven small white glazed earthenware mugs."

In the second place, simply putting a large number of sentences into a database does not indicate what it is that distinguishes them from non-sentences; it does not account for our intuitions, on seeing a novel string of words, as to whether that string is grammatical English or not.

So a 'database of all the grammatical sentences' is both impossible and unsatisfactory. The two disadvantages listed above converge in a common general observation, which is relevant to our requirement that our account of language be cognitively plausible. The human brain contains only a finite, even if awesomely vast, number of neurons, so human beings have a strictly limited memory. No single human brain, nor even the totality of all human brains, could hold in memory all the sentences of a language, since a finite space cannot contain an infinite number of objects. By the same token, we could not hope to put an infinite number of sentences into a computer database.

5.2.2   Pattern Matching

But we have already seen, in chapter 2, another way of going about things, that taken by ELIZA. In this method, we list not all the possible sentences in the language, but the possible *patterns* that sentences in English can have. This allows us to make far more general statements about the form of grammatical sentences in English, and to distinguish many grammatical strings from non-grammatical ones. For example,

```
[my ??words drinks ??more_words]
```

and

```
[you == me]
```

which match, respectively, the sentences

```
my aunt Mabel drinks pina colada
```

and

```
you never listen to me
```

seem plausible patterns for sentences in English, while

```
[drinks ??words my ??more_words]
```

and

```
[== you me]
```

do not, and would not be expected to match well-formed English sentences. Since sentences tend to be patterned in a small number of fairly regular ways in English, we might guess that a list of such patterns need not be cumbersomely vast.

Unfortunately, as we saw in chapter 2, *Eliza* does not much care what words fill up the spaces in the patterns marked by the variable **??something** and by the symbol **==**. The program is just as able to accept gibberish in those spaces as to accept meaningful English. Furthermore, this 'garbage in, garbage out' principle allows *Eliza* to respond with absolute nonsense. For example, if the form of *Eliza*'s response to

```
[my ??words drinks ??more_words]
```

is

```
[tell your ^^words to stop drinking ^^more_words]
```

and if the current input is

```
[my collection of drinks is legendary]
```

then the nonsensical output will be

```
[tell your collection of to stop drinking is legendary]
```

5.2.3 Grammars

There is, however, a third and more general way of describing languages. As native speakers of English, we know intuitively when a string of words is a possible sentence in the language, and when it is not, even though it may be a sentence we have never seen or heard before. Perhaps, then, it is a sensible strategy to try and specify a finite, and if possible small, number of abstract criteria that any sentence in English has to fulfill; criteria which we, as English speakers, draw on when making judgements about grammaticality.

This raises some interesting questions about the cognitive basis of linguistic knowledge. How is it that we are able to make such judgements? What does it mean to 'know a language' or to have 'learned a language'? Clearly, to learn a language is not simply to learn lists of sentences. A small child does not just memorize and imitate her parent's speech; indeed, children's language has its own unique features, and we can plot quite distinct stages of its development over time. Often, very small children correctly use irregular verb forms like 'came' and 'went' when they first begin to form simple sentences, but later mysteriously lapse into forms like 'comed' and 'goed'. Or they may form plurals like 'mouses' and 'foots' even though they have heard their parents use the words 'mice' and 'feet', and despite their parents' exasperated attempts to correct them. The psycholinguist Courtney Cazden (1972, p. 92) gives the following example of a conversation between an adult and child:

> Child: My teacher holded the baby rabbits and we patted them.
> Adult: Did you say your teacher held the baby rabbits?
> Child: Yes.
> Adult: What did you say she did?
> Child: She holded the baby rabbits and we patted them.
> Adult: Did you say she held them tightly?
> Child: No, she holded them loosely.

From this kind of evidence, it would seem that children gradually acquire some very general principles governing the forms of words in their language. They learn, for example, that the past tense of a verb can be formed by adding the sound '-ed'. Then they overgeneralize the rule, and produce incorrect forms like 'holded'. Or they acquire the rule that plurals can be formed by adding the sound '-s' to a noun, and again they overgeneralize. Only later do they learn specific exceptions to the rules. In chapter 8 we describe a program that attempts to model the development of children in forming the past tense of English verbs.

The same mechanism also applies to the learning of formal rules for the construction of sentences. How, for instance, do we learn to form questions? As children we might have heard sentences like

> The doll which is in the toy box is wearing a pink dress.

and know that to question statements like that, adults begin their sentence with "Is ...?" So we might hypothesize that to form a question, we move the first occurrence of 'is' to the front:

> Is the doll which in the toy box is wearing a pink dress?
> ↑_____|

But this is clearly wrong. It is not so much to do with the positions of words in sentences as with their grammatical function. We very quickly learn that the main verb in what grammarians call the main clause should be moved to the front, not the verb in the subordinate relative clause:

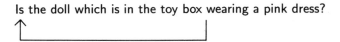

Is the doll which is in the toy box wearing a pink dress?

A theory of a natural language, then, is a theory about the underlying rules of word-structure and sentence-structure that its native speakers have acquired during infancy. These rules have been abstracted from actual utterances, and they can be used to produce and understand new sentences. This does not mean to say that a child can recite the rules that govern English language, but rather that people, children and adults, produce and understand language *as if* driven by rules. Whether the rules of language structure *do* exist in the mind, but are hidden from conscious inspection, or whether describing people's language as 'rule governed' is just a convenient way of saying that it 'shows regularity', in the same way that the orbit of a planet shows regularity, is a deep issue of philosophy and psychology.

Nevertheless, describing language in terms of underlying rules of structure makes sense: a string of words is a sentence in a language not according to whether it appears in some hypothetical database (and in any case, who would decide, and by what criteria, which strings should be in the list and which not?), nor whether it matches some pattern in a set of sentence patterns, but according to whether it meets certain conditions for sentence-hood, such conditions being implicitly known to speakers of the language and constituting, when formally expressed, the grammar of the language. This third method for describing languages has on its side not merely economy, productivity, and efficiency but also cognitive plausibility.

The conditions for sentence-hood can, as we shall see, be expressed quite simply and elegantly as sets of rules. Before we characterize these rules we shall explain the term 'grammar'. We may provisionally think of the grammar of a language as made up of three parts. (Do not worry if you find this difficult to follow now. It will become clearer, and the terms more familiar, as we work through the chapter.) First, there is a finite set of **terminal symbols**: the actual words in the language, and the ultimate constituents of sentences. Second, there is a finite set of **non-terminal symbols**, of which we can distinguish three types:

lexical category labels specifying the grammatical classes of the words in the language: 'noun', 'preposition', 'adverb', and so on;

Non-terminal symbols			Terminal symbols
Distinguished symbol	Syntactic categories	Lexical categories	
S (i.e., 'sentence')	Noun phrase	Noun	dog, chair, computer
	Prepositional phrase	Preposition	in, through, by
	Adverbial phrase	Adverb	very, directly, well

... etc. ... etc. ... etc. ...

Table 5.1
Summary of symbols in the grammar for a subset of English.

syntactic category symbols labelling permissible combinations of lexical categories: 'noun phrase', 'prepositional phrase', 'adverbial phrase', and the like; and

a special symbol, often called the **distinguished symbol** of the grammar (usually 'S' for 'sentence').

See table 5.1 for an illustration.

Third, a grammar will have a finite set of rules, frequently expressed as **phrase-structure** rules (sometimes called 'rewrite rules'), which specify all and only the permissible combinations of words in the language. The terminal symbols we shall call the dictionary, or **lexicon**, of the language; we shall call the set of non-terminal symbols together with the set of rules governing their combination, its syntax. (In the course of your further reading, you may find that many linguists prefer to use the word 'syntax' to refer to the study of the rules, rather than to the rules themselves.

In much the same way, the small number of pieces on a chess board (its 'dictionary'), together with labels for the types of pieces ('pawns', 'knights', 'rooks', ...) and the rules for moving and capturing (its 'syntax') account for the quasi-infinite number of possible chess games.

We shall say that the grammar of a language **generates** all and only well-formed strings in the language. That is, it will generate all the possible sentences and no nonsentences. By 'generate' we mean not only that the grammar is able to show the derivation of sentences from the rules for well-formedness but also that, as a consequence, it can 'assign a structural description to' those sentences. In other words, it will label the terminal symbols (the words) with lexical category names and show how these can be combined into larger units (syntactic categories) and how these can be ultimately combined together to form a sentence. The term 'generate' is in fact neutral as between the production and interpretation of sentences. Later in the chapter we will write a mini-grammar that generates a small subset of English, and leave it as an exercise to you to show how it assigns structural descriptions to sentences.

How might we go about discovering the rules governing the well-formedness of sentences in English? Try to follow the arguments below carefully, and you will get a sense of the method we are using, so that you will be able, as an exercise at the end of the chapter, to extend the grammar yourself. I presume we all intuitively feel that the sentences in (3) below share certain structural features, which are different from those shared by the sentences in (4) below. What is it that distinguishes the two groups of sentences?

3. a. My pet wallaby bit the postman.
    b. My mother got your letter.
    c. My girlfriend caught a bus.

4. a. My pet wallaby disappeared.
    b. My mother died.
    c. My girlfriend fainted.

One thing we might say is that the general form of the sentences in (3) is

SUBJECT + SOMETHING-ED + OBJECT

and of (4) is

SUBJECT + SOMETHING-ED

That is, sentences in (3) have a final 'direct object'. Since the subject in both groups of sentences can be the same, the difference between the two groups must lie in the rest of the sentence. The verb (the 'something' in the above patterns) in each of the sentences in (3) has different properties from that in the sentences in (4). Notice the strangeness of the sentences we get if, for example, we switch the verbs in (3) and (4) around (an asterisk conventionally indicates that the sentence is ungrammatical):

3′.   a. *My pet wallaby disappeared the postman.
      b. *My mother died your letter.
      c. *My girlfriend fainted a bus.

4′.   a. *My pet wallaby bit.
      b. *My mother got.
      c. *My girlfriend caught.

We can now say, then, that there is a lexical category called a 'verb', and that, of those words classified in the dictionary as verbs, some require an object while others do not. Verbs requiring an object are called 'transitive' verbs, and verbs not requring an object are 'intransitive' verbs.

Can we be more specific about the form of the subject and object? Let us go back to one of the *Eliza*-type patterns and look at some more examples of possible and impossible sentences in the English language. We began with the pattern

    [my ??words drinks ??more_words]

and decided that input sentence (5) below produced a grammatical response, shown below as (5′), but that sentence (6) below did not:

5.   My aunt Mabel drinks pina colada.
5′.   Tell your aunt Mabel to stop drinking pina colada.

6.   My collection of drinks is legendary.
6′.   *Tell your collection of to stop drinking is legendary.

To get a grammatical response, the subject and the object of the sentence have to be either 'noun-phrases' or other expressions which have the same **distribution** as noun-phrases. That is, they must be able to replace each other in the same position in the sentence. The words 'my collection of' do not form a noun-phrase; the words 'my aunt Mabel', 'the postman', 'pina colada', 'a bus', and 'your letter' do, and as such they all have the same distribution. For example, the sentences in (7) below are all perfectly grammatical sentences — that is, they are **syntactically well-formed** — even if one or two of them have slightly odd meanings:

7. a. The postman bit my mother.
    b. My girlfriend burned my pet wallaby.
    c. Your letter caught a bus.
    d. A bus bit my girlfriend.

So we can say that a possible sentence pattern in English is

NOUN-PHRASE + VERB + NOUN-PHRASE

and you can probably see already that this is a much more formal and specific description of a sentence than our original *Eliza*-like sentence pattern (we will describe later how a computer program would go about recognizing a noun-phrase or a verb). The sentences in (8) below, like those in (7), are also syntactically well-formed, but differ from those in (7) in having intransitive rather than transitive verbs as main verbs:

8. a. The postman disappeared.
    b. A bus died.
    c. Your letter fainted.
    d. My pet wallaby escaped.

The underlying pattern of these sentences is

NOUN-PHRASE + VERB

So we can see that an initial noun-phrase can be followed by either a transitive verb and another noun-phrase or an intransitive verb. Schematically, we can represent that rule as follows:

$$\text{NOUN-PHRASE} + \left[\begin{array}{l} \text{TRANSITIVE VERB} + \text{NOUN-PHRASE} \\ \text{INTRANSITIVE VERB} \end{array} \right]$$

In other words, a <TRANSITIVE VERB + NOUN-PHRASE> has the same distribution as an <INTRANSITIVE VERB>, and we can easily demonstrate this fact by listing two sentences which have the same meaning and which differ only in the transitivity of the verb:

9. a. My pet wallaby kicked the bucket.
    b. My pet wallaby died.

In each case, the sentence is made up of a subject and a predicate, and the predicate can have one of two forms, depending on the transitivity of the verb. In fact, predicates can be made up of other things as well, so we shall be more specific and say that, in the above cases, the sentence is made up of an initial noun-phrase and a following verb-phrase. We can write the phrase-structure rules that we have discovered so far in the following conventional form:

S	$\longrightarrow$	NP VP	(rule 1)
VP	$\longrightarrow$	Vtrans NP	(rule 2)
VP	$\longrightarrow$	Vintrans	(rule 3)

The rules are numbered for ease of reference in figure 5.1. The numbering has no other significance.

The non-terminal symbol S stands for 'sentence', NP for 'noun-phrase', VP for 'verb-phrase', Vtrans for 'transitive verb', and Vintrans for 'intransitive verb'. The arrow '$\longrightarrow$' means 'can be replaced by' or 'may be made up of'. Thus, the first rule can be read as "A sentence can be replaced by a noun-phrase followed by a verb-phrase." Notice, too, that we can establish a one-to-one correspondence between the lexical category symbols 'Vtrans' and 'Vintrans' and the lexical items 'kicked' and 'died', respectively. Consequently, we can add to our rewrite rules the following two **lexical rules**:

Vtrans	$\longrightarrow$	kicked	(rule 4)
Vintrans	$\longrightarrow$	died	(rule 5)

We can now draw a diagram, called a **phrase-marker** or **parse-tree**, to show how these rules capture the syntactic structure of the sentences in (9) (see figure 5.1). In (9a) we can identify a noun-phrase1 ('My pet wallaby'), followed by a transitive verb ('kicked') and a noun-phrase2 ('the bucket'). The verb and the following noun-phrase2 combine to make up a verb-phrase; the noun-phrase1 and the following verb-phrase in turn combine to make a sentence. You will notice that lines connect Vtrans and Vintrans to single words, while a triangle extends from NP over the words making up the noun-phrase; this is because we have not yet analyzed the internal structure of noun-phrases. Conventionally, linguists use such triangles from non-terminals to indicate that they are not concerned with the internal structure of a phrase. If you now compare the form of the parse-trees with the form of the phrase-structure rules, you will see that reading the parse-trees from top to bottom is much like reading the phrase-structure rules from left to right. The difference between the two formalisms is that a parse-tree indicates the structure of a single string of words, while phrase-structure rules specify all, and only, the permissible strings of a language.

Just as we have been able to analyze a VP into its ultimate constituents, so too we can analyze the structure of an NP. In the following sentences the initial NPs all have the same distribution — they can all occur in the same syntactic 'slot' in the sentence:

> 10. a. The grey squirrel drank a pink gin.
>   b. Harvey drank a pink gin.
>   c. He drank a pink gin.

Yet the three NPs have different forms: 'he' is a pronoun; 'Harvey' is a name or 'proper noun'; and 'the grey squirrel' is made up of the definite article 'the' (which we shall symbolize by 'Det' for 'determiner'), the adjective 'grey', and the noun 'squirrel'. Expressing these facts as phrase-structure rules, we get

NP	$\longrightarrow$	Pronoun
NP	$\longrightarrow$	PropN
NP	$\longrightarrow$	Det Adj Noun

It is quite possible, however, that a noun may be preceded by more than one adjective, as in 'long slow cold pink gin'. This would mean that we would have to write an indefinite number of NP rules to capture the fact, which goes against the spirit of our grammar. So instead of writing further rules such as

NP	$\longrightarrow$	Det Adj Adj Noun
NP	$\longrightarrow$	Det Adj Adj Adj Noun
NP	$\longrightarrow$	Det Adj Adj Adj Adj Noun

and so on, we can create a new syntactic category, called 'qualified noun', which may be preceded by zero or more adjectives. We shall use the symbol QNoun, and modify our grammar rules thus:

NP	$\longrightarrow$	Pronoun
NP	$\longrightarrow$	PropN
NP	$\longrightarrow$	Det QNoun
QNoun	$\longrightarrow$	Noun
QNoun	$\longrightarrow$	Adj QNoun

(9) a.

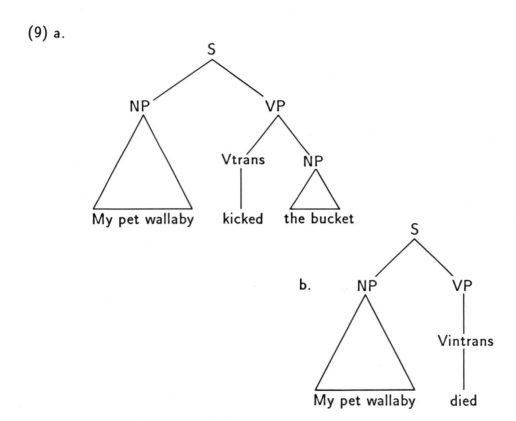

Figure 5.1
Parse-trees for sentences (9a) and (9b).

The last rule, in which the same symbol, QNoun, appears on both sides of the rewrite arrow, is an instance of a **recursive** rule — that is, a rule which allows itself to be reapplied to any depth of **embedding**. Although not a familiar concept, recursion does sometimes turn up in everyday descriptions, such as the story in which a quick-witted child is granted three wishes and replies, "I would like a huge ice cream, a holiday by the sea, and three more wishes." Repetitive events can be restated as recursions — for example, you could describe pacing out a square as "To pace out a square do the following: If you get back to your starting place then finish; otherwise walk forward ten paces, then turn left by 90 degrees, then pace out a square." Or another example — when playing a game of cards, dealing all the cards in your hand can be descibed by the following actions: if there are no more cards in your hand then stop; if it is the first card, then hand the card to the player on your right, turn to the next player on the right, and deal the cards; otherwise hand over the top card to the player you are facing, turn to the next player on the right, and deal the cards in your hand.

We can now add the new rules to the phrase-structure rules we have already discovered:

S	$\longrightarrow$	NP VP
VP	$\longrightarrow$	Vtrans NP
VP	$\longrightarrow$	Vintrans
NP	$\longrightarrow$	Pronoun
NP	$\longrightarrow$	PropN
NP	$\longrightarrow$	Det QNoun
QNoun	$\longrightarrow$	Noun
QNoun	$\longrightarrow$	Adj QNoun

The parse-tree for sentence (10b), for example, can then be represented in the manner shown in figure 5.2. Adding further lexical rules we get

S	$\longrightarrow$	NP VP
VP	$\longrightarrow$	Vtrans NP
VP	$\longrightarrow$	Vintrans
NP	$\longrightarrow$	Pronoun
NP	$\longrightarrow$	PropN
NP	$\longrightarrow$	Det QNoun
QNoun	$\longrightarrow$	Noun
QNoun	$\longrightarrow$	Adj QNoun

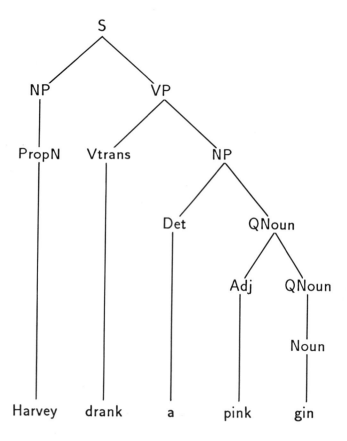

Figure 5.2
Parse-tree for sentence (10b).

N	$\longrightarrow$	man
N	$\longrightarrow$	squirrel
N	$\longrightarrow$	gin
N	$\longrightarrow$	lemonade
Pron	$\longrightarrow$	he
PropN	$\longrightarrow$	Ralph
Adj	$\longrightarrow$	old
Adj	$\longrightarrow$	pink
Adj	$\longrightarrow$	beautiful
Det	$\longrightarrow$	the
Det	$\longrightarrow$	a
Vtrans	$\longrightarrow$	kicked
Vtrans	$\longrightarrow$	drank
Vtrans	$\longrightarrow$	caught
Vintr	$\longrightarrow$	died
Vintr	$\longrightarrow$	evaporated

Let us now consider how we might supplement our grammar so as to enable it to parse (i.e., syntactically analyze) sentences such as the question with which we began this chapter. To avoid filling up pages of the book with parse-trees, we shall simplify our grammar, making the parse-trees slightly 'flatter'. In the first place, we shall omit the Pronoun and Qnoun rules for NPs, since we shall not need to to deal with pronouns and adjectives. This gives us

NP	$\longrightarrow$	PropN	(rule 1)
NP	$\longrightarrow$	Det Noun	(rule 2)

Next, we require a rule for handling prepositional phrases. We pointed out that the phrase

the gallery in the square containing the monument

is ambiguous; it has two interpretations according to whether we understand it to be the gallery or the square that contains the monument. A grammar to generate a large part of English will inevitably need to be ambiguous; that is, for some sentences it will assign two or more structural descriptions. But for the purposes of our Tourist Guide we only want a subset of English, and a single structural description of the phrase. We shall try out two NP rules for parsing prepositional

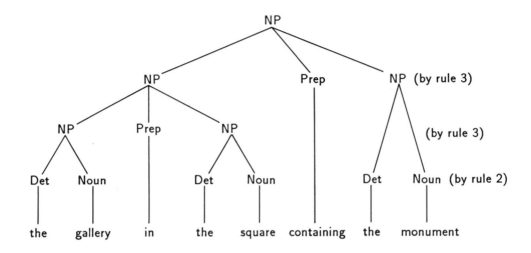

Figure 5.3
Parse-tree 1 for 'the gallery in the square containing the monument' obtained from
rule 3.

phrases, both of which will generate the sentence fragment, and then determine
which of the two rules gives us only the desired reading:

| NP | $\longrightarrow$ | NP Prep NP | (rule 3) |
| NP | $\longrightarrow$ | Det Noun Prep NP | (rule 4) |

Although the word 'containing', in the phrase 'the square containing the monument', is strictly speaking a present participle, for the sake of simplifying the
grammar, we shall treat it as though it were a preposition. The new rule 3, together with rule 2, gives us the parse-trees in figures 5.3 and 5.4; that is, rule 3
fails to filter out the reading we do not want. Rule 4, on the other hand, gives us
uniquely the parse-tree that we want (shown in figure 5.5).

As rule 3 will sometimes give us the wrong interpretation of the kinds of questions
we are asking of the Guide, we shall discard it (though it might well be a useful
rule in some other grammar). Since rule 4, on the other hand, gives us just the
desired reading, we shall retain this rule and so incorporate rules 1,2, and 4 in the
procedure in our program for recognizing noun-phrases.

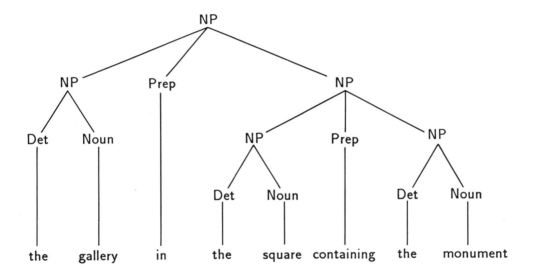

Figure 5.4
Parse-tree 2 for 'the gallery in the square containing the monument' obtained from
rule 3.

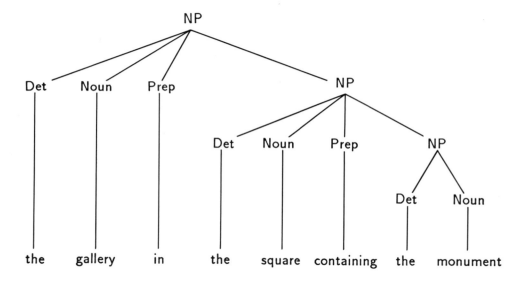

Figure 5.5
Single parse-tree for 'the gallery in the square containing the monument' obtained
from rule 4.

We shall restrict questions asking directions of the Tourist Guide to the form "How do I get to X?" or "Can you tell me how to get to X?" so we can specify the simple grammar of the Tourist Guide by the following rules:

S	⟶	How do I get to NP
S	⟶	Can you tell me how to get to NP
NP	⟶	PropN
NP	⟶	Det Noun Prep NP
NP	⟶	Det Noun
Noun	⟶	theatre
Noun	⟶	cinema
Noun	⟶	gallery
Noun	⟶	square
Noun	⟶	monument
Det	⟶	the
Det	⟶	a
Prep	⟶	in
Prep	⟶	containing
PropN	⟶	Trafalgar Square
PropN	⟶	The National Gallery
PropN	⟶	Nelsons Column
PropN	⟶	Hyde Park
PropN	⟶	The Serpentine Lake
PropN	⟶	The Tate Gallery

and so on. The 'S' rules, of course, are not proper 'S' rules for any serious grammar, insofar as they quote words rather than giving syntactic categories, and rely, to that extent, on *Eliza*-like pattern matching. This is merely a simplification we have permitted ourselves for the program we are developing. This set of grammar rules will now allow us to assign correct structural descriptions to a wide range of questions asking for directions, which in turn will permit us to obtain the meanings of the sentences.

5.3 Semantics

So far, we have been concerned only with the syntax of English. In this section we shall disscuss how to extract the meanings of sentences. First, we have to know what kinds of things 'meanings' are. There is no easy and uncontroversial answer to this, and indeed it is a question that has vexed linguists and psychologists for a century and philosophers for millennia. For a broad review of current semantic theories you might like to look at *Language, Meaning and Context* by John Lyons, or the denser and more detailed *Semantic Theory* by Ruth Kempson. In this book, we shall restrict our discussion to only one approach, called **formal semantics**, which is sometimes also called **compositional semantics** because of the crucial part played by the principle of **compositionality**: that the meaning of the whole sentence is composed from meanings of its parts.

5.3.1   The Meaning of Words

The smallest parts are the words of the sentence. What shall we take to be the meanings of words? In the case of a proper name, it seems intuitively right to regard its meaning as being that individual in the world to which the name refers. The meaning of 'Trafalgar Square', for example, will be just that square in London. But this cannot be quite right: consider that some individuals can be referred to by more than one name, but that we would not want to say that the names 'mean the same thing'. Consider the expressions 'Saint Peter' and 'the first Pope', both of which refer to the same person. The two expressions can not mean the same thing, for otherwise the sentence "Saint Peter was the first Pope" would be an uninformative tautology — which it obviously is not. Frege therefore distinguished between the reference (nowadays more commonly called the extension) of an expression, and its sense (or intension) — roughly, whatever it is that we need to know about an object to identify it. What the Automated Tourist Guide knows about Trafalgar Square is in fact given in its database:

```
[[trafalgar square] isa [square]]
```

The intension, or internal representation, of the expression is what connects that expression to an object in the world, and might thus be considered the meaning of the sentence.

Arguably, the database represents 'knowledge' rather than 'meanings'. In our simplified treatment of semantics, however, we shall not distinguish between the two, and permit ourselves the liberty of talking about database facts as though we were talking about meanings. What the intension of an expression is will vary from account to account according to the theoretical bias of the author and to how formal the semantics is. In Sowa's (1984) theory of conceptual graphs, for example, the intension of a word is a representation in semantic memory, something like a dictionary definition; thus the intension of 'mammal', for example, might be "warm-blooded animal, vertibrate, having hair and secreting milk for nourishing its young" (Sowa, 1984, pp. 10–11). In more mainstream formal semantics, the "intension of an expression is a function giving the reference of that expression in any world" (McCawley, 1981, p. 401). In the world of a science fiction novel, for example, the first Pope on Twin Earth might be Saint Thomas, in which case 'the first Pope' and 'Saint Peter' would not have the same referent. The intension of an expression, then, will contain an index that links it with particular individuals in particular worlds.

What about common nouns? The question at the beginning of the chapter made reference to the 'square'. As there are many squares in London, we could have been referring to any one of them. So let us say that the word 'square' simply picks out the set of all squares (its extension), and that the meaning of 'square' is the internal representation that allows the Tourist Guide to decide what is a member of that set and what is not. A fragment of the meaning of 'square' might then be

```
[[trafalgar square] isa [square]]
[[russell square] isa [square]]
[[berkeley square] isa [square]]
[[leicester square] isa [square]]
...etc.
```

In general, we may say that a common noun stands for the set of all those individuals that satisfy the description, and that to know the meaning of a noun is to know what things it can be used to refer to. We shall assume that the Tourist Guide knows about only one 'possible world', which is the London of this book. The intension is therefore simply a pointer to all the things in London that are squares.

5.3.2   The Meaning of Phrases

We can extend this account of meaning to other parts of speech, and show how the semantic values of larger constituents are built up compositionally from the semantic values of their sub-constituents. Think back to our discussion, in chapter 3, of the MSBLOCKS program, and in particular the set of unchangeable facts about the blocks-world:

```
[boxB isa box] [boxB size large] [boxB colour blue]
[boxb isa box] [boxb size small] [boxb colour blue]
[boxR isa box] [boxR size large] [boxR colour red]
```

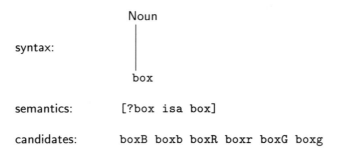

syntax:

Noun

box

semantics: [?box isa box]

candidates: boxB boxb boxR boxr boxG boxg

Figure 5.6
The parse and semantic value for 'box'.

```
[boxr isa box] [boxr size small] [boxr colour red]
[boxG isa box] [boxG size large] [boxG colour green]
[boxg isa box] [boxg size small] [boxg colour green]
```

The meaning of the noun 'box' is simply the relevant set of descriptions in the database, and its extension the set of individuals denoted by ?box when the pattern [?box isa box] is matched against the database. For the database above, these are the objects denoted by boxB, boxb, boxR, boxr, boxG, and boxg. What about the meaning of, say, 'small'? This is simply the set of descriptions picking out all individuals in the world that are small, in this case the objects denoted by boxb, boxr, and boxg. In the same way, the meaning of 'red' is the set of descriptions which identify all individuals whose colour is red: those represented by boxR and boxr. We are now in a position to work out the meaning of a noun-phrase like 'small red box', and we do so according to the **rule-by-rule principle** by which we build up the semantic value of a phrase in tandem with its syntactic parse. The parse and semantic value for 'box' is shown in figure 5.6.

We now build up the noun-phrase, such that the database facts about 'red' reduce the number of candidates (see figure 5.7). Finally, for the whole noun-phrase, the set of candidates is reduced further (see figure 5.8).

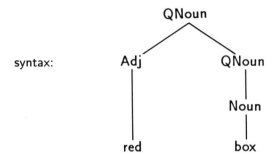

syntax:

semantics: [?box colour red] [?box isa box]

candidates: boxr boxR

filtered out: boxb boxB boxg boxG

Figure 5.7
The parse and semantic value for 'red box'.

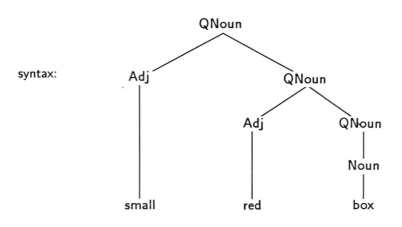

syntax:

semantics: [?box size small] [?box colour red] [?box isa box]

candidate: boxr

filtered out: boxR

Figure 5.8
The parse and semantic value for 'small red box'.

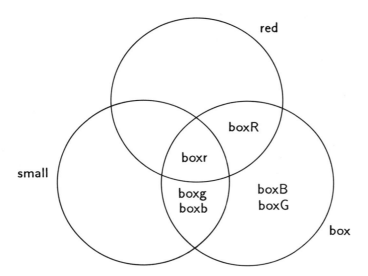

Figure 5.9
A set representation of meaning.

The meaning of 'small red box' is the description, or internal representation, which identifies that item which is at the same time a box, red, and small, or in other words the extension of ?box for the database query produced by the parse

```
[?box size small] [?box colour red] [?box isa box]
```

That object is the box denoted by boxr. An alternative way of representing this fact is as the intersection of the three sets (see figure 5.9).

One problem is what to do when there is more than one object known to the database that satisfies all of the conditions contained in a database query. For example, there may be more than one small red box (or another gallery in London which sits in a square containing a monument). One way of dealing with this type of indeterminacy is to look at the determiner of the top-level noun-phrase. If it is 'a' or 'an', as in "Is there a small red box on the table?" then the questioner is indicating that any small red box would be satisfactory. Similarly, the question "Is there a gallery near here?" indicates that the questioner will be happy with any nearby gallery (the questioner simply wants a day out looking at pictures) and any of the items that match the database query will be sufficient. On the other hand, if the determiner is 'the', then the questioner probably had a particular small red box (or gallery) in mind, and if there is more than one that could be referred to, the questioner should be asked which one is meant. This is not a problem we shall discuss further; in all our examples where we use the definite article 'the', there will be a unique object that satisfies the description.

5.3.3 Answering Questions

Let us now go back once again to the exchange at the beginning of the chapter, and see how we can use a form of the semantic theory sketched above for answering the question. Assume that our database contains facts such as the following:

```
[[the tate gallery] isa [gallery]]
[[the national gallery] isa [gallery]]
[[trafalgar square] isa [square]]
[[leicester square] isa [square]]
[[nelsons collumn] isa [monument]]
[[the albert memorial] isa [monument]]
[[the national gallery] in [trafalgar square]]
[[the natinal gallery] underground [charing cross]]
[[the tate gallery] underground [pimlico]]
[[trafalgar square] containing [nelsons collumn]]
```

and so on. According to our simplified semantic theory, the meaning of 'gallery' is the set of facts that will allow the Tourist Guide to identify all the values of `?place` found by matching the pattern `[?place isa [gallery]]`, in this case, `[the tate gallery]` and `[the national gallery]`. It is the same for 'square' and 'monument'. Put differently, part of the meaning of, for example, Trafalgar Square is that it is a square (just as part of the meaning of 'small red box' is that it is a box — if you are uncertain about this, look again at the earlier example of 'box'). By extension, we can now say that another part of the meaning of Trafalgar Square, for our Automated Tourist Guide at least, is that it contains Nelson's Column; or that a part of the meaning of the National Gallery, in this extended sense, is that it is in Trafalgar Square and close to Charing Cross underground station. To answer the question "Can you tell me how to get to the gallery in the square containing the monument?" then, we need to transform it into a set of patterns

```
[[?x underground ?destination]
[?x isa [gallery]]
[?x in ?y]
[?y isa [square]]
[?y containing ?z]
[?z isa [monument]]]
```

which can then be matched against the database until values are found for ?destination, ?x, ?y, and ?z such that each pattern is identical to an item in the database. If a consistent match can be found, then the value of destination will be the name of a station, which can be passed to the route finder, described in the last chapter, for determining the route. For the database above, the only consistent match gives [the national gallery] as the value of ?x, [trafalgar square] as the value of ?y, [nelsons column] as the value of ?z and [charing cross] as the value of ?destination.

Matching the patterns against the database is straightforward; the difficulty lies in the first stage — transforming an English sentence into patterns representing database items. The parse-tree for the sentence suggests a simple way of constructing this query from its constituent patterns. The idea is to turn each noun-phrase into a collection of patterns which capture the meaning of that phrase. Where there is an embedded noun-phrase, the corresponding collection of patterns is combined to form the new collection. Our program will therefore have a mechanism that translates linguistic expressions into database queries (for an example see figure 5.10).

The meaning of the entire noun-phrase is then a function of the meaning of each of its parts, as these are combined together by the syntactic rules. By adding the pattern

```
[?x underground ?destination]
```

for the 'canned' phrase "Can you tell me how to get to," we have built up a semantic representation that corresponds to the database query given.

In sections 5.4 and 5.5, we shall briefly discuss the pragmatics of language and the generating of natural language text. Since we shall not be concerned with pragmatics in designing the natural language interface to our Automated Tourist

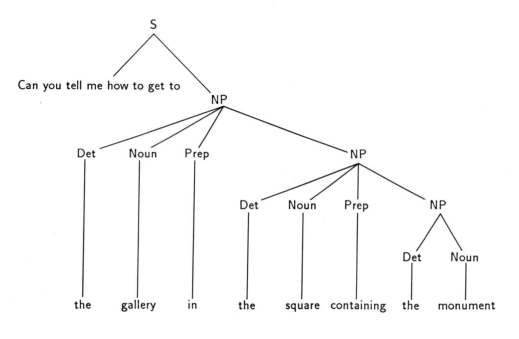

[?x isa [gallery]]   [?y isa [square]]   [?z isa [monument]]
[?x in ?y]   [?y containing ?z]

Figure 5.10
Parse-tree and database queries for "Can you tell me how to get to the gallery in
the square containing the monument?"

Guide, and since our program will generate replies using only stereotyped response patterns, we shall not go into any great detail in either section. If you are interested in finding out more about these topics, you might like to follow up the references cited in the text (McCawley, 1981; Sowa, 1984). But be warned: it is often very difficult reading!

5.4 Pragmatics

Pragmatics is concerned with the relation of utterances to the contexts in which they are uttered, including the identity of the speaker and hearer, their interests and intentions, the state of their knowledge, their physical surroundings, the business in hand, and so on. Whatever the literal meaning of a sentence might be, it is frequently the case that it acquires additional meaning, and sometimes a wholly different meaning, by virtue of the context in which it is produced. To take a simple example, the sentence "I love you madly" has a quite obvious literal meaning, but its full meaning on a given occasion will further depend on exactly who the referents of 'I' and 'you' are. When the reply comes back, "And I love you, too, darling," the identities of the 'I' and 'you' will have switched around. Such expressions whose referents change from one occasion of speech to another are called **deictic expressions**.

Some other deictic expressions are 'today', 'here', 'last month', and so on, whose interpretations depend on the time and the place at which the speaker is talking. Another kind of example of a sentence accruing meaning in addition to its literal meaning might be "Please check your change before you leave," seen in a shop. Its full meaning can only be understood by reference to commonsense knowledge about possible mistakes in counting coins, about standards of honesty, and so on.

5.4.1 Speech Acts

We noted at the beginning of the chapter that, although the question "Can you tell me how to get to the gallery in the square containing the monument?" taken literally, appears to be asking a yes-no question, it is in fact an indirect request for information. An important area of natural language processing in recent years has been that of understanding and generating so-called **speech acts**. The notion goes back to the Oxford philosopher J. L. Austin, who in a book entitled *How to Do Things with Words* (1962), noted that some sentences seem not simply to make statements, but, in their utterance, to perform the acts that they mention. When I say "I promise to fix your car for you" or "I bet you twenty pounds that it rains this afternoon," I am not simply saying that I promise or that I bet: I am actually making that promise or bet by uttering the sentence. This idea was generalized to cover all sentences by a student of Austin's, John Searle, in a book entitled *Speech Acts* (1969). For example, in saying "There's a fly in your soup," I am not simply uttering words; I am, subject to certain conditions being fulfilled, performing the act of making an assertion. (Searle calls these the 'preparatory', 'sincerity', and 'essential' conditions. We shall not discuss them here; you can find out more about the nature of speech acts by looking at Searle's book.) Likewise, in uttering "What's the time?" I am performing the act of making a request. Sometimes, however, the syntactic form of a sentence is not a good guide to the act it is performing. For example, "There's a fly in your soup" may not be a simple assertion but, in context, a warning not to drink it. Likewise, the question "What's the time?" might, in a situation in which you are looking for an excuse to get rid of an unwelcome guest, be intended as a suggestion that the guest leave. The use of direct and indirect speech acts in conversation has been well studied by a number of linguists, cognitive scientists, and philosophers, including Grice (1975), Cohen and Perrault (1979), and Allen and Perrault (1980).

5.4.2 Commonsense Knowledge

The second principal area of interest in pragmatics to which we briefly call attention is speakers' and hearers' use of commonsense knowledge to make sense of utterances. We have pointed out that the question asking for directions to 'the gallery in the square containing the monument' is syntactically ambiguous. There is nothing intrinsic in the semantics of the sentence, either, to dictate that we interpret it one way rather than the other. Yet clearly, we would only understand it in one way: that the monument is in the square and not in the gallery. We do so by appealing to our commonsense knowledge about the way things normally are in the world. There is no reason, I suppose, why monuments should not be housed in galleries; but it is much more likely that they would be found in squares. The cognitive scientist David Waltz has further suggested that the brain may use visual and spatial knowledge for interpreting sentences. He gives the following examples (Waltz, 1981):

> My dog bit the mailman's leg.
> My dachshund bit the mailman's ear.
> My doberman bit the mailman's ear.

The first sentence is easily understandable without recourse to visual imagery. The third sentence is probably reasonable, because a doberman is a large dog. But the second sentence may seem improbable because the hearer may find it very difficult to visualize a circumstance in which a small dog like a dachshund could possibly reach a mailman's ear.

If you wish to read further about pragmatics, you could look at *Pragmatics* (1983) by Stephen Levinson, which comprehensively covers the main topics in the field.

5.5   Producing a Reply

Generating a reply in English for the questioner is easier than coping with the question itself since we can invent a standard form of sentence. For answering questions about the route to a particular Underground station we shall define a procedure (given in the appendix to this chapter) which will output replies of the form

> Travelling by Underground, take the ... Line to ...
>   then change and take the ... Line to ...
>   then change and take the ... Line to ...

So, for example, the route from Victoria to Charing Cross would be described as follows:

> Travelling by Underground, take the Victoria Line to Green Park
>   then change and take the Jubilee Line to Charing Cross

The sentence divides naturally into fragments, each of which is defined by the name of a station at which the traveller gets off the train together with the name of the corresponding line. The fragments appear in the order in which the corresponding stations would be encountered during an actual journey, and this is the same order in which these stations are generated by the `route` procedure. In general, one way of conveying the order in which events occur is to order the occurrence of corresponding parts of a sentence.

The program constructs the output sentence by scanning the list of stations produced by `route` from the beginning to the end. For each station at which the traveller must get off the train a segment of output sentence is generated, by inserting the name of the line and the station into gaps in pre-defined lists of words.

Generating natural language is not usually so straightforward. The items needed to form the text may not be ordered in time, they may contain other types of knowledge, such as descriptions or hypotheses, they may be too detailed to be repeated in full, or they may already be known to the user and so could be omitted from the text. Having chosen the items to report, and an ordering for them, the program must then form a piece of text that is coherent and flowing, with the right level of formality and a consistent style.

To give you a flavour of the current state of natural language generation, here is part of the output from a program named TEXT (McKeown, 1985), which generates responses to questions about a military database. In this instance the user has asked for the definition of 'aircraft carrier':

> An aircraft carrier is a surface ship with a DISPLACEMENT between 78000 and 80800 and a LENGTH between 1039 and 1063. Aircraft carriers have a greater LENGTH than all other ships and a greater DISPLACEMENT than most other ships. Mine warfare ships, for example, have a DISPLACEMENT of 320 and a LENGTH of 144 ...

Though we shall not detail how TEXT works, you will appreciate that it goes well beyond the capabilities of our humble Automated Tourist Guide.

5.6   Conclusion

Behind even the simplest of conversations lies complex cognitive processing. In order to understand a comment or a question, and to respond appropriately, a person must recognize the type of utterance (whether, for example, it is a question, a statement, or a request), extract the correct meaning (from one or more possible interpretations), and form a reply that is matched to the context of the conversation. Syntax is that part of linguistics which deals with the structure of language: how words form into phrases and sentences, and how parts of words form into words. One aspect of computational linguistics is writing parsers: programs that can identify syntactically well-formed strings of words — that is, words which we, as English speakers, recognize as forming grammatical phrases and sentences. Normally, a parser will produce a description of the syntactic structure of the phrase or sentence; in this chapter we described one method of representing this, as phrase-structure rules. In tandem with the syntactic analysis, a parsing program will normally produce a semantic description. We described the method of compositional semantics, in which the semantic value, or meaning, of a sentence is built up from the semantic values of its sub-parts, which in turn are composed of the semantic values of individual words. In order to give an acceptable response, a natural language program may need to represent the pragmatics of an utterance: the identity of the person who produced the sentence; the physical surroundings; the business in hand, and so on. Finally, it must construct a grammatically well-formed and meaningful reply.

5.7 Appendix: Answering Questions

In this appendix we shall develop a POP-11 program to answer questions which are well-formed sentences according to the grammar developed in the body of this chapter. We shall make use of the following database for all the examples:

```
[
[[the national gallery] isa [gallery]]
[[the tate gallery] isa [gallery]]
[[the national gallery] in [trafalgar square]]
[[trafalgar square] isa [square]]
[[hyde park] isa [park]]
[[hyde park] containing [the serpentine lake]]
[[the serpentine lake] isa [lake]]
[[trafalgar square] containing [nelsons column]]
[[nelsons column] isa [monument]]
[[hyde park] underground [marble arch]]
[[the tate gallery] underground [pimlico]]
[[trafalgar square] underground [charing cross]]
[[nelsons column] underground [charing cross]]
[[the national gallery] underground [charing cross]]
[[the serpentine lake] underground [marble arch]]
] -> database;
```

First, we need a new POP-11 procedure, `which`. It takes a POP-11 variable name and a list of patterns and discovers all possible ways of matching these consistently against the POP-11 database, so that multiple occurrences of any variable have the same value. The procedure `which` returns a list of the values taken by the given variable in each complete match:

```
which("x", [[?x isa [gallery]]
             [?x in ?y]
             [?y isa [square]]
             [?y containing ?z]
             [?z isa [monument]]])=>
```

** [[the national gallery]]

Our top-level procedure for producing a response from a question is **answer**. Unlike
the versions of **answer** given in earlier chapters, this one does not match the question
against a series of patterns, but begins by passing it to procedure S, the combined
parser and meaning generator.

```
define answer(query) -> response;
    vars meaning, destination, routelist;

        ;;; parse and semantically analyse sentence
    S(query) -> meaning;
    if meaning /= false then
        if which("destination", meaning) matches
                                [?destination ==] then
            route([victoria], destination) -> routelist;
            if not(routelist) then
                [route not found] -> response
            else
                reply(routelist) -> response
            endif
        else
            [I do not know where that place is] -> response;
        endif;
    else

        ;;; cannot handle this question
        [Sorry I do not understand.
            Try rewording your question] -> response

    endif;
enddefine;
```

If the question is a well-formed sentence, S returns a list of patterns, stored as the value of **meaning**, to be matched by **which** against the database; otherwise it returns **<false>**.

When the procedure S returns a list of patterns, the first part of the following **if** statement is carried out. If **which** finds at least one consistent match, then a value has been found for **destination**, and this can be given as input to **route**. The result of calling **route** is a list of stations and times, and these can then be passed to a procedure **reply**, which composes an English sentence:

```
define reply(list) -> response;

    ;;;
    ;;; Convert route list into English description of form:
    ;;;
    ;;;     travelling by underground, take the ... line to ...
    ;;;         then change and take the ... line to ...
    ;;;         then change and take the ... line to ...
    ;;;                              ...
    ;;;

    vars line, station, line1, response;

    list --> [[[?line ??station] ==] ??list];
    [travelling by underground, take the ^line line to]
                                             -> response;
    while list matches [[[?line1 ??station] ==] ??list] do
        if line1 /= line then
            [^^response ^^station then change and
                take the ^line1 line to] -> response;
            line1 -> line;
        endif;
    endwhile;
    [^^response ^^station] -> response;
enddefine;
```

5.7.1   A Sentence Recognizer

Parsing and semantic analysis of the input sentence are performed in parallel and make heavy use of the POP-11 matcher. All this goes on within the call to procedure S. We shall begin by constructing a simplified version of S which returns <true> if the given list of words satisfies the grammar defined in the body of this chapter and <false> otherwise. In other words we can say that the simplified S 'recognizes' or 'accepts' sentences in our language. S attempts to match the word list against patterns, and, if a match is found, S returns <true>, otherwise <false>.

There is a pattern for each phrase-structure rule which has S on its left-hand side:

```
define S(list) -> found;
    vars np;
    if list matches [how do i get to ??np:NP] or
        list matches
                [can you tell me how to get to ??np:NP]
    then
        true -> found
    else
        false -> found
    endif
enddefine;
```

The patterns should be familiar except for one additional feature: a **restriction procedure**. This is indicated by the appearance of :NP following each pattern variable.

Until now we have used pattern variables like ??x in such a way that they match *any* sequence of words. If there is a restriction procedure associated with a pattern variable, then any potential match is offered to the procedure whose name appears after the colon; if this procedure returns <false>, the match is rejected, and otherwise it is accepted. We shall define NP to accept only word lists which are noun-phrases according to our grammar, and so S is guaranteed to accept only well-formed sentences.

The procedure NP is defined in exactly the same fashion as S, by constructing patterns from those rules which have NP on the left and comparing these with the given word list:

```
define NP(list) -> found;
    vars pn, d, n, p, np;
    if list matches [??pn:PROPN] or
        list matches [?d:DET ??n:NOUN] or
        list matches [?d:DET ??n:NOUN ?p:PREP ??np:NP]
    then
        true -> found
    else
        false -> found
    endif;
enddefine;
```

Again there are restriction procedures in the patterns to enforce the required syntactic categories. All three forms of the noun-phrase are taken into account, and the third involves a recursive call to NP as a restriction procedure.

If one of the patterns matches the series of words, then this must be a well-formed noun-phrase and <true> is returned; otherwise <false> is returned.

The definitions of restriction procedures DET and PREP are more simple.

```
define DET(word) -> found;
    member(word, [a the]) -> found;
enddefine;

define PREP(word) -> found;
    member(word, [in containing]) -> found
enddefine;
```

Each procedure is given a single word to check, and the phrase-structure rules define legal values for these words. member is a built-in POP-11 procedure that takes an item and a list as input, and returns <true> if the item is a member of the list, and <false> otherwise.

Procedures PROPN and NOUN are defined similarly, except that, to allow for the possibility of nouns and proper nouns containing more than one word, member checks that a given list of words is a member of a list of nouns or proper nouns.

```
define NOUN(list) -> found;
    member(list, [[gallery] [square] [monument] [lake]
                  [park]]) -> found;
enddefine;

define PROPN(list) -> found;
    member(list,
        [[trafalgar square] [the national gallery]
         [nelsons column] [hyde park]
         [the serpentine lake] [the tate gallery]
        ] ) -> found;
enddefine;
```

The grammar has now been defined, and S will return <true> for a well-formed sentence:

```
S([how do i get to the gallery in the square containing a
monument]) =>
** <true>


S([how do i get to the monument in trafalgar square]) =>
* <true>
```

The other procedures will also return <true> if given an appropriate word or phrase:

```
NP([the gallery in the square]) =>
** <true>


PREP("in") =>
** <true>
```

5.7.2   A Sentence Parser and Database Query Generator

The set of procedures given above enables us to recognize when we have a sentence which satisfies our grammar. But we need more than this. We want procedure S to produce a database query instead of <true>. We have seen how to do this by constructing the meaning of a sentence from the meanings of its syntactic constituents. The meanings of these constituents are in turn composed from the meanings of their syntactic constituents and so on.

This can be arranged within procedure S by extracting a meaning from the NP restriction procedure when there is a successful pattern match and composing it into a meaning for the entire sentence. To achieve this, NP must also be modified to return a meaning instead of <true>. If the noun-phrase is a proper name, the returned meaning is just a list containing that name. Otherwise, a list of database patterns is composed from the head noun in the noun-phrase and the meaning of an embedded noun-phrase if this is present.

The way in which this meaning is composed depends on which of the three phrase-structure rules with NP on the left-hand side describes the noun-phrase. We shall give new versions of S and NP which do just this. Although only one new term will be introduced, the procedures are *considerably more difficult* to follow than the ones we have given so far. We only show them here for the sake of completeness, and to demonstrate that a parser and meaning generator can be written in very few lines of POP-11.

To define the procedures there has to be some way of obtaining the value returned by a restriction procedure. Fortunately there is a feature of the pattern matcher that makes this possible. In normal use a pattern variable is set equal to the word or list of words with which it matches. When a restriction procedure returns <true>, this remains the case. However, when a restriction procedure returns anything other than <true> or <false>, the match succeeds, and furthermore the pattern variable is set equal to that value instead of the word or series of words appearing in the matched list.

```
define S(list) -> meaning;
    vars np, sym;
    if list matches [how do i get to ??np:NP] or
        list matches
            [can you tell me how to get to ??np:NP]
    then
        if np matches [[= ?sym isa =] ==] then
            ;;; meaning of noun-phrase is
            ;;; a list of patterns
            [ [? ^sym underground ? destination] ^^np ]
                                        -> meaning
        else
            ;;; meaning of noun-phrase is a proper name
            [ [^np underground ? destination] ]
```

```
                                                  -> meaning
        endif
    else
        ;;; unknown sentence form
        false -> meaning
    endif;
enddefine;


define NP(list) -> meaning;
    vars pn, d, n, p, np, sym1, sym2;
    if list matches [??pn:PROPN] then
        pn -> meaning
    elseif list matches [?d:DET ??n:NOUN]  then
        gensym("v") -> sym1;
        [ [ ? ^sym1 isa ^n] ] -> meaning
    elseif list matches [?d:DET ??n:NOUN ?p:PREP ??np:NP]
       then
        gensym("v") -> sym1;
        if np matches [[= ?sym2 isa =] ==] then
            ;;; meaning of noun-phrase is
            ;;; a list of patterns
            [ [? ^sym1 isa ^n] [? ^sym1 ^p ? ^sym2] ^^np]
                                          -> meaning
        else
            ;;; meaning of noun-phrase is proper name
            [ [? ^sym1 isa ^n] [? ^sym1 ^p ^np] ]
                                          -> meaning
        endif;
    else
        ;;; unknown noun-phrase form
        false -> meaning
    endif;
enddefine;
```

In both S and NP, when the returned meaning from an embedded NP is a list of patterns, the name of the first variable is extracted by matching it against ?sym, and this is used to form a new pattern which is tagged onto the front of the original list. This is necessary to ensure that certain variables in lists of patterns refer to the same objects.

In constructing new patterns a '?' must be inserted before pattern variable names which are themselves the values of ordinary procedure variables. As you can see this has been achieved using the up-arrow, in a list of the form:

```
[ ...?   ^sym ...]
```

to give

```
[ ...?   v5 ...]
```

where v5 is the value of **sym**. The list is now of a form that can be matched against the database (for example, [?v5 isa [park]]).

One small problem is the use of variable names within patterns. By virtue of our grammar, there may be an indefinite number of embedded noun-phrases within a place description. Consequently, an indefinite number of unique variable names will be required. A standard way of producing unique variable names is to append an increasing sequence of numbers onto the end of a word (e.g., v1, v2, v3 ...). The built-in POP-11 procedure **gensym** produces unique variable names which can be used in patterns. It is called with a word as argument and returns this word with a number appended onto the end. On subsequent uses of **gensym** the appended number is increased. Thus,

```
gensym("v") =>
** v1
gensym("v") =>
** v2
```

The procedures PROPN, NOUN, DET, and PREP could also be modified to return a meaning. It is not not necessary to do so for this example, since in each case the required meaning is identical to the input word or words. Hence, any pattern variable restricted by PROPN, NOUN, DET, or PREP will have as its value the desired meaning following a successful match. The versions of PROPN, NOUN, DET, and PREP in appendix B at the back of the book are slightly different in that they allow a greater range of words, including synonyms, and return one out of a list of synonyms, in order to facilitate matching against the database.

Here are some calls of the procedures:

```
 NP([the gallery in the square]) =>
 ** [[? v2 isa [gallery]] [? v2 in ? v1] [? v1 isa
 [square]]]
 NP([the park containing the lake])=>
 ** [[? v4 isa [park]] [? v4 containing ? v3] [? v3 isa
 [lake]]]
```

The result of each call is either <false> or a pattern which can be matched against the database using which. The main procedure S is now in the correct form to be called from within answer, with the following result:

```
answer([how do i get to the gallery in the square
containing the monument])=>>
travelling by underground,
take the victoria line to green park
then change and take the jubilee line to charing cross
```

5.8 Exercises

1. The phrase-structure rules listed on page 145 permit us to generate a fairly large number of different sentences, for example

   a. A beautiful squirrel drank the lemonade
   b. The pink gin evaporated
   c. The old man caught a beautiful pink squirrel

   and so on. Try to work out for yourself which rules, starting from the 'S' symbol, would have been used to generate the above sentences. Draw a phrase-marker for each sentence, labelling each sub-constituent in the manner of (9') and (10').

2. In our discussion of sentence ambiguity on page 148, we ourselves used (had you noticed it?) an ambiguous propositional phrase: "... the procedure in our program for recognizing noun-phrases." This expression manifests exactly the same kind of structural ambiguity as that on which this section comments. Using rule 2 with rules 3 and 4 on that page, respectively, draw

all the possible parse-trees for the expression, in the manner of the examples given in figures 5.3, 5.4, and 5.5. Does either of rules 3 or 4 give us uniquely the parse we want? If not, is it possible to write a rule that will do so?

3. We have said that we might regard the semantic value of a expression as the set of individuals to which that expression applies, and of a complex expression as the intersection of the sets denoted by its constituents. Try to write a simple POP-11 procedure that will take as input a pair of sets and return as a result their intersection.

4. We saw in this chapter how we would write a database query that would pick out blocks-world items such as 'the large green box'. Imagining that you have an appropriate database describing a state of the world, try now to write a set of POP-11 lists that would represent a database query for picking out an arch in that state description. To do this you will require a collection of blocks and relations such as 'isa', 'not-abutting', and 'supported by'.

5. Look at the POP-11 definitions of NP (first version), NOUN, DET, and so on. Referring to the phrase-structure rules given in this chapter, write similar procedures for VP, Vtrans, and Vintrans. If you have been able to do that, next try writing a new S procedure for recognizing declarative sentences, such as, "The old man saw a beautiful pink squirrel." Rules for VP on which you might base this exercise are given on page 145.

Chapter 6

Reasoning

6.1 Reasoning with Stored Knowledge

In chapter 3 we drew a distinction between two views of artificial intelligence: a performance model, concerned with reproducing the superficial aspects of human-like behaviour, and an internal representation model, covering most serious work in AI, which is concerned with representing the knowledge that underlies and gives rise to overt behaviour. In the present chapter we are going to discuss the semantic network as a means of reasoning about such stored knowledge.

Coming upon the word 'reasoning' in a book such as this, it is all too tempting to leap to premature conclusions about what is involved. In particular, you should note that deductive reasoning, whatever Aristotle and Sherlock Holmes may have thought of it, may not always be the most appropriate form of reasoning for the task in hand. Therefore, before we look in detail at semantic nets, we shall briefly say something about how human beings reason. In fact, there is no single uniform way in which humans reason. In differing circumstances, given different sets of known facts and goals, we use different tactics to reach solutions to our problems: we *generalize*, we *explain*, we *deduce*, we *visualize*, and so on. Although some reasoning strategies may not in fact be logically sound, they may in some circumstances be better than logic in getting us to the answers we need. Let us consider some concrete problems and how we go about solving them.

In the first place, we like to think that we live in a reassuringly orderly and predictable world. Indeed, it is only because it is in the main orderly and predictable that we are able to navigate our way through each day without too much conscious effort. Our behaviour and our perceptions, then, are largely based on expectation:

on the one hand, we have learned concepts and can recognize further instances of
them; on the other hand, we expect all further instances to be much like the ones
we have experienced before. If we know that this is a dog, or this is a picnic, or
that is a handshake, it is because we have seen innumerable instances of the same
thing before: it is another one of the same, and we expect this dog to be much
like any other dog, this picnic to happen much like any other, that handshake to
have the same social meaning as any other handshake. This form of reasoning is
called **induction** (or more familiarly a type of 'learning') and is typical of the kind
of reasoning we do in our everyday lives, from childhood on, in learning about the
world. Its typical form is

> if P is true of a,
> and P is true of b,
> and P is true of c,
> and ... P is true of n,
> then infer that P is true of all other entities
> of the same kind as a, b, c, ... n.

So if, in the course of our lives, every swan we see is white, we might inductively infer
that all swans are white. In this case, it is not a totally reliable form of inference, as
the discovery in Australia of black swans showed to a seventeenth-century Europe
used to seeing only white swans.

Inductive reasoning provides an account of how we are able to make generalizations and therefore how we recognize new objects or interpret the social acts of
others, but it does not account for other kinds of inference we may use in the course
of our everyday lives. Suppose I know that every time Bill has had an argument
with his wife he goes out to a bar and gets drunk. If I then meet Bill reeling drunk-
enly in the street I may infer that "Bill's been arguing with his wife again." I may
be right, but not necessarily so: he may have been out drinking for some wholly
different reason. What I am doing is reasoning back from a state of affairs that I
can perceive to a state or action that could have produced it. This second kind of
inference is an instance of **abduction** and, like induction, it is not a reliable form
of inference, though often both useful and necessary in our everyday lives, where
we more commonly think of it as 'explanation'. Its form is

> if b (normally) follows from a
> and b is known to be true,
> then infer a to be true.

Though abductive reasoning is, strictly speaking, not logical reasoning, it is often both an extremely useful and a highly plausible form of inference. As in the case of Bill's drunkenness, it provides a mechanism for understanding people's behaviour and analyzing the motives of their actions. Perhaps surprisingly, it also frequently used in solving professional problems by experts in engineering, medicine, and other skilled professions. For example, a doctor knows that someone suffering from, say, influenza, would have a temperature, an inflamed throat, muscular pain, and so on. The patient the doctor is examining has all of these symptoms; therefore the doctor has reason to suspect that the patient may be suffering from a bout of 'flu. We shall look at this kind of reasoning in more detail in chapter 7.

Suppose now I were to ask the questions "Is Moscow north or south of New York?" or "Are there more white notes lying between the nearest black note to C on the piano keyboard and the nearest black note to F above it, or between F and the nearest black note to B above it?" You would probably begin by visualising a map of the world or a piano keyboard and then, in the first case, working out which city is to the north and, in the second, counting off the white notes. In both instances you would be reasoning with *visual* rather than logical representations of the problem. You might, in each case, come up with perfectly good answers, though the answers would not have been arrived at by logical inference.

You may already have encountered **deductive** reasoning in the form of the classical Aristotelian syllogism, typically of the form

> All Xs are Ys.
> A is an X.
> Therefore A is also a Y.

You can no doubt intuitively recognize the validity of the following syllogism,

Premise 1:	All men are mortal.
Premise 2:	Clint Eastwood is a man.
Conclusion:	Therefore Clint Eastwood is mortal.

as perhaps you can of

Premise 1:	All those who believe in democracy believe in free speech.
Premise 2:	Fascists do not believe in democracy.
Conclusion:	Therefore fascists do not believe in free speech.

In the second example, you may be surprised to know that, even though you may intuitively feel, as for the first syllogism, the conclusion to be true, it does not follow logically from the premises. It is a curious fact about human reasoning that we tend to think that those conclusions we approve of are valid when they are not, while those of which we disapprove are false when they are not. Of course, much of our everyday reasoning is deductive — if the kettle whistles, the water has boiled; the kettle is whistling now, therefore the water has boiled — but we are seldom explicitly aware of it. Our second syllogism, on the other hand, points up the complexity of actual human reasoning, and the error of assuming that we can model human inferencing strategies purely on logic.

6.2   Reasoning with Semantic Nets

Now, to return to our knowledge representation formalism, we shall look in detail at semantic nets and suggest why they should be of interest to us and then see how semantic nets have been used for representing word and sentence meanings and for simple inferencing. We shall then give a more detailed description of the formalism and, in the appendix to this chapter, show how to use them in our Automated Tourist Guide. To begin with, why should we be interested in semantic nets?

In the first place, simple database commands are inadequate for doing inferencing. We can add items of knowledge, and then refer to them by matching patterns against the contents of the database, but we are merely asking the right questions to get the answers we want.

On the more positive side, there are three particularly good reasons for studying semantic nets in a course on AI. First, they are able to provide (with some caveats) an attractively simple representational format and inference mechanism.

Second, in one form or another semantic nets have been used in a large number of AI programs and are well documented in standard introductions to AI — for example, Rich (1983) and Winston (1984). *Associative Networks*, edited by N. V. Findler (1979), collects together a number of fairly recent papers on semantic networks for the more adventurous reader.

Finally, this very proliferation of programs using semantic networks of one form or another has given rise to a number of important theoretical studies which critically and productively examine the semantics of the formalism, making it probably the best understood knowledge representation formalisms in AI (even if one of the most carelessly used!). Particularly interesting (but, again, for the more adventurous reader) is "What's in a Link: Foundations for Semantic Networks" (Woods, 1975), as well as two papers by Ronald Brachman: "On the Epistemological Status of Semantic Networks" (1979), and "What IS-A Is and Isn't: An Analysis of Taxonomic Links in Semantic Networks" (1983).

Before we look in detail at semantic nets, it will be useful to pave the way by sketching out a brief history, and by clarifying what is meant by the 'semantics'of semantic networks.

6.2.1 What Are Semantic Networks? A Little Light History

The concept of a semantic network is now fairly old in the literature of cognitive science and artificial intelligence, and has been developed in so many ways and for so many purposes in its 20-year history that in many instances the strongest connection between recent systems based on networks is their common ancestry. The term 'semantic network' as it is used now might therefore best be thought of as the name for a family of representational schemes rather than a single formalism. A little light history will clarify how the network we shall use in our Automated Tourist Guide is related to other networks you may come across in your reading.

The term dates back to Ross Quillian's Ph.D. thesis (1968), in which he first introduced it as a way of talking about the organization of human semantic memory, or memory for **word concepts**. The idea of a semantic network — that is, of a network of associatively linked concepts — is very much older: Anderson and Bower (1973, p. 9), for example, claim to be able to trace it all the way back to Aristotle. Specifically, semantic networks were conceived as a "representational format [that would] permit the 'meanings' of words to be stored, so that humanlike use of these meanings is possible" (Quillian, 1968, p. 216), and, as with almost all mainline research in semantic nets since Quillian's original proposal, they were intended to represent the non-emotive, so-called 'objective' part of meaning: the properties of things, rather than of the way we may feel about them.

Quillian's basic assumption was that the meaning of a word could be represented by the set of its verbal associations. To see what this means, imagine that, in the course of reading a novel, you come across the word 'dugong' and the context does not make clear what the word refers to. So you look up the word in a dictionary, and there you find, not the object or the property or the action itself, but rather a definition made up of other words — in the present case,

To get some feel for semantic nets, think of a common, but evocative, word, say, 'castle'. Write it down in the middle of a sheet of paper. Now think of some words related to castle, say, 'king', or 'battlement'. Write down these words in a ring around 'castle', and join each of them with a line to 'castle'. Try and give each line a label that describes the relationship between the two words — for example, the line linking 'king' and 'castle' might be labelled 'lives in'. Continue outwards, writing down words relating to 'king', words relating to 'battlement', and so on. What you are constructing is, roughly, a semantic net.

DUGONG: *a herbivorous marine mammal of tropical coastal waters of the Old World, having flipperlike forelimbs and a deeply notched tail fin.*

You still have no clear idea of what a 'dugong' is, so you then look up each of the words making up the definition, and in turn each of the words making up the definition of each word in the definition of the original word, and so on, learning that 'herbivorous' means 'feeding on plants; plant-eating', that a 'flipperlike forelimb' is 'a wide, flat limb, as of a seal, adapted especially for swimming', that 'marine' means 'native to or formed by the sea', but that nonetheless it is not a fish but a 'mammal' which is 'a member of the class Mammalia', in turn 'a class of vertebrate animals ... distinguished by self-regulating body-temperature, hair, and, in the female, milk-producing mammae', and so on and so forth. As you follow through all the cross-references, so you build up a complex picture of the concept named by the word and of its relation to other concepts, say, that of manatee, whale, mammal, animal, life form.

Clearly, such a mental representation exceeds the mere dictionary definitions of the words you have looked up: semantic networks, as do dictionaries more indirectly, reflect the complex manner in which human knowledge is structured, every concept being defined in terms of its place in a web of relationships between concepts. We might picture a person's knowledge as a map, with points or nodes representing individual concepts and labelled links (called **arcs** or **pointers** in some texts) connecting those nodes together. Just as we know where Trafalgar Square is because we know how to get there from Picadilly Circus, or from Charing Cross, or from St. James Park, so too we know now what, for example, a dugong is because we 'know how to get there' from a tail fin, a herbivore, a flipper, and a mammal.

The foregoing 'map' analogy should not be pushed too far. In Quillian's original semantic networks, a relation between two words might be shown to exist if, in an unguided breadth-first search from each word, there could be found a point of intersection of their respective verbal associations. We would not, by contrast, wish to find a route from Tower Bridge to Trafalgar Square by blindly sending out search parties in all directions from each location in the hope that they might eventually meet! While Quillian's early nets might have appeared to be an attractive psychological model for the architecture of human semantic knowledge, they did not provide an adequate account of our ability to reason with that knowledge.

A couple of years later a psychologist, Allan Collins, conducted a series of experiments along with Quillian to test the psychological plausibility of semantic networks as models, both of the organization of memory and of human inferencing. The networks they used, such as that in figure 6.1, now gave far greater prominence than before to the hierarchical organisation of knowledge. (Don't worry too much on the first reading about trying to understand what the network in figure 6.1 means; it will become clearer on a second reading, after the network formalism has been explained.)

The network is displayed as a **taxonomic tree** or **isa hierarchy** (a term we introduced briefly in chapter 3). Each node (labelled by an underscored word) is connected upwards to its superset and downwards to its subset. A canary, in this schema, is a bird and, more generally, an animal. A shark, too, is shown to be an animal, but it is not a bird, as there is no link up from 'shark' to 'bird'. An ostrich is a bird because, like the canary, it is one of the **children** of the 'bird' node. The links sideways from each node state **properties** that are true of the node — that birds can fly, for example, or that canaries can sing — and properties of higher nodes are **inherited** by the lower nodes to which they are connected unless there is a property attached to a lower node that explicitly overrides it. Thus, we may infer from the tree that canaries can fly because birds in general can fly, whereas we are inhibited from making the same inference for ostriches since there is the explicit statement at the ostrich node that it 'can't fly'.

Collins and Quillian's experiments consisted in presenting subjects with sets of true and false sentences, and measuring their reaction time in deciding whether the sentences were true or false. Taking the number of links to be traversed between two nodes to be a measure of the semantic distance between concepts, they predicted that a person would require more time to decide, for example, that "A canary is an animal" or "A canary has skin" than to decide that "A canary is a bird" or "A canary can sing" since in the former cases the search for the relevant information requires rising through more links in the hierarchy. The experimental

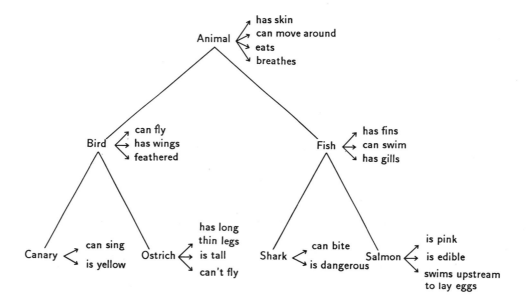

Figure 6.1
A taxonomic tree. From Collins and Quillian (1969).

Sentence type	True sentences	Mean reaction time (msec)
P0	A canary can sing.	1.3
P1	A canary can fly.	1.38
P2	A canary has skin.	1.47
S0	A canary is a canary.	1.00
S1	A canary is a bird.	1.17
S2	A canary is an animal.	1.23

Table 6.1
Reaction times for sentences with differing semantic distances. From Collins and Quillian (1969).

results met their predictions. Table 6.1 illustrates the kinds of stimulus sentences, with approximate reaction times, that were used in these experiments. While subsequent research on reaction times to sentences, such as that by Conrad (1972) and Smith, Shoben, and Rips (1974), raised doubts about the soundness of the model in the form it then had, Collins and Quillian's hierarchical nets were an important source of many good ideas for, and the direct forerunners of, more recent networks, particularly in the domain of language understanding.

One such network developed for the representation of sentence meaning was that of Robert Simmons and his co-researchers and successors. Quillian's hierarchical classification of world knowledge had no place in Simmons's networks, which were designed to capture the meanings of sentences by extending from a node representing the main verb a set of links to nodes representing the **cases** associated with the verb. Thus, to take a simple example, the meaning of the sentence "John gave

Mary an apple" might be represented by a net such as

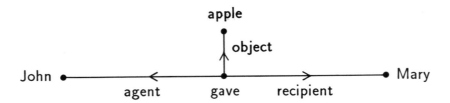

where the central node names the action, the remaining nodes are labelled by the
names of the participants in the action, and the links between the nodes indicate
the relationship of the participants to the action: it is John who does the giving, the
apple which is given, and Mary who receives the apple. Furthermore, the arrows
on the links indicate how the meaning should be read: that, for example, the apple
is the object of the act of giving and not that giving is the object of apple.

Because, in any act of giving, the underlying **case relationships** remain the same
— there is always someone who gives, something given, and someone to whom it
is given — we might see the network above as the filling in, for the sentence "John
gave Mary an apple", of a more abstract schema. That same schema also provides
an interpretation for numerous other sentences: "The boy gave his mother flowers,"
"Charlie gave his son a blank cheque," "Othello gave Desdemona a handkerchief,"
and so on. We might then say that the meaning of each of these sentences is 'give',
together with specific values filling the **case slots**, as follows:

> GIVE
>
> | | |
> |------------|---|
> | agent: | {john, the boy, charlie, othello} |
> | recipient: | {mary, his mother, his son, desdemona} |
> | object: | {apple, flowers, blank cheque, handkerchief} |

Among the developments from this form of the semantic network which deserve
mention, though we shall not discuss them further here, are Shapiro's distinction
between different kinds of relations between nodes, Hendrix's 'partitioned semantic networks' for dealing with quantification (as in "Every boy gave his mother
flowers"), and Schank's **conceptual dependency** representation which translates
natural language sentences into their underlying conceptual forms, expressed as
conceptual primitives. (For brief but illuminating descriptions of partitioned
semantic nets and of conceptual dependency, you could look at Rich, 1983).

Around the same time as Collins and Quillian as well as Simmons and his coresearchers were working on their respective semantic net representations of word meanings and sentence meanings, others were using net-like structures to express types of complex knowledge, though without Quillian's emphasis on cognitive plausibility. Patrick Winston at MIT designed a program which, from net-like **structural descriptions** of physical structures such as an arch, could infer the **concept** of arch; Jaime Carbonell adapted Quillian's networks as a data structure for a program called SCHOLAR, which gave tuition on the geography of South America.

6.2.2 A Description of Semantic Networks

In this section we shall describe the major features of semantic nets. Let us begin with a simple network; it is admittedly not much of a network, as it expresses only one simple relation, which is that the colour of canaries is yellow. The network is made up of two nodes and a link between them, showing that the nodes are related in some way.

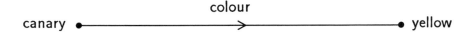

The nodes might be taken to represent concepts, or perhaps sets of individuals, or other kinds of entity; the differences between these are important, and we shall discuss them in the next section. For the time being, we shall informally interpret them as representing concepts.

The nature of the relation is specified by the label on the link and by the left-to-right direction of the arrow. A reading of the network in the direction of the arrow might be something like "A canary has a colour property, which is that it is yellow"; we might alternatively see the link as pointing out a particular kind of **feature** or **attribute** of canaries, and the node at the termination of the link as the value of that feature or attribute. If the arrow on the link were pointing the other way, of course, the meaning of the network would be "The colour of yellow is canary," which is nonsense; so it is quite important that we use *directed* links in our networks.

In addition to giving a link a simple word as a label, we may wish to show that the concept used to label the link also has some relations to other concepts, and is thus also a node. For example, we might wish to show that there are different ways

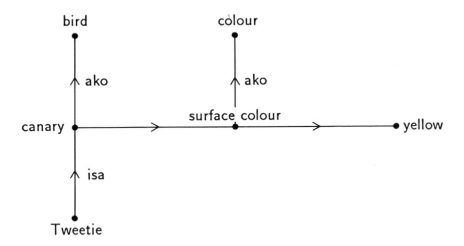

Figure 6.2
Semantic network for "Tweetie is a yellow bird."

in which a thing may have a colour; it may have that colour only on the surface, such as the yellowness of a canary, or it may have that colour all through, such as the greenness of grass. The network in figure 6.2 shows this distinction, by making the label on the link between 'canary' and 'yellow' be 'surface colour', which has the 'is a kind of' relation (abbreviated to *ako*) to the abstract idea of 'colour'. This network represents the fact that the surface colour of canaries is yellow, that surface colour is a kind of colour, and that yellow is a colour.

We might also use semantic nets to represent the meaning of referring expressions in the 'blocks-world' that we introduced in chapter 3. For example, the meaning of 'the big blue box' might be something like what is shown in figure 6.3. That same information, as we have shown in the discussion of the semantics of natural language, can be represented in the database by

        [boxB isa box] [boxB size large] [boxB colour blue]

where 'size' and 'colour' indicate attributes of the particular box, boxB, and 'large' and 'blue' represent the values of those attributes for that box. Other boxes will

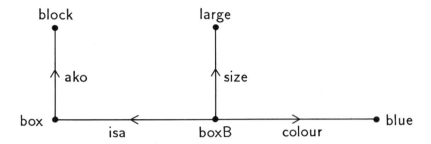

Figure 6.3
Semantic network for 'the big blue box'.

have different values.

The *isa* link, however, indicates a very different kind of information: that boxB is an instance of a more general class or concept, that of 'box'. This is a very useful sort of link in that it enables us to make simple kinds of inference.

In the two networks above we also have another type of link, *ako*. We have already seen an example of this, in our discussion of Collins and Quillian's psychological tests with semantic nets: Figure 6.1 implicitly conveyed the information that a bird is 'a kind of' animal, that a canary is 'a kind of' bird, that an ostrich is 'a kind of' bird, and so on. Since a bird is an animal, any properties or attributes that are generally true of animals will also be true of birds; for example, if animals in general have skin, breathe, move around, and eat, then, unless there is evidence to the contrary, so do birds. In the same manner, whatever is true of birds in general is therefore also likely to be true of particular types of birds. The process of inferring that something has a property because it is a particular type of something else which has that property is called **property inheritance**.

In terms of the deductive reasoning that we sketched above, we may therefore legitimately make the following inference:

> All animals have properties a,b, ... n.
> Birds are animals.
> Therefore birds have properties a,b, ... n.

We say that the concept 'bird' inherits the property of having skin or of breathing from the concept 'animal'. It may happen, however, that a particular kind of object will have peculiar properties that make it atypical of its superclass. A particular feature of ostriches that makes them atypical of birds, for example, is that they cannot fly. Attaching this information to the 'ostrich' node will prevent the inheritance of the property 'can fly' from the 'bird' node.

The *isa* and *ako* relationships are **transitive** — that is, if a relation holds between X and Y and between Y and Z, then it also holds between X and Z (but not necessarily between Z and X). For example, if a canary is a kind of bird and a bird is a kind of animal, then a canary is a kind of animal.

Suppose now we know that Tweetie is a canary. Even though we may not have been specifically told anything about Tweetie, we still know a great deal about him — for example, that like other canaries he is yellow and can sing, that he is a bird, and, like other birds, that he has wings, feathers, and can fly. This information is nowhere explicitly stated of Tweetie; rather, we have inferred it by exploring *isa*, *ako*, and attribute links extending from 'canary'.

So far in this section we have been talking about transitive relations between nodes, indicated by arrows pointing in one direction along the connecting links. Yet there are also occasions when we will wish to make inferences in both directions. For example, if Fred is the brother of Bill, then Bill is also the brother of Fred. Given the first fact, we will want to be able to infer the second. This kind of link is **commutative**: it indicates a symmetric relation between the nodes. In our Automated Tourist Guide, if we know that the London Underground station X is connected to station Y, we would want to infer that Y is also connected to X. The 'connects' link is, in fact, both commutative and transitive: if there is a route from X to Y and there is a route from Y to Z, then there is a route from X to Z (transitivity) and also from Z to X (commutativity). We can indicate a commutative relation in a semantic net by a bidirectional link:

```
        connects              connects
  X  •—<—>—•   Y  •—<—>—•   Z
```

6.2.3   Some Interpretations of Nodes and Links

In many programs using semantic nets, unfortunately, the meaning of nodes and links has been interpreted intuitively rather than described rigorously and system-

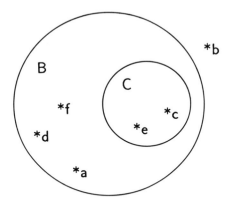

Figure 6.4
A set representation of a concept hierarchy.

atically. If we are using a semantic network to represent an area of knowledge, we ought to be clear about what kinds of things we are depicting in the nodes of our networks and what kinds of relations we are specifying in the links between nodes. That is, we ought to specify the semantics of our formalism. We will consider just two interpretations of nodes and links — though if you are interested, and are prepared for more advanced reading, you could look at Brachman (1983).

One interpretation of **generic** nodes (ones that refer to a general class or concept) is as sets. Thus the relation holding between a node at one level of a hierarchy and that at a higher level is that of subset to superset. If, for example, we indicate in our network that a canary is a bird, what we are in effect stating is that the set of all canaries is a subset of the set of all birds This is shown diagramatically in figure 6.4. Everything that lies within circle B is a bird; that is, circle B is the set of all birds. Within circle B lies circle C, which is the set of all canaries. Thus a, c, d, e, and f are all birds, since c and e, while contained by circle C, are also contained by the larger circle. But c and e are also canaries, while a, d, and f, because they lie outside that circle, are not. Whatever b is, on the other hand, it is not a bird, as it lies outside the larger circle.

If the generic node is interpreted as a set, then the relation of nodes representing individuals to generic nodes in the network is that of set membership. Thus, the

meaning of the network below

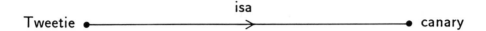

is represented in figure 6.4 by the relationship of c or e to the circle C.

A second interpretation of generic nodes is as prototypes, and of instance nodes as individuals for whom the generic nodes provide a prototypic description. Rather than describing an individual or picking out a class of individuals, a prototype describes what the typical exemplar of the class is like, in terms of physical characteristics, behaviour, diet, habitat, and so on. Individuals will then be more or less like the prototype. Thus, for example, mammals are prototypically thought of as land-animals which give birth to live young; a cow or a rabbit is a typical mammal in these respects, though a dugong is atypical on the first count, a platypus on the second. Canaries prototypically are yellow and can sing, so we recognize Tweetie, who is yellow and can sing, as a fairly typical instance of what we imagine canaries to be. A detailed model of human concept organization, based on prototypes, has been proposed by Rosch (1983).

6.3   Conclusion

In this chapter we briefly described the main methods of reasoning: induction, a type of learning by making generalizations from examples; abduction, or explanation by reasoning back from a situation to the state or action that produced it; spatial reasoning, by forming a mental image; and deductive reasoning using classical logic. One popular method of representing the meaning of words in a way that enables a computer to carry out reasoning is the semantic network. A semantic network describes the relationships between words, by means of directed links. We introduced three special types of link: *isa*, *ako*, and *connects*. The *isa* link relates an item (Tweetie, or boxB) to its general class (canary, box), and *ako* links a class (canary, box) to a super-class (bird, container). Both links are transitive — that is, they allow inferences like "If Tweetie is a canary and a canary is a kind of bird, then Tweetie is a bird." The *isa* and *ako* links permit propert inheritance, a form of inferencing whereby properties of a class or super-class are inherited by the subclass or instance. Given that Tweetie is a canary and canaries have the property 'yellow', an inference can be made that Tweetie has the property 'yellow'. The *connects* link is both transitive and commutative. If A connects B and B connects C, then we can infer that A connects C, C connects A, B connects A, and C connects B. The meaning of generic nodes (words like 'canary' that stand for a class of objects) can be interpreted in different ways, and we introduced two interpretations: sets ('canary' represents the set of individuals like Tweetie and friends, and is a subset of 'bird') and prototypes (a 'canary' is prototypically yellow and can sing).

6.4 Appendix: Inferences with a Semantic Net

A POP-11 library called **semnet** provides procedures for making inferences from items stored in the POP-11 database. For the procedures to work, the database must contain items in the form of triples, with the middle 'relation' item being a single word — for example,

```
[[the natural history museum] isa [museum]]
```

This is exactly the form that we have used for the examples in the previous chapters. The procedures names are the same as the normal database ones, plus an initial 's', and they perform in a similar manner. Certain key words, however, enable the inferences to be made; the ones that we shall be using in the examples are 'connects' and 'isa'. In this section we shall not make a distinction between *isa* and *ako* links, though often it is wise to do so, as properties of sets may not always also be properties of individuals. For example, while we know that there exist animals of both sexes, and that therefore there exist mammals and, after that, dogs of both sexes, we would not consequently want to deduce that Fido too is therefore of both sexes.

6.4.1 The connects Link

The standard procedure **present** cannot imitate our human intuition that, if X connects to Y, then Y also connects to X. The procedure **spresent**, however, can infer such commutative relations. For example, the Tourist Guide could answer a tourist's question, "What is near Madame Tussaud's," by constructing a query to the database of the form

```
present([?x near [madame tussauds]])
```

With the database containing the entry

```
[[the planetarium] near [madame tussauds]]
```

the call of **present** would return **<true>**. But the reverse query, "What is near the planetarium?" would produce **<false>**, unless the entry

```
[[madame tussauds] near [the planetarium]]
```

was explicitly put into the database. To save such duplication, we can instead form entries with the keyword **connects**. Thus, rather than the two entries above, we have the single item

```
[[the planetarium] connects [madame tussauds]]
```

You may think that this is a misuse of the word 'connects' to mean 'near', but the word is only a symbol used in the internal representation of the database. We might just as well have used 'cnncts' or 'xyzzy', providing that there is an appropriate translation from the internal form to a set of words that the human user (in this case our tourist) will understand.

The call of

```
present([?x connects [the planetarium]])
```

will still return **<false>**, since there is no matching entry, but a call of

```
spresent([?x connects [the planetarium]])
```

returns **<true>**. **spresent** acts *as if* the entry were explicitly in the database.

6.4.2   The isa Link

The new procedures are more powerful than the simple database ones, as we can now use them to carry out property inheritance via **isa** links. Given the following database,

```
[ [animal has skin]
  [bird isa animal]
  [bird can fly]
  [bird has wings]
  [canary isa bird]
  [canary can sing]
  [canary colour yellow]
  [tweetie isa canary]] -> database;
```

spresent can carry out inferences like

```
spresent([tweetie can fly])=>
** <true>
```

The **spresent** procedure works by recognizing the keyword **isa** in the the entries

```
[tweetie isa canary]
[canary isa bird]
```

and then associating the attributes of 'bird' with 'tweetie', as if the entry

```
[tweetie can fly]
```

was in the database.

The same kind of inference is also performed by **sallpresent**. just as **spresent** looks for single facts that are either in the database or that can be inferred from it, so **sallpresent** looks for collections of facts that are stored in, or can be inferred from, the database:

```
sallpresent([[tweetie has wings]
             [tweetie has skin]
             [tweetie can sing]]) =>
** <true>
```

For further examples, we shall use the property inheritance mechanism to work out the fare to any station from Victoria, given the fare zone of the station.

In order to work out the fare for a London Underground journey, we need to know certain facts. These are

1. London Underground stations are grouped into 'fare zones'.

2. The fare for a journey depends on how many fare zones you pass through on the journey.

3. If you are at Victoria, in Zone 1, and you want to go to a station in some other zone, the fare depends upon the zone you are going to.

4. Starting from Victoria (which is in Zone 1), the fare to any station in Zone 2 is 60 pence, and the fare to any (other) station in Zone 1 is 40 pence.

We can represent this by a database containing entries with fares for particular fare zones, and the fare zone for each station.

```
[[zone1 station] fare [40 pence]]
[[zone2 station] fare [60 pence]]
[[green park] isa [zone1 station]]
[[picadilly circus] isa [zone1 station]
  :
[[shepherds bush] isa [zone2 station]
[[goodge street] isa [zone2 station]]
[[brixton] isa [zone2 station]]
  :
```

Now we can ask, "Is the fare to Brixton 60 pence?" or in POP-11

```
spresent([[brixton] fare [60 pence]])=>
** <true>
```

In semantic network terms, the [brixton] node has inherited the 60 pence fare property from the [zone2 station] node. It is more likely that the tourist in London will want to ask something like "What is the fare to Brixton?" in which case the argument to spresent will be a pattern containing a variable:

```
vars fare;
spresent([[brixton] fare ?fare])=>
** <true>
```

The value of the variable is the required fare:

```
fare =>
** [60 pence]
```

Providing that the database entries are in the form of triples, with the connects and isa links where appropriate, then the Tourist Guide as it stands so far can be altered to carry out inferencing simply by substituting spresent for present and sallpresent for allpresent within the answer procedure.

6.5 Exercises

1. Figure 6.1 showed a very simple taxonomic tree for animals. Using a dictionary or encyclopedia if needed, try extending the tree to include 'platypus', 'iguana', and 'zebra'. What special problem is posed by trying to create a node for 'platypus' in the hierarchy? How might this be overcome? (Hint: Look again at the treatment of 'ostrich' in this chapter.)

2. In the second section of this chapter's appendix, we have shown how semantic networks can be represented as lists, and we have represented facts about Tweetie the Canary in this form. Complete the list representation of the ISA-hierarchy in figure 6.1 with facts about Percy the Platypus, Iggy the Iguana, and Ziggy the Zebra.

3. On page 179 we gave examples of syllogisms, and in figure 6.4 we showed how the set-theoretic interpretation of birds and canaries could be represented diagrammatically with circles. We might regard such a diagrammatic representation as a 'model' of facts given in syllogistic form. Draw similar diagrams to prove that the conclusions in the syllogisms below do not logically follow from the premises.

   (a) Premise 1: All who eat cream cakes get fat.
       Premise 2: Billy doesn't eat cream cakes.
       _____
       Conclusion: Billy isn't fat.

   (b) Premise 1: Anyone who studies AI is clever.
       Premise 2: Molly is clever.
       _____
       Conclusion: Molly studies AI.

4. Using the definition of **answer** in the appendix to this chapter, as a first model, try to write a procedure that, given your database of facts about animals, will answer questions such as

   Is a shark a fish?
   Does a zebra have gills?
   Can an iguana fly?

5. Suppose an impecunious tourist at Victoria wishes to know which tube stations can be reached for just 60 pence. You might imagine that one way for the Automated Tourist Guide to find out would be to use **spresent** as before, but this time inserting a variable in the place of the name of the station. For example, instead of

```
spresent([[brixton] fare 60]) =>
```

you might feel you could ask

```
spresent([[?station fare 60]) =>
```

However, when you then type in

```
station =>
```

you may be surprised by the answer:

```
** [zone 2]
```

Explain in detail why you get this response.

Chapter 7

Rule-Based Knowledge

7.1 Looking into the Black Box

In the present chapter, we shall describe the production system, which we introduced briefly in chapter 3, as a way of modelling human rule-based problem solving.
In particular, we shall look at how humans, and machines, can call on internal representations of task domains, in the form of production rules, to guide them towards
the solution to a problem, and on how they will act, at any step in a task, in specific
ways in response to specific conditions.

By way of example, consider how you might go about diagnosing a fault in your
hi-fi: you want to play a record, and you know that when you switch the power on,
a little red light appears on the amplifier; if the light is on and the tone-arm on the
record player does not respond to your pressing the button, you may know that it is
a good idea to check whether the lead between the record player and the amplifier
is properly connected; but on looking closely you notice that, in fact, the red light
has not come on, in which case it is a sensible idea to verify that the hi-fi is plugged
in; if it is not, you will do so, and try again; but if the hi-fi still does not work, you
know enough about electrical appliances and domestic electricity to suspect that a
fuse may have blown; and so on. At each step, you are invoking knowledge specific
to the domain, checking whether a certain condition holds and, if so, performing
the appropriate action. This kind of approach towards problem solving fits in well
with a view of humans as **information processing systems**, which we explain
more fully below, and contrasts with the state-space search procedures described
in chapter 4.

At the end of chapter 4 we pointed out that state-space analysis may not be the most appropriate way of solving, or describing, some kinds of problems. An alternative is to look at *why* people behave as they do, and to describe the mental states and cognitive processes of people engaged in problem-solving tasks. It is impossible to observe those mental states directly; indeed, as we mentioned in the introduction, behaviourism, for very many years the dominant movement in psychology, went so far as to deny that there were any such things as mental states, and proscribed all talk that seemed to refer to 'mentalistic' phenomena. But by the end of the 1950s there was active debate in psychology that ranged the behaviourists against a dissenting new generation of **cognitivists**, who maintained that it is possible to look into the 'black box' of the human mind, and that psychologists should be concerned with a person's internal representation of the world.[1]

The cognitivist view was not new, in spirit at least: Gestalt psychologists had earlier in the century sought to explain problem-solving behaviour in humans and animals by positing the existence of certain kinds of internal representation ('Gestalten'). Two factors that weakened their position were the lack of, on the one hand, a systematic technique for revealing the details of subjects' internal representations of the world and, on the other hand, an explanation for the relationship between cognition and action: how actions might be controlled by an organism's internalized image of its world. Renewed interest in cognitivism came at the end of the 1950s with the publication of papers by Newell, Shaw, and Simon (1958, 1963a), and of a seminal study by Miller, Galanter, and Pribram (1960). With them came the notions of **protocol analysis** and production systems, which together would provide mechanisms for eliciting subjects' internal representations and explanations of how these are linked to actual behaviour.

Miller and his co-researchers looked to the work of ethologists on instinctual behaviour in animals: an animal, it was argued, 'tests' to find whether a certain environmental condition holds and, if so, it performs the appropriate action. Different external conditions will trigger different associated responses of the form

if condition 1	then action 1
if condition 2	then action 2
if condition 3	then action 3
if condition 4	then action 4

---

[1]If you are interested in reading more about behaviourism, you might like to look at J. B. Watson's classic text, *Behaviorism* (1930), and at B. F. Skinner's more mature statement, *Science and Human Behavior* (1953). For some short critiques by cognitivists, you might like to look at Chomsky's classic "A Review of Verbal Behavior" (1959), and Dennett's "Skinner Skinned" (1978c).

Under this view of behaviour, there is no longer a problem of how cognition is related to behaviour: conditions and actions are paired together in such a way that, if the former is satisfied, the latter is automatically executed.

But humans do not just respond to the environment; they also devise **plans** for negotiating their way through the routine problems of everyday life. A plan is a program for behaviour that is triggered when certain conditions in the external environment are satisfied. For example, I have a plan for doing my shopping on a Saturday morning: picking up my cheque book, and walking to the shops if the weather is fine, taking the car if not. If walking, then I will need a sturdy shopping bag; otherwise I can just pack my shopping into the luggage compartment of the car. If driving, I will need to stop on the way at a service station if I need gas; go to the open market for fruit and vegetables, and the supermarket for pre-packaged goods; pack the bags at the supermarket checkout in such a way that the larger and heavier items are at the bottom, the smaller, lighter items at the top; and pay the cashier. Back home, I put the frozen items in the freezer, the perishable items in the refrigerator, the vegetables in the vegetable rack, and the rest in cupboards. But I do this with very little reflection; I do not need to re-plan my morning's activities each Saturday, since I have done it all so many times before. Thus I have a standard plan, or perhaps an interlinked group of plans, which 'as a rule' determine my behaviour. Such plans can be represented as condition-action rules, as above, or schematically as AND/OR trees and graphs. An AND/OR tree (or graph) is a way of representing solutions to problems by decomposing them into subsets of increasingly smaller problems. Arcs joined by curved ties link together AND nodes, and indicate that, in order to accomplish the goal in the parent node, each of the subgoals must be accomplished; arcs not so joined point to OR nodes, indicating that the goal in the parent node can be accomplished by accomplishing either of the subgoals. The difference between a tree and a graph is that each node of a tree has at most one parent node, while a node of a graph can have more than one parent. Figure 7.1 represents a fragment of the AND/OR tree that maps out my plan for Saturday morning shopping. A translation of the tree into English prose might begin along the following lines: "In order to go to do my shopping, I must either drive to the shops, OR walk AND take a strong shopping bag ... "

Complementing the contribution by psychologists, the computational metaphor of the human mind as a symbol-manipulating, information-processing system, pioneered by Newell and Simon, provided a way of talking about elusive internal cognitive structures and mechanisms and hence about the structure of human behaviour rather than about the structure of the problem alone. What was still needed was

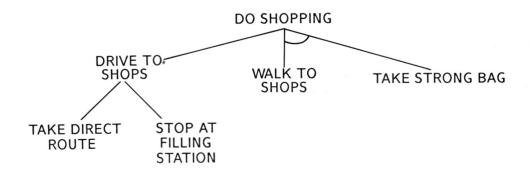

Figure 7.1
An AND/OR tree for a shopping plan.

some method of 'observing' human thought processes. Since they are not directly open to inspection, however, a less direct but still empirical method was required. One way, which we briefly mentioned in the last chapter, is to measure subjects' reaction time to stimuli. But it is also possible to study mental events by having subjects report what is going on in their minds during the performance of the task itself.

7.2   Protocol Analysis: Filling in the Black Box

We said at the end of chapter 4 that one factor which makes state space descriptions of problems inappropriate for subject-centred accounts of human problem solving is that, although we may be able to describe the state space of a problem independently of a human subject's attempts to solve it, the description alone cannot give us much of an indication of the subject's personal problem solving strategies. There is no way of predicting in advance the exact steps by which, for a novel task, a subject will proceed tentatively and thoughtfully towards a solution. Consider the puzzle shown in figure 7.2.

The state space for the problem is extremely large, corresponding to the set of all permissible tracings through the squares, but it is extremely unlikely that a human being would attempt to solve the problem by laboriously trying each possible path in turn until a word emerges. Rather, the person will draw on knowledge of English

Try the puzzle yourself now. While you are doing it, speak aloud what is going on in your mind. If you can stand the sound of your own voice, tape-record your thoughts as you solve the puzzle, and then afterwards replay the tape and try and work out what methods you used to solve the puzzle.

Figure 7.2
By moving up, down, sideways, or diagonally through the squares, order the letters to spell out a nine letter word.

spellings, fragments of words, and common prefixes and suffixes in order to try out various hypotheses. For instance, sequences of three consecutive consonants (unless the first is an S, which is not the case with the present puzzle) and sequences of vowels, such as -IOE-, -II-, and -EOI-, are atypical if not impossible in English; on the other hand, -ER and -TION are common suffixes and RE-, EN-, and NON- are common prefixes. Fragments like -TIND- and -DRIN- are neither inherently meaningful nor familiar sequences in the vocabulary of English, while -NINE and -REND- are. You should be able to solve the puzzle in a few minutes following this kind of reasoning, while a serial testing of all possible tracings would take very much longer. In the former case, however, you will not know exactly what your personal search tree looks like until, by working through the puzzle, you plot it out for yourself.

If you knew beforehand what your search tree for this kind of task looked like, you would, of course, be able to specify the kinds of information that constitute the knowledge states in the tree, together with the set of operations that allow you to move from one state to the next; and you could view your behaviour quite simply as a search within this space. Since these facts are unknown, how might you go about discovering them? Having discovered them, how might you go about representing them in such a way that a computer program might simulate human problem-solving activity?

Protocol analysis was developed by Allen Newell and Herbert Simon as a method of studying subjects' mental processes in the performance of tasks. It consists of having subjects say what is going on in their minds as they go about solving a problem. Their 'thinking aloud' is tape-recorded and later closely analyzed by the researcher. The analysis is a lengthy and complex process, since a protocol can run into hundreds of utterances. The researcher will break down the subject's protocol into what are taken to be the smallest, atomic, units of thought: discrete mental operations that cannot be further analyzed (or need not be for the purpose of understanding the subject's approach to the task). We shall from now on refer to these as **operators**. The application of an operator changes the problem state from one state of knowledge to the next. Taken together, the states and the operators applied to them constitute a **problem space**, and it is within this, rather than within a pre-given state space, that the search for a solution to a task or problem takes place. The problem space can be represented schematically by a **problem behaviour graph** (figure 7.3), a step-by-step reconstruction of the search, in which each node in the graph is a knowledge state (rather than, for example, a board position) and each directed link a mental operation (rather than a pre-defined legal move). At any moment the subject is viewed as being at some node in the problem behaviour graph, each node representing what the problem solver knows at that point, and each arrow representing a mental process that will put the problem solver in a new state of knowledge. Suppose that the problem is the one in figure 7.2. State1 will then correspond to the initial knowledge state of the subject faced with the puzzle; OP1 might be to look for a possible subpart of the word, leading to, say, the suffix -ER. The knowledge state has now changed, to state2. The subject may next look (OP2) for some sequence having a plausible syllable structure or meaning that will extend the word back from the suffix: say, -INNER (state3). It may be that the subject reasons into a 'blind alley' in which no further progress can be made (as is the case in the present puzzle); the subject may then give up on that line, and return to an earlier state of knowledge (state2) as a starting point for a new line of reasoning (state4), finding now (OP4) another possible extension back, -DINER (state5). This too is a blind alley; the correct solution is given at the end of the chapter.

It is unlikely that a subject uses a unique operator for each new problem state. We can assume that people do not possess an indefinitely large number of distinct mental operations for finding their way through a lifetime of everyday situations. The researcher will therefore look next for recurrences of similar operations (in this

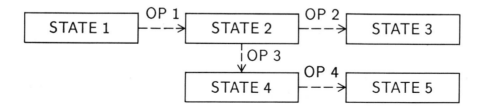

Figure 7.3
A problem behaviour graph.

example, ones like 'find a plausible suffix that has not already been tried') and assume these to be repeated uses of the same operator. Eventually, the researcher should be able to abstract from the subject's protocol a small number of distinct operators, some used more than once, that are sufficient to account for progress from the statement of the initial problem or task to its solution.

A good verbal protocol will allow a researcher to abstract a theory of how a subject went about solving the problem; the theory may then be viewed as a model of the problem solver's activities in tackling a task, and can be translated into a computer program. In this sense, Newell and Simon claim, "the theory performs the task it explains':

> A good information processing theory of a good human chess player can play good chess; a good theory of how humans create novels will create novels; a good theory of how children read will likewise read and understand. (Newell and Simon, 1972, pp. 10–11)

We shall have more to say about protocol analysis, and the use of production rules for the modelling of human problem solving, in the next chapter, but for the present we shall take up Newell and Simon's claim above, by sketching out the architecture of a production system, pointing out along the way some of the important features in its design, and illustrating through a series of examples of production rules how a theory about rule-based reasoning can be translated into programs. Finally, we shall describe how you might implement your own production system as part of the Automated Tourist Guide.

7.3 Production Systems: Simulating the Black Box

We have shown how subjects may solve problems by examining the current problem state and then choosing an appropriate and applicable rule to transform that state into a new state in the search for a solution. A production system is a means of codifying this rule-based knowledge. It has three major components that are analogous to the knowledge states, mental operations, and decision-making of the human problem solver:

1. a database of facts called the **working memory**,

2. a set of production rules, called the **rulebase**, that operate on those facts, and

3. a program called the **production system interpreter** that decides which rule to use in a particular problem state.

7.3.1 The Working Memory

The contents of the working memory represent what the system 'knows' about the problem at any one moment. At the start, this is the initial knowledge state, which is transformed into a new state each time an operator (production rule) is applied. At its simplest, working memory can be represented as a simple database of facts — for example,

```
[birdcage is open]
[tweetie is in birdcage]
[sylvester is in room]
```

At any one time the size of working memory is usually very small, just as the number of distinct items that the human mind can hold in short-term memory is small.

7.3.2 The Rulebase

The rulebase contains the system's equivalent of what we have previously called 'operators', the IF-THEN operations that change states of knowledge. In a production system, they are called production rules, or simply 'productions', the conditions (the IF part) sometimes being referred to as the **rule head** and the actions (the

THEN part) as the **rule body**. Although looking superficially like 'if ... then' statements in a programming language, they operate in a different manner. Each rule represents an independent 'chunk' of knowledge which can be initiated, or fired, when the entire condition matches items in working memory. Once the rule is fired, its actions are carried out, which usually (but not always) involves removing facts that are no longer true from working memory and adding new facts that have become true. A typical rule for the working memory given above might be informally written as

```
Rule 31
condition:
        [birdcage is open] and
        [tweetie is in birdcage] and
        [sylvester is in room]
action:
        remove: [birdcage is open]
        add: [birdcage is closed]
```

Translated into more natural English it reads, "If ever you discover that Tweetie's cage is open while Sylvester is in the room, and that Tweetie is still in his cage, then close the cage." That is, remove the fact that the [birdcage is open] and add the fact that the [birdcage is closed]. Firing the rule will change the database in such a way that the contents of working memory become

```
[birdcage is closed]
[tweetie is in birdcage]
[sylvester is in room]
```

In this example the actions to be taken on satisfying the conditions are simply to add facts to and remove facts from the database. This need not always be so; in other circumstances the actions might be of the form "Print this message to the terminal" or "Read what the user types on the terminal and add it to the database in some form"; or may just contain the instruction 'stop'. For example, an automated drink dispenser might use rules such as

Rule 1
condition:
        [user inserts coins]
action:
        print: "Would you like tea or coffee?"
        read: [RESPONSE]
        remove: [user inserts coins]
        add: [user wants RESPONSE]

Rule 2
condition:
        [user wants coffee]
action:
        print: "How would you like your coffee: black or white?"
        read: [RESPONSE]
        remove: [user wants coffee]
        add: [user wants RESPONSE coffee]

The capitalized RESPONSE in each rule would be a variable local to the production rule in which it is elicited. We shall see further examples of actions of this kind that permit interaction with the user, and use variables in rules, in our Automated Tourist Guide in the next section.

Production rules are unordered, in that irrespective of the order in which they are physically written into the production system rulebase (and hence the order in which they would appear, for example, on the printed page), the sequence in which they are used will depend on the current state of the working memory. (By way of analogy, think of how you might look for definitions in a dictionary or encyclopedia. Suppose the word you start with is 'dugong': the definition contains further unknown words, which in turn you look up under their alphabetical listings, and so on. Your search is guided by your current state of knowledge at each moment, in such a way that you move back and forth from one entry to another, and not serially from A to Z.) If more than one rule is **triggered** (its head matches the database), a **conflict resolution strategy** is used to decide which rule is to be fired. Three types of conflict resolution strategy are listed in the next section.

In certain production systems — for example, Waterman's PAS II system for doing addition, or Newell's PSG system, used to test psychological theories about human memory and recall — rule order *can* be important, and the rules are tried in the order in which they are written into the rulebase, so that conflict between rules does not arise.

7.3.3 The Production System Interpreter

The third component of a production system, the production system interpreter, is the program that applies the rules. It repeatedly performs the following steps:

1. **Match**: find the rules whose conditions are satisfied by the current contents of working memory.

2. **Conflict resolution**: decide which rule to use. If the condition part of none of the productions is satisfied, then halt the interpreter.

3. **Act**: perform the actions in the rule's body.

4. Go to step 1.

The cycle is usually repeated until either no rule can be found whose condition part is true — that is, whose head matches the database — or some rule is fired which has the action part 'stop'.

If more than one rule is triggered, then the interpreter will have to decide which of them it will fire. The choice of conflict resolution strategy may well depend on the nature of the task for which the particular system is being used. Three examples of possible conflict resolution strategies are

1. To select the first rule in the rulebase that matches the contents of the database. We might further stipulate that after it has been fired once, the same rule cannot be used again.

2. To use that rule amongst those triggered whose conditions for firing include all those of another plus some further conditions, on the grounds that it is more specialized. For example, there is little point in applying suntan lotion if you are still wearing your street clothes:

> Rule 1
> condition:
>   [temperature in sun hot]
> action:
>   add: [apply suntan lotion]

Rule 2
condition:
        [temperature in sun hot] and
        [clothes on] and
        [swimsuit off]
action:
        remove: [clothes on]
        remove: [swimsuit off]
        add: [clothes off]
        add: [swimsuit on]

3. To give priority to special case rules over more generally applicable rules. It may happen, perhaps, that two rule heads can be matched to the working memory, one fully specified and the other containing variables which might match a number of patterns. In this case the more specific rule would be applied first. Even when both rule heads are fully specified, one may be more general than the other. Consider, for example, rules 1 and 3 where rule 3 covers the more specific case of the sun being too hot for sunbathing:

Rule 1
condition:
        [temperature in sun hot]
action
        add: [apply suntan lotion]

Rule 3
condition:
        [temperature in sun greater than 100]
action:
        add: [stay in the shade]

7.4 Production Systems and Artificial Intelligence

Quite apart from their cognitive plausibility, production systems have advantages over conventional programming languages that make them ideal for task domains in which knowledge may change or grow over time, and in which the initial problem state and final solution state may differ from user to user: they are flexible, modular, and plausible.

7.4.1 Production Systems Are Flexible

Production systems use the same basic IF-THEN format to represent knowledge in very different domains. An informal Automated Tourist Guide rule, for example, expresses a very different content from the rules, given earlier, for closing Tweetie's cage or for applying suntan lotion:

```
rule centre_theatre
condition:
        [entertainment type theatre] and
        [entertainment place centre]
action:
        add: [location piccadilly circus]
```

Yet all three rules have the same underlying form: whether its function is to infer conclusions from premises or to perform actions in response to given circumstances, in each case the 'condition' side of the rule is matched against working memory and, if the match succeeds, the action specified in the rule body is executed.

7.4.2 Production Systems Are Modular

In an ordinary computer program one procedure calls another, in such a way that a change to one procedure may entail the modification of any others that call it. Simply removing a procedure may well result in the collapse of the whole program. In contrast, the functional units of a production system — the set of rules in its rulebase — are independent, self-contained chunks of knowledge, any one of which can be altered or replaced without disabling the entire production system and without requiring the modification of other rules. Such alterations might modify or restrict the behaviour of the system, but will not cripple it. This is because the rules in a production system are separate from the program that runs them: the rules do not interact with one another directly but only through changes to the working memory. By way of illustration, figure 7.4 contrasts the *flow of control* in an ordinary program with that of a production system. Modularity is especially important in large production systems; as knowledge of a domain is modified or extended, new rules can be added in a fairly straightforward manner. Failure of a system to perform some primitive action or draw some inference can be remedied

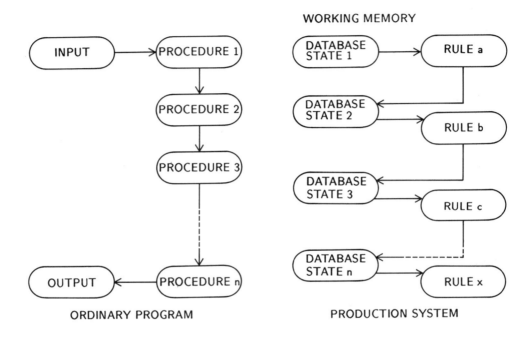

Figure 7.4
Flow of control in ordinary programs and production systems.

simply by writing a new rule whose head matches the relevant items in the database and whose body executes the appropriate action.

The most important development in production systems has been in the building of expert systems: computer programs that have the knowledge and expertise, in the form of hundreds or even thousands of rules, that will enable them to operate at the level of the human expert in some specialist domain. This makes them valuable as consultants in medicine, management, engineering, computer-system configuration, and chemical analysis, to name but a few areas where expert systems are in regular use. Such systems provide the support of expert knowledge that is relatively cheap (a full-time human consultant commands a much higher salary!), reliable (humans do make mistakes), portable (human experts are scarce, and sometimes too busy to come on call), and untiring (human experts have to sleep sometimes; eventually they die); and, because of the modularity of such systems, they can be extended to become more proficient than any human expert whose knowledge has been 'written into' the rulebase. Expert systems need not store information uniquely in the form of production rules. For example, the PROSPECTOR system to analyze geological data codes much of its knowledge in a semantic net; other systems have used frames or a form of predicate logic.

7.4.3 Production Systems Are Plausible

Human experts do not simply apply their knowledge to problems; they can also explain exactly why they have made a decision or reached a particular conclusion. This facility is also built into the expert systems that simulate human expert performance: they can be interrogated at any moment and asked, for example, to display the rule they have just used or to account for their reasons in using that rule. That a system is able to explain its reasoning is in itself no guarantee that the human user will understand the explanation: if the advice is to be of use, it is important that the system be able to justify its reasoning process in a cognitively plausible manner, by working through a problem in much the same way as a human expert would. Production systems, and the more sophisticated expert systems, can be made to reason either forwards, from initial evidence towards a conclusion, or backwards, from a hypothesis to the uncovering of the right kind of evidence that would support that hypothesis, or by a combination of the two. One significant factor which will determine whether a system will use forward or backward reasoning is the method used by the human expert.

If all the necessary data are either pre-given or can be gathered, and if it is possible to state precisely what is to be done in any particular set of circumstances, then it is more natural and likely that a human being — and hence any machine modelling human performance — would work forward from the data towards a solution. An expert system which reasons forward in this way is R1, which configures DEC-VAX computer systems. R1 reasons forward until a single good system configuration is found (others may be possible, but are not considered so long as one good solution is found). Medical diagnosis, on the other hand, normally proceeds abductively from a patient's symptoms back to the possible causes of the illness, and hence to an appropriate course of treatment. This was a crucial factor in the design of, for example, MYCIN, a system that diagnoses blood infections. MYCIN is a moderately large expert system, having around 450 rules, of which the following is typical. (The rule is shown in its English form, which is used by MYCIN to generate explanations to the user. For reasoning, the system calls on rules coded in an extension of the LISP programming language.)

IF: 1) THE STAIN OF THE ORGANISM IS GRAMNEG AND
           2) THE MORPHOLOGY OF THE ORGANISM IS ROD AND
           3) THE AEROBICITY OF THE ORGANISM IS AEROBIC

THEN: THERE IS STRONGLY SUGGESTIVE EVIDENCE (0.8)
           THAT THE CLASS OF THE ORGANISM IS
           ENTEROBACTERIACEAE

You will notice that in the 'actions' part of the MYCIN rule, the certainty of the conclusion is not absolute: it is simply a hypothesis or estimate supported by the premises stated in the conditions. The parenthesized number represents the degree of certainty of the inference made by the rule: if evidence is found that satisfies the premises, then there is a (0.8) likelihood that the hypothesis is correct (a likelihood of 1.0 being absolute certainty). Being able to use statistical and probabilistic reasoning in this manner is important in real-world situations where, for example, there is some factor of randomness in the situation itself, or where we do not have access to sufficient data to be able to know with any real certainty that our conclusions are correct. Medical diagnosis is a clear instance of such a class of problems: a complex domain in which medical knowledge is incomplete, and in which the diagnostician may not have all the data needed. Often, inexact reasoning is necessary if the doctor is to make any diagnosis at all. Various methods exist for estimating the certainty of conclusions: Bayes' theorem for calculating probabilities (used by PROSPECTOR), Zadeh's fuzzy logic, and Shortliffe's scheme based on measures of 'belief' and 'disbelief', which is used in MYCIN. Values attached to rules can be passed on to further rules, and combined in various ways with other values, so as to produce final values for conclusions. For a highly readable overview of MYCIN and other expert systems, you might like to look at Feigenbaum and McCorduck (1984). Rich (1983) and Charniak and McDermott (1985) give more technical accounts of statistical and probabilistic reasoning.

7.5   Conclusion

In this chapter we described the production system as a method of modelling human problem solving. When trying to solve everyday problems, people may respond to an external condition with appropirate actions; they also form plans to guide their behaviour. One way to uncover a person's problem-solving strategies is to collect a protocol: the problem solver's own account of thoughts and intentions, spoken while solving the problem. From these 'think aloud' protocols, the researcher tries to construct a problem space consisting of the person's states of knowledge and the operators needed to move from one state to another. A production system is one means of encoding a problem space, in a form that can be run on a computer. It has three main components: a database, called the working memory, that represents a person's current state of knowledge; a set of production rules that operate on the working memory; and an interpreter that decides which rule to fire in a particular state. Production systems have certain advantages — flexibility, modularity, and cognitive plausibility — over conventional computer programs that make them suitable for use in expert systems: programs that simulate the performance of human experts.

Note that the word formed by the nine letters of the puzzle in figure 7.2 is 'rendition'.

7.6 Appendix: Production Rules

POP-11 has a production system called PRODSYS, with rules of the form

```
rule <name/number> [ <condition> ] ;
     <action> ;
     <action> ;
     ...
endrule;
```

Their appearance is similar to those we presented earlier in our more informal notation. Here are two of the earlier rules, rewritten in PRODSYS form:

```
rule 31 [birdcage is open] [tweetie is in birdcage]
     [sylvester is in room];
     remove([birdcage is open]);
     add([birdcage is closed]);
endrule;
```

```
rule get_drink [user inserts coin];
    vars response;
    [Would you like tea or coffee?]  =>>
    readline() -> response;
    remove([user inserts coins]);
    add([user wants ^^response]);
endrule;
```

Like a POP-11 procedure definition, a rule has a header line, which determines the circumstances in which it will be used, followed by a body containing some POP-11 code specifying what is to be done when the rule is invoked. Also, like a POP-11 procedure, it has a pair of terms — **rule** and **endrule** — which mark the beginning and end of the rule. The header line represents the condition part of the rule, and the commands between the header line and **endrule** represent the actions to be carried out if the rule is fired. Working memory is the standard POP-11 database, and the patterns in the condition are matched, using the standard POP-11 matcher, against items in the database. **rule 31**, for example, will be available for use if there are three items in the database which match:

```
[birdcage is open]
[tweetie is in birdcage]
[sylvester is in room]
```

PRODSYS uses a very simple conflict resolution strategy: rules are tried one by one in the order in which they were loaded, i.e., reading from the beginning to the end of the rulebase. This means that the same rule could be used on more than one occasion. If the built-in variable **repeating** is set to false, however, the system will not trigger the same rule on the same database items twice.

So far, all the rules we have seen in this appendix contain completely specified conditions and actions; we can, however, use variables to make the rules more general. Consider rule 7:

```
rule 7 [take umbrella] [sun shining];
    remove([take umbrella]);
    add([wear sunglasses]);
endrule;
```

It says in effect that if the sun is shining and you are carrying an umbrella, put it down and put on your sunglasses. Suppose we generalize the rule to say that, whatever you are carrying, if the sun is shining, all you need to take with you is a bucket and spade:

```
rule 4 [take ??x] [sun shining];
      remove([take ^^x]);
      add([take bucket and spade]);
endrule;
```

Given the database

```
[[take umbrella] [sun shining]]
```

`rule 4` will fire, changing the database to

```
[[take bucket and spade] [sun shining]]
```

What will happen next? Unless the control variable `repeating` is set to `<false>`, `rule 4` will be triggered and fired again, since the pattern `[take ??x]` will still match the fact `[take bucket and spade]`.

Consequently, the same rule will continue firing forever, unless the program is interrupted. The moral is that you should be cautious in the design of your rulebase (if using variables in your rules, it is wise to avoid, if possible, an action whose result might be matched against a condition in the same rule). `repeating` should be set to `<false>` if there is a risk of the same rule being fired repeatedly in a never-ending cycle.

7.6.1   Using a Production System in the Automated Tourist Guide

Since production rules are useful for representing human rule-based knowledge, an example related to the Automated Tourist Guide might be a What's-On Guide to London. The 'action' part of some of the production rules can prompt the user for information about, for example, preferred kinds of entertainment and the area to visit. Applying the rules will deduce suitable events. To begin with the working memory must indicate that the system knows neither the type of entertainment the user might want nor the area of London:

```
[ [entertainment type unknown]
  [entertainment place unknown]] -> database;
```

The rule `find_type` (which, being the first to be loaded and given the conflict resolution strategy already described, will be the first that is fired by the database) will establish what type of entertainment the tourist wishes. The only acceptable responses to the rule as given below are 'cinema' and 'theatre', though of course the rulebase could be enlarged and modified to allow other options, such as pubs, parks, or nightclubs:

```
rule find_type [entertainment type unknown];
     vars ent_type;
     [What type of entertainment would you like:
      cinema or theatre?]  =>>
     readline() -> ent_type;
     remove([entertainment type unknown]);
     add([entertainment type ^^ent_type]);
endrule;
```

Having established the type of entertainment the tourist is seeking, the system next finds out the desired location:

```
rule find_place [entertainment place unknown];
     vars place;
     [Where do you want to go in the city:
      centre or suburbs?]  =>>
     readline() -> place;
     remove([entertainment place unknown]);
     add([entertainment place ^^place]);
endrule;
```

A good place for looking for theatres in the centre of London is in the environs of Piccadilly Circus:

```
rule centre_theatre [entertainment type theatre]
     [entertainment place centre];
     add([location piccadilly circus]);
endrule;
```

Alternatively, if the tourist has indicated a wish to go to the cinema, then Leicester Square is a good place to start:

```
    rule centre_cinema [entertainment type cinema]
        [entertainment place centre];
        add([location leicester square]);
    endrule;
```

Whichever the city centre location, the tourist now needs to know how to get there:

```
    rule suggest_centre [location ??x];
        [I suggest you take the underground to ^^x
        and look around] =>>
    endrule;
```

If, on the other hand, the tourist has expressed a preference for the suburbs (irrespective of whether or not cinema or theatre has been asked for), then the following rule is fired:

```
    rule suggest_suburbs [entertainment place suburbs];
        [I suggest you look at the entertainments
            section of the London Standard] =>>
    endrule;
```

The production system can then be run by calling the procedure **run**:

```
    run();
    What type of entertainment would you like :  cinema or
    theatre ?
    ?  cinema
    Where do you want to go in the city :  centre or suburbs ?
    ?  centre
    I suggest you take the underground to leicester square and
    look around
```

The production system can then be incorporated into the Automated Tourist Guide. The system should be initially triggered by a tourist's query, such as, "What entertainments are there in London?" The **answer** procedure needs to be altered to match the query and run the production system. It should look something like this:

```
define answer(query) -> response;
  if query matches [what == entertainments ==] then
    [[entertainment type unknown]
     [entertainment place unknown]] -> database;
    run();
    flush([entertainment ==]);
    [Consultation finished] -> response;
    ...
  else
      [i cannot answer that] -> response;
  endif;
enddefine;
```

Now, whenever the user asks an appropriate question, the database will be loaded with the initial content of working memory, and the production system will be set in action. Since the system relies on the POP-11 database, which is already full of facts about London, then, to avoid confusion, all the items added by the production system begin with [entertainment ...]. The flush command acts like remove but remove *all* the items in the database that match the pattern, in this case all the items added by the production system.

7.7   Exercises

1. Think of some simple task or goal involving up to 6 steps, such as the 'shopping trip' described on page 201, and draw and annotate an AND/OR tree for it. Here are some suggestions:

   stacking a pile of different size blocks
   eating a pizza
   acquiring a bicycle (by any means!)
   opening a bank account

2. Using as a model the rules schematized in the chapter, write a set of POP-11 style production rules for holidaying on the beach in Florida (where it does, sometimes, rain!). Let your initial database have you, for example, sitting in your hotel room with the sun shining brightly outside.

3. Explain what the following rule does:

```
rule 1 [temperature in sun is ?val];
    add([apply suntan lotion screening factor
         ^(val/10)]);
endrule;
```

How would you stop this rule repeating? The calculation probably works plausibly for temperatures between about 80 and 100 degrees Fahrenheit; but is ludicrously wrong for temperatures lower than that. How would you modify the calculation?

4. In a POP-11 production rule, the action part typically contains a **remove** list and an **add** list. Suppose we wished to streamline the rule by simply having a command **changes**, which made the appropriate changes to the database. Define a procedure for updating the database

```
changes(Old_Fact, New_Fact)
```

but without using, in the body of the procedure, the commands **add** and **remove**.

Chapter 8

Models of Cognition

The previous chapters have formed a progression, from programs that at first sight *appear* intelligent, but are driven by simple pattern matching, to ones which store and process symbolic representations of knowledge. Whether in the form of search spaces, semantic nets, or production rules, this stored knowledge has been **competence knowledge**: what a person *ought* to know about some subject, or how an expert *should* perform, rather than what any one person actually *does* know and do. In this chapter we shall consider some of the qualities and limitations of the human mind, and look at some models of human cognition that can account for individual differences in performance.

8.1   Building Minds

Computer programs can now play chess at better than club tournament level. The Eurisko program (Lenat, 1983) beat human competitors for two years running to win a United States national tournament to design battle fleets for a space warfare game. The MYCIN medical expert system performed better than Stanford doctors in diagnosing bacterial infections of the blood. Yet no program has been written with the general intelligence, learning ability, and range of language of a two-year-old child.

Most of the successes of AI have been in building programs to match or beat human performance on a carefully defined and restricted task, and even within these limits they are not intended as accurate models of human cognition. In tuning such programs to their tasks the designers have used heuristics, programming techniques, and representation schemes that seem to have no parallel in the human mind. Chess playing programs, for example, search and evaluate a large number of possible board states for each move; the size and speed of this search is far greater than that of a human player. But studies of human chess experts show that they choose a move not by searching a large space of possible moves, but by recalling previously remembered groupings of pieces (Simon and Gilmartin, 1973, estimate that chess masters have learned some 50,000 different patterns of chess pieces) and by a detailed comparison of the few most promising strategies.

For some tasks, such as winning games of chess, it may be acceptable to design non-human intelligences, but generally there are good reasons to create more accurate models of the human mind. (Even chess playing programs could benefit from more human strategies. Good players find them frustrating, at times producing an unbeatable series of moves, and at other times making elementary mistakes.) A computer must communicate on human terms. It is not enough for a medical expert system simply to offer a diagnosis; the user, normally a qualified doctor, will want some justification, particularly if in disagreement with its decision; so its explanation needs to be presented in a form that corresponds to the doctor's own thinking. For expert systems, then, the aim is to reproduce the reasoning and explanations of an expert problem solver and teacher, the more accomplished the better. Methods of acquiring and modelling this competence knowledge have been the main concern of this book so far.

But if, instead of packaging expertise, we want to discover the full range of human cognition, then our models need to reproduce both the qualities and the limitations of the human mind. Some of the more important ones are listed below.

Before reading on, try and list some of the general limitations of the human mind — restrictions on memory, for example. Some of them can be overcome by training, but some seem to be an inevitable consequence of 'being human' and so might not apply to 'non-human intelligences'. Are any of these limitations useful (for example, in coping with stress)?

8.1.1 Qualities of the Human Mind

Flexibility When faced with a new type of problem the human mind does not give up, but can conjure up possible solutions out of commonsense knowledge.

Learning From a jumble of visual impressions a baby rapidly learns to distinguish complex and changing objects like faces and bodies; a little later it acquires a language out of the grunts and noises it hears. Later still the child passes through the stages of cognitive development described by Piaget (Boden, 1979) and other developmental psychologists. An accurate model of learning must describe the learning that takes place within each stage of development, including the acquisition of skills and expertise, and be able to account for the transition from one stage to the next.

Graceful degradation If the mind is impaired by fatigue, distractions, or brain damage, it does not simply stop working, but finds ways to cope by, for example, taking longer to solve a problem, reducing the accuracy of the solution, or reducing the frequency of success. Similarly, if it receives an unexpected input, then the mind tries to cope by reinterpreting it, or modifying strategies, or asking for help.

Generative power Minds are not confined to repeating old information, but can generate an unlimited number of, for example, meaningful sentences, correct arithmetic expressions, or tuneful pieces of music.

Parallelism We can perform two or sometimes more activities simultaneously, such as singing while dancing, or talking while driving a car.

8.1.2 Limitations of the Human Mind

Short term memory span We can hold around seven new items in conscious attention. For example, given a random seven-digit number, a person can generally repeat it back exactly a few minutes later, but the recall will rapidly get worse as the number of digits to remember increases. A strange aspect of short term memory is that an 'item' is a single chunk of meaning, so that people can equally well remember seven random letters, or seven series of letters, providing the series form meaningful words. People *can* learn to remember longer strings of random elements by mentally attaching them to meaningful items (mnemonics).

Brain speed Compared to a computer, the human brain works very slowly. A good computer can perform one basic operation every nanosecond (10^{-9} second), whereas neurons (human brain cells) operate at times measured in milliseconds (10^{-3} second). Assuming that a neuron carries out a function roughly equivalent to a single computer instruction (a big assumption, but from what we know of neural activity it cannot be *more* complex), it follows that the brain works about 1 million times slower than a computer. The only conclusion we can reach is that, unlike a computer, the brain must carry out many different computations simultaneously in order to give the *overall* performance it does.

Sloppiness Humans are bad at following rules accurately. They suffer from lapses of concentration, take mental short-cuts, and forget or change rules. It seems that evolution has selected minds that are flexible rather than thorough. It may even be that controlled sloppiness is an important part of creativity. An accurate cognitive model must be sloppy in the same way as a human, making the same type of slips and lapses.

A study of human error may lead not only to a better understanding of the mind but also towards AI programs that can cope with a wide range of everyday problems. For example, the only way a person can survive in a complex and fast moving environment, such as when driving a car or teaching a classroom of children, is by selectively ignoring most sensory data — sights, sounds, smells — to concentrate on the important ones, and by employing imaginative heuristics to find quick, ready solutions to everyday problems. As Aaron Sloman points out in the foreword to this book, such 'productive laziness' may cause errors, of over-generalization, prejudice, and the like, but it is also one of the major motivations for scientific research, as well as an important way of coping with the demands of life.

8.2   Computer Models of Mind

Creating a working model of the human mind is a grand intellectual challenge. A complete model would have to account for substantially different types of activity, such as hand-eye coordination, speech, and reasoning; it would accept sensory data from a rapidly changing environment and would learn from experience; and it would make the same kind of errors and creative leaps as human thinkers.

Although we are far from that goal, there are some tentative theories of the 'cognitive architecture' of the human mind. This section sketches two very different models: one employs production rules and the other a **connectionist network** of simple distributed processors. For each model we shall begin with a practical example and then describe the general approach.

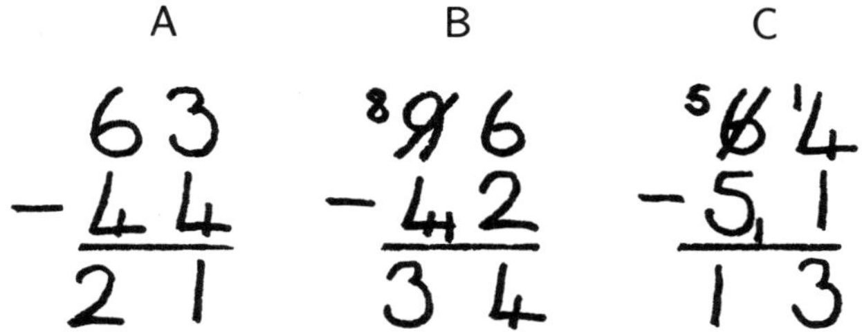

A   B   C

$$
\begin{array}{r}
63 \\
-44 \\
\hline
21
\end{array}
\qquad
\begin{array}{r}
{}^{8}\!\!\not{9}6 \\
-42 \\
\hline
34
\end{array}
\qquad
\begin{array}{r}
{}^{5}\!\!\not{6}\,{}^{1}\!4 \\
-5\,1 \\
\hline
13
\end{array}
$$

Figure 8.1
Subtraction sums with errors.

8.2.1   Errors in Children's Subtraction

Some of the arithmetic errors made by children are due to carelessness or a lack of concentration, but many result from a child carefully carrying out an arithmetic process, but following the wrong set of rules. Young and O'Shea (1982) have produced a model of children's subtraction that accounts for over two-thirds of such rule-governed subtraction errors (from an analysis of 1,500 subtraction sums done by 10-year-old children). Subtraction is taught in school mainly by one of two methods — 'decomposition' and 'equal addition'. In both methods the columns are processed from right to left, but they differ in the way 'borrowing' is carried out. In decomposition, when borrowing to the units column the top number in the tens column is decreased by 1; in equal addition the bottom number is increased by 1. The examples are all from children taught the decomposition method. Figure **??** shows some of the children's errors, taken from the paper. A is an example of a very common error, where the child always subtracts the smaller number from the larger in a column (in this case subtracting 3 from 4 in the units column, producing 1 as a result). Example B is the opposite case, where the child ought not to borrow, but does. The child deals with the problem of subtracting 2 from 16 by carrying over 10 into the tens column as if it were an addition sum. In example C the child has also mistakenly borrowed and carried over a 10. But in the tens column the bottom number is greater than the top, so the child just subtracts the smaller, 5, from the larger, 6, coincidentally getting the right answer.

The basis of Young and O'Sheas's model is a set of production rules. Figure **??** shows the complete set of rules, adapted from Young and O'Shea, to carry out correct subtraction. The rules are written in the same format as those in chapter 7, except that they are laid out in columns to make them easier to compare. The

CONDITION	ACTION
rule ac [Result 1 X]	add:[Result X] *Carry
rule b2c [TOP equals BOTTOM]	add:[NextColumn] add:[Result 0]
rule done [NoMore]	*Halt
rule wa [Result X]	*Write X
rule ts [FindDiff]	*TakeAbsDiff
rule nxt [NextColumn]	add:[ProcessColumn] *ShiftLeft
rule in [ProcessColumn]	*ReadTopandBottom
rule cm [Top TOP][Bottom BOTTOM]	*Compare
rule bs2 [Borrow]	*Decrement
rule bs1 [Borrow]	*AddTenToM
rule b2a [BOTTOM greater TOP]	add:[Borrow]
rule fd [Top TOP][Bottom BOTTOM]	add:[NextColumn] add:[FindDiff]

Figure 8.2
A set of production rules to model children's subtraction.

rule name, followed by the condition, is on the left side, and the actions to be taken when the rule fires on the right.[1] Variables, such as TOP and BOTTOM, are in uppercase. For the rule to fire, the condition must match an item in working memory. The initial content of working memory is

[ProcessColumn]

Some of the conditions represent states of the subtraction sum (for example, [BOTTOM greater TOP] can fire if the bottom number in the column under inspection is greater than the top number); others represent the child's goals, such as [ProcessColumn]. Those actions marked with a star are procedures to carry out operations like comparing two numbers or shifting attention to the next column of figures. For the purpose of this example these procedures are assumed to be 'primitive' mental operations; that is, they are not decomposable into sets of production rules. Some of them do, however, affect working memory: for example, *ShiftLeft adds NoMore to memory when the last column is reached.

In English, the rule fd says, "Once the top and bottom number in a column are known, then the action is to place into working memory symbols representing the

---

[1] The format is slightly different from that in the Young and O'Shea paper, the main differences being that the actions in the Young and O'Shea production system are read from right to left, and the ordering of the rules is altered to allow for the conflict resolution strategy described below.

two goals of finding the difference between two numbers and then moving to the next column." The other rules can similarly be translated into recognizable sub-parts of the subtraction process (with the exception of rule ac, which is part of the child's rule set for addition — rules for the different areas of arithmetic may well overlap in a child's mind, and the ac rule copes with the carry problem of example B).

So, given the first problem in figure 8.1 (63 − 44), the rule in would fire. The action part carries out the operation ReadTopandBottom, which loads [Top 3] and then [Bottom 4] into working memory. Since each new item is added to the front, working memory is now

   [Bottom 4][Top 3][ProcessColumn]

Rules fd and cm are now triggered, as well as in.

The conflict resolution strategy is to ignore a rule that has already fired for a particular item in working memory, and otherwise choose the most recent rule (the one at the top of the list); so cm fires and the *Compare procedure is called, which represents the child comparing two numbers. The procedure places [Bottom greater Top] at the front of working memory. Figure 8.3 shows the behaviour of the production system for the first few firings. The subtraction continues until [NoMore] is added to working memory and the system halts.

Figure 8.3 shows the behaviour of the production system for the units column: comparing the top and bottom number, borrowing, and writing out the result, 9. Try and continue the process, working through the rules for the tens column to convince yourself that the production system produces the correct answer.

The beauty of this set of rules is that it not only models the process of Subtraction by Decomposition but, by making slight modifications to the rule set, it can also model Subtraction by Equal Addition, and it can generate children's systematic errors. For example, if we take out the rule b2a, then the rules still operate, but they produce errors of the type shown in figure 8.1, example A. The reason is easy to see: removing b2A means that the borrowing rules bs1 and bs2 are never fired, so the rule ts steps in to subtract the smaller Top digit from the larger Bottom one. Young and O'Shea describe other simple modifications to the rules to generate most of the errors made by their sample 10-year-old children.

WORKING MEMORY	RULE FIRED	ACTION
[ProcessColumn]	in	*ReadTopandBottom
[Bottom 4][Top 3][ProcessColumn]	cm	*Compare
[Bottom greater Top][Bottom 4] [Top 3][ProcessColumn]	b2a	add:[Borrow]
[Borrow][Bottom greater Top] [Bottom 4][Top 3][ProcessColumn]	bs1	*AddTenToTop
[Borrow][Bottom greater Top] [Bottom 4][Top 13][ProcessColumn]	bs2	*Decrement
[Borrow][Bottom greater Top] [Bottom 4][Top 13][ProcessColumn]	fd	add:[NextColumn] add:[FindDiff]
[FindDiff][NextColumn][Borrow] [Bottom greater Top][Bottom 4] [Top 13][ProcessColumn]	ts	*TakeAbsDiff
[Result 9][FindDiff][NextColumn] [Borrow][Bottom greater Top] [Bottom 4][Top 13][ProcessColumn]	wa	*Write 9

Figure 8.3
The behaviour of the production system for 63 − 44.

How a child acquires a wrong rule in the first place is an interesting issue. Young and O'Shea suggest that one of the more puzzling errors, that of always borrowing, may arise from the way children are taught subtraction. In many school workbooks, as soon as the topic of borrowing is introduced, the child is given a long series of sums, *all of which require borrowing*. It is not surprising, therefore, that some children pick up the false idea that one should always begin a subtraction sum by borrowing.

Brown and VanLehn (1980) have proposed a more comprehensive theory, called **Repair Theory**, to explain how someone learning a new skill can acquire a faulty set of rules. They suggest that a learner will sometimes miss, or forget, a crucial rule. On reaching the point that the rule is needed, the learner copes by calling on **repair heuristics** to complete the task. If a child is trying to subtract a larger number from a smaller one in a column and does not know how to borrow, then the child can get over the impasse by, for example, giving up, or moving on to the next column, or mentally swapping the two numbers so taking the smaller one from the larger. These heuristics — 'give up', 'move on', and 'swap data' — are all general purpose and, apart from 'give up', at least allow the learner to continue with the problem.

8.2.2 Anderson's ACT

A far-reaching model which incorporates production rules has been developed by John Anderson over the past 20 years. Unlike the Young and O'Shea system, ACT is intended as a general model of cognition. Although comprehensive, ACT is far from complete and has seen a number of versions, the latest being ACT* (pronounced 'ACT Star'). The ACT theory is described in *The Architecture of Cognition* (Anderson, 1983).

ACT consists of a large long-term memory component in the form of a semantic network, a small 'working memory' of active items, and a production system that operates on the memories. A feature of ACT's long-term memory is that only part of it is active at any one time and the condition part of a production rule can only match an active element. The action part can cause a change to memory, or some other action such as reporting a result. Activation can spread through the network as elements activate their neighbours; for any element, the greater the 'fan out' (the number of its immediate neighbours), the weaker the activation. Activation gradually decays in elements that are not probed by the production rules.

Central to ACT is the notion that, from a little knowledge about a new domain, plus general problem-solving rules (modelled as production rules) and a rule interpreter, a mind can acquire procedures to carry out highly specialized activities like recognizing a particular word or proving a theorem in geometry. According to Anderson a skill is acquired in three stages. At first the learner calls on general-purpose rules, like the one (shown very informally) below, which are part of each person's cognitive equipment:

> rule
> condition:
> > [solve a list of problems]
>
> action:
> > add: [do the first problem in the list]

These rules interpret facts about the problem and guide the problem solving. The facts, called **declarative representations**, may have been gained from examples, or they may be learned verbal descriptions and definitions like '10 minus 5 equals 5'. This method should be adequate to solve a new problem, but it will be demanding on memory and slow, since the facts must be recalled in order to solve the problem.

At the second stage, the learner has built up a set of production rules (which Anderson calls **compiled representation**) specific to the task. The Young and O'Shea subtraction rules represent a transition to this second stage of skill development. Finally, the rules are 'tuned' to speed up and extend the performance. What is interesting about Anderson's theory is that it offers a small number of quite general mechanisms to account for a learner's transition from one stage to the next.

To give just a taste of ACT, consider subtraction again. At the same time as acquiring a set of rules for subtraction like those described by Young and O'Shea, a child will be learning particular number combinations. ACT suggests that the child starts with a general rule for completing a subtraction pattern,

> rule
> condition:
> > [ProcessColumn] [TopNumber TOP] [BottomNumber BOTTOM]
> > [SuccessfulColumn TOP BOTTOM RESULT]
>
> action:
> > add: [Result RESULT]
> > add: [NextColumn]

plus number facts, such as [SuccessfulColumn 7 0 7] and [SuccessfulColumn 8 0 8]. When the child is presented with a new sum, these facts are called, in turn, into working memory until the Top and Bottom numbers match those of the sum. At this stage of learning the child may well need to keep looking back at previous sums as sources of examples.

As the child becomes experienced, she builds up more specific rules. One mechanism to do this is what Anderson calls 'proceduralization'. This involves removing those conditions in the rule that require number facts to be retrieved from memory, and also replacing the variables to form new, more specific, compiled rules:

```
rule
condition:
        [ProcessColumn] [TopNumber 7] [BottomNumber 0]
action:
        add: [Result 7]
        add: [NextColumn]

rule
condition:
        [ProcessColumn] [TopNumber 8] [BottomNumber 0]
action:
        add: [Result 8]
        add: [NextColumn]
```

There are then a number of methods by which a learner might tune these compiled rules to improve performance. One of these is 'generalization', a form of inductive learning whereby the range of the rules is broadened to cope with novel situations. For example, having acquired the rules shown above, a child might generalize them to form the new rule

```
rule
condition:
        [ProcessColumn] [TopNumber TOP] [BottomNumber 0]
action:
        add: [Result TOP]
        add: [NextColumn]
```

This can now cope with new number combinations, such as $9 - 0$, without having to recall number facts from long-term memory. (This final rule is identical to one which the Young and O'Shea paper suggests children do actually acquire.) Anderson and various colleagues have tested the ACT theory by building working programs to model the learning of varied skills and then comparing the output of the programs with protocols of human learners. The results are impressive, with essentially the same program being able to mimic the reports of, for example, students learning geometry and the verbal utterances of Anderson's young son as he learned to speak, but the theory is not well enough developed to cope with individual variations in learning ability or the issue addressed by Brown and VanLehn of how a learner acquires incorrect rules.

8.2.3 Learning the Past Tense of English Verbs

As human beings we are attuned to a single level of description in the world, that which is directly accessible to our senses, and in which events happen at a rate we can interpret. For anything slower than a drifting cloud, faster than a running horse, or much smaller than a mosquito, our direct knowledge gives out and we have to rely on recollections, or the probes of instruments, to reveal beautiful patterns: the flow of history, the shape of a water splash, or the structure of an atom. Although, when building models of the world, we tend to treat different descriptive levels as independent, they fit together into a coherent picture. For example, the movement of gas molecules at one level gives rise to the concept of gas pressure at a higher level. Whether there is a level of cognition below symbol manipulation and, if so, what form it takes, has been the subject of much debate. This section outlines a model of subsymbolic cognition that has a form very different from ones we have presented so far.[2]

The new model (or more correctly models, since there are a number of related ones, referred to by the general title of **connectionist models** or **neural networks**) has been devised to account, in a straightforward way, for some of the qualities of the human mind, particularly parallelism and graceful degradation, and also some of its limitations, such as speed of processing. It consists of a network of processing units (loosely based on the arrangement of neurons in the brain), each one carrying out a simple computation, and all interconnected and working in harmony. (A connectionist model is not the same as a semantic net. The latter consists of passive symbols pushed around by a central processor; the former is an arrangement of active processors.) Intelligence emerges from the changing connections between these processing units, and it is this pattern of connections that constitutes what the system 'knows' and how it will respond to an input. Because

---

[2]A review of connectionism can be found in Smolensky, 1987.

knowledge is distributed amongst the units, removing units one by one does not rapidly bring the system to a halt (as would removing symbols one by one from the memory of a conventional computer) but gradually degrades the performance (an analogy is employees one by one falling ill in a large busy office).

Most of the example connectionist systems constructed so far have been for perception, and some of the theory is mathematical and difficult to appreciate, but the one described here is fairly straightforward and concerns a puzzling aspect of language learning: the acquisition of the past tenses of English verbs. The system is described in detail in chapter 18 of McClelland, Rumelhart, and the PDP Research Group (1986, Vol. 2). Before describing the system, it is important to clear up what appears to be an absurdity. A connectionist system represents human subsymbolic processing, yet the example below was programmed on a normal symbolic computer! We have already seen, however, that the computer is a versatile mimic. In this case it provides a poor imitation of the human mind. It took Rumelhart and McClelland's powerful computer about 30 minutes to produce the past tense of a new verb, a task which takes a person less than a second. More powerful computers are coming along, but the way the network described below deals with inputs strongly suggests that a system very different from a conventional computer is needed — one which is organized more like the neurons in the human brain and which can carry out hundreds of simple computations simultaneously.

The past tense of most English verbs can be found by adding -ed to the root form of the verb (for example walk/walked), but many common verbs have irregular past tense forms (get/got, eat/ate, see/saw, go/went), and it is these common verbs, along with a few regular ones such as look/looked, that children learn first. At this stage, when they are beginning to speak English, there is no evidence that children make use of the -ed rule; they simply know a small number of separate words. Then, the child learns a range of less-common verbs, and most of these are regular, (for example pull/pulled, wipe/wiped, drop/dropped). The child can now follow the -ed rule. That does not mean that she can explain the rule itself, but that she acts *as if* her language were governed by it. For example, if persuaded to link an invented word with an action ("Look how I rick this book"), then she will generate a regular past tense for the word ("What have I just done?" "You ricked the book"). Moreover, the child may incorrectly add regular past-tense endings (forming words such as 'eated') to words that a few months previously she had pronounced correctly. Finally, as the child matures further, she regains the correct use of the irregular past tense.

The connectionist model suggests that, rather than a child having explicit but

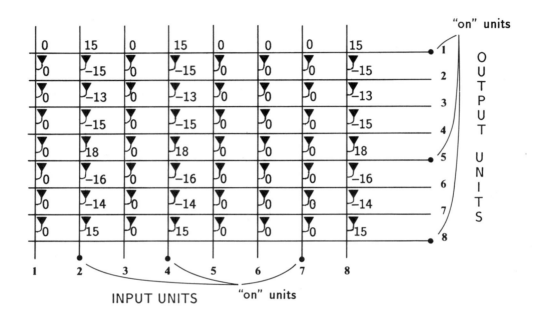

Figure 8.4
A learning network.

inaccessible rules for language, the child's rule-like behaviour arises from a network of simple cognitive processes. A much-simplified version of the network used by Rumelhart and McClelland (McClelland, Rumelhart, and the PDP Research Group, 1986, Vol. 2, Chap. 18) is shown in figure 8.4.

The Rule of 78 We shall begin by describing how such a system can learn a simple number rule and then show how a more sophisticated version can be made to learn the rules for forming the past tenses of verbs.

Along the bottom are the input units, each one of which is connected to every output unit. A connection can be either 'excitatory' (marked by a positive number), in which case it makes a positive contribution to the output, or 'inhibitory' (marked by a negative number), in which case it restrains the output, or zero (marked by a 0), in which case that input unit has no effect on the output unit. The strength of each connection (positive or negative) is shown by the number above it. Figure 8.5

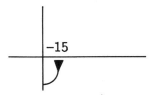

Figure 8.5
A single inhibitory connection.

shows a single inhibitory connection, of strength 15. Each unit has only two possible states: 'on' (indicated by a filled blob) or 'off'. Given a pattern of inputs, the network generates a pattern of outputs. Take output unit 1 as an example. Four of the eight inputs are 'off', so they can be ignored. Each of the 'on' units (numbers 2, 4, and 7) is linked to output unit 1 by a positive connection of strength 15. The total input is found by adding the individual strengths, and it is this total, 45, that determines whether the output unit will be 'on' or 'off': the higher the total, the greater the probability that the output unit is 'on'.

The probability that a particular output unit is 'on' is given by this formula:

$$probability = \frac{1}{1 + e^{-(net-\Theta)/T}}$$

where 'net' is the sum of the input strengths (45 in this case), Θ is a 'threshold value' (this allows for the possibility of an output being on even when there is no input — but to make things simple, in our example it is set to 0) and T represents the variablility of the system. If T is set to 0, then an output unit is 'on' if the inputs simply exceed the 'threshold' value. The larger the value of T, the greater is the uncertainty as to the state of the output unit; in the example here it is set to 15. Putting figures into the formula, the probability that the output unit 1 is 'on', given the 2 4 7 pattern of inputs, is 0.95; that is, on 95% of the occasions that the network receives input on units 2,4 and 7 the output unit will be 'on':

$$0.95 = \frac{1}{1 + e^{-(45-0)/15}}$$

We can calculate similar probabilities for each of the other output units and then multiply them together to get a probability for a particular output pattern. In

```
Input pattern?  2 4 7
Output: 1 3 5 8
Input pattern?  2 4 7
Output: 1 5
Input pattern?  2 4 7
Output: 1 5 8
Input pattern?  2 4 7
Output: 1 5 8
Input pattern?  2 4 7
Output: 5 8
```

Figure 8.6
A test of the network shown in figure 8.4.

this case 1,5,8 is the most likely output pattern, given an input of 2,4,7, with a probability of 0.68. In other words, the network behaves as though it 'almost knows' the rule 2 4 7 ⟶ 1 5 8. It will fairly often make mistakes and produce output like 1 5 or 1 3 5 8 (see figure 8.6), but the higher the connection strengths, the more likely it is to produce 1 5 8 in response to an input of 2 4 7. Notice that, unlike production rule systems, there is no stored symbolic rule of the form

```
rule
condition:
        [2 4 7]
action:
        print: [1 5 8]
```

The knowledge of a connectionist system is entirely contained in the pattern of connection strengths, and the response is probabilistic rather than predetermined.

If the network could only represent a simple association between a single input and a single output, then it would not be of much use as a cognitive model, but one network can store many associations, providing they conform to a general rule. Here is a made-up rule for number pairing, which Rumelhart and McClelland call the 'Rule of 78' (because when the input is 7 the output is 8, and vice versa):

Divide the input units into 3 groups:

A: 1 2 3
B: 4 5 6
C: 7 8

An input pattern always contains one active unit from each group — e.g., 2 5 7. To follow the rule, an output pattern must have the same unit as the input for group A, the same unit as the input for group B, and the other unit for group C. So, examples of input-output pairs that follow the rule are

INPUT		OUTPUT
2 4 7	$\longrightarrow$	2 4 8
1 6 8	$\longrightarrow$	1 6 7
3 5 7	$\longrightarrow$	3 5 8

An exception to the rule is, for example, 1 4 7 $\longrightarrow$ 1 4 7 because the last digit of the output is the same as that of the input.

Figure 8.7 shows a network that has learned the Rule of 78, with the examples to test it below. Each number in the network represents the connection strength between the corresponding input and output unit. As the figure shows, it sometimes produces the wrong response, but in general it gives a correct response to the input number.

Learning the Rule The way the network learns a rule is quite simple. At the beginning the connection strengths are all set to 0; in this condition, given any input pattern, it will produce a random output. It then learns by example. The network is presented with an input pattern and its correct output pattern. The network then generates an output from the input, and if its output differs from the correct one, then the connection strengths are adjusted. Taking each output unit in turn, if the correct output is 1, and the network generated a 0 then we want to increase the probability that, next time, the output will be 1, so all the strengths on that output unit are increased by 1. If the current input is 0 and the network

```
  44   -34   -28    -5    -5    -8   -11    -7
 -28    46   -34    -6    -4    -6    -8    -8
 -28   -33    44    -4    -5    -8    -8    -9
  -7    -1    -6    42   -28   -28    -1    -2
  -3    -9    -4   -29    41   -28    -2   -14
  -3    -4    -7   -28   -27    41    -7    -7
  -5     0     3     0     0    -2   -43    41
   2    -1     1     1    -1     2    45   -43
```

```
Input pattern?  2 4 7
Output: 2 8
Input pattern?  1 4 7
Output: 1 4 8
Input pattern?  2 5 7
Output: 2 5 8
Input pattern?  2 5 8
Output: 5 7
Input pattern?  1 3 7
Output: 1 3 6 8
Input pattern?  1 4 7
Output: 1 4 8
Input pattern?  3 4 7
Output: 3 4 8
```

Figure 8.7
A test of a network that has learned the 'Rule of 78'.

	REGULAR PAIRS			EXCEPTION	
	INPUT	OUTPUT		INPUT	OUTPUT
				1 4 7	1 4 7
	1 4 8	1 4 7			
	2 4 7	2 4 8			
	2 4 8	2 4 7			
	3 4 7	3 4 8			
	3 4 8	3 4 7			
	1 5 7	1 5 8			
	and so on.				

Figure 8.8
The Rule of 78, with an exception.

has generated a 1, then all the strengths for that output unit are decreased by 1. Figure 8.4 shows a network after some 30 trials learning the pair 2 4 7 $\longrightarrow$ 1 5 8.

Now for the experiment. We want the network to learn regular and irregular number pairs, in a manner similar to that of a child learning regular and irregular verbs. There are 18 different number pairs that correspond to the Rule of 78, but let us assume that one of the pairs is an exception to the rule. Instead of 1 4 7 $\longrightarrow$ 1 4 8 we have the irregular pair 1 4 7 $\longrightarrow$ 1 4 7 (see figure 8.8). As we have seen, a child learning to speak first learns mainly irregular verbs, but the less common verbs are generally regular, and so as the child learns more words the proportion of regular verbs that the child uses increases. We can present our number learning network with a similar situation. The network is first given two different pairs of numbers to learn. One of these, 2 5 8 $\longrightarrow$ 2 5 7, corresponds to the Rule of 78; the other, 1 4 7 $\longrightarrow$ 1 4 7, is irregular. After 60 learning trials for each pair, the network gives the right response about 50% of the time to the two learned numbers 258 and 147 (see figure 8.9), but it has not acquired any rule to deal with the other 16 numbers.

At this point it is like the child learning individual words with no sense of a rule. Then the network is given 40 further trials of all 18 pairs, 17 of which correspond to the Rule of 78 and one (1 4 7 $\longrightarrow$ 1 4 7) of which is an exception. Even though this irregular pair of numbers is still being taught to the network, after the 40 trials its performance on that pair is worse than before. The probability of it getting

After the first 60 trials with 1 4 7 $\longrightarrow$ 1 4 7 and 2 5 8 $\longrightarrow$ 2 5 7:

```
Input pattern?  1 4 7
Output: 1 4 7
Input pattern?  1 4 7
Output: 1 4 5 7
Input pattern?  1 4 7
Output: 1 4 7
```

After 40 further trials with the Rule of 78 pairs, and the exception:

```
Input pattern?  1 4 7
Output: 1 4 8
Input pattern?  1 4 7
Output: 1 4
Input pattern?  1 4 7
Output: 1 2 4 7 8
```

Figure 8.9
Performance of the network after 60 and 100 trials.

the right answer with an input of 1 4 7 has gone down from 0.48 to 0.14. In fact, given 1 4 7 it more often produces 1 4 8 than 1 4 7. Now, however, is it acquiring the Rule of 78 and is beginning to give a correct response to all 18 numbers. The reason that performance on the 147 $\longrightarrow$ 148 exception has worsened is that the network has been swamped with examples that correspond to the Rule of 78, and these have outweighed the one exception. However, if the learning trials continue, still with all 18 pairs, then eventually the network adjusts its connection strengths to cope with the exception. After 500 trials the network gives a correct response both to the regular numbers, and to the irregular 1 4 7.

The Past Tenses of English Verbs Rumelhart and McClelland's verb learning model is similar in principle to the number learning network. They first converted each common verb and its past tense into a phonetic code which represented the pronunciation of the word. Then the network (somewhat like the one above, but with more input and output units) was trained by providing it with pairs of phonetic patterns, standing for a word and its past tense. In the first phase of the experiment the network was given only the ten commonest verbs and their past tenses, those that a child would learn first. Of these words (come, get, give, look, take, go, have, live, feel) eight of them are irregular. After ten trials with each pair of verbs, the network was then presented, for 190 trials, with a mixture of these common verbs, and 410 less common verbs, such as 'walk', 'smile', and 'drink', most of which happen to have regular -ed past tenses.

The model performs remarkably like a young child. Early in its learning it responded equally well in giving the past tense of regular and irregular verbs. Next, after it was given the series of mainly regular verbs, it became worse at producing the past tense of irregular verbs, even the common ones, and then it gradually improved. Not only does it show behaviour similar to that of a child, but it can also correctly generate the past tenses of new verbs. After it had been given the learning trials and could cope with regular and irregular verbs, it was presented with 86 entirely new uncommon verbs, some regular, some irregular. It produced the correct response for over half of the regular ones, and also managed the correct past tense for some of the irregular ones, such as 'bid $\longrightarrow$ bid', 'weep $\longrightarrow$ wept', and 'cling $\longrightarrow$ clung'.

8.2.4 Connectionist Models

Connectionism is not new. The foundations were laid down in the 1940s by McCulloch and Pitts who proved that logical expressions can be computed by networks of simplified neurons. It was already known that any expression in propositional logic can be constructed from combinations of AND, OR, and NOT functions; McCulloch and Pitts constructed arrangements of simple simulated neurons to compute each of these functions.

In the same decade Hebb showed how neural networks could form a system that exhibited memory and learning. Memory, he suggested, may not be formed by each neuron storing a single concept, but by patterns of interconnection within groups of neurons. Learning is then a process of altering the strengths of connection to form and transform these neural patterns.

Rosenblatt extended the McCulloch and Pitts neuron to form a 'perceptron', which can carry out useful pattern recognition tasks, and by the mid-1960s people were building connectionist machines to recognize visual patterns and classify signals. Connectionism and symbolic AI stood side-by-side in the academic journals.

Then, in 1969, Minsky and Papert published *Perceptrons* (1969), a carefully-worded analysis of the Rosenblatt perceptron and similar models. They proved that perceptrons and related 'single-layer linear threshold systems' are unable to compute important classes of function and so cannot serve as general purpose computing and pattern recognition devices. Although Minsky and Papert acknowledged that more complex 'multi-layer' systems can act as general purpose computers, they saw no easy way to form them into useful models of human learning and cognition.

The reaction to *Perceptrons* was swift. Funding for research in connectionist models dried up and promising projects were abandoned. So it remained throughout the 1970s, with a few important theoretical advances, but no strong undercurrent of interest. The resurgence of connectionism came with the publication of *Parallel Distributed Processing* (McClelland, Rumelhart, and the PDP Research Group, 1986), which reported the work of the PDP Research Group at the University of California, San Diego. Not only did they claim that Minsky and Papert had "incorrectly tainted more interesting and powerful networks of linear threshold and other nonlinear units" (Vol. 1, p. 65), but they also described working connectionist systems that can, they claimed, provide models of human learning and memory, of sentence processing, and of speech perception. In the opening pages, McClelland, Rumelhart, and Hinton state (Vol. 1, p. 11)

> One reason for the appeal of PDP models is their obvious 'physiological' flavor: They seem so much more closely tied to the brain than are other kinds of information-processing models.

8.3   Two Models of Cognition

In this chapter we have looked at two very different models of cognition: one in which knowledge is represented as production rules, controlled by a rule interpreter, the other in which rule-like behaviour emerges from a network of many simple processes. Which one is correct? The answer seems to be both. At the lower level of the subconscious, the mind appears to reflect the structure of the brain, and a network of simple processors seems to provide the most natural model. To describe the mind at the level of conscious intellectual reasoning, we need a model that can carry out a single sequence of symbolic operations.

These are, however, only models of cognition, not explanations of how the mind or brain works. Other models may offer yet more accurate explanations. For example, the verb learning program seems, in its present form, to be too general: it is capable of learning regularities that the human mind cannot handle. Many questions still remain to be answered. What is the relation between a connectionist network and the arrangement of neurons in the human brain? What kind of model is appropriate for cognitive processes, like language understanding, that lie on the boundaries of consciousness? How does conscious thought emerge from the ever-changing patterns of neural activity? At some point in her cognitive development, a child becomes able not only to form words *as if* they were governed by rules, but also consciously to state a rule like 'regular past tenses end in -ed' and check words against that rule. She can also control and alter these rules; for example, she can *pretend* to be a young child and use 'runned' as the past tense of 'run', even though she knows it to be incorrect. 'Playing pretend' cannot simply involve altering one's neural network for producing past tenses — otherwise we would never be able to tell reality from pretense. A full model of cognition must be able both to react and to reason, and not confuse the two, and as yet no such model has been developed.

8.4 Conclusion

In this chapter we drew a distinction between the knowledge and problem-solving processes of idealized 'experts' and those of real human beings. The human mind has limitations — of memory, speed, and accuracy — that may produce errors with even quite simple problems, but may also result in novel and imaginative solutions. It also has qualities — such as flexibility, graceful degradation (ways of coping), generative power (creating novel ideas), and parallelism (carrying out two or more activities at once) — that give it great power and range. We described two different models of human cognition: a production system for children's subtraction and a connectionist system for learning the past tenses of verbs. Both models can account for some of the behaviour of children when doing subtraction or learning language — in particular, their systematic errors — and both models can be extended to cover other aspects of human cognition. The fundamental difference between the two models is that one represents knowledge as explicit rules and the other as a pattern of connections between units in a network. It is still too early to say whether one type will be successful, or whether some new model, possibly combining symbolic rules with patterns of interaction, is needed to account for the wide range of human cognitive activities.

8.5 Appendix: The Tourist Guide and Human Tourists

We have reached the end of our Tourist Guide project. Piecing together the parts described in each chapter, we have a system that will answer queries about places, events, and routes. Appendix B shows a complete Tourist Guide (based on ideas from an undergraduate's project) and here is a dialogue with that program:

```
converse();
Hello , this is the automated London tourist guide
I can offer information on the following
cinema
theatre
museums
galleries
places of interest
routes and fares on the underground
Please ask about any of the above and I will try to help
you
Type in your question using lowercase letters only
and then press RETURN
If you want to exit please type " bye " and press RETURN
? where is the lake in the park
the serpentine is in hyde park
?  how do i get to the serpentine
travelling by underground , take the VICTORIA line to green
park then change and take the PICCADILLY line
to hyde park corner
?  what entertainment is there in london
what type of entertainment would you like :  cinema or
theatre ?
?  theatre
would you like western , drama or horror
?  drama
world go away is on at the phoenix .
slaving over a hot keyboard is on at the lyric .
I hope you enjoy the show
?  where is the lyric
the lyric is in shaftesbury avenue
```

There are still obvious improvements to be made. Its handling of language could be enhanced by improving the parser, and the database could be extended beyond the centre of London. In the present state it is a demonstration system, one that could be shown off to the British Tourist Authority or grant-awarding bodies in the hope of gaining funds to design a full prototype. To take the project further we would need to discover what type of advice human tourists really require. One way to find out is to study successful human tourist guides at work and to build a model of their mental representations and operations. Another way is to concentrate on tourists and to discover what planning strategies they employ, what form of questions they ask, and how they make use of the information given.

The protocol below is taken from a person (S) planning a daytime visit to London with a young child. Speaker E is the experimenter, who is also acting as a human guide and information giver.

> S: First of all I'd list about five or six places that I'd go to and I'd pick first of all, Madame Tussaud's perhaps. Then the Science and Natural History museums ... is that what they're called? The ones with the dinosaurs and the whale and the one with all the scientific experiments. I think they're next door to each other.
>
> E: That's right. The Natural History Museum and the Science Museum.
>
> S: Right. And possibly the Planetarium. Yes, I think those four would be my choice. And it would be the museums in the morning which would wear us out. First thing I need to do is find out where the museums are. I think they're around Kensington.
>
> E: The Science Museum is in Exhibition Road and the nearest Underground station is South Kensington.
>
> S: OK. Next I need a tube map.
>
> E: You can ask me.
>
> S: OK. I arrive at Victoria. I need to know what line to, sorry, what was it?
>
> E: South Kensington.
>
> S: South Kensington.
>
> E: Right. You can take the District or Circle line west two stops from Victoria to South Kensington.
>
> S: Without changing?
>
> E: Without changing. Just directly west two stops.
>
> S: OK. Do I have to remember this or can I write it down?

E: Yes, write it down.

S: Is it the third stop?

E: The third stop, yes.

S: OK. So, now before I think about what we're doing in the museum I need to think about where to go next. The next thing I need to know is where Madame Tussaud's and the Planetarium are.

E: Right. They are actually right next to each other. Let's have a look.

S: Oh, I know what else I will probably want to do in between these two.

E: It's in Marylebone Road, next to Baker Street. The nearest tube station is Baker Street.

S: OK, so I need to know. Now, I've just thought of something else I'd like to do in between, which would depend on where it's located and how awkward it is to get to. But assuming I'm going to go from South Kensington to Baker Street, is Fortnum and Mason's anywhere in between? For tea.

E: Right. It's in Piccadilly. Nearest stop is Piccadilly Circus or Green Park.

S: Right. Now I really need a map of the relationship between South Kensington, Baker Street, and Green Park. [S is shown an Underground map of Central London.] Now assuming I can do all these things, that is, go from Victoria to South Kensington, then to Green Park then to Baker Street, that is the order in which I would like to do them. The museums first, then Fortnum and Mason's, then the Planetarium and Madame Tussaud's.

There is no set way to analyze such a protocol; it depends on the purpose and level of detail needed. In this case a good starting point is to divide up the protocol into sections that appear to indicate the main strategies.

First, the subject makes use of a common problem-solving technique known as **problem reduction**, which involves splitting the problem into manageable parts. This he does by recalling interesting trips that could fill out the day. Assuming that each visit is straightforward, he is left with the reduced problem of linking together the visits. Next, beginning with the words "First thing I need to do is find out where the museums are," he asks for a route between Victoria and the museums. Then, from "The next thing I need to know," he locates Madame Tussaud's and the Planetarium, with the aim of linking them to the museum visits. At this point he notices a gap in the plan — he has not allowed for a tea break! — and from "Now I've just thought of something else" he plans how to insert tea at Fortnum and Mason's into the itinerary. Finally, from "So now I really need a map" onwards, he plots a route between all the stops.

A good tourist guide, computer or human, should be able to help at any point in the planning process, and the protocol indicates that a tourist needs suggestions for main visits (in different circumstances such as daytime, evening, weekends, or for children), routes from Victoria to a specified location, a suggested route between a number of locations, and ways to fill a gap in the plan (such as where to take a tea or lunch break). From the protocol we can also gain ideas on presenting the information: for instance, this subject clearly preferred a map of his chosen locations and the routes between them, rather than a verbal description, and he needed a constant reminder of the plan so far. A parallel study of human tourist guides could suggest successful strategies for meeting these needs.

Because it is concerned with studying the process of thinking rather than just the end results, protocol analysis can be time consuming, and such studies generally involve small groups of subjects, perhaps six or less. The experimenter forms a tentative model on the basis of a few protocols and then gradually refines it, perhaps by studying a part of the task, or selected groups of subjects. For the Tourist Guide the end result would be a completely redesigned system, whose information, reasoning capabilities, and style of presentation is matched to the needs of tourists. If, inspired by this, you succeed in building such a system, in London or elsewhere, we look forward to using it!

8.6 Exercises

1. On page 229 we said that removing 'b2a' from the set of rules for subtraction, given in figure 8.2, produces the systematic errors shown in figure 8.1, where a child always subtracts the smaller number from the larger one. Produce a table like that in figure 8.3 for the sum 63 − 44, using the modified rules, to show that they produce the incorrect answer 21. The other example errors in figure 8.1 can be produced by adding a rule which says 'borrow when the bottom number is smaller than the top'. Write this as a production rule, add

it to the top of the list, and show that the rules now produce the incorrect answers for sums B and C.

2. Find a young child who only just knows how to subtract and still makes mistakes. Give the child a variety of two digit subtraction sums to do, and record the answers — e.g.,

$$
\begin{array}{ccccccc}
63 & 96 & 64 & 72 & 71 & 21 & 70 \\
-44 & -42 & -51 & -57 & -52 & -19 & -47
\end{array}
$$

See if you can spot any patterns in the mistakes. Give further sums to see if the child produces wrong answers that are consistent with the pattern you have hypothesized. Talk to the child to see if you can elicit the rules being used. Which of the incorrect answers could be generated by the modifications to the production system described in exercise 1? Suggest alterations to the production system that would produce at one of the new types of mistake that you have discovered.

3. Given the learning network shown in figure 8.4, for each of the output units what is the probability that the unit is 'on' with an input of 2 4 7?

4. Choose a town or city that you know well, and write a version of the Tourist Guide for it, based on the example in appendix B. Take on the role of a tourist guide and record two or three interviews with newcomers to the town, answering their questions about events and places to visit. Write a report describing ways in which the the Tourist Guide might be improved to take account of tourists' needs.

Chapter 9

Computer Vision

9.1 Finding the Underground

Imagine you have arrived at one of London's railway stations and now wish to continue your journey by the Underground. You are confronted by the scene shown in figure 9.1.

As a seasoned traveller you know that a sure way of finding the entrance to the Underground station is to look for the London Underground logo (figure 9.2), and so you scan the scene before your eyes until the sign is spotted and then begin to move towards it, avoiding obstacles in your path, until the entrance is reached.

How does your visual system make this possible? Certainly, it seems to require very little effort, and it is tempting to believe that whatever is going on inside your head must be quite different from the mechanisms proposed in the previous chapters of this book. This chapter shows that, on the contrary, internal representations (chapter 3), search strategies (chapter 4), and structural descriptions (chapter 5) all play a central role in recent computational models of visual perception. For example, we show that the same depth-first search strategy used to plan a route through the London Underground system (chapter 4) can be used to recognize the London Underground sign in a street scene.

9.2 A Seeing Machine

The advent of the computer has introduced a new way of finding out about human vision systems: by building a machine that can 'see' and investigating this as a model of human vision. But what does this mean in practice? If we are to learn anything about human vision, what should the machine vision system be made to do?

Figure 9.1
An image of the forecourt at Victoria Station.

A plausible answer is to select a task performed routinely by people, and then to build a machine to do the same thing. With this in mind, we consider the problem of building a mobile tourist guide (MTG), and, in particular, the task of recognizing and moving towards a visible Underground sign. If we succeed in building a machine to perform this task, then we have a possible model (which may of course be wrong) for the way in which people do the same task.

The MTG is equipped with a TV camera which feeds a stream of snapshots of the scene into an on-board computer. In practice, the 'intelligence' of mobile robots is

Figure 9.2
The London Underground sign.

often situated off-board, remaining in contact with on-board sensors and actuators using a radio link or wire, but this does not alter the task of the visual sub-system with which we are concerned.

The basic problem is how to turn images from the TV camera into commands to control the MTG's transport mechanism. We have seen already, in earlier parts of this book, that we need an internal representation of the world to answer questions intelligently. It is hard to imagine how the MTG could possibly perform correctly without itself forming some kind of internal representation of the scene before its 'eye', although the form of this representation is unclear. We suppose therefore that the role of the visual sub-system of the MTG is to produce an internal representation of the scene which is updated as changes occur in the world (e.g., the MTG moves to another position) and further suppose that a second sub-system, controlling the vehicle guidance mechanism, interrogates this representation to decide how to move the MTG and thereby guide it towards the Underground sign. The function of the visual sub-system is summarized by the following mapping:

TV images → Internal Representation of Scene

9.2.1   Digitized Images

We begin by looking at the way in which TV images are fed into the visual sub-system. The human eye is often likened to a camera in that light from a scene passes through a lens and is cast onto a light sensitive surface — the film in the camera or the retina in the eye. We bring this analogy up to date for the MTG and use a TV camera connected to a box known as a video digitizer which converts the video picture into a stream of numbers which are fed directly to the computer. Each number, or **grey-level**, is a measure of the light intensity over a small square patch of the picture, known as a **pixel**, and a complete image is built up from a large number of adjoining pixels arranged into rows and columns; like a jigsaw puzzle with square pieces of the same size.

Figure 9.3 shows the array of numbers produced by our video digitizer for a small part of the image shown in figure 9.1 in the vicinity of the Underground sign. Each number is a measure of the light intensity at the pixel in the corresponding position in the TV picture. The numbers range from 0 to 99; 0 is the darkest and 99 is the lightest — intermediate values correspond to the greys in between.

We shall not address all of the technical problems involved in setting up the video digitizer and connecting it to the computer and assume instead that the grey-levels of figure 9.3 are available as an array of numbers inside the computer.

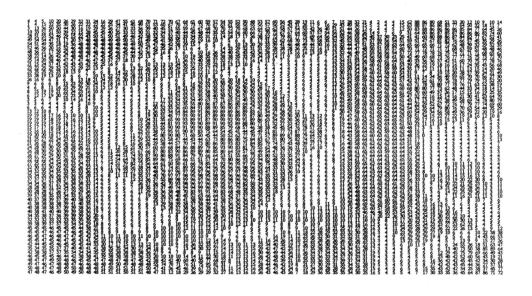

Figure 9.3
An array of numbers corresponding to the Underground sign in figure 9.1.

9.2.2   Internal Representation

Several kinds of internal representation have been employed as the output from machine vision systems, depending to some extent on the task to be performed. Similarly, there have been many proposals for the kind of internal representations that may be generated by the human visual system for the wide range of tasks for which it is used.

Chapter 3 introduced the idea of representing the world by a data base of facts. For the purpose of describing the location of the Underground sign to the transport sub-system of the MTG, a fact like the following may be all that is necessary:

```
[SIGN at [35 40 10] ]
```

The three numbers specify the position of the sign with respect to the MTG in terms of the distance to the sign, the angle between the direction in which the MTG is facing and the direction from the MTG to the sign, and the height of the sign above ground.

A general purpose vision system will need many such descriptions, and much more besides, in order to navigate a robot around a cluttered environment containing many objects. For the remainder of this chapter, we examine two methods for producing a part of this rudimentary kind of representation, namely, the fact a particular object is visible to the TV camera. In particular, we shall be concerned with the part of the MTG's visual sub-system for recognizing Underground signs. The appendix to this chapter shows how to implement the first method and part of the second method in POP-11. We concentrate on the problem of recognizing the Underground sign in a single image and do not address the problems and benefits of recognizing objects through sequences of TV images.

9.3   Method 1: Template Matching

Our problem is to recognize that the Underground sign is visible given an array of grey-levels from the MTG's camera. One way of doing this to store away an idealized image of an Underground sign like that shown in figure 9.2 and to compare this image with the input image, looking for a match. This is somewhat analogous to a botanist trying to identify a particular specimen in a field by alternating gaze between the field and a text book picture of the desired plant. We call the idealized image a **template** and represent it inside the computer as an array of grey-levels in just the same way as we did for input images. Figure 9.4 shows the array of grey-levels representing the idealized image or template shown in figure 9.2.

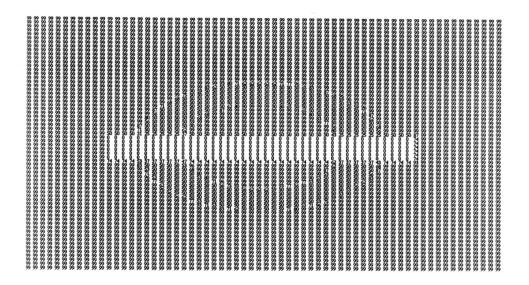

Figure 9.4
The array of grey-levels of the stored template.

Since they are in the same form, input images can be compared with the stored template looking for the pattern of grey-levels of the template within the array of grey-levels of the input image. An easy way of doing this is to slide the template over the input image from left to right and from top to bottom moving a single pixel at a time and at each position looking to see whether the numbers lying above one another from each image are the same.

Trace over the edges of the underground sign in figure 9.1 and then compare it with the template sign in figure 9.2. How would the template need to be altered so that its edges fit exactly under your tracing?

A moment's inspection of figures 9.1 and 9.2 should convince you that nowhere
will the template and the input image match up exactly. Indeed we should be surprised if they did since in general it is very unlikely that two images of Underground
signs will exhibit precisely the same array of grey-levels. There are at least three
reasons for this:

- The appearance of the Underground sign, and therefore the pattern of grey-
  levels, is crucially dependent on viewing angle and size. As we move away
  from the sign or as the sign gets smaller, its image becomes smaller, and as
  we move around the sign its image becomes elliptical. Try rotating a round
  saucer in front of your eyes and observe how its projected shape changes. It
  is quite difficult to convince oneself of this, since we are so used to perceiving
  things as they are in three dimensions. (For the sake of this discussion we
  have ignored perspective effects within images of Underground signs.)

- The grey-levels are affected by the pattern of light falling on the surface of
  the sign. The same sign will look different in the morning when the sun is
  rising in the East from in the evening when the sun is setting in the West.

- No two Underground signs are exactly alike. There will always be imperfec-
  tions and surface markings which distinguish one from the other (aside from
  the different types of sign which can be seen around London).

In the case of the appearances of the signs in the stored template (figure 9.2)
and input image (figure 9.1), the former has a higher contrast and extends over
a greater number of pixels than the latter, and furthermore has a circular shape
whereas the latter has an elliptical shape. There are also many details on the real
sign which are not represented in our stored template — in particular, the word
'Underground' appears across the middle of the real sign. What we need to do is
to transform one or both of the arrays of numbers (i.e., the input image and the
template) to make them comparable.

9.3.1 Dealing with Differences in Viewing Angle and Size

First we consider the problem of variations in viewing angle and size. Our template depicts an underground sign from straight on and with a set image size. By
deforming this template, according to simple geometric rules, we can predict what
the same sign would look like at different distances and viewing angles. To predict
the appearance of a more distant sign (or a smaller sign), we just shrink the size
of the template. To predict the appearance of a sign viewed at an oblique angle,

we rotate and compress the template. In this way, new templates can be produced for Underground signs viewed at any angle and with any image size. A selection of templates depicting signs viewed at different angles is shown in figure 9.5.

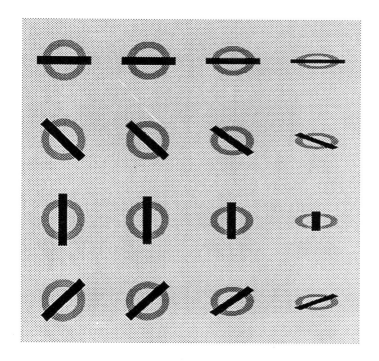

Figure 9.5
Templates for signs viewed at different angles.

This suggests a way of finding the Underground sign in an image. First produce a catalogue of templates depicting an Underground sign viewed at a range of angles and for a range of different image sizes. The catalogue should be comprehensive so that for an arbitrary image of an Underground sign it will include a sign from a similar viewing angle and of a similar image size. Now compare each of the templates from the catalogue, one after the other, with the input image. As before this may be achieved by sliding the templates over the input image, looking at the corresponding grey-levels at each position.

Figure 9.6 shows the grey-levels of a 'best-fit' template, produced by manually adjusting the deformation applied to the original template (with the help of a computer) to find a good approximation to the projected shape and size of the Underground sign depicted in figure 9.1. Unfortunately, the grey-levels of this 'best-fit' template are still significantly different from those derived from the Underground sign in our input image.

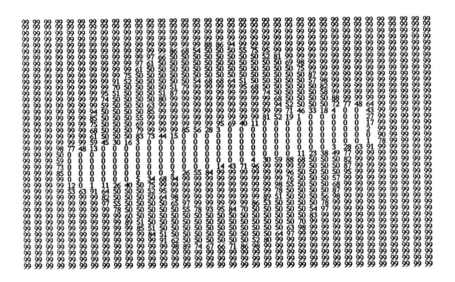

Figure 9.6
A 'best-fit' deformation of the original template.

Although the ability to deform the original template enables us to predict the shape and size of the image of a London Underground sign seen at different viewing angles and distances, it cannot predict the actual grey-levels since these will depend, among other things, on the prevailing lighting conditions. Consequently, it is very unlikely that any of our catalogue of derived templates will match with any sub-array of grey-levels from an input image.

9.3.2 Dealing with Variations Due to Lighting

Fortunately there are ways of dealing with the dependence of grey-level values on prevailing lighting conditions. If you examine figures 9.1 and 9.2, one thing they have in common is the image contours defining the characteristic shape of the London Underground sign and along which the intensity changes abruptly. Such image contours are known as **edges**. Some of these edges are caused by the use of paints of different colours, while others are just the silhouette of the sign against its background, but all are characterized by changes in grey-level between adjacent pixels of the digitized image. Since the edges in figures 9.1 and 9.2 correspond to the same features in the world, there is a strong basis for comparison and we are no longer subject to the vagaries of variable lighting.

In perhaps the most widely known computational account of visual perception, Marr (1982) suggests that intensity changes are detected and described as the first step in interpreting an image. This view is supported by biological studies of various animal visual systems, most notably in the work of Hubel and Wiesel (1968).

We have observed that edges may be useful for matching an input image with a stored template, but how do we detect edges in a methodical fashion? There has been a long search for the ideal edge finding procedure — that is, one which responds only to the meaningful edges in an image. All edge finders are essentially looking for step changes in intensity, but they vary as to the way such changes are characterized formally and the need for efficiency as well as correctness.

The search for edges normally proceeds by examining groups of neighbouring pixels, looking for the smallest pieces of edge, known as **edge elements**, and then grouping these into chains to form complete edges.

We consider a simple procedure for detecting edge elements, which produces an array of the same size as the digitized image with a 1 at each location for which there is an edge element in the vicinity of the corresponding pixel and 0's elsewhere. This array is called an **edge map** (strictly speaking this should be edge element map). The procedure works by repeating an identical operation at each pixel in the image. Consider one such pixel — the current pixel — valued a and two of its neighbours situated above and to the left, with values b and c:

	b
c	a

If there is a horizontal edge in the region of the current pixel, there should be a significant difference between a and b, while there may be very little difference between a and c. Similarly, if there is a vertical edge in the region of the current pixel, there should be a significant difference between a and c, while there may be little difference between a and b.

The difference between two numbers, a and b, expressed as a positive number, is called the 'absolute difference'; this is written $|a - b|$. We can test for both horizontal and vertical edges at once by adding together the absolute difference between a and b, and the absolute difference between a and c and testing to see whether this exceeds some pre-determined threshold value t. Formally, we can write this condition as:

$$|a - b| + |a - c| > t$$

When this condition is satisfied, 1 is recorded in the edge map at the position corresponding to the current pixel; otherwise 0 is recorded.

This works fine for vertical and horizontal edges, but what about diagonal edges? In this case, the absolute differences will be smaller than for optimal horizontal or vertical edges but when added together they have a similar chance of exceeding the threshold t.

Figure 9.7 shows the edge map produced from the grey-levels shown in figure 9.3 corresponding to part of figure 9.1.

The threshold value t was 10. For clarity, small squares are shown surrounding the pixels where edge elements are present (i.e., 1's in the edge map).

Figure 9.8 shows the edge map produced from the template with the array of grey-levels shown in figure 9.6. Again, a threshold value of 10 was used.

By substituting edge maps for the input image and the template, we have eliminated the worst effects of variable lighting and so are now in a much better position to make a comparison. Again an easy way to compare the two edge maps is to slide one over the other, looking for a position in which edges from the two line up with one another. A good match is one in which most 1's in the first edge map lie directly above 1's in the other edge map. We will accept some failed matches between 1's due to extra markings on the physical sign and errors in the assumed viewing angle and image size used to generate the template.

Now if we place the top left-hand corner of the edge map derived from the template over the 10th column and the 12th row of the edge map derived from the input image, there is a good match between the two maps. Indeed over 60% of the edges in the first edge map are found to be in the second edge map.

Given the size of the physical sign and information about the camera optics, we could in principle compute the 3-dimensional position of the Underground sign

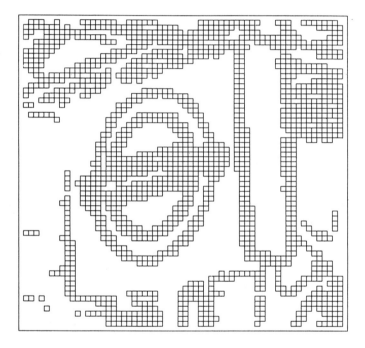

Figure 9.7
The edge map produced from the Underground sign of figure 9.1.

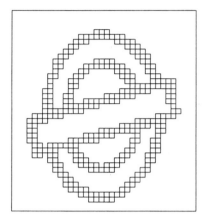

Figure 9.8
The edge map produced from the template of figure 9.6.

depicted in figure 9.1 given its image location and size. This position could be outputted from the vision sub-system and used to guide the MTG towards the entrance to the Underground station (assuming, as is the case here, that the entrance to the station is roughly underneath the sign!).

A major problem with this method is the need to generate and scan through a catalogue of templates. This is can take up a great deal of computer time and is suited only to situations in which the position of a target object is known to be restricted to a narrow range. This might be the case, for example, in applications within production engineering. The problem would be alleviated if some means could be found for focusing on a restricted range of viewing angles, image locations, and sizes using fast but reliable heuristics.

Another problem arises when we deal with objects which are non-planar (i.e., 3-dimensional, unlike the Underground sign). For planar objects it is straightforward to predict how they will appear from different viewing angles, but this is not the case for non-planar objects. One solution is to develop an idealized 3-D model for the non-planar object (similar to those used in the design of motor cars) from which its appearance from different viewpoints can be predicted. Again this method has been shown to work for a variety of everyday objects.

In conclusion, method 1 is highly predictive, in that no attempt is made to examine the image prior to matching with a catalogue of stored templates. It seems implausible that the human visual system could operate such a scheme to recognize familiar objects, if only because it would be overloaded by the vast number of comparisons between objects and templates. By way of contrast, we now examine a different approach to recognizing Underground signs which does try to make some sense of the image before attempting to find the sign.

9.4   Method 2: Matching Descriptions

It has long been known that the human visual system is sensitive to certain salient spatial features of an image, so that, for example, a white blob on a dark background stands out as a single entity. This process by which the visual system segments images into collections of salient features seems to go on no matter what is being looked at and appears to be fundamental to visual perception. The Gestalt psychologists documented many examples of this phenomenon, and, in recent years, computational mechanisms have been proposed to account for it (e.g., Marr, 1976).

The close relationship between those features salient to people and the images of objects in a scene leads us to believe that such features play a central role in recognizing objects. Could it be that our visual systems detect salient features as a precursor to recognizing the objects in a scene? One piece of evidence for this may be found in the way in which we describe images using language. If you were asked to describe the image of the Underground sign in figure 9.2 as concisely as possible you might say something like "There is a ring intersected by a bar."

In general, the images of many everyday objects, from a limited range of viewpoints, can be characterized by listing a number of salient features and their properties (e.g., shape and size), together with topological and spatial relationships between these. We call such a characterization a **model**. Notice that models are kinds of structural description, of which we are already familiar from earlier chapters.

We have seen that images are represented inside the computer as arrays of numbers (i.e., grey-levels). Can you think of a way of detecting salient features by examining only these numbers?

The existence of a model for a familiar object leads to a powerful method for recognizing that object from an image — namely, to look for a collection of salient features of the image having the necessary properties and satisfying all of the spatial and topological relationships required by the model.

9.4.1   Regions and Edges

Before looking at the recognition method in more detail, we need a well defined procedure for locating salient features without first recognizing what is depicted. Two kinds of feature have been particularly important in computer vision: **edges** and **regions**.

We have already met the notion of an edge earlier in this chapter, as an image contour along which there is a step change in intensity. For most everyday scenes, there is a close correspondence between such edges and the boundaries between objects and parts of objects in the scene. For example, in figure 9.7 there are edges corresponding to the markings and border of the Underground sign and other objects in the background. As we have discussed, edges are detected by first looking for edge elements and then grouping these elements into longer edges. For the purposes of matching image features with models, we must identify edges which 'stand out' as single entities from the network of adjacent edge elements; otherwise there is no reason to expect that discovered edges will match with the edges specified in the model. A promising approach is to break the chains of adjacent edge elements at sharp corners and places where three or more chains are joined together (i.e., at junctions). For example, the half-rings of the Underground sign give rise to four smoothly curved chains of edge elements terminated abruptly where they join with edge elements derived from the central bar (see figure 9.7). Rather than pursue this further, we turn our attention to another kind of salient feature.

In some ways complementary to edges, regions are connected groups of pixels over which intensity or texture is nearly homogeneous. For example, although the grey-levels on the ring of the Underground sign differ from point to point, they are nevertheless confined to a narrow band of values ranging from around 20 to 45 (ignoring those 'mixed' pixels on the border of the ring), whereas the background of the sign ranges from around 3 to 8.

This observation suggests a simple algorithm for detecting regions. First draw up a list of non-overlapping grey-level ranges corresponding to the desired regions and then label each pixel according to the range in which its grey-level lies. Of course, the grey-level ranges are chosen carefully to ensure that pixels within individual target regions are given the same label. Unfortunately, the ranges must be chosen before a segmentation into meaningful regions is derived, but nevertheless this can be achieved automatically. The idea is to look at the distribution of grey-levels in the input image to find ranges where large numbers of values are clustered. The expectation is that such clusters of values will be derived from one or more non-adjacent image regions.

Figure 9.9 shows the regions derived from the array shown in figure 9.3 using the above algorithm with grey-level ranges determined manually. Pixels with grey-levels in the range 3–8 are labelled 1, those in the range 20–45 are labelled 2, those in the range 45–80 are labelled 3 and those in the range 85–99 are labelled 4. Pixels with grey-levels falling outside all of the ranges are labelled 0. An array of labels as in figure 9.9 representing the segmentation of an image into regions is known as a **region map**.

As required, most pixels on the ring have been assigned the label 2, those on the two half-discs within the ring the label 4, and those on the background the label 1. Notice, however, that many pixels in other parts of the image have been assigned these labels. A large proportion of the pixels on the bar have the label 3 although some have been labelled 2 and 0, because this part of the image is not completely homogeneous.

Figure 9.10 shows an alternative depiction of the region map, in which lines are drawn between pixels with different labels. This shows clearly that the half-rings and half-discs have been extracted by the segmentation algorithm as single regions. Unfortunately the central bar of the sign appears as several regions of which the largest 'leaks' into the narrow band of mixed pixels on the inner boundary of the ring.

If you would like to read more about edge and region finding algorithms, there are useful sections on the subject in the book *Computer Vision* by Ballard and Brown (1982).

9.4.2 Matching

Having identified salient image features, an object is recognized by matching these with a stored model in which a number of required features are listed together with necessary properties and relationships between the features. Models will be expressed using a semantic net, where the nodes are the required salient features and the arcs are the relationships between features as well as the properties required of individual features (represented by an arc from a node to itself). Figure 9.11 shows a model for a London Underground sign, in which the required features are regions labelled hring1, hring2, hdisc1, hdisc2, corresponding to the upper and lower

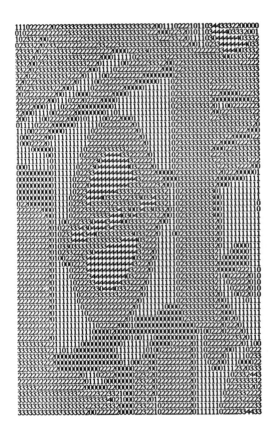

Figure 9.9
A region map produced from the Underground sign of figure 9.1.

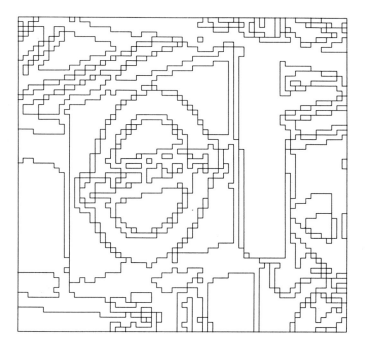

Figure 9.10
An alternative depiction of the region map in figure 9.9.

half-rings and the upper and lower half-discs of the sign.

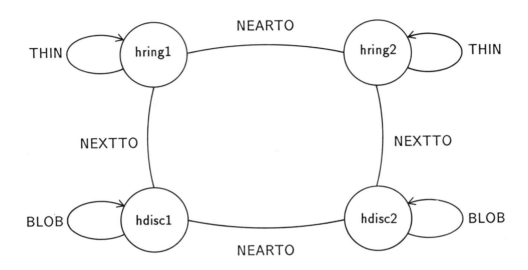

Figure 9.11
A model for an Underground sign.

We test for blob-like regions and thin regions by looking at the ratio of region boundary length to area enclosed (assuming the boundaries are reasonably smooth) and define two regions as 'nearto' one another when the closest distance between them is less than some threshold (which may depend on the sizes of the regions).

One way of matching the model would be to find all combinations of assignments of regions to nodes, and then, for each combination, to check that all properties and relationships are satisfied. This would be very time-consuming since there will in general be a large number of possible combinations of assignments. However, there is a much better way of finding consistent matches, using a depth-first search strategy (chapter 4) in which large parts of the space of possible matches are eliminated by testing partial matches for consistency.

The depth-first matching strategy works as follows. One of the model nodes is selected and all regions are assigned to this node in turn. If a region does not satisfy all necessary properties associated with the node, the region is skipped and we move on to the next one. A second node is now selected, and for each successful region assignment to the first node, all regions are now assigned in turn to this second node. Again, region assignments to the second node are skipped if they do not satisfy all necessary properties associated with this node. Now, for each remaining assignment to the second node and the current assignment to the first node, any necessary relationships between these nodes are checked, and if not satisfied, the region assignment to the second node is skipped and the next one selected. For each assignment to the first and second nodes which satisfies all properties and relationships between the nodes, all possible regions are assigned to a third node. Again the required properties and relationships between this assignment and the first two are checked, and so the process continues until all nodes have been assigned a region and all properties and relationships are satisfied.

The depth-first search can be represented by a tree in which each level corresponds to a model node and each of the branches corresponds to a region assignment to that node which satisfies all properties and relationships with assignments of regions to nodes on the path to the root of the tree (figure 9.12).

Returning to our example, we have already observed in figure 9.10 that the segmentation process extracts a number of regions which correspond well with meaningful parts of the Underground sign. In particular, the top and bottom segments of the ring, and the top and bottom half-discs within the sign, have been identified as single regions: call these a, b, c, and d, respectively. The search tree in figure 9.12 shows the successful match in which these regions are assigned to nodes hring1, hring2, hdisc1, and hdisc2.

As with method 1, a satisfactory match locates the Underground sign in the image, but for much less effort. However, there are problems. First, all properties and relationships must be satisfied; there is no room for error. A more sophisticated matching procedure is needed to get around this.

A second important problem with the kind of model described is that it does not take account of variations in the appearance of an object from different viewing angles. For example, when an Underground sign is looked at obliquely, the semi-circular regions within the sign become more like thin regions. Consequently, in practice, it is necessary to have a separate model corresponding to each substantially different viewpoint. Nevertheless, it is worth noting that there are relationships, like 'nextto', which are not affected by viewing angle.

A more effective solution to this problem is to use stored models of the 3-dimensional structure of objects from which the characteristic arrangement of salient features from a particular viewing angle can be predicted. An object is

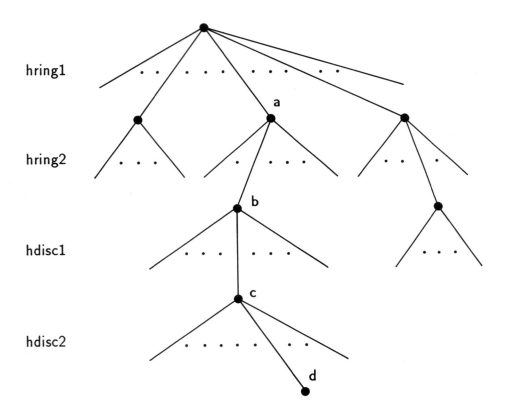

Figure 9.12
The search tree for matching model of Underground sign.

recognized by looking for a collection of salient features which is consistent with the appropriate model for some viewing angle (see, for example, Brooks, 1981).

9.5 Describing Shape and Position

The two methods described above deal with the problem of building a vision system to recognize familiar objects within a scene. This is only one of the tasks that the visual sub-system of our MTG would have to deal with. An equally important task is generating an internal representation of the shapes and positions of visible objects, including unspecified objects that may be obstacles in the path of the MTG, thereby enabling the MTG to plan and execute a path to the Underground entrance. For example, how could the MTG find out about the structure of an unfamiliar building for which a stored model could only be loosely specified (for example, "buildings have a floor and walls which usually meet at right-angles")?

One valuable source of information is the use of binocular vision, in which a pair of images of the same scene are taken from slightly differing viewpoints. If the projection of a point in space can be identified in each image, by, say, matching edge elements derived from a fragment of texture on a visible surface, then the actual 3-D location of that point can be determined using simple geometry. This technique works for unspecified objects and clearly provides a useful starting point from which to map out the surrounding world.

Another valuable source of information about the surrounding world is the shading across visible surfaces caused by variations in surface orientation. Under certain conditions, measurements of these variations can be turned into precise descriptions of surface orientation (see Horn, 1975, for more details).

A time sequence of images depicting one or more objects moving with respect to the camera provides yet another means for discovering something about the the disposition of the object surfaces. The situation here is similar to that for binocular vision since objects are viewed from more than one direction. It is therefore hardly surprising that methods developed for binocular vision can often be adapted to deal with sequences of images and vice versa.

More information on binocular vision, shading analysis, and the use of image sequences can be found in Marr (1982), Frisby (1979), and Bruce (1985).

9.6   Conclusion

Our intention in this chapter has been to show the magnitude of the task carried
out by the human vision system by getting down to the 'nuts and bolts' of possible
(although not always plausible) mechanisms. We have addressed the problem of
designing a vision system for a mobile tourist guide and looked in detail at two
ways of recognizing a familiar object: the London Underground sign. One way of
recognizing a particular object in a TV image is to match a series of templates
corresponding to idealized versions of the object, viewed from different angles and
distances, against areas on the image. To compensate for variations in lighting,
the image and the templates can be reduced to the form of edge maps: abrupt
variations in light intensity that correspond approximately to the edges of objects.
Another approach is to extract a range of features, such as edges and regions, from
the scene, and then to match these against models of possible objects in the scene,
stored in the form of knowledge representation structures such as semantic nets.

9.7   Appendix: Recognizing   an   Underground Sign

In this appendix we shall develop programs in POP-11 for generating edge maps,
matching templates (from method 1), and finding regions (from method 2).

We first need some way of representing images obtained from the video digitizer
and also the stored templates. The POP-11 array is the ideal construct for this.
An array is a data-structure containing a collection of POP-11 items indexed by
integers. For example, we can store the names of the months of the year as an
array in which each name is indexed by the number of that month. The array is
first created using the POP-11 procedure **newarray**, which takes as argument a list
containing the desired upper and lower bounds of the index numbers. Then each
array cell is filled with the name of a month of the year:

```
vars months;
newarray([1 12]) -> months;
"January" -> months(1);
"February" -> months(2);
  :
"December" -> months(12);
```

Now to find out the name of the 6th month we write

```
months(6) =>
** June
```

There will be a mishap if you try to access an array cell which is outside the declared bounds of the array.

The built-in POP-11 procedure **boundslist** returns a list containing the upper and lower bounds for a particular array — for example,

```
boundslist(months) =>
** [1 12]
```

Instead of using arrays to store the names of the months we could have used lists. However, arrays are a very efficient means for accessing data that have to be indexed by number, and for this reason they are preferable when large amounts of data are to be stored, as with the grey-levels of an image.

Cells of the array **months** are accessed by a single integer argument. Arrays of this type are known as 1-dimensional arrays. However, because an image is essentially a 2-dimensional array of pixels, we shall use 2-dimensional arrays to store the grey-levels: that is, arrays which require two integer arguments to access or update their elements. The first argument is the number of the column and the second argument is the number of the row.

The same POP-11 procedure **newarray** is used to create 2-dimensional arrays. The single argument is a list specifying the upper and lower bounds for each of the two indices. Thus, to make an array for storing an image which is 64 × 64 pixels in size we do the following:

```
vars image;
newarray([1 64 1 64]) -> image;
```

We could assign grey-levels to this array by inserting them one by one into the array cells using 4096 (64 × 64) assignment statements

```
4 -> image(1,1);
4 -> image(2,1);
5 -> image(3,1);
⋮
72 -> image(64,64);
```

but that would be very laborious, so instead we make a list of the grey-levels and assign this to a POP-11 variable and then transfer the numbers from this list into the array using a general procedure `fillimage`, defined as follows:

```
define fillimage(image, list);

    /* to transfer numbers from list into array */
    vars x, y, g, xsize, ysize;

    boundslist(image) --> [1 ?xsize 1 ?ysize];

    /* scan array from top-left to bottom-right
       inserting grey-levels from list */
    for y from 1 to ysize do
        for x from 1 to xsize do
            list --> [?g ??list];
            g -> image(x,y)
        endfor
    endfor
enddefine;
```

The first argument to `fillimage` (the array **image**) is a newly created image array into which grey-levels are to be inserted, and the second argument (`list`) is a list of grey-levels ordered from the top-left pixel to the bottom-right pixel, moving from left to right and from top to bottom. For example, a list of the grey-levels shown in figure **??** would appear as

```
[4  4  5 ...
 1  4 15 ...
 ...86 71 72] -> grey_levels;
```

The procedure `fillimage` generates the row and column indices for each image array cell (pixel) in turn using two **for** loops, one nested within the other. The outer **for** loop iterates over the rows and the inner **for** loop iterates over the columns, thereby selecting each pixel in the current row. The pattern matcher is used to extract grey-levels from the front of `list` one at a time and to replace `list` with the values remaining (both these operations are achieved by a single use of the pattern matcher).

First, we shall produce an edge map from a given image. The procedure `findedgels` returns an array which is the same size as the image array given as its argument, with a 1 in those cells for which there is a nearby edge element in the corresponding point in the image array, and 0 otherwise.

```
define findedgels(image, thrshld) -> edgemap;
  vars x, y, xsize, ysize;

  /* find the width and height of the given image */
  boundslist(image) --> [1 ?xsize 1 ?ysize];

  /* make an edge map of the same size as the
     given image and initialize each entry to 0 */
  newarray([1 ^xsize 1 ^ysize], 0) -> edgemap;

  /* scan each pixel in turn */
  for y from 2 to ysize-1 do
    for x from 2 to xsize-1 do

      /* does sum of differences between horizontally
         and vertically adjacent pixels exceed a given
         threshold? */
      if abs(image(x,y) - image(x-1,y))
        + abs(image(x,y) - image(x,y-1)) > thrshld
      then
        /* yes so record a 1 in current position */
        1 -> edgemap(x,y)
      endif
    endfor
  endfor

enddefine;
```

We now need to define a procedure for comparing an edge map derived from a stored template image with an edge map derived from an input image. First we define a procedure for performing the comparison at a particular position of one edge map with respect to the other. The position is specified by the location of the pixel in the second edge map which lies under the top left-hand corner of the first edge map. A pair of counters are initialized to zero. When all corresponding entries in each edge map have been compared, counter `maxtotal` will contain the number of edge elements that should have been found (i.e., those in the edge map derived from the template), and the other counter, `hittotal`, will contain the number of times that an edge element is found in the corresponding location in both edge maps. The quality of the match is obtained in numerical form by dividing `hittotal` by `maxtotal`:

```
define match_at_xy(edgemap1, edgemap2, x, y) -> goodness;
  vars xx, yy, xsize, ysize, maxtotal, hittotal;

  /* find the size of the edge map from the template */
  boundslist(edgemap1) --> [1 ?xsize 1 ?ysize];

  0 -> maxtotal; 0 -> hittotal;

  /* scan each element of edgemap1 */
  for yy from 1 to ysize do
    for xx from 1 to xsize do

      /* is there an edge element at (xx,yy) in edgemap1 */
      if edgemap1(xx,yy) = 1 then

        /* increment running total of edges */
        1 + maxtotal -> maxtotal;

        /* is there a matching edge at
           corresponding position of edgemap2 */
        if edgemap2(x+xx-1, y+yy-1) = 1 then
    /* yes so increment running total of matching edges */
          1 + hittotal -> hittotal;
        endif
      endif
    endfor
  endfor;

  /* compute goodness of match by dividing number of matching
```

```
        edges by number there would be in an ideal match */
    hittotal / maxtotal -> goodness;

enddefine;
```

The next procedure, `match_image`, finds an edge map from the stored template and from the input image and then matches these by sliding one over the other applying `match_at_xy` at each position. When the quality of the match exceeds a threshold value, which is given as an argument to `match_image`, the position of that match is printed out:

```
define match_image(template, image, thrshld);
  vars xsize, ysize, xxsize, yysize, x, y, edgemap1, edgemap2;
  findedgels(template, 10) -> edgemap1;
  findedgels(image, 10) -> edgemap2;
  boundslist(template) --> [1 ?xxsize 1 ?yysize];
  boundslist(image) --> [1 ?xsize 1 ?ysize];
  for y from 1 to ysize-yysize+1 do
    for x from 1 to xsize-xxsize+1 do
      if match_at_xy(edgemap1, edgemap2, x, y) > thrshld then
        [There is a good match at position ^x ^y] =>
      endif
    endfor
  endfor
enddefine;
```

Using the arrays shown in figures 9.3 and 9.6, and with a threshold value of 0.6, a handful of positions are printed, all in the vicinity of the correct position:

```
    ** [There is a good match at position 10 11]
    ** [There is a good match at position 11 11]
    ** [There is a good match at position 9 12]
    ** [There is a good match at position 10 12]
    ** [There is a good match at position 8 13]
    ** [There is a good match at position 9 13]
```

In this case the method seems to work!

9.7.1   A POP-11 Procedure to Find Regions

In the second part of this chapter, a region finding procedure is described which takes a list of ranges and labels each pixel of an image according to which of the ranges the corresponding grey-level is contained within or 0 if it is not contained within any of the ranges.

The following procedure performs this labelling for a given image and list of ranges:

```
define findregions(image, ranges) -> regionmap;
  vars a, b, table, i, label, xsize, ysize, x, y;

  /* build a table mapping grey-levels to labels   */
  /* (2nd arg. to newarray initializes cells to 0) */
  newarray([0 99],0) -> table;
  0 -> label;
  foreach [?a ?b] in ranges do
    label + 1 -> label;
    for i from a to b do
      label -> table(i)
    endfor
  endforeach;

  /* construct a region map from image by assigning label
     from table to each pixel according to grey-level */

  boundslist(image) --> [1 ?xsize 1 ?ysize];
  newarray([1 ^xsize 1 ^ysize]) -> regionmap;
  for y from 1 to ysize do
    for x from 1 to xsize do
      table(image(x,y)) -> regionmap(x,y)
    endfor
  endfor;

enddefine;
```

9.8 Exercises

1. List as many different kinds of use for human vision as you can (e.g., looking for something, noticing the sudden appearance of an object, planning a route down a mountain).

2. Design a model for the appearance of an object in your immediate environment. You will need to force yourself to think about the object in terms of its 2-dimensional projection on your retina rather than as a 3-dimensional entity. Express your model as a semantic net of the form shown in figure 9.11.

3. Write a program to turn an image into its negative version. You will need to replace each grey level by the difference between that level and the level representing maximum intensity (99 in our case).

4. Outline a set of rules for finding closed edge contours in an image by hopping between neighbouring edge elements. If you are feeling ambitious, turn this outline into a program.

5. Think about how you might set about blurring an image and write a program to achieve this. (Hint: You will need to replace each grey-level with a new value computed from grey-levels at neighbouring pixels.)

6. One way in which to model the 3-D structure of objects is in terms of a number of primitive shapes glued together. For example, we can represent the limbs and body of many animals using cylinders (see Marr, 1982). Try to draw up a list of primitive shapes with which to model the objects in a typical office scene. For example, you could use a series of rectangular faced shapes to construct the tables.

Chapter 10

AI and the Philosophy of Mind

The advent of 'intelligent' computers has given several new twists to the tangle of problems which constitute the Philosophy of Mind. Some writers have proposed that computation can provide us with a new explanation of the nature of the mind. It is not difficult to see why. It has become commonplace to use mental terms about computational processes. At many points in this book we have talked of understanding, decision, searching, and other cognitive processes in relation to computer programs we have described or referred to. Can such cognitive or intellectual ascriptions be taken literally? Or are we simply indulging in poetic (or philosophic) licence?

10.1   Mind and Body

It is easy for people who have grown up, as we have, in an intellectual environment which takes scientific **materialism** for granted to be dismissive of old-fashioned views of the mind, such as those held by René Descartes (see chapter 1). He provided a picture of a human being as a combination of a material body and an immaterial soul. The body functioned according to strict mechanistic physical laws, while the soul was the seat of cognition, emotion, will, and sensation. Descartes wanted to defend the traditional canons of Christian belief against a rising tide of secular thought, this latter engendered by the growing successes of the young physical sciences in the seventeenth century. But he also had, as he saw it, some excellent reasons of a purely philosophical kind for believing in a soul, or 'spiritual substance', to use his term.

His most famous argument was based on issues of *doubt* and *certainty* (Descartes, 1642). There is a lot that I can feel reasonably sure of, but little of which I can have absolute, unquestionable certainty. I assume that my physical body, and the various states that I observe it to undergo, are real occurrences in a real physical world. But all I can observe is a sequence of *subjective sensations* of these states. I cannot get behind the sensations to the physical reality which I assume to be their cause. I infer from a certain kind of sensation that something is pressing on my right foot. But amputees can have such sensations of non-existent 'phantom limbs'. I sense myself as sitting at a desk, typing at a keyboard — but maybe I am asleep, and merely dreaming of the episode. By some even more extravagant supposition, my firm belief that I do have a real body may be an illusion implanted in my mind by an all-powerful Evil Demon. This is highly unlikely, but the mere possibility of such a thing is sufficient to make it possible for me to say that I do not know for certain that my body exists.

Can I, then, be certain that I exist at all? Perhaps this same Evil Demon has duped me into thinking that I exist, when I do not. Well, my body may be an illusion — but what about *my existence as such*? Surely I must exist — in some form or other — in order to be able to *think* the thought "Maybe I don't exist." Thus, Descartes concluded that the part of me which engages in reflection and cogitation must be independent from, and in a sense privileged with respect to, my physical body — since it appears that it cannot be doubted away in the way that my body can. And that privileged part of me is my mind.

Another argument, inspired by Descartes, if not directly attributible to him, concerns, not cognition, but sensations, such as pain. Just pinch your arm hard, hard enough for it to hurt. Various bodily processes are presumably occurring: local traumas to blood vessels in your arm, impulses to your central nervous system, etc. (We are now once again assuming that you do have a body after all!) An expert physiologist could give a good hour's lecture on the various things which will be happening. But besides the physical processes, something else seems to be occurring, something of which you are directly aware, and to know about which you need no understanding of the physical processes: the feeling of pain itself. Indeed, according to followers of Descartes, this feeling of pain is, *conceptually*, or *logically*, completely distinguishable from any of the accompanying physical processes. An amputee who is feeling pain in a phantom limb is still feeling pain, even if the physical source of the pain is misidentified.

We take it as a well founded scientific hypothesis that the pain results from a particular assortment of physical causes. But do we have any good reasons for *equating* the pain with those physical causes? Well, first, a small child can know she is in pain without knowing anything about the physical causes. Second, if you tried to observe all the physical causes of that child's pain, you would not, for all that, observe the pain itself. To observe the pain directly, surely, you would have to *be* the child — for only she can observe her own pain. Pain — and other mental states, such as thoughts, wishes, emotions, and so on — seem to possess a special kind of subjectivity or 'privacy', which physical processes do not. To *identify* the pain with the physical processes is, it is claimed, a confusion, the result of failing to think clearly enough about one's own personal experiences.

This, at least, is how people who agree with Descartes' philosophical outlook would argue. We may not feel like agreeing with Descartes that our mental processes reside in a 'spiritual substance'. But it does seem difficult, after some reflection, to avoid accepting that mental processes are *special* in some way, and not completely reducible to physical processes.

Anyone who feels at all sympathetic to the above train of thought (I only ask you to be sympathetic, not to be convinced!) will find it hard to see how even the most intelligent or versatile of artificial intelligence programs could endow a digital computer with real mental states — with genuine subjectivity.[1] Surely, it may be said, however closely a computer might model the outward manifestations of human thought processes, the machine would not really be thinking, since that involves being able to have subjective, inner processes. We certainly seem to have this subjective, inner experience of ourselves as mental beings. But how could a program provide a computer with similar sorts of subjective experience?

What good AI programs do is make computers *perform* in certain ways. But we saw in earlier chapters that AI programs do more than that. They *also* provide computers with an elaborate structure of internal representations, and internal mechanisms for manipulating those representations. But have we any right to conclude that a machine under the control of an AI program (even an extremely complex one) must also be having subjective experiences or conscious states? For surely that is what would be necessary in order for us to be able to say that such machines really do have mental states, and not just capabilities of performing in mind-like ways.

It might be said in reply to this that when we are talking of internal representations in computers we are, by that very token, talking of genuine mental states. But this would surely be a difficult position to defend. By internal representations

---

[1] See Dennett, 1978b, for a more detailed discussion.

we mean data-structures — for example, list structures of various sorts — which facilitate the transformation of different kinds of inputs (e.g., a sentence like "What is the quickest way to Marble Arch?") into appropriate outputs (e.g., the response "Take the Victoria Line to Oxford Circus ... "). It would be a bad pun on the word 'internal' to say that whatever internal representations are operating here must, *because* they are internal, be subjective states of consiousness. So *if* it is necessary to have subjective states of awareness in order to qualify as having a mind, it would not follow from the fact that machines can perform intelligently and operate with elaborate structures of internal representations (in the sense outlined), that they therefore must have minds.

It looks at this stage as though we have to accept that, in order to undergo genuine mental processes of any kind, it is necessary to have subjective, conscious states of experience. Should we, then, conclude that computers and AI have nothing useful to tell us about the nature of the human mind, despite the promising and innovative nature of so much that is currently being discovered in AI research? This would be premature.

First, as we have seen at length in this book, and as was explored in detail in chapter 8, AI programs have been instructive in explaining and modelling the functional operations of thinking, even if we were not to accept that machines which are running such programs are literally thinking. Second, it may be that the points we have just looked at, which seem to argue against granting mentality to AI systems under any circumstances, do not survive closer examination. One possibility, for example, might be that there are (at least) two quite different kinds of mental states or mental properties. On the one hand, there would be subjective states of consciousness, which we have already talked about. But on the other hand, when we talk, in an idiomatic way, of 'things going on in our minds', we are often talking, surely, not about qualitative states of awareness, but rather of cognitive operations of various kinds, of which we are not, or need not be, fully conscious. Perhaps processes of this latter sort *are* much closer to the internal processes of working AI systems.

10.2   Consciousness and the Puzzle of Other Minds

Consider again the case of the pinched arm. The child whose arm has been pinched will have a familiar enough mental state. We can use the example to construct a venerable old philosophical puzzle — the problem of 'Other Minds' (see the editor's introduction to Chappell, 1962). We are unable to observe the child's pain directly, although we can observe all the outward behavioural manifestations and, with the right equipment, various related physiological changes. So we cannot be absolutely certain that the child really does have that inner, subjective feeling of pain — as certain, that is, as we can be of the existence of our own pain. This is what is meant by saying that the experience of pain is 'private', whereas the outward manifestations are 'public'.

We have a similar problem, it would appear, with *all* mental states of people other than ourselves. Only my own mental states, it seems, are directly observable by me. But then how can I possibly be sure that there *are* any other minds besides my own? I cannot simply infer it from the fact that the outward signs are the same in the case of myself and of others, for this begs the very question which is at issue — namely whether I have any right to take it for granted, as I do, that other human beings are like me in having both the outward manifestations *and* the inner subjective states. Maybe, on the contrary, I am a very special human being (perhaps unique, or perhaps one of a small minority), and that most people do not have any of this inner stream of conscious experiences at all.

There are many ways of dealing with this puzzle, and we shall not go into them here. (See Chappell, 1962, and Shaffer, 1968, for representative discussions.) Let us limit ourselves to one underlying difficulty. Suppose we change the initial example upon which the puzzle is constructed. Imagine this time, not a child whose arm is being pinched, but someone sitting across the table playing chess with you. Once again we can suppose that there are various externally observable processes — physical movements of various sorts, and no doubt certain characteristic physiological processes. Again, too, there would seem to be various internal processes. But here it is not at all clear that the sorts of 'inner' processes of thinking which are attributable to a person playing chess are so very different from the kinds of 'inner' processes which are attributable to a computer which is running a good chess-playing program. Of course there are various characteristic sensations — a certain quivering feeling in the pit of one's stomach, for instance — which may occur whenever you play chess. But these are not an inseparable part of the cognitive process of chess playing. If you do not have such experiences or sensations, but still play a good game of chess, we would still allow that you were genuinely playing the game, and indeed that you were playing it 'with your mind'. In the case of 'chess'-type mental states, all that seems to be essential is that the person is capable of having various sorts of internal representations and cognitive processes, and these appear to be much closer to the sorts of processes which we attribute to a computer chess program. So the puzzle about Other Minds seems much harder to launch if you use examples like chess playing as a departure point, rather than examples like arm pinching.

Suppose I consider my chess opponent and wonder whether there really are chess-like thoughts in her mind underlying the external appearances? If she is playing chess in the normal way (that is, assuming she is not under post-hypnotic suggestion, using a hidden auto-cue, etc.), could such a possibility be coherently entertained? She may lack the usual characteristic (but inessential) sensations, but can she fail to be performing the sorts of cognitive operations which are necessary ingredients of normal chess play? Can she fail, that is, to be doing things like considering alternative possible moves, reviewing different strategies, making inferences about her opponent's likely moves, and so on? This all seems to render more plausible the suggestion made earlier that there are two rather different classes of mental processes or mental states: experiential processes (like pains) and cognitive processes (thoughts about chess, etc.); and that perhaps computer systems are at least capable of having genuine mental states of the latter kind, if not the former.

I said 'perhaps'. All we are doing here is removing one obstacle to admitting computers with minds. There is an alternative kind of response, of course, which is to say that computers *could*, after all, have conscious mental experiences. It is not clear whether this has been seriously claimed by anyone. (For an interesting discussion of this issue see Dennett, 1978a). But the claim has certainly been made that the notion of consious experience is so difficult to pin down that, in the end, the issue of whether or not computers could have conscious experiences simply becomes a practical, or ethical issue, hinging on how we decide to treat them. What has been argued is that if it became a widespread practice to treat certain kinds of extremely sophisticated machines as conscious beings, because of the richness and depth of their behaviour, it would then not make any sense to ask the further question "But are they *really* conscious?" This, the argument goes, would be like asking whether my hand is occupying *the very same point in space* now as it was five minutes ago, and refusing (as relativity theory says you must) to accept any answer that was relativized to a given inertial frame (Sloman, 1986).

10.3   Syntax, Semantics, and Intentionality

We shall return to the general issue of whether computers can experience pains and other experiential states towards the end of the chapter. Instead we now direct our attention to the claim that, even if computers could not literally be conscious, they might still be able to have genuine mental states insofar as their computational processes mirror the cognitive processes in our minds. So the next part of our discussion leaves consciousness entirely out of the picture, and concentrates on the nature of cognition, which is the prime territory of AI.

When we think, we think about things. For instance, Jane's belief that Tom is sprinkling salt on his French fries is a belief about something. Jane's thought — in this case a belief — has, as its content, the proposition

> Tom is sprinkling salt on his French fries.

Similarly, if Jane wants to buy a pair of green leg-warmers later today, she has a thought — this time a wish, rather than a belief — whose content is

> Jane buys a pair of green leg-warmers later today.

If Tom also wants Jane to buy green leg-warmers today, then he too has a wish, which has the same content as Jane's wish. Different thought, same content.

Many philosophers have thought that possessing a content in this way is a defining feature of mental states, at least of those mental states which we have been calling 'cognitive processes', if not of conscious experiences as well. The term **intentionality** has often been used to refer to this characteristic, and some philosophers have seen it as providing a key to the essence of 'mind'. The word 'intentionality' is supposed to indicate the way in which thoughts are directed at objects or circumstances outside themselves. That is, 'intentionality' connotes 'aboutness' (see Searle, 1983).

The notion of intentionality is also used in order to explain the meaningfulness of language: the difference between meaningless utterances and meaningful communication. When we talk or write things down, our utterances have certain formal properties — phonological and syntactical properties, which can be discussed completely in isolation from their meaning. For example, when Jane speaks or writes the sentence "Tom is sprinkling salt on his French fries," we can talk of the fact that the sentence has eight words, that the sentence contains an embedded adverbial phrase, and so on. These are observations about the symbols in themselves, and do not make any reference to their meaning, to the fact that the sentence is about certain objects and events in the world, namely, Tom, salt, and French fries. To talk about the sentence's meaning is to talk on the level of semantics, and it is relatively easy to characterize meaning in terms of intentional content. So the notion of intentionality can be used in order to explain both inner mental states and external spoken or written utterances.

People who doubt that computers can tell us much of interest about the nature of the mind have frequently appealed to the intentionality of human mental activity and of meaningful communication as a way of denying mentality in machines. On the face of it, it may seem obvious to people who have read through this book that computers *can* have states which possess intentionality. The symbol-structures that a computer operates with are surely not necessarily mere collections of uninterpreted tokens, but will often be understandable in terms of meanings, or contents. The structures will refer to objects or circumstances outside themselves. We have seen, for example, how programs can be written to engage in natural language dialogues which do not merely operate on the level of syntax, but also on the level of semantics. Also we have observed that machines running AI (and other) programs operate with many internal representations which can only be understood in an 'intentionalistic' way: they construct plans about the manipulation of objects, perform searches, compare, choose among alternatives, apply rules, and so on. All these operations are characterizable in terms of their reference to various subject-matters which are distinct from the symbolic structures which constitute the operations themselves.

In response to this, philosophers who are sceptical about machine mentality retort that such programs do not have genuine semantics or intentionality, but only pseudo-intentionality. Consider, first of all, the sentences of a book or of a letter. If we came across the sentence about Tom and the French fries in a letter written by Jane, we would say that the words in the letter 'had meaning', but by this we would really be intending to refer to Jane's using the words to express *her* meaning — or alternatively, to the meaning which *we* derived from the words on reading them. The piece of paper and the marks on it would not possess meaning or intentionality in their own right, or at least they would do so only in a derivative sense. They would simply be a vehicle to express the intentional contents of Jane's thoughts. Surely, the argument goes, a computer is just a more complicated kind of device for transmitting symbols whose meanings originate in their human users, rather than in the device itself. However complex we might make the computer and its software, and however life like its external behaviour, it will always be in essence simply a device for manipulating and transmitting strings of symbols which are, from the computer's point of view, merely formal patterns of tokens, to which meaning is given by us, the human users. This, in outline, is the position of those who are against attributing genuine intentionality to computers. Naturally enough, people have been quick to come forward in defence of the machines.

10.4   The Intentional Stance

In a paper called "Intentional Systems" (Dennett, 1978a), Daniel Dennett suggested the following line of thought. Consider a computer running a chess-playing program. We might consider this machine from a number of different points of view. We might adopt the 'design stance': this will be our point of view if what we are interested in is primarily the construction of the program, how it is implemented in the hardware, and so on. Then there is the 'physical stance': this will be our perspective if we are interested in the chemical or electronic properties of the semiconductor devices in the machine's circuit board, and so on. But apart from these perspectives there is what Dennett calls the 'intentional stance'. This is the point of view you would adopt if you were actually playing chess with the machine: in this case you would consider its goals, strategies, the beliefs that it might have about your strategy, and so on.

When we adopt the intentional stance, we are treating the machine *as if* it had desires, beliefs, purposes, representations, etc., that is, intentional states. But this, says Dennett, is not just a luxury. It is a necessary condition of our being able to use the machine for its intended purpose — namely, to play chess (or whatever). If we chose to limit ourselves to the design stance or, worse, to the physical stance, we would find it difficult or even impossible to play a good game with the machine. We need the intentional stance in order to make proper explanations and predictions of the machine's actions.

But if the intentional stance is necessary in one sense, in another sense it is, or *need be*, merely a product of our own predictive purposes. When reflecting "It's threatening my knight, so it obviously wants to trap me into exposing my queen," we do not have to be attributing literal beliefs and desires to the machine. The issue of whether or not there really are such entities inside the computer will not in the slightest affect our game.

So the attribution of intentionality to the chess-playing machine is merely the product of the adoption of a certain sort of stance to the machine, a stance which is appropriate because of its predictive and explanatory value, and therefore to that extent objectively justified, but which need have no deeper 'metaphysical' basis. But, insists Dennett, the same may just as well be true of intentionality in human beings. We need to make intentional characterizations of one another (and of ourselves), in order to make sense of each other's actions. So the adoption of the 'intentional stance' is, for this reason, unavoidable in humans just as it is in the case of the chess machine. But do we therefore need to conclude that there must be metaphysically real intentional entities in our minds? Surely the cases are comparable. In each case intentionality appears to function as an indispensable descriptive and explanatory framework, but in each case, too, we have no especial need, once we have realized the nature of this explanatory framework, to wonder whether or not there is any inherent reality to the phenomena referred to in the framework.

Dennett's view is an example of what has been called the **eliminativist approach** to mental states. Eliminativists tend to be rather sceptical about the traditional vocabulary of mental states, such as 'beliefs', 'wishes', 'intentions', 'meanings', and so on, believing that such concepts belong to an outmoded, pre-scientific, 'folk psychology'. (See chapters 2 and 3 of Churchland, 1984). Dennett believes that philosophers' notions of intentionality (among other commonsense notions of the mind) are infected by the mythologies of our folk psychology and that, as a result of findings in AI, neurophysiology, and the cognitive sciences in general, they will be replaced by other, more adequate notions in a fully scientific account of human nature and of the mind. This is not to say, of course, that there is any harm in using such notions on a day-to-day basis: obviously they have, as we have seen, an indispensable heuristic role to play. As long as we continue to recognize that our intentional ascriptions do have to play this heuristic role, nothing will be lost by supposing that there is no such thing — in scientific or metaphysical fact — as real intentionality, whether in machines or in humans.

10.5   Searle's Chinese Room

Not surprisingly, not all philosophers are happy with the idea of eliminating our 'folk psychology'. There has been a strong tradition in recent decades of English-speaking philosophy of giving the concepts of common sense the greatest amount of respect. The idea that AI or neurophysiology or any other new-fangled subject could simply come along and supplant our time-honoured concepts of mind is regarded by these philosophers with great suspicion. In his famous paper "Minds, Brains and Programs" (Searle, 1980), the philosopher John Searle has offered a sustained counterblast to the eliminativist's dismissal of commonsense psychological notions. In it (and subsequently in his Reith Lectures — Searle, 1984) he attempts to show why intentional notions are not so easy to give up, and why human intentionality must necessarily be in a privileged position with respect to machine intentionality. It is Searle's arguments that we shall now consider, after a brief diversion to the Turing Test.

It is now becoming common for people to communicate with each other by electronic mail, and no doubt it will soon be relatively easy for people to write AI programs which can join in on the act in a way that makes their contributions indistinguishable, to a greater or lesser extent, from those of humans. As we have already mentioned, Alan Turing (Turing, 1950) proposed a criterion, or benchmark, for machine intelligence and hence, by extension, for machine intentionality. The ideas that Turing put forward were outlined in chapter 1 of this book, so we need not dwell on them here. Turing's claim was, in essence, that if a program could be written which was flexible enough to participate in an extended electronic mail dialogue, and if it could do so in a way which was not easily ascertainable by other participants in the dialogue, then we could take the machine in question as displaying genuine intelligence. (This is a generalization of the test proposed by Turing in his paper, but one which keeps to the spirit of his proposal.)

It is probable that Turing would have been sympathetic to the eliminativist's claim that our common notions of 'folk psychology' are confused and not capable of scientific justification. It was, indeed, partly to bypass the, as he saw it, hopelessly vague nature of questions such as "Can machines think?" that Turing proposed his test in the first place. Also he believed that our psychological terms were liable to change their meanings as a result of advances in computing and other sciences, and he predicted that, by the end of the current century, most educated people would agree without question that computers were capable of thinking.

Searle, by contrast, does not think there is anything vague about questions like "Can machines think?" Sure, he says, machines can think. We are machines, and we can think. But the key question is, "Can digital computers think?" or more precisely, "Could a machine think merely by virtue of the fact that it was a digital computer programmed in a certain way?" This is the question which Searle thinks is neither vague nor difficult to answer, and the answer is negative.

In order to show why that question has to be answered negatively, Searle describes an imaginary situation, rather like Turing's Imitation Game, but with some special features added. Searle pictures someone (whom we shall call 'the operator') in a room equipped with a large number of pieces of paper on which are written various symbols that are unintelligible to the operator. There are slots in the wall of the room, through which more slips of paper with such symbols can be passed, both into and out of the room. The operator also has an elaborate set of rules giving precise instructions on how to build, compare, and manipulate symbol-structures, using the pieces of paper inside the room, in conjunction with those coming in from the outside. These instructions also tell the operator to send sets of symbols out of the room on occasion. The instructions are all expressed in terms of the formal properties of the symbols which, as we have said, have no significance in themselves to the operator.

In fact, the instructions correspond to a computer program which simulates the linguistic ability and understanding of a native speaker of Chinese. The sets of symbols being passed into and out of the room correspond to sentences in a meaningful dialogue (rather like a Turing Test dialogue, but in Chinese). The operator, however, understands no Chinese; the instructions for manipulating the Chinese symbols are, we assume, written in English or some other language which the operator understands. We are to suppose that the behaviour of the operator inside the room (the 'Chinese Room', as it has been dubbed) is identical to the behaviour of an electronic computer running the same program. (In order to get round problems of speed we shall suppose that the operator is special in being able to work prodigiously fast.) The operator is, in effect, one particular implementation (albeit a rather strange one) of a particular program which supposedly 'understands' Chinese.

To summarize: Searle's position can best be understood by imagining the following three changes made to Turing's imitation game:

- Have the correspondents communicating, not in English, but in Chinese.

- Have the electronic computer hardware replaced by a human being who (working at superhuman speeds, alone in the 'Chinese Room') is operating all the rules of the program by hand, faithfully reproducing the computer's output. That is, in place of a computer simulating a human being, have a human being simulating the computer's simulation of the human being.

- Assume that the human program operator understands only English.

We assume that the program we are dealing with can pass the Turing Test with flying colours: so that, for example, many native Chinese speakers fail to tell that the person they are apparently having extended intelligent conversations with over the electronic mail system is in fact a person simulating a computer simulating a native Chinese speaker.

Turing's claim was, in essence, this. Providing the program is of a sufficient degree of richness or complexity, the computer playing the imitation game will have, roughly, the mental states which we would have attributed to the human whose dialogue has been imitated. One such mental state is *understanding the words of the language which you are using to communicate in*. So if the dialogue is going on in English, you would expect the computer (or its human simulator) to understand English. If the dialogue is going on in Chinese, you would expect the computer, or its human simulator, to understand Chinese. But under our assumptions, this surely will not be the case. The human computer simulator, sitting inside the 'Chinese Room', will be operating with various symbols, perhaps written on bits of paper or card. These symbol manipulation operations will be formally equivalent to those performed by our computer program which passes the Turing Test. However, it is apparently neither a necessary nor a sufficient condition of the human opertator's successfully replicating the computer's performance that the operator be able to understand any of the input or output sentences in the dialogue.

As Searle puts it, the person inside the Chinese Room has (or need have) only a **syntax**, as opposed to a **semantics** — that is, a knowledge of various *formal* properties of the collections of linguistic tokens being manipulated, rather than an understanding of how the symbols relate to a reality lying outside the symbols themselves. Yet it is semantics, rather than syntax alone, which would be necessary in order for the symbol operator to be able to fix any content to the symbols — that is, in order for there to be any genuine intentionality. But, says Searle, semantics cannot be derived from syntax.

Of course, the program whose operations are being simulated inside the Chinese Room is likely to contain many so-called 'semantical' rules. But these rules are not 'semantical' in the true sense, says Searle: all they can do is establish interrelationships between various purely formal operations. We, the human users of this formal system, can apply semantic interpretations to the input and output strings which are passing through the computer (or its analogue, the Chinese Room). But the semantics, or intentionality, which is thus generated is on the outside of the system — imposed upon it rather than contained within it. If you directly ask the person inside the Chinese Room what all these symbols mean, the answer is likely to be: "Search me — they're just a bunch of meaningless squiggles to me." If you ask the *system*, which the operator is operating, whether it understands Chinese, the answer will come back, in Chinese: "Of course I do, what do you think I'm speaking now?"

Here, then, we have a very clear proposal of how to demonstrate the difference between intentionality in humans and intentionality in computers. If Searle is right, the intentionality of computers must be derivative upon the intentionality of the human creators and users of those machines — more like the derivative intentionality of a book or letter than like the intrinsic intentionality of real thinkers and communicators.

10.6   Responding to Searle

One possible response to Searle is to try to insist that the operator in the Chinese Room *does* understand Chinese after all, despite the operator's most insistent assurances to the contrary. Suppose we were playing chess with someone who, as it turned out, had no conscious knowledge of the rules of chess, but was operating under post-hypnotic suggestion. Would there not, perhaps, be a case for saying that this person did know how to play chess, even though that knowledge was not possessed by the player in a standard fashion? It has, after all, been known for people under post-hypnotic suggestion to deny most vehemently that they have a certain ability or motivational pattern, and then to exhibit that ability or motivation. Might our Chinese Room operator not be in a similar position? We could perhaps say that the operator understood Chinese, but that the operator's understanding was incorporated in a non-standard set of operational dispositions. The trouble with this reply, however, is that it is self-defeating. The aim of the original Turing Test simulation was to show how human psychological characteristics could be embodied in a digital computer. What we wanted to be able to conclude was that the computer could understand Chinese, in the straightforward fashion in which normal Chinese speakers understood the language. But if all we could conclude concerning the human simulator of the program was that the simulator understood Chinese in this non-standard way, then surely we would only have the right to ascribe, at best, this non-standard form of Chinese understanding to the computer — a hollow victory.

One popular response to Searle's argument — dubbed by him the 'Systems Response' — has been to concede that the human symbol operator inside the Chinese Room does not understand Chinese, but to claim that the operator is merely part of a larger system, and that it was 'the system as a whole' which understood Chinese. One version of this response was made by Dennett, in conjunction with Douglas Hofstadter, in their joint compilation *The Mind's I* (Hofstadter and Dennet, 1981, pp. 373–382). The nub of their argument is that Searle has failed to take account of the different *levels* of a computational system. It may be correct to say, of one level of the system, that it is operating merely upon the formal or syntactic properties of the symbols that it is manipulating. But it may also be appropriate to apply a more full-bloodedly intentional or semantic description of its operations when considering the system at a higher level. Bearing that in mind, the total computational system of which the human symbol operator is just a part, may possess higher-level psychological or cognitive properties that are not attributable directly to the symbol operator in the operator's own right. This, at least, is something which Searle would have to show independently to be false, before his argument could be accepted without question.

Searle dismisses the 'Systems Response' in forthright terms, but it is not clear that he has very much in the way of sound argument, rather than rhetoric, with which to reject it (this is not to say that the Systems Response is correct). One consideration he brings to bear is this: what could the 'system' be other than the person, the various pieces of paper which are being shuffled about inside the Chinese Room, and the room itself? If the symbol operator does not understand Chinese, how can the symbol operator *plus bits of paper plus room* understand Chinese? But this is to assume that the only way you can characterize a system is in terms of the physical entities which make the system up, rather than in terms of the *functional relationships* between those entities. After all, what is a human being other than a whole load of carbon and oxygen molecules, and a few other odds and ends? Described in such terms, it would seem pretty unconvincing to suppose that a human being could understand things, or indeed have any other mental states! The point at issue is just that the person in the room, operating the symbols in the appropriate ways, produces a functional system whose properties cannot be described purely in terms of the physical constituents in their own right. Searle may dislike the claim that there is such a functional system, but he cannot just dismiss the idea without begging the very question at issue.

10.7   Artefacts

At the centre of the debate between followers of Searle and his opponents is the question of the status of *artefacts*. The Chinese Room argument seems to depend for at least some of its plausibility upon the picture of computers, together with their programs, as objects which originate in *us*, their human creators, and whose properties must therefore be derivative upon our purposes. There can be no such thing as machine intentionality, so the claim goes, because the states of machines are purely dependent upon our ends: they cannot have *their own* goals. Everything they do, it is claimed, is done (ultimately, at least) because we created them and designed them to follow our 'instructions'. Even if we were to imagine computers which were themselves designed and built by other computers — and which were, perhaps, the product of very many generations of computer design and manufacture — they would still be our artefacts originally. Therefore, it is argued, since intentionality and meaning are intimately bound up with goals and purposes, such machines cannot have their own inherent intentionality. The symbols that they operate with have meaning only when given interpretations which map on to our, human, purposes.

Opposed to this is a contrasting picture of machines which can and do have their own independent purposes and goals: machines to which it is, so it is believed, perfectly proper to ascribe a full-blooded 'intentionality'. Anyone who has wrestled with even a moderately complex AI program will have experienced the feeling that one is confronting a being with a will of its own, with its own purposes and finality. For Searle this would just be a case of over-enthusiastic anthropomorphism, similar to that of the enraged driver who begins to attribute malign purposes to a misbehaving car.

And yet: it seems conceivable that, at least in principle, we might well be obliged to attribute independent or intrinsic goals or purposes to certain kinds of artefacts. Suppose it became possible one day to create human beings by some process of biochemical synthesis. We can imagine the people so created to be as similar to us as you like in physiological terms (that is, they are not composed of miniaturized electronic circuits, for instance, but of the same kind of DNA-based cell tissue as us). It is quite possible that such beings would possess all the same sorts of mental states that we do: they would have pains, emotions, cognitions, purposes, and desires, just like us, since (unlike computers, as presently conceived) they share exactly our physiology.

So it is not the fact that something is an artefact which prevents it from having intrinsic goals, or intrinsic intentionality. Can we, then, conclude, after all, that ordinary digital computers — at least if they are capable of passing something like the Turing Test — do, after all, possess intrinsic intentionality (or at least as much of it as we do)? This is doubtful. What makes the suggestion unconvincing is that the sorts of systems which are being considered as falling within the scope of the Turing Test (at least as it is usually conceived) have a very limited mode of operation. All that they are designed to do is to receive, manipulate, and transmit symbols or tokens, and this really is a very slender basis on which to assert that they have a cognitive existence of a sort which is equivalent to our own. Of course we might attribute to them a sort of intentionality: something which is more than the completely secondary, or derived, intentionality of the contents of a filing cabinet, while yet not in any way approaching the full-blooded intentionality of real human lives. But because their existence is so purely to do with the operation of symbols, their intentionality would be of a decidedly attenuated kind. When dealing with purely 'intellectual', or symbol-related, activities — such as playing games or solving problems in logic — their intentionality more closely approaches ours, since the nature of the purposes in hand are more purely encapsulated in a world of pure symbols. But insofar as they are simulating our world-directed cognitions, as opposed to our symbol-directed cognitions, their intentionality would be but a poor simulacrum of our own.

Of course we can adorn such symbol-processing mechanisms with various accessories which will enable them to engage, in ever more sophisticated ways, with the real world. We can give them sensors which will provide environmental inputs, and motor effectors to act on the environment in various ways. As we do so we will progressively deepen their intentionality. But of course it will also be true that we will progressively be weakening the sense in which we are dealing with merely computing systems, as opposed to systems of a rather richer sort. How far could we take such a progression without wandering away from the original perspective and philosophy of the computational approach to mind? How far would it still be true that we were offering a *computational* account of mentality at all?

And again: what limits might there be to this progressive enrichment of such systems? How far could we reproduce real emotions, consciousness, pleasures, pains? It might well be considered that even the most sophisticated and agile robotic system would not really possess intentionality in its fullest sense if the only world it shared with us was the outer physical spatial world, rather than the inner world of feelings, hopes, fears, and satisfactions. There does seem to be an intimate relationship between notions, such as 'purpose', 'goal', 'intention', and so on, and experiential notions, such as 'satisfaction', 'pleasure', and 'grief'. Perhaps the notions of intentionality and semantics cannot be dissociated from consciousness.

Further, perhaps it might be said that there were at least two distinct kinds of purposes or goals: purposes related to output (for want of a better word) and purposes related to satisfaction. For an example of a goal (or a hierarchy of goals) of the first sort, consider an expert system which has asked you a question concerning a patient's condition for whom you are seeking a diagnosis. If you ask it why it asked you the question, it may explain the hypothesis it is currently seeking to confirm or disconfirm; it is, in other words, explaining its goal. You might then ask it why it wants to confirm that hypothesis, and it might reply in terms of some higher-level goal or goals. Eventually, such explanations will peter out; in the end, the highest-level goal that it can have (at least if it is the sort of expert system currently in use) will be that of producing the answer that you requested. In this sense all of its goals deal with generating a certain sort of output.

A doctor, on the other hand, conducting a similar kind of diagnostic dialogue, is likely to have additional sorts of goals, expressible perhaps in terms of job satisfaction, desire to eradicate disease or ease suffering, intellectual fascination with the scientific issues involved, and so on. People will claim, no doubt, that one day expert systems (or their successors) will possess such inner, satisfaction-oriented goals. But it is not clear what it would be for a system really to have such goals (as opposed to giving outward verbal expression of them). And it may be said that unless they were to do so, the sense in which you can ascribe goals or purposes to them at all is rather weak.

10.8   'Pure' and 'Impure' Functionalism

It has become increasingly fashionable, in recent years, for people in AI to embrace the view that hardware, or the computer architecture, has to be borne in mind in the understanding of how computational models relate to human thinking — particularly in relation to parallel distributed processing, as opposed to the sequential processing which has characterized most computing systems up to now. We saw in chapter 8 how recent work on connectionist machines has suggested some extremely rich (if, at the moment, rather embryonic) models for cognition. The bulk of the work in connection with parallel distributed processing is still to be done. However it does suggest an alternative current of philosophical thinking which may recommend itself to people who wish to use AI as a stepping-stone towards understanding and explaining the mind.

In the dawn of the computer era, and of the era of AI, it was supposed that the notion of mind could be explained entirely in terms of the formal, or functional, properties of a computational system. The term 'functional', as used here, communicates the idea that, in order to have a mind, a system did not have to have a specific *physical* makeup; it just had to be so organized that it was capable of realizing a specific sort of *abstract* computational structure. This computational structure might be implemented on different kinds of physical device: electronic circuits or human brains, or on other kinds of more exotic hardwares yet to be discovered. This sort of approach — which might be called 'pure' **functionalism**, or 'pure' **computationalism** — claimed that the mind could be discussed in terms which were entirely *implementation-independent*. Pure functionalism offered an exciting new approach to the solution of those age-old problems in the philosophy of mind which we talked about at the beginning of this chapter (Putnam, 1960, 1965).

It was partly in order to show up the inadequacy of 'pure functionalism' that Searle produced his 'Chinese Room' argument. If the nature of the hardware was irrelevant to the origination of mental states, then a human agent could substitute for the electronic mechanism performing the operations in a given computational system without altering the supposed thinking states of that system. It was the absurdity of that result that Searle was attempting to demonstrate.

While many of Searle's opponents strove to defend 'pure functionalism' against his attack, many replies to him in effect conceded that that rather extreme view had to be given up. That is, they conceded that while, in the case of his imaginary Chinese Room symbol operator, no genuine mental states would be present, it may still be the case that, in an electronic realization of the same computational operations, real mentality would result. One typical response along these lines was given by Aaron Sloman, in a paper entitled "Did Searle Refute Strong Strong or Weak Strong AI?" (Sloman, 1986), in which he argued that what differentiated the Chinese Room case from a standard case of a computational mechanism was, essentially, the free will of the human operator inside the room. In a conventional computer system the processing device is under the *control* of the program, whereas, in the Chinese Room case, the operator's actions are only *guided* by the rules in the program. This is one of a number of different ways in which it could be argued, with some plausibility, that what Searle says may be true as far as his example goes, but irrelevant to the larger issue of whether a 'real' computer — a VAX, or a Cray, say — could possess mental states.

As might have been expected, many people have also made appeal to the new developments in parallel and neural architectures in order to block the sorts of conclusions Searle wishes to draw. The argument that is often used is that human cognitive processing appears to possess certain characteristics — such as being able to carry distributed representations, susceptibility to graceful degradation, and so on — that could be practically realizable only within an architecture which, like that of the human brain, involves a network of very many simple processors linked up together. Although, abstractly, the computational characteristics of such connectionist networks could be simulated on a serial machine, in practice the time taken for the processing would be far too slow to be appropriate for the real time needs of an intelligent agent operating in a real time environment. Insofar as we interpret connectionism as proposing a criterion for the occurrence of genuine mentality (as opposed merely to a fertile new paradigm for the *modelling* of cognition), this involves an even more radical departure from 'pure functionalism' than Sloman's suggestion considered above. For it would rule out the possibility that today's large single-processor machines (even if their speed and memories were considerably extended) could ever genuinely possess mental states, since their hardware architecture is so different from that of a genuine cognizer (Thagard, 1986). For some excellent philosophical discussions of the implications of connectionism, see Boden (1984), Clark (1987) and Clark (forthcoming).

Clearly, there is room for equivocation here. In practice many of those people who have defended an AI-flavoured philosophical account of mind have tended to vacillate somewhat between the 'pure functionalist' position and the comparatively impure position which is suggested by some of the new developments in connectionism. Obviously you could depart quite radically from 'pure functionalism', while still holding that certain sorts of electronic computing machines were capable of being the subjects of genuine mental states.

10.9   AI as an Account of Mind

So there is a lot of scope for variation on the issue of how much relevance you are going to give to hardware considerations in formulating a computational account of mental states. But this is not the only issue on which there is scope for different views. Another issue concerns the *range* of mental states which are considered to be subject to some sort of computational explanation. As we saw earlier, there seems to be a radical difference between experiential mental states, such as pains, and cognitive mental states, such as planning moves in a chess game. Mental states of the former kind seem to be much more resistant to computational explanation than do those of the latter. (This distinction between just two kinds of mental states is only intended to be a rough-and-ready preliminary division: there may be lots of other categories which it is important to delineate — but it is a start.)

Many supporters of a computationalist account of mind would want to hold that *all* mental states are ultimately explicable in computational terms; others hold that only *some* are (the cognitive ones). We could distinguish between 'full' and 'partial' computationalism here. There are obviously difficulties with partial computationalism. The main problem is that it seems rather uncomfortable to hold that 'the Mind' encapsulates processes of (at least) two such radically different types: those which are computational and those which are not. We certainly do not seem to experience such a division in our own firsthand experience: when we undergo a complex of states — such as, for example, anger when some possessions are stolen — the cognitive and the experiential aspects appear to be interwoven into a single unity.

On the other hand, it does seem to be utterly implausible to suppose that the nature of states of experiential awareness can be explained in computational terms. The considerable degree of credit that AI earns for itself in the context of, for example, sentence parsing or visual recognition, completely evaporates in the context of pleasure or pain. So if *any* kind of computationalism is to be accepted — that is, any view which maintains that a given class of mental state is computational in nature — then maybe one casualty will be the assumption that the mind is a unified field, and that all those processes traditionally classed as 'mental' (and distinguished from the 'physical') have a single fundamental essential characteristic.

Where does this leave us? How much weight *should* we give to AI, and computer science, in deepening our understanding of the mind? One thing is clear: there are a number of different alternative philosophical conclusions that might be drawn from AI. Rather more tentatively, we can conclude that pure functionalism is very unlikely to be a correct view. It is very unlikely that mental states can be explained in the purely abstract terms of computational structures, without any reference at all to how those computations are implemented. Another suggestion is that computationalism is unlikely to provide an account of all those phenomena which have traditionally been grouped under the notion of 'mind'.

It may be, then, that one casualty in all of this will be our traditional notion of 'mind' itself. We have been hanging on to this notion since Descartes, and indeed since long before. Even the most urbane of modern materialists — who rejects the divinity, the immortality, or the immateriality of the soul, who rejects the idea of the mind as any kind of independent entity not completely explicable ultimately in physical terms — may still be sufficiently imprisoned by the historical vestiges of the metaphysical, religious, and ethical roles once played by that grand old notion as to be incapable of believing that perhaps there is, after all, no such thing as a correct theory *of mind* as such. Perhaps the truth is that there is no such sphere as 'the mental', but rather only a collection of disparate phenomena for which different sorts of explanations are appropriate. For the understanding of some among these phenomena AI is likely to be central; for the understanding of others it may play only a relatively minor role.

Chapter 11

Artificial Intelligence — What Next?

In chapter 1 we began a brief history of AI and cognitive science but, apart from a couple of references to expert systems and neural modelling, did not take it beyond 1980. Now we shall return to the history and then cast a glance into the future. With a grounding in the theory, techniques, and philosophy of AI you should be able to make your own judgment as to whether the widespread adoption of AI systems will result in prosperity, chaos, or business as usual.

By the mid-1970s, the early hopes that AI would soon provide the world with general-purpose thinking machines had evaporated. Researchers accepted that programs such as SHRDLU, which performed so impressively within the limits of a **microworld** whose objects, actions, and rules were all predefined, or easily constructed, could not capture the complexity of everyday human reasoning. From designing cute-looking programs, many turned back to the fundamental problem of representing knowledge and modelling human reasoning.

11.1   Commercial Expert Systems

What changed the prevailing mood to one of optimism was the realization that many commercially important domains *are* microworlds, amenable to rule-based reasoning. This led, in the late 1970s, to the development of expert systems. Expert systems are now in regular commercial use: the Caisse d'Epargne bank in France uses one at sixty of its branches to give advice on home loans, and other banks and moneylenders use them to assess the credit-worthiness of people seeking loans; Thomas Cook has a system which plans journeys on the Australian railway network and offers guidance on suitable train schedules; other systems are being coupled directly to information sources — for example, to monitor fluctuations in exchange rates and alert the user when there is a likelihood of making a profitable currency deal.

Almost all the developments in expert systems have been towards making standard AI techniques more accessible, through graphical displays, natural language interfaces, and explanation facilities, and towards providing tools to help in the design of new expert systems. The simplest of these is the *expert system shell*, which is essentially an expert system with the knowledge base and rules removed, leaving the rule interpreter and explanation facility, to which new rules and facts, in a different domain, can be added. In the early days of research in expert systems it was hoped that such shells could be fitted to a wide range of problems, by doing little more than pouring in new facts and rules. In fact, domains that are superficially similar may require very different types of reasoning and forms of explanation. Nevertheless, as the tools become both more powerful and easier to use, designing expert systems may become a cottage industry, with 'home repair guides', and 'tax advice systems' being developed by individuals on their personal computers.

11.2   The Fifth Generation Initiative

In October 1981, the Japanese announced a ten-year national plan, with a budget of $855 million, to develop a 'fifth generation' of computers. Figure 11.1 shows the structure of the proposed computer. The hardware will directly support AI techniques such as 'knowledge base management', 'problem solving and inferencing', and 'intelligent interfacing' by holding a very large database of stored knowledge and carrying out fast logical inferencing. The most controversial proposal is to write the AI software in an extension of the logic programming language Prolog. The decision had U.S. academics reaching for their conference reports since, until then, LISP had been by far the most popular AI language, with Prolog little-known outside of a few European AI departments.

The response of Western nations to this perceived 'invasion of cheap Japanese knowledge' was swift. In the United States, a consortium of companies, inluding DEC, NCR, Motorola, and National Semiconductor, set up the Microelectronic and Computer Technology Corporation (MCC), with an annual budget of over $50 million, to carry out collaborative research in computer-aided design, image

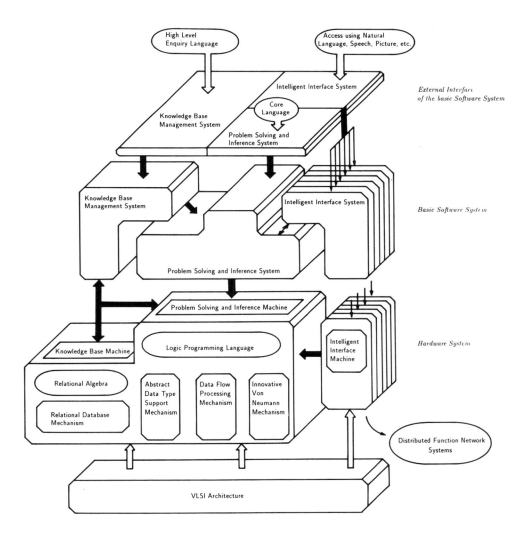

Figure 11.1
The structure of the proposed 'fifth generation' computer.

processing, and expert systems. Through the Defense Advanced Research Project Agency (DARPA), the US Government channelled funds for long-term research in AI, and in 1983 the Strategic Computing Initiative (SCI) was launched. Costing $600 million, the aim of SCI is to sponsor the research and development of three specific military AI systems:

1. an automated co-pilot (a system that assists a human fighter/bomber pilot in tracking targets),

2. an autonomous tracked vehicle (i.e., a robot tank), and

3. a battlefield management system.

In Europe, the EEC set up the European Strategic Research Programme in Information Technology (ESPRIT), a ten year research programme on Information Technology involving consortia drawn from industry and academia, and in Britain the government launched the Alvey Programme of advanced information technology. Costing £350 million, of which £200 million came from public funds and £150 million from industry, its aim was to stimulate research and development in information technology through four main themes: intelligent knowledge-based systems, the man/machine interface, software engineering, and very large scale integration (the design of computer chips with a very high density of components).

To give an example of the type of AI research, leading to saleable products, that these national programmes intend to promote, the Alvey Programme set up four well-funded 'Demonstrator Projects' (Alvey, 1986):

1. The Design to Product Demonstrator will use AI techniques to help designers at any stage of product development, from initial design through manufacture to in-service support.

2. The DHSS Demonstrator will produce three systems for Department of Health and Social Security officers and Social Security claimants. The first will assist DHSS local officers in processing claims and help them to interpret the mass of regulations governing Supplementary Benefits. The second will advise claimants on their likely eligibility for benefits, the procedures they should follow, and the documents they need to take in support of a claim. It will also offer help in filling out the DHSS forms. The third system will assist a DHSS policy officer in investigating the consequences in a change in benefits in terms of consistency and overlap with other benefits.

3. The Speech Input Word Processor and Workstation will be a system that can turn human speech into text for a word processor.

4. The Mobile Information System is intended to bring the benefits of information technology to a mobile user. Its sub-projects include a Mobile Electronic Office, and a Traffic Information Collator, which will take police traffic incident reports (such as notification of accidents or road blockages) and, from them, prepare messages suitable for broadcasting by local radio.

Perhaps the most far-reaching is the speech-input word processor, which could transform office practices. A prototype has been produced which works much more slowly than would be acceptable, takes speech from "an adult male reading prepared sentences in a relatively quiet accoustic environment," and produces "up to five best guesses about the sentence actually input to the machine." There is every hope that some of these limitations will be overcome, and the prototype turned into a more general and flexible speech recognition system, but one of the lessons learned from the short history of AI has been that such generalization is always far more difficult and time-consuming than it first appears.

11.3 The New Connectionists

The short history of AI has been colourful and turbulent. It has been marked by surges of enthusiasm, in the early 1970s following successes such as Winograd's SHRDLU, and in the mid-1980s with the commercial exploitation of expert systems and Japan's Fifth Generation Project. It has suffered waves of recrimination, in the late 1970s when it was realized that the techniques used for small-scale specialized AI systems could not easiiy be transferred to more general ones, and in the late 1980s, when funding agencies began to doubt that some of the more extravagant predictions for symbolic AI could be turned into working products. It has undergone sudden changes in direction, in 1969 when Minsky and Papert halted the growth in connectionist research, and in 1986 when the publication of *Parallel Distributed Processing* sparked off the new connectionism.

In 1986 Rumelhart and McClelland submitted a report to DARPA which argued that connectionist research had been seriously underfunded for over a decade. In 1988 DARPA announced a connectionist research initiative with a budget of $390 million over 6 years. The result has been a sudden shift of interest in some important US research institutions from symbolic AI to connectionism.

The reason why the US AI community (academic as well as commercial) has taken up the neural-net model so enthusiastically is quite straight-forward. It is primarily because the Department of Defense has decided that neural net computing is a high priority strategic technology. As an example the UCLA [University of California, Los Angeles] AI lab has recently started ten new projects concerned with neural networks while seven (Schank-style) symbolic AI projects are due to be termi-nated shortly. This switch did not come from inside the University, it happened as a result of strong prompting from DARPA and other funding bodies (Forsyth, 1988, p. 12).

A new sect needs its icons and Sejnowski's NETtalk system (Sejnowski and Rosenberg, 1986) may serve as a reference point both for advocacy and for criticism of connectionism, just as Winograd's SHRDLU has done for symbolic AI. The pro-gram converts text to speech and, connected to a speech synthesiser, can pronounce typewritten words. It was trained by given examples of text and its spoken form, and over 10 hours of learning it progressed from a formless babble to intelligble pronounciation. The audio tape of its performance is a convincing demonstration of the practical worth of connectionism.

11.4   Into the Future

In 1986 the Office of Technology Assessment, US Congress (1986) carried out a survey of leading AI researchers, asking them to forecast the state of the field in the first half of the next century. The majority of them held the view that there are "few fundamental barriers for machine intelligence and thus that over the long term intelligent machines would meet or surpass humans in most cognitive skills." For the shorter term (the next fifty years) their views were mixed. On the one hand, there was the "minimum progress" scenario, that speech recognition systems will be available for somewhat restricted subject areas, that expert systems will be widely deployed as decision-making aids but in very limited subject areas; the problems of mobility and control algorithms for robots will not be fully solved, but robots will be widely used in, for example, warfare, and vision will improve but will be somewhat primitive compared with that of humans. On the other hand, the "maximum progress" view was that the fundamental problems of knowledge representation, commonsense reasoning, and learning will be essentially solved, computer systems will have a language proficiency better than many humans, intelligent machines will be near-constant companions and assistants to most humans, and robots will be freely mobile.

One of the problems with predictions about the future of technology is that they almost invariably omit some crucial social or political factor which alters the entire course of research and development. The image of the 'thinking machine' still gives rise to both fascination and repulsion, and these attitudes could have an important influence on the future course of AI, as would moves towards economic or political decentralization, a thirst for computer-provided knowledge, or conversely a rejection of the 'information society'. Whatever the technical advances, AI could be called on to fill a variety of roles, some pleasant, some unpleasant.

11.4.1   The Optimistic View

Much of the optimism towards AI is not because of its proven success, but because of its potential. Tremendous benefits could be brought to industry, government, medicine, education, voluntary groups, and ordinary people in their homes by the cheap and easy availability of knowledge and assistance directly relevant to a problem: about which set of actions is appropriate to the circumstances, about how to perform a task, and about the consequence of each possible decision. At present specialist knowledge is very unevenly distributed, concentrated in universities, teaching hospitals, company head offices, government departments, and specialist advice centres. One way to ensure its spread is to provide non-specialists, such as school teachers, general practitioners, and sales representatives, with a source of knowledge applicable to their immediate needs, in the form of an AI system supplemented by a referral service to the human expert for the particularly difficult cases. There is a danger that the non-specialist may not be able to spot a problem requiring the intervention of a human expert, but the alternative to the limited expertise of a non-specialist plus expert system may be no expertise at all.

Donald Michie has warned of situations where a sudden 'flood of information' can completely overwhelm a human monitor. During the emergency at the nuclear power plant at Three Mile Island over 100 warning lights were flashing simultaneously; the operators wrongly interpreted the warnings and, instead of drenching the reactor core with water, switched off the emergency cooling system, with disastrous results. Michie argues the complex systems like power plants, chemical installations, or aeroplanes, need a 'human window' which, in an emergency, can give the human operator an intelligible précis of the situation. AI systems have the ability to interpret large amounts of data, turning it into usable knowledge to guide action. The system need not carry out the action itself (though such 'automated decision making systems' already exist) but merely offer an analysis, and maybe a set of remedies.

In the home an AI system could be the modern equivalent of a 'general factotum', replacing do-it-yourself books, car maintenance manuals, and self-study guides by offering knowledge in the context in which it is needed. Indeed that expertise may in time become a property of the device. Already there exist packages of electronics capable of directly monitoring car engines, and reporting faults, and in the future these could not only provide a warning of an engine fault, but also offer advice on a remedy. The development of speech recognition systems could lead to the availability of a wide range of computer-provided telephone services: intelligent telephone answering machines that could operate central heating or switch on the oven from voice commands; and automated telephone enquiries, entertainment guides, and travel information. Each domestic appliance may in the future be a little more intelligent, with the central heating system automatically minimizing heat loss, the vacuum cleaner automatically steering itself around the house, the oven recommending the best cooking method for a particular dish, or the front door telephoning to announce that it has been inadvertently left open.

If the thought of accepting advice from an oven or conversing with a door appals, then there is the consolation that each wave of innovation — the train, the automobile, electronics — has, in the short term, brought with it dissonance and disruption of traditional work patterns, but has quickly been assimilated and accepted.

11.4.2   The Pessimistic View

As a result of five thousand years of literacy most people are now able to read, and to detect some of the lies, assumptions, and fallacies buried in text. Even so a good writer can bend the mind of his reader with a well-turned analogy, a subtle distortion, or some false logic. Commercial AI systems have been with us for a mere five years, and there is no equivalent base of literacy. Users have not learned the skills of 'reading' the rules of expert systems, uncovering false assumptions, or detecting gaps in stored knowledge. Such literacy will evolve, but not in the near future, since the methods of representing and organizing knowledge are still changing.

The result is that the user of an AI system must take its conclusions largely on trust. Most expert systems have rudimentary rule justification and explanation facilities, but these do little more than list the rules used to form a conclusion. They cannot comment on whether each rule is a correct representation of the real world; nor can they comment on whether the reasoning itself is complete and reliable.

These issues of the adequacy and correctness of knowledge are particularly important for systems, such as for plant monitoring or battlefield management, that act on the basis of data gathered from the real world. The benefits, mentioned in the previous section, of providing a 'human window' in the form of an AI system that can monitor and offer advice on a complex process, rest on the assumption that the system is itself understandable and reliable. If it is not (and the first sign that it is faulty may come in the very emergency it was supposed to assist), then the human user may not be able to call up the raw data quickly, or may have lost the skill in interpreting it; the user may not even be able to tell whether the fault has occurred in the underlying machine or in the 'human window'. So the term 'window' is highly misleading; a monitoring AI program is no sheet of glass, but a complex system, interpreting another complex system to the human user. Using an AI system to monitor a nuclear plant may give the appearance of simple efficiency, but so would removing 90% of the gauges and warning lights.

Battlefield management systems raise even more important social issues, since the consequences of a failure are great (it could literally start World War III). They provide a good example of the general problems and ethical issues involved in employing autonomous decision making systems.

As Bundy (1987) has pointed out, a Battle Management System would have to be a *general-purpose* system:

> It might have to reason about the nature, purpose, and destination of previously unknown objects. It might have to reason about the intentions of an adversary, taking into account the general political situation. It might have to use analogy to cope with an unforeseen situation by adapting an existing plan. Thus battle management is not the sort of restricted domain that lends itself to expert systems technology.
>
> That is not to say that a rule-based Battle Management System could not be built — it could, but it would be a special-purpose system not able to cope with unpredicted circumstances. One could regard the problem of detecting and reacting to missile attack as one of fault diagnosis and correction and adapt an existing expert system shell to do the task. But the resulting system would be subject to precisely the same criticisms about reliability as a conventional, non-AI, Battle Management System, in fact more so.
>
> The behaviour of an expert system is inherently less predictable than that of a conventional program. Because the rules can be com-

bined in many different ways by the inference mechanism according to
the circumstances, the order of rule firing may be different from any
anticipated by the programmer. The unpredictability is increased if
certainty factors are used to facilitate the search strategy (they usually
are).

Because of its complexity and the impossibility of testing it in a realistic setting,
we can never know if a battlefield AI system will work properly until it is too late.

AI systems designed to manage a major war cannot be given that realistic testing.
We have no spare world on which to try out nuclear conflict. Using simulated data
is not an adequate test: the same (possibly wrong) assumptions that governed the
programming may also be behind the choice of test data. Even if the assumptions
are good, concocted data are no substitute for the complex interactions of signals
from many different remote sensors (for example, a common source of problems is
the time delays in signals sent from different parts of the globe).

So far, the criticisms of AI can be construed as technical objections, to be overcome when the next, or the next but one, generation of systems arrives. But there
are dangers *inherent* in the attempt to build 'thinking machines', dangers which
will increase as AI systems become more human-like. People have becoming accus-
tomed to computers producing the truth. One may doubt the accuracy of a bank
statement, but not the arithmetic associated with it; computers are still accused of
making errors, but the public is being trained to blame the data, or the programmer who has specified the wrong set of instructions. Once the 'bugs' in the system
have been removed, once the program performs according to specification, then it
produces a correct result.

But now all this carefully nurtured public acceptance must be thrown out; AI
systems are *designed* to be inexact, to offer part truths, to make errors. Their
output must be judged by the criterion of *adequacy*, not correctness. Certainly,
as knowledge acquisition techniques improve, so will the quality of the computer's
reasoning, but until a system can be designed to acquire its own knowledge, in
some worthwhile domain such as medicine, the system will be bounded by human
understanding. Even if it can learn for itself, it will not be perfect. Indeed, Sloman
(1984) argues that an inevitable consequence of designing larger and more general
purpose systems is that they will take on human characteristics, such as emotion:

> It can also be argued that there is no way to build a super-intelligent
> robot which also copes with a complex set of different sorts of motives,
> in a partly unpredictable world, without giving that robot mechanisms

which are capable of producing emotional states, as a result of performing the cognitive tasks for which they are required. That is, the possibility of having emotions may be a by-product of being able to cope with a complex and unpredictable world in an intelligent way. (This does not mean that every intelligent robot will necessarily be emotional, only that it will have the ability — and abilities are not always exercised.)

Emotions are not necessarily harmful or unproductive, but they do not square with the image of computers as efficient and accurate. Even if *in most cases* it performs better than a human expert, an AI system that is designed to be uncertain, or emotional, may not win public acceptance, particularly if its decisions may affect people's welfare or, in the case of military systems, threaten their lives.

Alternatively, people may come to believe and trust the pronouncements of an AI program. The uncertainties involved in reaching a decision can be easily hidden, with the system reporting only its final conclusion. This is less likely in a decision support system; even with present-day ones the human user can demand justification and alternative suggestions. But once AI systems are designed to take action based on a decision, they may appear to perform *as if* driven by the truth. Imagine an AI system in some hospital of the future that, given the diagnosis of a patient's conditions (perhaps provided by another AI system), will not only prescribe drugs but also administer them. All kinds of difficult decisions must be taken — whether to use a drug with general or specific action, what dosage to give, perhaps even what drugs can be afforded given the current state of the hospital's finances — but all the patient receives is a shot in the arm.

Even if these fears prove groundless, if AI systems become highly regarded assistants and colleagues, there is still one problem. Inevitably the spread of technology will not be uniform. The industrialized and technologically sophisticated nations will be the first to design and sell such tools for the mass market. The remaining countries, particularly in Africa and Latin America, will not only increase their dependence on high technology but will also on alien assumptions about the content, structure, and purpose of knowledge. An agricultural expert system, for example, may suggest solutions in the form of proprietary brands of feedstuff, or be governed by questionable assumptions, like the need for artificial fertilizer. The problems of 'knowledge imperialism' are not unique to AI, but as has been pointed out, the assumptions implicit in an AI system may be hard to detect.

11.5   Computers and Thought

In the near future, the succeful applications of artificial intelligence are likely to be small in scale but broad in range: expert systems to support decision making in commerce, finance, science, and medicine; flexible production control systems; industrial robots with limited powers of vision; advice-giving systems in shops, workplaces, and homes; connectionist systems for visual pattern recognition and signal processing. But perhaps the most profound contribution to society from the attempts to build thinking machines will not be the technology of AI — medical diagnosis systems, home robots, personal financial advisors, and automated tourist guides — but a greater appreciation of the human mind. There is a widespread belief that in comparing the human mind to a computer you are reducing human freedom and spontaneity to a dull repetitive mechanism. That belief (which Margaret Boden, among many, has argued against so trenchantly — see Boden, 1986) is one that we have tried to dispel, by showing you what it is like to *do* AI.

After reading this book it should no longer seem paradoxical that a study of machine intelligence can lead to a more humane understanding of ourselves. Much of modern psychology has been an attempt to represent the mind as a mechanism, but until the advent of AI psychologists have never been in the position of *implementing* their theories. An AI model does not constitute a proof of any claim concerning psychological function, but it can be used to generate new hypotheses, and to test the adequacy of existing theories. And each time we try, and fail, to build an accurate replica of some small part of cognition, we affirm the power of the human mind. When we do achieve the first great successes in artificial intelligence, when we can regard an automaton as a trusted friend and mentor, when we can entrust a machine to enrich our culture through song, dance, and literature, then we will have learned vastly more about our own strengths and limitations.

Appendix A

The POP-11 Reference Guide

This guide lists the words, symbols, and structures of the subset POP-11 used in this book. Those items not enclosed in angle brackets <> are POP-11 reserved words (i.e., they have a special meaning to POP-11).

Item	Description	Example

<Word>	A letter followed by a series of letters or digits (including the underscore). It may also be a series of signs such as $. A word is put in double quotes, except within a list.	`"cat"`
		`"a_long_word"`
		`"M1"`
		`"#$#$#$#"`

<Number>	One or more digits, with an optional decimal point.	`55` `3.14159`

<List>	A series of text items, such as words, numbers, and other lists, within square brackets.	`[a b c d]`
		`[1 Acacia Avenue]`
		`[[CAT CHAT] [DOG CHIEN]]`

;;;	Begins a comment (text that will be ignored by POP-11). The comment ends at the end of the line.	`;;; This is a comment.`

Item	Description	Example
`vars`	Used to declare variables.	`vars x, y, z;`
`;`	Terminates commands.	`vars a; 100->a;`

`undef`	Printed out for a variable that has been declared, but not had a value assigned to it.	`vars xxx;`
		`xxx=>`
		`** <undef xxx>`

`=>`	Print arrow.	`3+4=>` `** 7`
`==>`	Pretty print arrow (prints a long list tidily).	
`=>>`	Print lists without the brackets.	`[[the] [cat] [sat]]=>>` `the cat sat`
`->`	Assignment arrow. Assigns a value to a variable.	`vars a;` `100->a;`

`^`	Includes the value of a variable in a list.	`vars animal;`
		`"cat"->animal;`
		`[the ^animal sat]=>`
		`** [the cat sat]`

`^^`	Includes the value of a variable (which must be a list) inside another list.	`vars animal;`
		`[orang utang]->animal;`
		`[the ^^animal sat]=>`
		`** [the orang utang sat]`

`<Procedure>`	A 'package' of POP-11 commands, usually with a name.	

`define`
`enddefine`
	Mark the start and end of a procedure definition	`define perim(w,h)->p;`
		`2*w + 2*h->p;`
		`enddefine;`

Item	Description	Example
`readline()`	A POP-11 procedure that prints a ? and then waits for input from the terminal. Any words typed on the line after the ? are returned as a list.	`readline()` `->input_words;`

`length(<item>)`	A procedure that returns the length of an item.	`length`
		    `([the cat sat])=>`
		`** 3`
		`length("iguana")=>`
		`** 6`

`<Subscript>`	An element can be picked from a list by giving its position in brackets after the name.	`vars sentence, animal;`
		`[the cat sat]`
		    `->sentence;`
		`sentence(2)->animal;`

`oneof(<list>)`	Returns an element picked at random from a list.	`vars throw;`
		`oneof([1 2 3 4 5 6])`
		    `->throw;`

`+`	Adds one number to another.	`width+height` `->half_perim;`
`*`	Multiplies two numbers.	`3.14159*d->circum;`
`/`	Divides one number by another.	`total/items` `->average;`
`//`	Divides one integer by another to get dividend and remainder.	`10//3 ->dividend` `->remainder;`
`**`	Raises one number to the power of another.	`2**3=>` `** 8`

Item	Description	Example
( )	Round brackets have two uses. They can alter the order of evaluation in expressions or they can enclose the arguments to a procedure.	`3+(2*4)=>` `** 11` `perim(45,23)=>` `** 136`
\<Boolean\>	A variable whose value is either true or false, used in conditionals and loops.	`<true>` `<false>`
?\<variable\>	Matches one item inside a list pattern and makes that the value of the variable.	`mylist matches` `  [?first ==]`
??\<variable\>	Matches zero or more items within a list pattern and makes the list of matched items the value of the variable.	`alist matches` `  [?first ??rest]`
=	Has two uses. It tests whether two items are equal. It also matches one item inside a list pattern.	`a=100` `mylist matches` `   [= cat sat]`
==	Has two uses. It tests whether two items are identical. It also matches zero or more items inside a pattern.	`a==[cat]` `mylist matches` `   [== cat ==]`
/=	Tests whether two items are unequal.	`a /= b`
/==	Tests whether two items are not identical.	

Item	Description	Example
`>`	Compares two numbers. The result is true if the first is greater.	
`>=`	Compares two numbers. The result is true if the first is greater or equal.	
`<`	Compares two numbers. The result is true if the first is smaller.	
`<=`	Compares two numbers. The result is true if the first is smaller or equal.	
`and`	Forms the 'conjunction' of two boolean expressions.	`x>0 and x<100`
`or`	Forms the 'disjunction' of two boolean expressions.	`word="cat" or` `    word="puss"`
`not`	Negates a boolean expression.	`not(list matches` `    [== cat ==])`
`if`	Marks the start of an `if` conditional.	`if english="cat"` `  then "chat"=>`
`then`	Ends the condition part of an `if` conditional.	`endif;`

`elseif`	Begins a second (or subsequent) condition in an `if` statement.	`if english="cat"`
		`  then "chat"=>`
		`elseif english="dog"`

`else`	Marks the beginning of the alternative course of action in a conditional.	`  then "chien"=>`
		`else`
		`  [I dont know]=>`

`endif`	Marks the end of a conditional.	`endif;`

Item	Description	Example

`matches`	Compares a list with a pattern. It returns `<true>` if they match, `<false>` otherwise.	`vars sentence;`
		`[the cat sat]`
		`    ->sentence;`
		`sentence matches`
		`    [= cat =] =>`
		`** <true>`

`database`	A POP-11 variable whose value is the database.	`database==>`
`add(<list>)`	Puts an item into the database.	`add([john loves mary]);` `add([mary loves ian]);`
`remove(<pattern>)`	Removes the first item matching the pattern from the database.	`remove([john loves =]);`
`flush(<pattern>)`	Removes all items matching the pattern from the database.	

`present(<pattern>)`	Searches the database for an item matching the pattern and returns `<true>` if it is found, and `<false>` otherwise.	`if present`
		`   ([?x loves mary])`
		`  then`
		`   x=>`
		`endif;`

`allpresent(<list of pattern>)`	Searches the database for items that consistently match all the patterns and returns `<true>` if a a match is found, and `<false>` otherwise.	`if allpresent`
		`   ([[= loves ?x]`
		`    [?x loves = ]])`
		`then`
		`   x=>`
		`endif;`

Item	Description	Example
it	A variable that is set by add, remove, present and foreach. Its value is the last item found in the database.	``` if present ([?x loves mary]) then it=> endif; ```
repeat	Marks the start of a repeat loop.	``` repeat readline()->line; quitif(line/=[]); ```
endrepeat	Marks the end of a repeat loop.	``` endrepeat; ```
times	Indicates the number of times a loop is to be repeated. (If it is omitted then looping is forever, unless halted by quitif).	``` repeat 4 times; "."=> endrepeat; ```
quitif(<expression>)	If the expression is true then quit the loop. This example and the one using the while loop below are equivalent (ie they give the same result).	``` 2->n; repeat; quitif(n>1000); n=> endrepeat; ```
while	Marks the start of a while loop.	``` 2->n; while n<=1000 do ```
do	Ends the condition part of a while, for, or foreach loop.	``` n=> n*n->n; ```
endwhile	Marks the end of a while loop.	``` endwhile; ```
for	Marks the start of a for loop.	``` for x in [paris london] do [^x is a city]=> ```
endfor	Marks the end of a for loop.	``` endfor; ```

Item	Description	Example

`foreach`	Marks the start of a foreach loop, which matches a pattern against each item in the database.	`vars x, y;`
		`foreach [?x loves ?y]`
		`    do`
		`    it=>`

`endforeach`	Marks the end of a foreach.	`endforeach;`
`<array>`	Multi-diemnsional data object accessed by numerical subscript	
`newarray`	Creates a new array.	`newarray([1 10 1 10],0)` `    ->ten_by_ten;`

`boundslist`	Returns a list containing the upper and lower bounds for an array.	`boundslist`
		`    (ten_by_ten)=>`
		`** [1 10 1 10]`

`abs`	Returns the magnitude of a number.	`abs(-10)=>` `** 10`
`trace <names of procedures>`	A command that alters procedures so they print out helpful information. (NB. You can trace built-in procedures like **add**).	`trace add` `     first_and_last;`
`untrace <names of procedures>`	A command that switches off tracing of the named procedures.	`untrace add` `     first_and_last;`
`untraceall`	Switches off any traces.	`untraceall;`

Appendix B

The Automated Tourist Guide

This appendix gives a listing in POP-11 of a complete Tourist Guide based on one programmed by a student. It makes use of the 'prodsys' and 'semnet' POP-11 libraries. The program can be called by the command `converse();`

```
/******************************************************
        Defines the pretty print arrow =>>
******************************************************/


define ppr(x);
  if x=nil then sp(1)
   elseif ispair(x) then applist(x,ppr)
  else spr(x)
  endif;
enddefine;

define macro =>> ;
  ".", "ppr", ";", "nl", "(", 1, ")", ";"
enddefine;


/******************************************************
  Rule-Based Advisor on Entertainment - see Chapter 7
******************************************************/
;;; following rules deal with entertainment in London
[] -> rulebase; false -> chatty; false -> repeating;
```

```
rule find_type [entertainment medium unknown];
    vars enttype;
    [what type of entertainment would you like:
     cinema or theatre?] =>>
    readline() -> enttype;
    remove([entertainment medium unknown]);
    add([entertainment medium ^^enttype]);
endrule;


rule find_style [entertainment style unknown];
    vars styletype;
    [would you like western, drama or horror]=>>
    readline() -> styletype;
    remove([entertainment style unknown]);
    add([entertainment style ^^styletype]);
endrule;


rule cinema_western [entertainment style western]
    [entertainment medium cinema];
    [soldier blue is on this week at the eros.] =>>
endrule;


rule cinema_horror [entertainment style horror]
    [entertainment medium cinema];
    [[the amazing doctor vulture is on this week
      at the classic and abc1.]
     [i was an american vulture in london is on
      this week at abc2.]] =>>
endrule;
```

```
rule cinema_drama [entertainment style drama]
    [entertainment medium cinema];
    [[twenty tiny ants is on this week at the carlton.]
     [dog on a shed roof is on until thursday at the rialto.]
     [sharp shooter the prequel
       is on for two weeks at dominion.]]=>>
endrule;


rule theatre_western [entertainment style western]
    [entertainment medium theatre];
    [home on the range is on at the criterion.]=>>
endrule;


rule theatre_horror [entertainment style horror]
    [entertainment medium theatre];
    [[cant slay wont slay is on at the adelphi.]
     [sweaters is on at the piccadilly.]]=>>
endrule;


rule theatre_drama [entertainment style drama]
    [entertainment medium theatre];
    [[world go away is on at the phoenix.]
     [slaving (ver a hot keyboard is on at the lyric.]]=>>
endrule;
```

```
/*********************************************************
    Syntactic and Semantic Analysis of Noun-Phrases
                  - see Chapter 5
*********************************************************/


define DET(word) -> found;
    member(word, [a the]) -> found;
enddefine;


define PREP(word) -> found;
    if member(word, [near by]) then
        "near" -> found;
    elseif member(word, [in containing]) then
        word -> found;
    else
        false -> found;
    endif;
enddefine;


define NOUN(list) -> found;
    if member(list, [[avenue] [street] [road]]) then
        [road] -> found;
    elseif member(list, [[gallery] [square] [museum]
                        [theatre] [cinema] [monument]
                        [lake] [park]] ) then
        list -> found;
    else
        false -> found;
    endif
enddefine;
```

```
define PROPN(list) -> found;
    member(list,
        [[the abc1] [the abc2] [the carlton]
            [the odeon] [the rialto] [the dominion]
            [the classic] [the eros] [the haymarket]
            [the criterion] [the phoenix] [the adelphi]
            [the savoy] [the piccadilly] [the lyric]
            [the royal albert hall]
            [the royal opara house]
            [the british museum]
            [the natural history museum]
            [the victoria and albert museum]
            [the science museum] [the tower of london]
            [hms belfast] [the houses of parliament]
            [st pauls cathedral] [westminster abbey]
            [london zoo] [the serpentine]
            [st katherines dock] [the national gallery]
            [nelsons column] [hyde park] [the serpentine]
            [the tate gallery] [shaftesbury avenue]
            [leicester square] [haymarket]
            [piccadilly circus] [coventry street]
            [tottenham court road] [trafalgar square]
            [jermyn street] [the strand] [denman street]
            [kensington gore] [floral street]
            [great russel street] [cromwell road]
            [exhibition road] [millbank] [tower hill]
            [st catherines way]
            ] ) -> found;
enddefine;


define NP(list) -> meaning;
    vars pn, d, n, p, np, sym1, sym2;
    if list matches [??pn:PROPN] then
        pn -> meaning
    elseif list matches [?d:DET ??n:NOUN]  then
        gensym("v") -> sym1;
```

```
          [ [ ? ^sym1 isa ^n] ] -> meaning
    elseif list matches [?d:DET ??n:NOUN ?p:PREP ??np:NP]
      then
          gensym("v") -> sym1;
          if np matches [[= ?sym2 isa =] ==] then
              ;;; meaning of noun phrase is
              ;;; a list of patterns
              [ [? ^sym1 isa ^n] [? ^sym1 ^p ? ^sym2] ^^np]
                                            -> meaning
          else

              ;;; meaning of noun phrase is proper name
              [ [? ^sym1 isa ^n] [? ^sym1 ^p ^np] ]
                                            -> meaning
          endif;
      else
          ;;; unknown noun phrase form
          false -> meaning
      endif;
enddefine;



define referent(meaning) -> thing;

    ;;;
    ;;; find the thing referred by meaning structure
    ;;;

    vars sym, vals, x;

    if meaning matches [[= ?sym isa =] ==] then
        ;;; meaning is a list of patterns

        which(sym, meaning) -> vals;

        if vals matches [?x ==] then
            ;;; at least one thing referred to
```

```
            x -> thing
        else
            ;;; nothing referred to
            false -> thing
        endif;
    else
        ;;; meaning is a proper name
        meaning -> thing;
    endif
enddefine;
```

```
/**********************************************
        Finding a Route on the Underground
                - see Chapter 4
**********************************************/

vars verychatty;
false -> verychatty;

/* first set travel and change times */
vars travtime, changetime;
2 -> travtime;
3 -> changetime;

define addonefuture(newplace,newtime,comefrom);
    ;;; This records in the database a single pending
    ;;; arrival at a place (where place means
    ;;; a line-station combination as in the database),
    ;;; unless there has already been an
    ;;; arrival at that place.
    ;;; Also protects against inserting the same future event
    ;;; twice, as could happen when looking at
    ;;; line changes due to the fact that the
    ;;; information that a station is on a given line can
    ;;; appear twice in the database.
    ;;; Can also say what it's doing.
    vars futureevent;
    [will arrive ^newplace at ^newtime mins from ^comefrom]
        -> futureevent;
    if not(present([arrived ^newplace at = mins from =]))
    and not(present(futureevent))
    then
        add(futureevent);
        if verychatty then
            [ . . will arrive ^newplace at ^newtime mins] =>>
        endif;
    endif;
enddefine;
```

```
define addfuture(event);
    ;;; Given an event, adds the pending events that
    ;;; follow it into the database
    vars place, newplace, time, station, line, newln;

    ;;; Get breakdown of event
    ;;; Note that the matcher arrow --> could be
    ;;; replaced by MATCHES except that it
    ;;; does not return a TRUE/FALSE value.
    ;;; We know that the event passed to
    ;;; ADDFUTURE will have the right format.
    event --> [arrived ?place at ?time mins from =];
    place --> [?line ??station];

    ;;; First get all the connections on the same line
    foreach [^place connects ?newplace] do
        addonefuture(newplace,time+travtime,place);
    endforeach;

    ;;; This repeats the last bit for patterns
    ;;; the other way round
    foreach [?newplace connects ^place] do
        addonefuture(newplace,time+travtime,place);
    endforeach;

    ;;; Then all the changes to other lines
    foreach [[?newln ^^station] connects =] do
        addonefuture([^newln ^^station], time+changetime,place);
    endforeach;

    ;;; And again for patterns the other way round
    foreach [= connects [?newln ^^station]] do
        addonefuture([^newln ^^station], time+changetime,place);
    endforeach;
enddefine;
```

```
define next();
    ;;; This looks at all the future events in the database
    ;;; and finds the one that will happen next - that is,
    ;;; the one with the smallest value of time, and returns
    ;;; a list giving the corresponding actual event.
    vars leasttime, place, time, lastplace, event;
    ;;; leasttime has to start bigger than any likely time
    100000 -> leasttime;

    foreach [will arrive ?place at ?time mins
             from ?lastplace] do
        if time < leasttime then
            [arrived ^place at ^time mins from ^lastplace]
                                            -> event;
            time -> leasttime;
        endif;
    endforeach;

    return(event);
enddefine;

define insertnext(event);
    ;;; Takes an event returned by NEXT and inserts it
    ;;; into the database, then removes all pending events
    ;;; which would cause later arrivals at the same station.
    ;;; Can also print out the event.
    vars place;
    ;;; addition
    add(event);

    ;;; removal
    event --> [arrived ?place at = mins from =];
    foreach ([will arrive ^place at = mins from =]) do
        remove(it);
    endforeach;
```

```
        if chatty or verychatty then
            event =>>
        endif;
    enddefine;


    define start(station);
        ;;; This sets up the database ready to start by inserting
        ;;; pending arrivals at the starting station
        vars line;
        foreach [[?line ^^station] connects =] do
                addonefuture([^line ^^station],0,[start]);
        endforeach;

        ;;; This is the same as the first half but
        ;;; for the other sort of patterns
        foreach [= connects [?line ^^station]] do
                addonefuture([^line ^^station],0,[start]);
        endforeach;
    enddefine;


    define search(startstat,deststat);
        ;;; Inserts information into the database till the "tree"
        ;;; as far as the destination station has grown
        vars nextevent, destline;
        start(startstat);
        repeat
            next() -> nextevent;
            insertnext(nextevent);
        quitif (nextevent matches
                [arrived [?destline ^^deststat]
                 at = mins from =]);
            addfuture(nextevent);
        endrepeat;
        add([finished at [^destline ^^deststat]]);
    enddefine;
```

```
define traceroute();
    ;;; Assuming the tree has been grown in the database,
    ;;; and event is the arrival at the destination station,
    ;;; return a list of the stations through which the
    ;;; quickest route passes
    vars place, lastplace, time, ok, routelist;

    ;;; ok will always be true
    present([finished at ?place]) -> ok;

    present([arrived ^place at ?time mins from ?lastplace])
                                                    -> ok;
    [[^place at ^time mins]] -> routelist;

    until lastplace = [start] do
        lastplace -> place;
        ;;; the next line is there for its side effects.
        ;;; ok will always be true
        present([arrived ^place at ?time mins from
                ?lastplace]) -> ok;
        [[^place at ^time mins] ^^routelist] -> routelist;
    enduntil;

    return(routelist);
enddefine;


define checkstat(station);
    ;;; simply checks that a station is present
    ;;; in the database
    return(present([[= ^^station] connects =])
        or present([= connects [= ^^station]]));
enddefine;
```

```
define tidyup();
    ;;; this removes any previous route-finding information
    ;;;from the database, in order to clear the way
    ;;; for a new route

    foreach [will arrive = at = mins from =] do
        remove(it);
    endforeach;
    foreach [arrived = at = mins from =] do
        remove(it);
    endforeach;
    foreach [finished at =] do
        remove(it);
    endforeach;
enddefine;


define route(startstat,deststat);
    ;;; this is the overall calling program for route finding
    ;;; this sets up the database for the other routines.

    ;;; checking
    if not(checkstat(startstat)) then
        [start station ^^startstat not found] =>>
        return(false);
    endif;
    if not(checkstat(deststat)) then
        [destination station ^^deststat not found] =>>
        return(false);
    endif;

    ;;; tidy the database in preparation
    tidyup();

    ;;; do the search
    search(startstat,deststat);
```

```
    ;;; return the result. Note that the database is left
    ;;; with all the search stuff still in it
    return(traceroute());

enddefine;


define reply(list) -> response;

    ;;;
    ;;; Convert a route list into
    ;;; an English description of the form:
    ;;;
    ;;;   travelling by underground, take the ... line to ...
    ;;;        then change and take the ... line to ...
    ;;;        then change and take the ... line to ...
    ;;;                             ...

    vars line, station, line1, response;

    list --> [[[?line ??station] ==] ??list];
    [travelling by underground, take the
        ^line line to] -> response;
    while list matches [[[?line1 ??station] ==] ??list] do
        if line1 /= line then
            [^^response ^^station then change and
             take the ^line1 line to] -> response;
            line1 -> line;
        endif;
    endwhile;
    [^^response ^^station] -> response;
enddefine;
```

```
/******************************************************
          Top-Level Procedures of the
          Automated Tourist Guide
 ******************************************************/


define setup();

    ;;;
    ;;; Setup the database of facts about London
    ;;;

    [

;;; cinemas

        [[the abc1] in [shaftesbury avenue]]
        [[the abc1] underground [leicester square]]
        [[the abc1] isa [cinema]]
        [[the abc2] in [shaftesbury avenue]]
        [[the abc2] underground [leicester square]]
        [[the abc2] isa [cinema]]
        [[the carlton] in [haymarket]]
        [[the carlton] underground [piccadilly circus]]
        [[the carlton] isa [cinema]]
        [[the odeon] in [haymarket]]
        [[the odeon] underground [piccadilly circus]]
        [[the odeon] isa [cinema]]
        [[the rialto] in [coventry street]]
        [[the rialto] underground [piccadilly circus]]
        [[the rialto] isa [cinema]]
        [[the dominion] in [tottenham court road]]
        [[the dominion] underground [piccadilly circus]]
        [[the dominion] isa [cinema]]
        [[the classic] in [piccadilly circus]]
        [[the classic] underground [piccadilly circus]]
        [[the classic] isa [cinema]]
```

```
[[the eros] in [piccadilly circus ]]
[[the eros] underground [piccadilly circus]]
[[the eros] isa [cinema]]
```

;;; theatres

```
[[the haymarket] in [haymarket]]
[[the haymarket] underground [piccadilly circus]]
[[the haymarket] isa [theatre]]
[[the criterion] in [jermyn street]]
[[the criterion] underground [piccadilly circus]]
[[the criterion] isa [theatre]]
[[the phoenix] in [charing cross road]]
[[the phoenix] underground [tottenham court road]]
[[the phoenix] isa [theatre]]
[[the adelphi] in [the strand]]
[[the adelphi] underground [charing cross]]
[[the adelphi] isa [theatre]]
[[the savoy] in [the strand]]
[[the savoy] underground [charing cross]]
[[the savoy] isa [theatre]]
[[the piccadilly] in [denman street]]
[[the piccadilly] underground [piccadilly circus]]
[[the picadilly] isa [theatre]]
[[the lyric] in [shaftesbury avenue]]
[[the lyric] underground [piccadilly circus]]
[[the lyric] isa [theatre]]
[[the royal albert hall] in [kensington gore]]
[[the royal albert hall] underground
 [south kensington]]
[[the royal albert hall] isa [theatre]]
[[the royal opera house] in [floral street]]
[[the royal opera house] underground [covent garden]]
[[the royal opera house] isa [theatre]]
```

;;; museums

    [[the british museum] in [great russel street]]
    [[the british museum] underground
     [tottenham court road]]
    [[the british museum] isa [museum]]
    [[the natural history museum] in [cromwell road]]
    [[the natural history museum] underground
     [south kensington]]
    [[the natural history museum] isa [museum]]
    [[the victoria and albert museum] in [cromwell road]]
    [[the victoria and albert museum] underground
     [south kensington]]
    [[the victoria and albert museum] isa [museum]]
    [[the science museum] in [exhibition road]]
    [[the science museum] underground [south kensington]]
    [[the science museum] isa [museum]]

;;; galleries

    [[the national gallery] in [trafalgar square]]
    [[the national gallery] underground [charing cross]]
    [[the national gallery] isa [gallery]]
    [[the tate gallery] in [millbank]]
    [[the tate gallery] underground [pimlico]]
    [[the tate gallery] isa [gallery]]

;;; places of interest

    [[the tower of london] near [tower hill]]
    [[the tower of london] underground [tower hill]]
    [[the tower of london] isa [place of interest]]
    [[hms belfast] near [the tower of london]]
    [[hms belfast] underground [london bridge]]
    [[hms belfast] isa [place of interest]]
    [[the houses of parliament] near [parliament square]]
    [[the houses of parliament] underground [westminster]]

```
[[the houses of parliament] isa [place of interest]]
[[st pauls cathedral] in [newgate street]]
[[st pauls cathedral] underground [st pauls]]
[[the houses of parliament] isa [place of interest]]
[[westminster abbey] in [millbank]]
[[westminster abbey] underground [westminster]]
[[westminster abbey] isa [place of interest]]
[[st katharines dock] near [st katharines way]]
[[st katharines dock] underground [tower hill]]
[[st katharines dock] isa [place of interest]]
[[nelsons column] in [trafalgar square]]
[[nelsons column] underground [charing cross]]
[[nelsons column] isa [place of interest]]
[[nelsons column] isa [monument]]
[[london zoo] in [regents park]]
[[london zoo] underground [camden town]]
[[london zoo] isa [place of interest]]
[[the serpentine] in [hyde park]]
[[the serpentine] underground [hyde park corner]]
[[the serpentine] isa [lake]]

;;; roads

[[shaftesbury avenue] isa [road]]
[[haymarket] isa [road]]
[[coventry street] isa [road]]
[[tottenham court road] isa [road]]
[[jermyn street] isa [road]]
[[the strand] isa [road]]
[[denman street] isa [road]]
[[kensington gore] isa [road]]
[[floral street] isa [road]]
[[great russell street] isa [road]]
[[cromwell road] isa [road]]
[[exhibition road] isa [road]]
[[millbank] isa [road]]
[[tower hill] isa [road]]
```

```
        [[st catherines way] isa [road]]

;;; squares

        [[leicester square] isa [square]]
        [[piccadilly circus] isa [square]]
        [[parliament square] isa [square]]
        [[trafalgar square] isa [square]]

;;; parks

        [[hyde park] isa [park]]
        [[regents park] isa [park]]

;;; underground topology for route finder

        [[JUBILEE charing cross] connects [JUBILEE green park]]
        [[JUBILEE green park] connects [JUBILEE bond street]]
        [[JUBILEE bond street] connects [JUBILEE baker street]]
        [[BAKERLOO embankment] connects [BAKERLOO charing cross]]
        [[BAKERLOO charing cross] connects
         [BAKERLOO piccadilly circus]]
        [[BAKERLOO piccadilly circus] connects
         [BAKERLOO oxford circus]]
        [[CIRCLE embankment] connects [CIRCLE westminster]]
        [[CIRCLE westminster] connects [CIRCLE st jamess park]]
        [[CIRCLE st jamess park] connects [CIRCLE victoria]]
        [[CIRCLE victoria] connects [CIRCLE sloane square]]
        [[CIRCLE sloane square] connects
         [CIRCLE south kensington]]
        [[PICCADILLY south kensington] connects
         [PICCADILLY knightsbridge]]
        [[PICCADILLY knightsbridge] connects
         [PICCADILLY hyde park corner]]
        [[PICCADILLY hyde park corner] connects
         [PICCADILLY green park]]
        [[PICCADILLY green park] connects
```

```
    [PICCADILLY piccadilly circus]]
    [[CENTRAL lancaster gate] connects [CENTRAL marble arch]]
    [[CENTRAL marble arch] connects [CENTRAL bond street]]
    [[CENTRAL bond street] connects [CENTRAL oxford circus]]
    [[CENTRAL oxford circus] connects
     [CENTRAL tottenham court road]]
    [[VICTORIA warren street] connects
     [VICTORIA oxford circus]]
    [[VICTORIA oxford circus] connects [VICTORIA green park]]
    [[VICTORIA green park] connects [VICTORIA victoria]]
    [[VICTORIA victoria] connects [VICTORIA pimlico]]
    [[VICTORIA pimlico] connects [VICTORIA vauxhall]]
    [[NORTHERN charing cross] connects
     [NORTHERN leicester square]]
    [[NORTHERN leicester square] connects
     [NORTHERN convent garden]]

;;; fare and zones for fare finder

    [[zone1 station] fare [40 pence]]
    [[zone2 station] fare [60 pence]]
    [[green park] isa [zone1 station]]
    [[picadilly circus] isa [zone1 station]]
    [[shepherds bush] isa [zone2 station]]
    [[goodge street] isa [zone2 station]]
    [[brixton] isa [zone2 station]]

    ] -> database;

enddefine;
```

```
define introduction();

    ;;;
    ;;; output welcome and instructions to user
    ;;;

    [Hello, this is the automated London tourist guide]=>>
    [I can offer information on the following]=>>
    [cinema]=>>
    [theatre]=>>
    [museums]=>>
    [galleries]=>>
    [places of interest]=>>
    [routes and fares on the underground]=>>
    [Please ask about any of the above
     and I will try to help you]=>>
    [Type in your question using lowercase letters only]=>>
    [and then press RETURN]=>>
    [If you want to exit please type "bye"
     and press RETURN]=>>

enddefine;


define answer(query) -> response;

    ;;;
    ;;; produce a response to query
    ;;;

    vars list, museums, response, x, y, place, routelist;


    if query matches [== places of interest ==] then

        ;;; this is a query about places of interest
```

```
      [] -> list;
      foreach [?place isa [place of interest]] do
          [^^list , ^place] -> list;
      endforeach;
      ;;; strip off leading comma from reply
      list --> [, ??list];
      [I know about the following places of interest:
       ^^list] -> response;

  elseif query matches [== where is ??np:NP] or
          query matches [== where ??np:NP is] then

          ;;; a query about where somewhere is

          ;;; find the place referred to by noun-phrase
          referent(np) -> place;

          if place and present([^place in ?y]) then
              [^^place is in ^^y] -> response;
          elseif place and present([^place near ?y]) then
              [^^place is near ^^y] -> response;
          elseif place and present([^place underground ?y])
            then
              [^^place is near ^^y underground station]
                                              -> response;
          else
              [I do not know where that place is]
                                              -> response;
          endif;

  elseif query matches [== get to ??np:NP] then

      ;;; route finding query

      ;;; find place referred to by noun-phrase
      referent(np) -> place;
```

```
    if place and present([^place underground ?y]) then
        route([victoria], y) -> routelist;
        if not(routelist) then
            [route not found] -> response
        else
            reply(routelist) -> response
        endif
    else
            [I do not know where that place is]
                                        -> response;
    endif

elseif query matches [== fare to ??x] then

    ;;; query about fare to a given underground station

    if spresent([^x fare ?y]) then
        [The fare to ^^x is ^^y] -> response
    else
        [I do not know about the underground station ^^x]
                                        -> response
    endif

elseif query matches [== entertainment ==] or
        query matches [== cinema==] or
        query matches [== theatre==] or
        query matches [== theatres ==] or
        query matches [== cinemas ==] then

        ;;; answer query about entertainment in London
        ;;; using LIB PRODSYS

    ;;; add initial entertainment facts to database

    add([entertainment medium unknown]);
    add([entertainment style unknown]);
```

```
        ;;; run production system
        run();

        ;;; remove database entries created by
        ;;; production system
        flush([entertainment ==]);

        [I hope you enjoy the show] -> response;

    elseif query matches [] then

        ;;; blank line input

        [please type in your question and press RETURN]
                                        -> response

    elseif query matches [bye] then

        ;;; produce response to terminate session

        [bye] -> response

    else

        ;;; cannot handle this query

        [Sorry I do not understand. Try rewording
         your question] -> response

    endif;

enddefine;
```

```
define converse();

    ;;;
    ;;; main calling procedure
    ;;;

    vars query, response;

    ;;; setup the database of facts about London
    setup();

    ;;; output welcome and instructions to tourist user
    introduction();

    ;;; read and answer queries until done
    repeat

        ;;; read in query from keyboard
        readline() -> query;

        ;;; produce an answer to query
        answer(query) -> response;

        ;;; output answer to user
        response =>>

        ;;; quit if answer indicates end of session
        quitif(response = [bye]);

    endrepeat;
enddefine;
```

Glossary

Abduction
A form of reasoning by which, given a fact or state, we can hypothesize some prior fact or state which might have given rise to it. For example, if we know that the streets are always wet after it has been raining, and that the streets are wet now, we can guess that it has recently been raining. The streets could be wet, of course, for some other reason entirely, so abduction is not always a reliable form of reasoning. See also **Logic**, **Rules of Inference**.

Agenda
A list of possible tasks for a system to perform, ordered according to usefulness. An agenda may be used, for example, in a **search** program to determine the next path to investigate.

Algorithm
A fixed set of operations on numbers or symbols – of a sort that can be automated on a **digital computer**. See also **Heuristic**.

Analogue computer
See **Digital/Analogue Computer**.

Analogical
In an analogical representation there is a direct correspondence between the important properties of the representation and the properties of the **domain** — for example, by using a 2-dimensional array to represent a 2-dimensional picture.

Arc/Link/Pointer
Nodes in a **semantic network** are connected by labelled directed arcs (also sometimes called links or pointers), which indicate the nature of the connection between adjacent nodes. In **isa-hierarchies**, the most basic links are taxonomic (isa) and

partonomic (ispart) relations; others name features or attributes; their values are given by the node pointed to by the link.

Architecture
(As applied to **computers**), the structured organization of elements in a computational mechanism — for example, the difference between **sequential processing** and **parallel distributed processing** machines is said to be a difference in archi-- tecture. See also **Computation, (non-) von Neumann Architecture**.

Argument/Result
A **procedure** may take **input** values and produce **output** values. The former are called the procedure's **arguments**; the latter its **results**. Thus the **POP-11** procedure call length([1 2 3]) has one argument (the **list** [1 2 3]) and produces one result (the number 3). In **logic**, an argument represents individual entities, such as 'John', or 'apple'. A **predicate** is applied to one or more arguments to produce a **formula**. See also **Axiom/Theorem**.

Array
A **data object** consisting of an ordered series of elements that can be accessed by number index.

ASCII Code
The widely used American Standard Code for Information Interchange (ASCII Code) assigns a number to each character that can be typed on a **computer** keyboard. The code aids programming and communication between computers.

Assignment
The operation in **computer** programming of giving a **value** to a **variable**.

Attribute/Feature/Property
An attribute (or feature, or property) is a distinguishing aspect, quality, or characteristic of an object. An attribute of a canary, for example, is yellowness.

Axiom/Theorem
Most logical systems contain fundamental propositions or axioms, which cannot themselves be justified from within the system itself. Any conclusions derived from these axioms by the system's **rules of inference** are called theorems. See also **Logic, Predicate Calculus/Predicate Logic, Propositional Calculus**.

Backtracking
Returning to a previous state in a computation in order to try an alternative strategy. In terms of a **search tree**, backtracking occurs when the end of a branch is reached without a solution being found, and a different branch is chosen.

Backup Memory
See **Main Memory/Backup Memory**.

Behaviourism/Behavioural Psychology
An influential twentieth-century school of thought in psychology and in the philosophy of mind that claimed that only the outwardly observable aspects of human behaviour produced scientific data for the study of the mind. Behaviourists thus rejected **introspectionism**.

Binary Digit (Bit)
Most modern **computers** use the binary counting system — employing only 1's and 0's — to represent any number or other character. Binary numbers can be easily stored in electronic form. See also **Central Processor**.

Boolean
A **data object** which represents whether some condition is true or not. There are only two such objects: `<true>` and `<false>`.

Branch and Bound
A **search strategy** in which the 'lowest cost' **node** in the **agenda** is always considered first. This strategy is guaranteed to find the lowest cost solution if more than one solution to a problem exists.

Branching
See **Conditional**.

Breadth-First
A **search strategy** in which each level of the **search tree** is considered in turn. All the **nodes** at any given level of the search tree are considered before any nodes at a deeper level.

Built-In/User-Defined

Most programming languages have a variety of terms which are primitive to the language; these are the **built-in** terms. Many languages, such as **POP-11**, allow you to define your own terms or **procedures**. These are known as **user-defined** terms.

Calling a Procedure

Instructing a **computer** to **interpret** the series of instruction defined in a **procedure**. See also **Argument/Result**.

Case/Case Relationship/Case Slot

The case is the functional relationship of noun-phrases to the main action of sentences as expressed in the verb. Every verb has a certain number of case slots. For example, the verb 'cut' presupposes someone cutting (the 'agent' case slot), something cut (the 'object'), and something with which the act of cutting is performed (the 'instrument').

Central Processor

That part of a conventional **digital computer** which performs the direct operations upon sequences of sysmbols stored as sets of **binary digits (bits)**. See also **Architecture, Compilation/Interpretation, Computation, Hardware, Main Memory/Backup Memory, Parallel Distributed Processing, Sequential Processing, Software**.

Children

The relation of nodes to the node that immediately dominates them in an **isa hierarchy** is that of children to a parent node. See also **Taxonomic Tree**.

Cognitivism

In contrast to **behaviourism** this school of thought claims that psychology should be concerned with a person's internal representations of the world and with the internal or functional organization of the mind. See also **computationalism, functionalism**.

Command

Procedural programming languages such as **POP-11** are composed of statements that can be interpreted as commands to the **computer** to perform various operations — for instance. adding two numbers and assigning the result to a variable.

Commutative

A commutative relation in a **semantic network** is one which is symmetric. That is, for any relation R, if xRy is true, then yRx is also true. For example, if Frank is married to Hilda, then Hilda is also married to Frank.

Competence Knowledge

An abstract description of the knowledge characterizing a particular **domain**. See also **Performance Knowledge**.

Competence/Performance

A person's linguistic competence is the ability to produce and understand an indefinite number of novel sentences, to detect ambiguities, and to recognize grammatical errors. Performance refers to a person's use of language in particular situations. The distinction is mirrored in natural language processing by **grammars**, which are usually stored **declarative** representations of the rules governing the well-formedness of sentences, and **parsers**, which are **programs** that process utterances by reference to such rules.

Compilation/Interpretation

Two widely adopted methods for converting the instructions of a **program** into **binary** machine code instructions specifying basic operations on the machine's **central processor**. Compilation involves converting a program as a whole, whereas interpretation involves translating each instruction singly.

Compiled Representation

A representation of human knowledge in the form of an automatic process that runs without calling on **declarative** knowledge nor making demands on **working memory**.

Compositionality

The principle that the meaning (or **semantic value**) of a sentence is a function of the meanings of its constituents together with their mode of combination (just as the meaning of a complex expression in propositional calculus is a function of the truth-value of the atomic propositions together with the truth-functional connectives by which they are combined together).

Computation
The manipulation of numbers or symbols according to fixed rules. Usually applied to the operations of an automatic electronic **computer**, but by extension to some processes performed by minds or brains. See also **Cognitivism**.

Computationalism
The notion that the operation of the mind can be explained entirely in terms of the formal, or functional, properties of a computational system. See also **Cognitivism, Eliminativism, Functionalism, Materialism, Turing Test**.

Computer
A machine for performing operations on numeric or symbolic data. Nowdays the term usually refers to **digital computers** capable of being instructed by stored **programs**. See also **Algorithm, Hardware, Software**.

Concept
A concept is a stable mental representation of objects, classes, properties, and relations. When we encounter a new object or event for the first time, we draw upon our mental store of concepts in order to identify it. One of the most important parts of the human learning process is concept-formation, where, after a number of distinct experiences of the 'same' object or event, we acquire, by a process of **induction**, a concept for it.

Conceptual Dependency Representation
A formalism for representing the meanings of sentences, in a manner similar to that of a **semantic network**, as structured configurations of basic language-independent conceptual elements, or **conceptual primitives**. See also **Knowledge Representation, Semantics**.

Conceptual Primitive
One of a small number of fundamental sorts of action or event, such as the physical movement of an object (*ptrans*) or the transfer of some mental content (*mtrans*). Used in conjunction with **scripts** as a method of **knowledge representation**.

Conditional
Used to describe an instruction, or a sequence of instructions, that is only to be executed when certain specified conditions are met. For instance, the Automated Tourist Guide should only print information about the river when the user has asked

a question about the river. Programming languages often introduce a conditional instruction by means of the word `if`. The possibility that a program can carry out different actions under different circumstances is called **branching**.

Conflict Resolution Strategy
A strategy used by a **production system interpreter** for deciding which production rule is to be fired if the heads of more than one rule match the contents of **working memory**.

Connectionist Model/Neural Network
A system consisting of a network of processing units each of which carries out a simple computation. The units are all interconnected and knowledge is represented as patterns of connection. See also **Parallel Distributed Processing**.

Constant
See **Variable/Constant**.

Data Object
Computer **programs** involve operations on different kinds of symbolic entities, known as data objects or types. In **POP-11** the data objects include numbers, **words**, **booleans**, and **lists**.

Data Structure
A specific **data object** used as an object of **computation**.

Database
A means of recording and accessing large amounts of relatively simple items of data, such as bibliographical information. In **POP-11** the database package contains a set of **built-in** procedures for accessing list-structured items.

Declarative/Procedural
A declarative representation contains knowledge in the form of facts or images. In a procedural representation, knowledge is stored as processes or procedures. Different programming languages can be characterized as having a declarative or procedural style. See also **Procedural, Prolog, POP-11**.

Declare

When a variable name is declared by means of the `vars` instruction, **POP-11** enters the word in its list of variable names and allocates memory for the variable.

Deduction

A form of logical reasoning by which, from a given set of facts (premises), certain consequences (conclusions) can be inferred. For example, if I know that on every occasion on which it rains the streets get wet, and that it is raining now, then I can deduce that the streets are now wet.

Define

To specify the set of instructions associated with a **procedure**, as used in **computer** programming.

Deictic Expression

An expression which picks out some individual, time, or place relative to the context of utterance. For example, 'I', 'you', 'here', 'these', 'yesterday' have no intrinsic semantic value; the reference of each on an occasion of speech is determined by the appropriate component of the speech situation.

Demon

A type of procedure associated with a **frame**. The two main types are if-needed and if-added demons.

Depth-First

A **search strategy** in which all the **nodes** on one branch of the **search tree** are considered before **backtracking** to try nodes on other branches. All the successors of a given node are considered before any other nodes at the same level as the given node.

Digital/Analogue Computer

An analogue computer uses continuously variable quantities, such as voltages, to represent similarly varying enities in the **domain**. Digital computers operate upon discrete, coded symbols.

Distinguished Symbol

In a generative **grammar**, the distinguished symbol is the only **non-terminal** symbol which can appear at the **root** of a **parse-tree**. It is conventionally 'S' for 'sentence'.

Distributed Processors
See **Parallel Distributed Processing**.

Distribution
Two syntactic items have the same distribution if they can be substituted for each other in the same context within a sentence.

Domain
The area of enquiry and associated tasks to which an artificial intelligence system is applied. (For instance, MYCIN has as its problem domain the diagnosis of blood disorders.) See also **Domain-Independent/Domain-Specific Knowledge**, **Heuristic**, **Knowledge-Based System**.

Domain-Independent/Domain-Specific Knowledge
Many artificial intelligence systems operate within a specific domain — i.e., their knowledge is mainly domain-specific. However, they may also contain domain-independent knowledge, in the form of principles of common sense, or general scientific laws common to many areas of expertise.

Dualism
A philosophical theory of mind associated with the philosopher Descartes according to which human beings are constituted by two distinct metaphysical substances or realms: Thought and Extension. See also **Functionalism, Materialism**.

Dynamic Value
In game playing, the estimated value of a **state**, arrived at by considering the results of a **static evaluation function** applied to possible future states. These static values are propagated back in time using, for instance, a **minimax** strategy.

Edge
An image contour along which intensity changes abruptly.

Edge Element
The smallest piece of edge detectable by examining neighbouring **pixels** in an image.

Edge Map
A 2-D array recording the position of edge elements derived from an image. Typically there is a one-to-one correspondence between array cells and image pixels at the centre of edge elements.

Eliminativism
An approach to understanding the mind in which it is claimed that terms like 'beliefs' and 'intentions' belong to an outmoded 'folk-psychology' and are not capable of scientific justification. See also **Functionalism, Intentional System/Intentional Stance, Materialism.**

ELIZA
A program which can be taught to respond to sentences typed by a user in a way that can give the illusion of understanding them, but which in fact relies on **pattern matching** and **substitution** to produce answers based on a pre determined set of stock phrases. ELIZA was originally developed by Joseph Weizenbaum in the mid-1960s, and now serves as a demonstration of the technique and as a warning against taking the responses of a **computer** at face value.

Embed
When a syntactic constituent has another of the same category nested within it as one of its constituents, the nested constituent is said to be embedded within the larger one.

Evaluate
To perform an operation on given **arguments** producing a canonical (or simplified) **result**. For example, given an appropriate definition for the procedure `maximum`, the expression `maximum(5,7)` will evaluate to 7.

Expert System
A **computer program** that incorporates the rule-governed expertise of human experts such as doctors, engineers, or economists within a restricted problem **domain**. See also **Heuristic, Knowledge-Based System.**

Expression
In a **computer program**, a combination of **data objects** linked by **operators**.

Feature
See **Attribute/Feature/Property**.

Fire
(Pertaining to production rules.) See **Trigger**.

Flow of Control
The sequential behaviour of a **program**, as it carries out the processing of **input**.

Formal semantics
A theory of meaning based on the analysis of a natural language as though it were a formal language, such as the propositional and predicate calculi. Typically, it is **truth-conditional** and **compositional**.

Formalism
A set of symbols and a collection of systematic rules governing their uses and interrelations. See also **Knowledge Representation**, **Logic**.

Formula
In **predicate logic** a formula consists either of a **predicate** applied to one or more **aguments**, or a combination of such 'atomic' formulae linked by the connectives 'not', 'or', and 'and'. See also **Axiom/Theorem**.

Frame
Frame systems are a particular kind of **knowledge representation** formalism, consisting of structured descriptions of stereotyped objects or situations, with **slots** filled in with particular values. See also **Demon**, **Script**.

Functionalism
A philosphical view of mind according to which mental processes are characterized in terms of their abstract functional (opr computational) relationships to one another, and to sensory inputs and motor outputs. See also **Cognitivsm**, **Computationalism**, **Eliminativism**, **Turing Test**.

Generate
A formal set of rules which explicitly defines the grammatical sentences of a language is said to generate that language. Such a set of rules constitutes a generative **grammar**.

Generic
A generic term is one which picks out a class of individuals, or the prototype of the individual, rather than the individual itself. For example, in the sentence "The wolf has disappeared from northern Europe," we are referring to the genus rather than to a particular wolf.

Grammar
A grammar may be informally thought of the set of words and category symbols in a language, together with the rules governing their combination into sentences. It is, in human terms, what speakers know of their language independent of their ability to use that knowledge. See also **Competence Knowledge**, **Competence/Performance**, **Syntax**.

Grammatical
A grammatical sentence is one which is well-formed with respect to the rules ('grammar') for generating the sentences of the language. See also **Syntax**.

Grey-Level
A numerical measure of the intensity of a single pixel. The number is typically an integer between 0 and 63 or 0 and 255, where 0 signifies minimum intensity and 63 or 255 signifies maximum intensity.

Hardware
The physical machinery of a **computer** and its associated devices. See also **Algorithm**, **Central Processor**, **Computer**, **Program**, **Software**, **Visual Display Unit (VDU)**.

Heuristic
A rule of thumb which may help in solving a problem, but is not guaranteed to find a solution. A method for cutting down useless searching amongst possibilities. Heuristics provide much of the knowledge contained in **expert systems**. Constrasts with **algorithmic** procedures. See also **Knowledge-Based Systems**.

Heuristic Search
Any **search strategy** which makes use of **heuristics** to suggest the best **nodes** to consider at each stage of the search.

Induction
A form of reasoning by which we derive general principles from particular facts
or instances sharing common properties. For example, if all ravens of which we
have had experience are black, then we might inductively reason that all ravens are
black.

Information Processing System
Generally speaking, any system which operates on symbolic data given as its input
so as to generate an appropriate output. See also **Computer**, **Program**.

Inherit
See **Property Inheritance**.

Input/Output
(a) The values that are passed into a procedure, and which are returned as the
results of the operation of a procedure.
(b) In general, those aspects of a **computer** system which involve the transmission
of data into the system, and the communication of results back to the outside world.
See also **Argument/Result**, **Calling a Procedure**.

Intentional System/Intentional Stance
Some philosophers claim that intentionality should be understood instrumentally
as a feature of certain kinds of systems; these would include intelligent computers
as well as people. It is necessary use terms such as 'intending', 'believing', 'wanting' in order to explain the behaviour of such systems. Adopting this 'intentional
stance' does not commit one to believing that there really are intentional states as
such. See also **Cognitivsm**, **Computationalism**, **Eliminativism**, **Functionalism**, **Turing Test**.

Intentionality
The quality of 'aboutness', or 'world-directedness', that has been claimed to be a
distinguishing feature of mental processes as opposed to physical ones. It has been
proposed that 'intelligent' **computer** performances possess only a secondary, or
derivative, intentionality: this has been used as an attack on the pretensions of
artificial intelligence to explain the human mind. See also **Computationalism**,
Functionalism, Intentional System/Intentional Stance, Turing test.

Internal Representation
A symbolic representation in a **computer** of the states and processes of problem solving, search, etc. See also **Cognitivsm, Knowledge Representation**.

Interpretation
See **Compilation/Interpretation**.

Introspection
A process of inward attention or reflection, so as to examine the contents of the mind. Introspectionism, as a method in psychology, is contrasted with, and was supplanted by, **behaviourism**.

isa Hierarchy
A series of nodes joined by links of the form 'X isa Y' in **semantic networks**, which allow efficient forms of inference. See also **Knowledge Representation, Property Inheritance, Structural Description**.

Keyword
In a program based on **pattern matching**, a keyword is a word in the input sentence which determines the actions to be taken. In a simple program such as **ELIZA**, recognition of a keyword may completely determine the response of the program; in more sophisticated programs the keyword may determine the context in which further analysis is undertaken.

Knowledge Representation
The term used in artificial intelligence to cover the study of **formalisms** which model human forms of knowledge. See also **Frames, Predicate Calculus/Predicate Logic, Production Systems, Scripts, Semantic Networks**.

Knowledge-Based System
A **computer program** which represents relatively complex kninds of information, often as rules governing judgements in particular problem **domains**. See also **Database, Expert System, Knowledge Representation**.

Lexical Category
Every word in the language belongs to some lexical category, that is, instances some part of speech. Thus, 'dog', 'brain', and 'syllogism', for example, all belong to the lexical category 'noun'.

Lexicon
The lexicon of a language is dictionary of all the words in the language, and may contain many types of information about each word, for example, what part of speech it is (its **lexical category**), and what its distributional properties are.

Link
See **Arc/Link/Pointer**.

LISP
A programming language that uses the **list** as its primary **data object**. The most widely used language for artificial intelligence.

List
A special kind of **data object**, found in **POP-11** and other artificial intelligence languages. A list consists of a sequence of zero or more elements, each of which may be any kind of data object (including another list).

Local/Global
In **POP-11** procedures, **variables** can be defined as local to a given **procedure**. These variables lose their values outside the context of the procedure itself. Global variables, however, retain their assigned values after the procedure terminates.

Logic
The study of formal principles of rasoning. The two fundamental systems of logic are **propositional calculus** and **predicate calculus**, although many extensions to these systems exist. Logic is used extensively in computer science and artificial intelligence. See also **Axiom/Theorem**, **Rules of Inference**.

Main Memory/Backup Memory
The part of the **computer's** circuitry which provides instructions and data to be fed into the **central processor**, and which stores the output of the latter's operation, is known as the main memory. By contrast, the backup memory, such as disc or tape, contains information in a form which can be transported from one machine to another.

Materialism
A general philosophical view that only physical processes exist. The term is also applied to philosophical theories of mind which claim that mental states are identical

with brain states. See also **Dualism**, **Eliminativism**, **Functionalism**.

Microworld
A representation of some well-defined **domain**, such as Newtonian physics, such that there is a simple mapping between the rules and structures of the microworld and those of the domain.

Minimax
A strategy to determine good moves in computer game playing by choosing the move that minimizes the loss the player can expect to incur, under the assumption that the player's opponent is adopting the same strategy (and hence trying to cause the maximum loss). The possible gain or loss for a sequence of moves is usually assessed using a **static evaluation function** applied to the state of play at the end of the sequence. See also **Dynamic Value**.

Model
In vision, an internal description of the structure of an object, whether in terms of the structure of image features in a 2-dimensional image or solids in 3-dimensional space.

Naive Physics
People's commonsense knowledge about the behaviour of physical objects in the world — for example, that a liquid spreads out when it pours onto a flat surface.

Neural Network
See **Connectionist Model**.

Node
A single **state** in a **state-space** representation. In **search**, a junction point in the **search tree**, representing a **state** which may need to be considered either as a possible solution to a problem or en route to reaching such a solution.

Non-terminal Symbol
In a generative grammar, a non-terminal symbol labels a syntactic or lexical category, and is used in the formulation of the rules of the grammar. Examples of non-terminals are Prep, VP, Det, Pronoun, NP.

Operator

(a) A symbol to denote an operation, such as multiplication or comparison, which is applied to numbers or other **data objects** in a **computer program**.

(b) A discrete atomic mental operation that transforms one knowledge state, or state of **working memory**, into another. See also **Problem Behaviour Graph**.

Operator Schema

A **knowledge representation formalism** similar to a **frame** representing the type, preconditions, and actions of an operation. Used in artificial intelligence planning and problem solving systems.

Parallel Distributed Processing

Computing by means of a network of simple computational elements, working in parallel, each of which influences the other elements and is influenced by them. See also **Connectionist Model, Sequential Processing**.

Parser

A **program** which, given as input a **grammar**, a **lexicon**, and a word-string, will output, if the string is a well-formed sentence, a structural description of the sentence. Otherwise, the parser will reject the string. The structural description is often represented as a **parse-tree**, also called a **phrase-marker**, a diagrammatic representation of the sentence's constituent structure.

Parse-Tree

See **Parser**.

Pattern Matching

A programming method for matching a list of words (or other symbols) against a template, to discover whether particular words or combinations of words occur in the list. Pattern matching is built into **POP-11**. See also **Wild Card**.

Performance

See **Competence/Performance**.

Performance Knowledge

The knowledge posessed by a particular person which determines what or how they will perform on a given task See also **Competence Knowledge**.

Phrase-Marker
A diagrammatic representation, in the form of an inverted schematic tree, of a
sentence's constituent structure. See also **Parser**.

Phrase-Structure Rule
A rule which specifies the internal structure of a **syntactic category**. Rules are
generally written in the following manner: X $\longrightarrow$ Y Z, where X, Y, and Z are
syntactic category symbols, and Y and Z can replace X in its context within a
sentence. A set of such phrase-structure rules, where at least one of the rules
has the **distinguished symbol** on the left-hand side of the arrow, constitutes a
phrase-structure **grammar**.

Pixel
A tiny patch of an image. Images are normally broken down into a rectangular
lattice of square pixels like tiles on a wall, although hexagonal tessellations have
also been used.

Plan
A routinized program for behaviour that is triggered when certain specific environ-
menal conditions are satisfied.

Planning
The selection of a sequence of operations in order to bring about one or more
goals. An important area of enquiry of artificial intelligence. See also **Problem
Behaviour Graph**, **Problem Reduction**.

Pointer
See **Arc/Link/Pointer**.

POP-11
A programming language for artificial intelligence teaching and research.

Pragmatics
Those aspects of the study of language that pertain to the identity and intentions of
the speaker and hearer, and the context in which speech takes place. The context
is sometimes most narrowly regarded as the body of world knowledge to which
speakers and hearers have access in generating and interpreting speech. Pragmatics
belongs to the study of linguistic **performance**. See also **semantics**, **speech act**,

syntax.

Predicate

In **logic**, a function whose value is is either 'true', or 'false'. It specifies a relatioship between **arguments**. See also **Axiom/Theorem, Formula**.

Predicate Calculus/Predicate Logic

A system of **logic** in which one can formalize inferences by representing relationships between predicates such as '...is happy' and '...is wise'. Predicate calculus incorporates, but extends, **propositional calculus**. See also **Axiom/Theorem, Logic, Quantifier/Quantification**.

Problem Behaviour Graph

A schematic representation of a subject's **problem space**, in the form of labeled boxes denoting knowledge states, and directed **links** representing the mental operations that transform each such state into a new state. See also **Knowledge Representation, Planning**.

Problem Reduction

A method of solving problems by splitting them into more manageable parts.

Problem Space

A set of knowledge states, including a start-start and a goal-state, and a set of admissible problem-specific operations which can be performed on these states. The problem space can be represented schematically by a **problem behaviour graph**.

Procedural

See **Declarative/Procedural**.

Procedural Programming Language

A programming language such as **POP-11** consisting **procedure** definitions together with sequences of **commands** for invoking them.

Procedure

A sequence of instructions in a programming language designed to carry out a coherent operation or set of operations. Procedures often operate on data, passed to them through **arguments**, and return results, which may be used by other parts of the program. Procedures are first **defined**, to establish the actions they take, then **called** to carry out those actions.

Production System
A **knowledge representation formalism** consisting of collections of condition-action rules (called production rules), a **database** which is modified in accordance with the rules, and a **production system interpreter** which controls the operation of the rules. See also **Conflict Resolution Strategy**.

Production System Interpreter
The 'control mechanism' of a **production system**, determining the order in which production rules are fired.

Program
A set of abstract instructions or procedures for a **computer** to perform. When the instuctions are written in a high-level language like **POP-11**, they have to be converted, either by **compilation** or **interpretation**, into basic operations that the computer can perform. See also **Algorithm, Hardware, Software**.

Prolog
A programming language with a strongly **declarative** style, which is based on **predicate calculus**. See also **Resolution**.

Property
See **Attribute/Feature/Property**.

Property Inheritance
A process by which **features** attached to parent **nodes** (more general concepts or inclusive classes) in an **isa hierarchy** are passed down to ('inherited by') their children (more specific concepts or sub-classes) in such cases where no properties or attributes of the same type are associated explicitly with the children nodes. For example, if we know that birds can fly and that canaries are birds, then we can infer that canaries too can fly.

Propositional Calculus
A simple but powerful system of **logic** for representing implications between logically compound sentences, such as 'either A or not B', 'if B then A', etc. The system will prove, for example, that each of these two sentences implies the other.

See also **Predicate Calculus/Predicate Logic, Rules of Inference**.

Protocol Analysis

A method of studying subjects' mental processes in the performance of tasks by recording their spontaneous 'thinking aloud' and subsequently segmenting the running commentary into the discrete atomic mental operations that the subjects have used in the accomplishment of the tasks. See also **Operator, Problem Space**.

Quantifier/Quantification

Quantifiers play an important role in **predicate calculus** logic. There are two kinds of quantifier: the universal quantifier (as in 'all dogs are mammals') and the singular or existential quantifier (as in 'some mammals are dogs').

Recursion

Self-reference, particularly in the form of a **procedure** containing, within its body, a call to iteslf. A recursive **phrase-structure rule** is one in which the symbol on the left-hand side of the arrow also appears on the right-hand side — for example, NP $\longrightarrow$ NP Prep NP, which says that a noun-phrase can be made up of two **embedded** noun-phrases joined by a preposition.

Region

An area of an image which is homogeneous in intensity or texture.

Region Map

A 2-D array representing a segmentation of an input image into regions. The array is typically the same size as the input image, so that there is a one-to-one correspondence between array cells and image pixels. Array cells belonging to the same region contain a label which is unique to that region.

Repair Heuristic

A general-purpose **heuristic** used to effect a **repair**.

Repair Theory

An analysis of errors, based on the assumption that a learner who reaches as impasse, as a result of following a wrong method, will devise a repair to be able to continue solving the problem.

Repeat Loop
A structure in a program which allows an instruction, or a sequence of instructions, to be carried out repeatedly. The repetition may continue indefinitely, or for a fixed number of times, or may end when some condition specified in the program becomes true. See also **Until Loop**, **While Loop**.

Resolution
A popular technique used in automated theorem proving systems. A version of resolution underlies the **logic** programming language **Prolog**.

Restriction Procedure
Matching of **variables** in **lists** can be constrained, in **POP-11**, by a restriction procedure, which specifies some property or feature a variable must have.

Result
See **Argument/Result, Input/Output**.

Root
The **node** of a **search tree** from which all other nodes can be reached by moving down the branches. Often represents the starting **state** of a problem or game.

Rule Body
The 'action' part of a production rule, which specifies what actions are to be performed if the rule is fired (i.e., there is a successful match of the **rule head** against the contents of the **working memory**). Most typically, these are actions which change the contents of the working memory by *adding* and *removing* facts. See also **Conflict Resolution Strategy, Production System**.

Rule Head
The 'condition' part of a production rule (in the **POP-11** production system formalism, the first line of a production rule) consisting of one or more facts which the **production system interpreter** attempts to match against the contents of the **working memory**. See also **Conflict Resolution Strategy, Rule Body**.

Rule-by-Rule Principle
Maintains that the meaning of a sentence can be compositionally built up by semantic rules in tandem with the syntactic parse. See also **Formal Semantics**.

Rulebase
The set of rules in a **production system**. See also **Rule Body, Rule Head**.

Rules of Inference
Any system of **logical** deduction uses general **rules of inference** to allow logical **formulae** to be derived from others. For instance, a rule of inference in many systems of **propositional calculus** is *modus ponens*, which, given the propositions 'if P then Q' and 'P', allows one to infer 'Q'.

Script
A structure rather like a **frame** which represents situations or events, and which is used as a **knowledge representation** formalism. It is particularly suited to natural language understanding systems. See also **Conceptual Primitive**.

Search
A technique of problem solving in which possible solutions are explored in a systematic way, in effect by asking a series of "What if . . . ?" questions. Asking each a question corresponds to trying out a possible **state** of the **domain** in which the program operates to see if it leads to a solution of the problem.

Search Strategy
Any way of organizing the questions asked in problem solving by **search**, so as either to find a solution as rapidly as possible or to find a particularly good solution when more than one solution is possible.

Search Tree
The exploration of possibilities in problem solving by **search** generally leads to a branching structure, in which each **state** may give rise to a new set of states (sometimes called successor states) and each of these may give rise to successor states of its own, and so on. This structure is not usually represented in full in **computer** memory, but is implicit in the problem itself. Finding a solution involves systematically traversing this tree.

Semantic Network
A **knowledge representation** formalism which describes objects and their relationships in terms of a network consisting of labelled **arcs** and **nodes**.

Semantic Value
In **formal semantics**, the semantic value of an expression is the individual(s) or
state(s) in the world to which the expression refers, or which make that expression
true.

Semantics
The study of meaning in language. See also **formal semantics**, **pragmatics**,
syntax.

Sequential Processing
A **computer architecture** in which a **central processor** carries out a series of
operations in sequence. See also **Computation, Parallel Distributed Processing**.

Set-Value Variable
In **POP-11** a set-value variable in a pattern matches an equivalent element in the
list being matched. If there is a correct match, then the item in the list is **assigned**
to the variable. See also **Use-Value Variable, Wild Card**.

Slot
An element in a **frame**, which can be filled with a value. For instance a 'chair'
frame may have a 'number of legs' slot, perhaps filled with the default value of 4.

Software
A **program** for a **computer**, together with the data upon which the program
operates. See also **algorithm, hardware**.

Speech Act
The theory of speech acts views natural language utterances as actions — for example, questions, orders, statements — on the part of speakers. Speech act theory
belongs to the field of **pragmatics**.

State
A description of a possible arrangement of a **domain**. For instance, in game playing,
a state may correspond to a position of pieces on the board; in route finding, a state
may correspond to arrival at a specified place at a specified time; in planning, a state
may correspond to an arrangement in space of some objects to be manipulated.

State-Space
The set of all the **states** which could possibly need to be considered in the course of solving a particular problem.

Static Evaluation Function
In computer game playing, any method of determining the advantage to the player of a given state of play, without looking ahead at possible future moves.

Structural Description
A description of the formal constituents, **features**, and relationships that exhaustively account for the structural integrity and cohesion of an object. A structural description of, for example, an arch will include such terms as 'block', 'supported by', and 'abutting'. See also **Knowledge Representation, Semantic Network**.

Substitution
In a program such as **ELIZA**, using part of the user's input sentence to produce response. In general, replacing part of a string of words or other symbols by different symbols, depending on context.

Successive Refinement
A method of **software** design characteristic of artificial intelligence **program** development, which involves starting with a relatively crude working program and gradually increasing its complexity and sophistication.

Syntactic Category
A grammatical class determined on the basis of the syntactic role it fills in the construction of sentences, used in the formal description of language. It is labelled by a category symbol, such as NP, VP, PrepP. See also **Phrase-Structure Rule, Syntax**.

Syntactically Well-Formed
See **Grammatical**.

Syntax
(a) In programming, the rules by which the words in a program are combined to form **commands** to a **computer**.
(b) For natural languages, the study of the rules governing the way in which words and phrases are combined to form sentences in a language. The word is also some-

times used to refer to the rules themselves; thus one may speak of 'English syntax', 'the syntax of German', and so on, to mean much the same thing as 'English grammar', 'the grammar of German', and so forth. See also **Grammar**.

Taxonomic Tree
See **isa Hierarchy**.

Template
In vision, a stored sub-image with which to compare incoming images.

Terminal Symbol
Terminal symbols are the output of the syntactic component of a grammar, and are usually identified with the words and grammatically meaningful sub-parts ('morphemes') of words. In a phrase-structure **grammar**, they will only ever appear on the right-hand side of lexical rules. See **Lexical Category**, **Lexicon**, **Phrase-Structure Rule**, **Syntax**.

Theorem
See **Axiom/Theorem**.

Transitive
A relationship which, for any relation R, if xRy and yRz, then xRz. For example, if a canary is a bird and a bird is an animal, then a canary is an animal.

Trigger
A production rule is said to be triggered if there is a successful match of the **rule head** against the facts in **working memory**. See also **Conflict Resolution Strategy**, **Production System**.

Truth-Conditionality
The assumption that meaning can be defined in terms of the conditions in the real world under which a sentence may be used to make a true statement. See also **Formal Semantics**.

Turing Test
A hypothetical test for **computer** intelligence, proposed by Alan Turing in 1950, involving a **computer program** generating a conversation which could not be distinguished from that of a real human.

Until Loop
A structure in a **computer program** which allows a sequence of instructions to be repeated until some condition becomes true. See also **Repeat Loop, While Loop**.

Use-Value Variable
In **POP-11** when a use-value variable occurs in a list, the value of the variable is inserted at that place in the list. See also **Set-Value Variable, Wild Card**.

User-Defined
See **Built-In/User-Defined**.

Value
The actual data which have been stored in a section of *computer* memory and which are associated with a **variable**. The value can change as new **assignments** to the variable are made.

Variable/Constant
In many programming languages, there is a class of terms which do not have a fixed **value**, but to which values can be **assigned**. These are called variables. Constants, on the other hand, are terms whose values are fixed. See also **Local/Global**.

Visual Display Unit (VDU)
A screen, usually like a TV set, that displays text or pictures representing the output of a **program** while it is running on a **computer**. See also **Hardware, Input/Output**.

von Neumann Architecture
The 'classic' design for **computer hardware**, named afer the mathematician John von Neumann, who formulated the main elements of the standard, sequential, stored program, computer **architecture** in the late 1940s. Non–von Neumann architectures are now being developed that exploit various forms of **parallel** or **distributed processing**. See also **central processor, computation, connectionist model, parallel distributed processing**.

While Loop
A structure in a **computer program** that allows a sequence of instructions to be repeated while some condition remains true. See also **Repeat Loop, Until Loop**.

Wild Card
In **pattern matching**, an element in a pattern which can match any element in the equivalent section of the **list** being matched. See also **Set-Value Variable**, **Use-Value Variable**.

Word
A particular kind of **data object**. In **POP-11**, a word identified by sequences of symbols within double quotation marks, such as `"fred"`, `"abc123"`. Each word used by a program is stored in an internal dictionary.

Word Concept
The stored mental representation of a word.

Working Memory
Sometimes also called 'short term memory' by psychologists, it is a mental workspace consisting of a small set of data items representing the current state of knowledge of a system at any stage in the performance of a task, and which is transformed into a new set, in humans by the application of a discrete mental operation (**operator**), and in production systems on the firing of a new production rule. See also **Production System**.

Suggested Readings

General Texts on Artificial Intelligence

- Boden, M. A. (1986). *Artificial Intelligence and Natural Man* [Second Edition]. Brighton: Harvester Press and Basic Books.

  Now somewhat dated (the second edition is identical to the first, 1977, edition, except for an additional preface and chapter) but still a good introduction to AI techniques and issues, including psychological and philosophical implications.

- Charniak, E., and McDermott, D. (1985). *Introduction to Artificial Intelligence.* Reading, Mass.: Addison-Wesley.

  A thorough introduction to artificial intelligence techniques, aimed at people from a mathematics or computing background. It uses LISP for its programming examples.

- Rich, E. (1983). *Artificial Intelligence.* New York: McGraw-Hill.

  Provides a good grounding in artificial intelligence techniques for students with a background in mathematics or computer science. Particularly good on problem solving and knowlege representation. It gives no programming examples, but uses logic and diagrammatic representations.

- Winston, P. H. (1984). *Artificial Intelligence.* Reading, Mass.: Addison-Wesley.

  Knowledgeable, but somewhat quirky, textbook which refelects the author's own interests. Good coverage of search and constraint propagation. No programming examples; these are contained in a companion book:

- Winston, P. H. and Horn, B. K. P. (1981). *LISP.* Reading, Mass.: Addison-Wesley.

- Barr, A., and Feigenbaum, E. A. (1982). *The Handbook of Artificial Intelligence,* Volumes I and II. Los Altos: William Kaufmann Inc.

- Cohen, P. R., and Feigenbaum, E. A. (1982). *The Handbook of Artificial Intelligence,* Volume III. Los Altos: William Kaufmann Inc.

The three handbooks provide *the* reference guide to artificial intelligence. They are authoritative and well organized. Volume I introduces the main AI techniques; Volume II covers programming and applications of AI in science, medicine, and education; Volume III includes bits and pieces left out of the other two volumes, such as vision, planning, learning, and models of cognition.

General Texts on Cognitive Science

- Stillings, N. A., Feinstein, M. H., Garfield, J. L., Rissland, E. L., Rosenbaum, D. A., Weisler, S. E., and Baker-Ward, L. (1987). *Cognitive Science: An Introduction.* Cambridge, Mass.: MIT Press.

A textbook that spans the field, from neuroscience to artificial intelligence to the philosophy of cognitive science, with particular emphasis on language acquisition and processing. But the topics are not well integrated; the chapters on AI, in particular, have few links to the rest of the book.

- Fischler, M. A., and Firschein, O. (1987). *Intelligence: The Eye, the Brain, and the Computer.* Reading, Mass.: Addison-Wesley.

A lavishly produced book on intelligence in people and machines. Discussion of AI and cognitive science is well integrated. It includes a major section (about one-third of the book) on the physiology and psychology of human vision, and computational vision. The text is well supported by a large number of illustrations.

Performance without Knowledge

- Weizenbaum, J. (1976). *Computer Power and Human Reason: From Judgement to Calculation.* San Francisco: Freeman.

This is Weizenbaum's personal view of the limitations of computer programs and their relationship to thought, and includes some discussion of his program ELIZA.

Stored Knowledge

- Jackson, P. (1986). *Introduction to Expert Systems.* Reading, Mass.: Addison-Wesley.

  A survey of some of the practical and theoretical problems in the area of knowledge-based systems. Chapters 3–5 give clear overviews of the main approaches to knowledge representation.

- Brachman, R., and Levesque, H. [Eds.] (1985). *Readings in Knowledge Representation.* Los Altos: Morgan Kaufmann.

  A collection of important articles covering the whole area of knowledge representation, including classic papers by Quillian, Woods, Brachman, and Minsky.

- Bobrow, D. G., and Collins, A. [Eds.] (1975). *Representation and Understanding: Studies in Cognitive Science.* New York: Academic Press.

  Another collection of classic papers on knowledge representation.

Search

- The Handbook of AI (Barr and Feigenbaum, 1982) contains a summary of the different search strategies.

- Winston (1984) gives a thorough account with precise algorithmic descriptions of search methods. It goes on to analyze game playing in some detail. This would form a good complement to the approach taken in the present book, at a more advanced level.

- Charniak and McDermott (1985) relate search to parsing — in particular, game playing and problem solving — and give a search program in LISP.

- Rich (1983) has a detailed and fairly formal account, with many diagrammatic examples and careful discussion, of different search strategies.

Natural Language

- Fromkin, V., and Rodman, R. (1983). *An Introduction to Language,* [Third Edition]. New York: Holt, Rinehart and Winston.

  A good general (i.e., non-AI) introduction to linguistics and the nature of language, with a broad but fairly detailed coverage of the main topics in the subject. Includes sections on the historical, psychological, philosophical, and biological aspects of language, as well as good chapters on syntax and semantics.

- Winograd, T. (1983). *Language as a Cognitive Process,* Volume 1:*Syntax.* Reading, Mass.: Addison-Wesley.

  An excellent introduction to natural language processing, with a good general opening chapter on language as a knowledge-based system, and covering all of the main approaches to syntax and parsing. Each chapter is supplemented with a number of very useful exercises. Winograd's idiosyncratic specialized representation language, DL, very effectively guides the reader towards the writing of natural language processing programs.

- Lyons, J. (1981). *Language, Meaning and Context.* Glasgow: Fontana Paperbacks.

  There is no book on semantics from an AI perspective that is easy reading. The above book, however, is a good general introduction to semantics, which includes clarificatory discussion of some of the semantic theory we have sketched out in the chapter, as well as quite an extensive overview of the main issues in pragmatics.

- Grosz, B. J., Sparck Jones, K., and Ebber, B. L. [Eds.] (1986). *Readings in Natural Language Processing.* Los Altos: Morgan Kaufmann.

  A massive (664 pages) volume bringing together key papers in all areas of natural language processing (syntax, semantics, discourse, speech acts, generation) together with descriptions of milestone natural language systems. Much of it is tough reading, but it makes an excellent reference and resource book.

Reasoning

- Findler, N. V. [Ed.] (1979). *Associative Networks: Representation and Use of Knowledge by Computer.* New York: Academic Press.

  A collection of papers, each illustrating the use of semantic networks in some area of AI. The collection is interesting in that the basic semantic net formalism is adapted to quite disparate domains — e.g., story-understanding (Reiger) and qualitative reasoning (Kuipers).

- Johnson-Laird, P. N., and Wason, P.C. [Eds.] (1977). *Thinking: Readings in Cognitive Science.* Cambridge: Cambridge University Press.

Although fairly old now, the book collects together some major papers in human reasoning supporting, and supplementary to, the discussions in our chapter including Winston's structural descriptions of arches using semantic networks, Minsky's description of 'frames', Rosch's of prototypes, and Schank and Abelson's of 'scripts'.

Rule-Based Knowledge

- Alty, J. L., and Coombs, M. J. [Eds.] (1984). *Expert Systems: Concepts and Examples.* Manchester: NCC Publications.

A clearly written tutorial introduction to expert systems. The early chapters, with sections on first-order logic, search, rule-based reasoning, and knowledge representation, lay the foundations for the fairly detailed case studies of expert systems (including MYCIN, PROSPECTOR, and R1) occupying the main body of the book.

- Nilsson, N. (1982). *Principles of Artificial Intelligence.* Berlin: Springer-Verlag.

Despite the very general title, the principal focus and organizing theme of the book is production systems. Topics covered include search strategies for production systems, AND/OR graphs, forward vs. backward deduction, and plan generation. The book will be of particular interest to readers wanting to know more about formal methods in artificial intelligence.

- Hayes-Roth, F., Waterman, D. A., and Lenat, D. B. [Eds.] (1983). *Building Expert Systems.* Reading, Mass.: Addison-Wesley.

A very readable, fairly recent, collection of papers on expert systems, containing some good general references.

Models of Cognition

- Aitkenhead, A. M., and Slack, J. M. [Eds.] (1985). *Issues in Cognitive Modelling.* London: Lawrence Erlbaum.

A collection of readings, including important papers on mental imagery, mental models, memory organization, and analogical problem solving. The readings have been abbreviated, often drastically.

- Anderson, J. R. (1983). *The Architecture of Cognition.* Cambridge, Mass.: Harvard University Press.

  An attempt to set out the basic principles of operation for the human cognitive system, including memory and problem solving.

- Rumelhart, D. E., McClelland, J. L., and the PDP Research Group (1986). *Parallel Distributed Processing,* (Two Volumes). Cambridge, Mass.: MIT Press.

  The books that started the resurgence of interest in parallel distributed processing. Volume 1 lays the foundations and introduces the techniques. Volume 2 describes models of perception, memory, language, and thought.

Computer Vision

- Bruce, V., and Green, P. (1985), *Visual Perception, Physiology, Psychology and Ecology.* London: Lawrence Erlbaum Associates.

  A good introduction to visual perception, covering neurophysiological studies, psychological and computational models of vision, and the use of vision in interacting with the environment.

- Ballard, D. H., and Brown, M. B. (1982), *Computer Vision.* Englewood Cliffs, N.J.: Prentice Hall.

  A textbook of computer vision that includes descriptions of many standard algorithms. The book is a also a useful reference for those involved in building vision systems.

- Marr, D. (1982). *Vision.* San Francisco: W. H. Freeman.

  A coherent, computational theory of human vision, motivated by the physics of image formation, together with known physiology and psychology.

Philosophy of Mind

- Two classic papers in the area are

  - Turing, A. M. (1950). "Computing Machinery and Intelligence," *Mind,* LIX, pp. 433–460. Reprinted in Anderson, A. R. [Ed.] (1964). *Minds and Machines,* Englewood Cliffs, N.J.: Prentice Hall.

– Searle, J. R. (1980). "Minds, Brains and Programs" (with peer commentaries), *Behavioral and Brain Sciences*, 3, pp. 417–457. Reprinted in Haugeland, J. [Ed.] (1981). *Mind Design,* Cambridge Mass.: MIT Press/Bradford Books.

• Churchland, P. M. (1984). *Matter and Consciousness: a Contemporary Introduction to the Philosophy of Mind.* Cambridge Mass.: MIT Press/Bradford Books.

A short and readable survey of key issues in this area, oriented towards the cognitive and neural sciences. Particularly good at explaining the various 'isms' which abound in philosophical discussions about mind.

• Hofstadter, D. W. (1979). *Gödel, Escher, Bach: An Eternal Golden Braid.* New York: Basic Books.

One of the most remarkable pieces of writing of the twentieth century. Hofstadter, a computer scientist by training, sheds light on many interesting issues in philosophy, art, mathematics, music, mysticism, and biology. A primary theme of the book is the role of logic, paradox, contradiction, and self-reference in understanding the mind.

• Dennett, D. C. (1978). *Brainstorms: Philosophical Essays on Mind and Psychology.* Cambridge Mass.: MIT Press/Bradford Books.

A collection of essays by one of the best known philosophers of cognitive science. Particularly worth reading are the essays "Intentional Systems," "Why You Can't Make a Computer That Feels Pain," and the concluding science fiction story on brain replication and personal identity.

Future Trends

• Yazdani, M., and Narayan, A. [Eds.] (1984). *Artificial Intelligence: Human Effects.* Chichester: Ellis Horwood.

A series of essays on the social implications of artificial intelligence.

• Feigenbaum, E. A., and McCorduck, P. (1984). *The Fifth Generation.* London: Pan Books Ltd., and Reading, Mass.: Addison-Wesley.

A manifesto for artificial intellligence. It claims that reasoning machines will change the world for the better, that the Japanese have farsighted plans for exploiting this new technology, and that the United States should respond with its own ambitious programme of research and development.

References

Aleksander, I., and Burnett, P. (1987). *Thinking Machines: The Search for Artificial Intelligence.* Oxford: Oxford University Press.

Allen, J., and Perrault, C. R. (1980). "Analyzing Intention in Utterances." *Artificial Intelligence*, 15, 143–178.

Alvey Directorate (1986). *Alvey Annual Report 1986.*

Anderson, J. R. (1983). *The Architecture of Cognition.* Cambridge, Mass.: Harvard University Press.

Anderson, J. R., and Bower, G. H. (1973). *Human Associative Memory.* New York: John Wiley and Sons.

Austin, J. L. (1962). *How to Do Things with Words.* Oxford: Oxford University Press.

Ballard, D. H., and Brown, M. B. (1982). *Computer Vision.* Englewood Cliffs, N.J.: Prentice Hall.

Barrett, R., Ramsay, A., and Sloman, A. (1985). *POP-11, a Practical Language for Artificial Intelligence.* Chichester: Ellis Horwood.

Bobrow, D. G., and Collins, A. (Eds.) (1975). *Representation and Understanding.* New York: Academic Press.

Boden, M. A. (1979). *Piaget.* Glasgow: Fontana/Collins.

Boden, M. A. (1984). "What Is Computational Psychology?" *Proceedings of the Aristotelian Society*, Supplementary Volume, 1984, 17–35.

Boden, M. A. (1986). *Artificial Intelligence and Natural Man.* [Second Edition]. Brighton: Harvester Press and Basic Books.

Bowden, B. V. (Ed.) (1953). *Faster Than Thought. [Lady Lovelace's Memo].* London: Pitman.

Brachman, R. J. (1979). "On the Epistemological Status of Semantic Networks." In Findler, N. V. (Ed.) (1079). *Associative Networks: Representations and Use of Knowledge by Computers.* New York: Academic Press.

Brachman, R. J. (1983). "What IS-A Is and Isn't: An Analysis of Taxonomic Links in Semantic Networks." *Computer,* 16, 30–36.

Brooks, R. A. (1981). "Symbolic Reasoning among 3-D Models and 2-D Images." *Artificial Intelligence,* 17, 285–348.

Brown, J. S. and VanLehn, K. (1980). "Repair Theory: A Generative Theory of Bugs in Procedural Skills." *Cognitive Science,* 4, 397–426.

Bruce, V., and Green, P. (1985). *Visual Perception: Physiology, Psychology and Ecology.* London: Lawrence Erlbaum Associates.

Bundy, A. (1987). "The limitations of Artificial Intelligence and the Distinction between Special-Purpose and General-Purpose Systems." Report prepared by the Edinburgh Computing and Social Responsibility Group.

Burton, M., and Shadbolt, N. (1987). *POP-11 Programming for Artificial Intelligence.* Wokingham: Addison-Wesley.

Cazden, C. (1972). *Child Language and Education.* New York: Holt, Rinehart and Winston.

Chappell, V. C. (Ed.) (1962). *The Philosophy of Mind.* Englewood Cliffs N.J.: Prentice Hall.

Charniak, E., and McDermott, D. (1985). *Introduction to Artificial Intelligence.* Reading, Mass: Addison-Wesley.

Chomsky, A. N. (1959). "A Review of Verbal Behavior." *Language,* 35, 26–58.

Chomsky, A. N. (1966). *Cartesian Linguistics.* New York: Harper and Row.

Chomsky, A. N. (1975). *Reflections on Language.* Glasgow: Fontana/Collins.

Chomsky, A. N. (1980). *Rules and Representations.* Oxford: Basil Blackwell.

Churchland, P. M. (1984). *Matter and Consciousness: A Contemporary Introduction to the Philosophy of Mind.* Cambridge, Mass.: MIT Press.

Clark, A. (1987). "The Kludge in the Machine." *Mind and Language*, Vol. 2, No. 4. Winter 1987.

Clark, A. (in press). *Microcognition: Philosophy, Cognitive Science, and Parallel Distributed Processing.* Cambridge, Mass.: MIT Press/Bradford Books.

Clocksin, W. S., and Mellish, C. S. (1981). *Programming in Prolog.* Heidelberg: Springer-Verlag.

Cohen, P., and Perrault, C. R. (1979). "Elements of a Plan-Based Theory of Speech Acts." *Cognitive Science*, 3(3), 177–212.

Collins, A., and Quillian, R. (1969). "Retrieval Time from Semantic Memory." *Journal of Verbal Learning and Verbal Behavior*, 8, 240–247.

Conrad, C. (1972). "Cognitive Economy in Semantic Memory." *Journal of Experimental Psychology*, 92, 149–154.

Cottingham, J., Stoothoff, R., and Murdoch, D. (Translators) (1985). *Discourse on Method — the Philosophical Works of René Descartes.* Cambridge: Cambridge University Press, pp. 139–140.

Dennett, D. C. (1978a). "Intentional Systems." In Dennett, D. C. (1978). *Brainstorms: Philosophical Essays on Mind and Psychology.* Cambridge, Mass.: MIT Press.

Dennett, D.C. (1978b). "Why You Can't Make a Computer that Feels Pain." In Dennett, D. C. (1978). *Brainstorms: Philosophical Essays on Mind and Psychology.* Cambridge, Mass.: MIT Press.

Dennett, D.C. (1978c). "Skinner Skinned." In Dennett, D. C. (1978). *Brainstorms: Philosophical Essays on Mind and Psychology.* Cambridge, Mass.: MIT Press.

Descartes, R. (1642). "Meditations 1 and 2." In Anscombe, G. E. M., and Geach, P. T. (Eds.) (1954). *Descartes' Philosophical Writings.* Edinburgh: Thomas Nelson and Sons Ltd.

Dreyfus, H. L. (1979). *What Computers Can't Do.* [Revised Edition]. New York: Harper and Row.

Duda, R., Gaschnig, J., and Hart, P. (1979). "Model Design in the PROSPECTOR Consultant System for Mineral Exploration." In Michie, D (Ed.) (1979). *Expert Systems in the Microelectronic Age.* Edinburgh: Edinburgh University Press.

Ericsson, K. A., and Simon, H. A. (1980). "Verbal Reports as Data." *Psychological Review,* 87, 3.

Ernst, G. W., and Newell, A. (1969). *GPS: A Case Study in Generality and Problem Solving.* New York: Academic Press.

Feigenbaum, E. A., and Feldman, J. (Eds.) (1963). *Computers and Thought.* New York: McGraw-Hill.

Feigenbaum, E. A., and McCorduck, P. (1984). *The Fifth Generation.* London: Pan Books Ltd., and Reading, Mass.: Addison-Wesley.

Findler, N. V. (Ed.) (1979). *Associative Networks: Representation and Use of Knowledge by Computers.* New York: Academic Press.

Forsyth, R. (1988). "AI: East/West Conference Report." In *AISB Quarterly,* 66, Autumn 1988.

Frisby, J. (1979). *Seeing: Illusion, Brain and Mind.* Oxford: Oxford University Press.

Gibson, J. (1984). "POP-11: an AI Programming Language." In Yazdani, M. (Ed.) (1984). *New Horizons in Educational Computing.* Chichester: Ellis Horwood.

Grice, H. P. (1975). "Logic and Conversation." In Cole, P., and Morgan, J. L. (Eds.) (1975). *Syntax and Semantics 3: Speech Acts.* New York: Academic Press.

Hayes-Roth, F., Waterman, D. A., and Lenat, D. B. (Eds.) (1983). *Building Expert Systems.* Reading, Mass.: Addison-Wesley.

Hofstadter, D. W. (1980). *Gödel, Escher, Bach: An Eternal Golden Braid.* Harmondsworth: Penguin Books.

Hofstadter, D. W., and Dennett, D. C. (Eds.) (1981). *The Mind's I: Fantasies and Reflections on Self and Soul.* Brighton: Harvester Press.

Horn, B. K. P. (1975). "Obtaining Shape from Shading Information." In Winston, P. H. (Ed.) (1975). *The Psychology of Computer Vision.* New York: McGraw-Hill.

Hubel, D. H., and Wiesel, T. N. (1968). "Receptive Fields and Functional Architecture of Monkey Striate Cortex." *J. Physiology (London)*, 195, 215–243.

Kempson, R. M. (1977). *Semantic Theory.* Cambridge: Cambridge University Press.

Laventhol, J. (1987). *Programming in POP-11.* Oxford: Blackwell Scientific Publications.

Lenat, D. B. (1983). "EURISKO: A Program that Learns New Heuristics and Domain Concepts." *Artificial Intelligence*, 21, 61–98.

Levinson, S. C. (1983). *Pragmatics.* Cambridge: Cambridge University Press.

Lyons, J. (1981). *Language, Meaning and Context.* London: Fontana.

McCawley, J. D. (1981). *Everything That Linguists Have Always Wanted to Know about Logic *but Were Ashamed to Ask.* Oxford: Basil Blackwell.

McClelland, J. L., Rumelhart, D. E., and the PDP Research Group (1986). *Parallel Distributed Processing,* Volume1: *Foundations;* Volume 2:*Psychological and Biological Models.* Boston: MIT Press.

McKeown, K. R. (1985). *Text Generation: Using Discourse Strategies and Focus Constraints to Generate Natural Language Text.* Cambridge: Cambridge University Press.

Marr, D. (1976). "Early processing of visual information." *Phil. Trans. Royal Soc. London B,* 275 (1976), 483–524.

Marr, D. (1982). *Vision.* San Francisco: W. H. Freeman.

Miller, G. A., Galanter, E., and Pribram, K. H. (1960). *Plans and the Structure of Behaviour.* New York: Holt.

Minsky, M. (Ed.) (1968). *Semantic Information Processing*. Cambridge, Mass.: MIT Press.

Minsky, M. (1975). "A Framework for Representing Knowledge." In Winston, P. H. (Ed.) (1975). *The Psychology of Computer Vision*. New York: McGraw-Hill.

Minsky, M. (1986). *The Society of Mind*. London: Heineman.

Minsky, M., and Papert, S. (1969). *Perceptrons*. Cambridge, Mass.: MIT Press.

Newell, A., and Simon, H.A. (1972). *Human Problem Solving*. Englewood Cliffs, N.J.: Prentice Hall.

Newell, A., Shaw, J. C., and Simon, H. A. (1958). "Elements of a Theory of Human Problem-Solving." *Psychological Review*, 65, 151–166.

Newell, A., Shaw, J. C., and Simon, H. A. (1963a) [first published 1958]. "Chess-Playing Programs and the Problem of Complexity." In Feigenbaum, E. A., and Feldman, J. (Eds.) (1963). *Computers and Thought*. New York: McGraw-Hill.

Newell, A., Shaw, J. C., and Simon, H. A. (1963b). "Empirical Explorations with the Logic Theory Machine: A Case History in Heuristics." In Feigenbaum, E. A., and Feldman. J. (Eds.) (1963). *Computers and Thought*. New York: McGraw-Hill.

Office of Technology Assessment, US Congress (1986). "Artificial Intelligence: A Background Paper." US Government Printing Office, Washington, DC. [Cited in *The Encyclopedia of AI*, pp. 1050–1051.]

O'Shea, T., and Eisenstadt, M. (1984). *Artificial Intelligence: Tools Techniques and Applications*. New York: Harper and Row.

Papert, S. (1980). *Mindstorms*. Hassocks, Sussex: Harvester Press.

Putnam, H. (1960). "Minds and Machines." In Hook, S. (Ed.) (1960). *Dimensions of Mind: A Symposium*. New York: New York University Press.

Putnam, H. (1965). "Psychological Predicates." In Capitan, W. H., and Merrill, D. D. (Eds.) (1967). *Art, Mind and Religion*. Pittsburgh: University of Pittsburgh Press.

Quillian, M. R. (1968). "Semantic Memory." In Minsky, M. (Ed.) (1968). *Semantic Information Processing.* Cambridge, Mass.: MIT Press.

Ramsay, A., and Barrett, R. (1987). *AI in Practice: Examples in POP-11.* Chichester: Ellis Horwood.

Rich, E. (1983). *Artificial Intelligence.* New York: McGraw-Hill.

Robinson, J. A. (1965). "A Machine Oriented Logic Based on the Resolution Principle." *Journal Assn. of Computing Machinery*, January 1965, 23–41.

Rosch, E. (1983). "Prototype Classification and Logical Classification: The Two Systems." In Scholnick, E. (Ed.) (1983). *Trends in Cognitive Representation: Challenges to Piaget's Theory.* Hillsdale, N.J.: Lawrence Erlbaum Associates, pp. 73–86.

Schank, R. C., and Abelson, R. P. (1977). *Scripts, Plans, Goals, and Understanding.* Hillsdale, N.J.: Lawrence Erlbaum Associates.

Schank, R. C., and Riesbeck, C. K. (Eds.) (1981). *Inside Computer Understanding: Five Programs Plus Miniatures.* Hillsdale, N.J.: Lawrence Erlbaum Associates.

Searle, J. R. (1969). *Speech Acts.* London: Cambridge University Press.

Searle, J. R. (1980). "Minds, Brains and Programs" [with Peer Commentaries]. *Behavioral and Brain Sciences*, 3, 417–457.

Searle, J. R. (1983). *Intentionality: An Essay in the Philosophy of Mind.* Cambridge: Cambridge University Press.

Searle, J. R. (1984). *Minds, Brains and Science: The 1984 Reith Lectures.* London: BBC Publications.

Sejnowski, T. J., and Rosenberg, C. R. (1986). *NETtalk: A Parallel Network that Learns to Read Aloud.* JHU/EECS-86/01. The John Hopkins University, Electrical Engineering and Computer Science Department.

Sergot, M. J., et al. (1986). "The British Nationalities Act as a Logic Program." *Comms. ACM.*, 29 (5), 370–386.

Shaffer, J. A. (1968). *Philosophy of Mind.* Englewood Cliffs, N.J.: Prentice Hall.

Shepard, R. G., and Metzler, J. (1971). "Mental Rotation of Three-Dimensional Objects." *Science*, 171, 701–703.

Shortliffe, E. H. (1976). *Computer-Based Medical Consulations: MYCIN*. New York: American Elsevier.

Simon, H. A., and Gilmartin, K. (1973). "A Simulation of Memory for Chess Pieces." *Cognitive Psychology*, 51, 29–46.

Skinner, B. F. (1953). *Science and Human Behavior*. New York: Macmillan.

Sloman, A. (1978). *The Computer Revolution in Philosophy*. Hassocks, Sussex: Humanities Press.

Sloman, A. (1984). "Towards a Computational Theory of Mind." In Yazdani, M., and Narayan, A. (Eds.) (1984). *Artificial Intelligence: Human Effects*. Chichester: Ellis Horwood.

Sloman, A. (1985a). "Why We Need Many Knowledge Representation Formalisms." In M. Bramer, M. (Ed.) (1985). *Research and Development in Expert Systems*. Cambridge: Cambridge University Press.

Sloman, A. (1985b). "Real-Time Multiple-Motive Expert Systems." In Merry, M. (Ed.) (1985). *Expert Systems 85*. Cambridge: Cambridge University Press.

Sloman A. (1986). "Did Searle Refute Strong Strong or Weak Strong AI?" In Cohn, A. G., and Thomas, J. R. (Eds.) (1986). *Artificial Intelligence and Its Applications*. Chichester: John Wiley.

Sloman, A. (1987). "Motives, Mechanisms Emotions." In *Emotion and Cognition*. 1(3), 217–233.

Sloman, A., and Thwaites, G. (1986). "POPLOG: A Unique Collaboration." In *Alvey News*, June 1986.

Smith, E. E., Shoben, E. J., and Rips, L.J. (1974). "Structure and Process in Semantic Memory: A Feature Model for Semantic Decisions." *Psychological Review*, 81, 214–241.

Smolensky, P. (1987). "Connectionist AI, Symbolic AI and the Brain." *Artificial Intelligence Review*, 1, 95–109.

Sowa, J. F. (1984). *Conceptual Structures.* Reading, Mass.: Addison-Wesley.

Thagard, P. (1986). "Parallel Computation and the Mind-Body Problem." *Cognitive Science*, 10, 301–318.

Turing, A. M. (1950). "Computing Machinery and Intelligence." *Mind*, 59, 433–460. Also in Feigenbaum and Feldman (1963).

Waltz, D. (1981). "Towards a Detailed Model of Processing for Language Describing the Physical World." *Proceedings IJCAI-81*, 1-6.

Watson, J. B. (1930). *Behaviorism.* [Revised Edition]. Chicago: Chicago University Press.

Weizenbaum, J. (1984). *Computer Power and Human Reason: From Judgement to Calculation.* Harmondsworth: Penguin Books.

Winograd, T. (1972). *Understanding Natural Language.* New York: Academic Press.

Winograd, T. (1983). *Language as a Cognitive Process.* Reading, Mass: Addison-Wesley.

Winston, P. H. (1984). *Artificial Intelligence.* Reading, Mass.: Addison-Wesley.

Woods, W. A. (1975). "What's in a Link? Foundations for Semantic Networks." In Bobrow, D. G., and Collins, A. (Eds.) (1975). *Representation and Understanding.* New York: Academic Press.

Yazdani, M. (Ed.) (1984). *New Horizons in Educational Computing.* Chichester: Ellis Horwood.

Young, R. M., and O'Shea, T. (1982). "Errors in Children's Subtraction." *Cognitive Science*, 5, 153–177.

Index

The MIT Press, with Peter Denning, general consulting editor, and Brian Randall, European consulting editor, publishes computer science books in the following series:

ACM Doctoral Dissertation Award and Distinguished Dissertation Series

Artificial Intelligence, Patrick Henry Winston and J. Michael Brady founding editors; J. Michael Brady, Daniel G. Bobrow, and Randall Davis, current editors

Charles Babbage Institute Reprint Series for the History of Computing, Martin Campbell-Kelly, editor

Computer Systems, Herb Schwetman, editor

Exploring with Logo, E. Paul Goldenberg, editor

Foundations of Computing, Michael Garey and Albert Meyer, editors

History of Computing, I. Bernard Cohen and William Aspray, editors

Information Systems, Michael Lesk, editor

Logic Programming, Ehud Shapiro, editor; Fernando Pereira, Koichi Furukawa, and D. H. D. Warren, associate editors

The MIT Electrical Engineering and Computer Science Series

Research Monographs in Parallel and Distributed Processing, Christopher Jesshope and David Klappholz, editors

Scientific Computation, Dennis Gannon, editor

Technical Communication, Edward Barrett, editor

Order form for software to accompany

Computers and Thought
by Mike Sharples, David Hogg, Chris Hutchison, Steve Torrance, and David Young

A demonstration version of AlphaPop, along with programs from the book is available. Programs include the Automated Tourist Guide, the Route Finder, and Eliza.

Program diskette (3.5 in. double-sided) is only available in Macintosh™ version. Memory requirements, 512K or more. System 4.2 or later.

Please send

_____ copies of program diskette (SHACDM) $15.95   _____

                                               Postage $2.50

                                               Grand total _____

All prices in U.S. dollars. Checks must be drawn on a U.S. bank.

_____ Check enclosed payable to The MIT Press.

_____ Bill my MasterCard   _____ Bill my Visa

Credit card No. _____ Signature _____

Ship to   Name _____

           Address _____

           City _____ State _____ Zip _____

Special Instructions _____

_____

Send Order to
Textbook Manager, The MIT Press, 55 Hayward Street, Cambridge, MA 02142